D0553953

HANDBOOK OF INTERNATIONAL CREDIT MANAGEMENT

Handbook of International Credit Management

Edited by
Brian W Clarke

Gower

Published by
Gower Publishing Company Limited
Gower House
Croft Road
Aldershot
Hants GU11 3HR
England

Gower Publishing Company
Old Post Road
Brookfield
Vermont 05036
USA

British Library Cataloguing in Publication Data
Handbook of international credit management
   1. International credit management
   I. Clarke, Brian W.
   658.8'8

   ISBN 0–566–02764–X

Library of Congress Cataloging-in-Publication Data
Handbook of international credit management / edited by Brian W.
  Clarke.
     p. cm.
  Includes index.
  ISBN 0–566–02764–X (U.S.)
   1. International business enterprises—Finance. 2. Credit—
Management. I. Clarke, Brian W.
HG4027.5.H35   1989
658.8'8—dc19   88–24526
          CIP

Printed and bound in Great Britain at
The Camelot Press Ltd, Southampton

Contents

Contents

assessment – Credit limits – Credit risk categories – Day-to-day risk control – Opening a credit account – Doing business with marginal risk accounts – Controls for risky accounts – Risk control on overseas accounts – A checklist for good export risk control – Summary

PART III LAYING OFF THE RISK

PART IV TERMS AND CONDITIONS OF SALE

Contents

Anatomy of countertrade – Countertrade checklist –
Conclusion – Recommended reading

Contents

PART IX   INTERNATIONAL LAW

Foreword

Sir James Cleminson, Chairman, British Overseas Trade Board

There must be very few countries in the world whose well-being and prosperity, existing and future, does not depend on healthy free trade.

As Chairman of the British Overseas Trade Board, the export promotion arm of the Department of Trade and Industry, I am, of course, particularly anxious to encourage British firms to make the most of the export potential of their products and services. But I also see it as part of my role to foster international trade generally.

There is one element of the international trade process that is crucial to the success of the whole operation. If you get it wrong, it tends to make all the efforts somewhat pointless. It is, of course, making sure that you get paid *and* get paid without undue delay.

The difficulties associated with getting paid can often be overestimated, and sadly this puts many businesses off exporting altogether. There are some markets where there is a considerable inherent risk in providing credit. But firms can generally insure against such risks, through private insurers or government agencies, such as, in the United Kingdom, the Export Credits Guarantee Department.

But very often, non-payment or delayed payment for exports arises not because of the inability of the customer to pay or a dishonest desire not to do so, but because the supplier fails to get the paperwork right. For exporting frequently involves complex documentation where, in some extreme cases, even a missing comma on a vital piece of paper can lead to a hold-up in payment – on letters of credit, for example.

Much is being done to simplify the documentation and management of international trade as, for instance, in the UK by the Simpler Trade Procedures Board (SITPRO). The Board's work is not only to simplify the paperwork, but where possible, to remove it altogether.

Despite all this, we shall never reach the stage when the need for efficient international credit management will disappear. It will always be a vital part of international trade. That is why I welcome this handbook as an important contribution to world trade in that it addresses the key question on which it all hinges – How can I make sure I get paid?

Preface

An anonymous but beautiful and uplifting poem, now called 'Desiderata', found some three hundred years ago in a Baltimore church, entreats us to 'exercise caution in our business affairs, for the world is full of trickery'. It is a fascinating poem mixing high ideals with the realities of life and the industry of mankind; and near its end the poem reminds us that 'with all its shams, drudgery and broken dreams, it is still a beautiful world'.

Indeed it is, though some parts of the world are of course more beautiful than others. Nature has endowed some with such scenic beauty as to provide an asset forming the basis of a modern-day tourist industry. Other parts of the world are unusually endowed with those other bounties of nature (and industrial feedstocks), the wide variety of mineral deposits and fossil fuels. Climate can make or mar a country's claim to riches, fostering or hampering the growth of valuable crops and vegetation. And to all this must be added the ingenuity and labour of mankind not simply adding to nature's bounties but often indeed compensating for the lack of them.

Throughout the world, however, there have always been, and always will be local imbalances between the supply of, and demand for, the goods and services which are generated by those riches and talents; and the desire to satisfy the demand and achieve the supply is the basis for international trade.

In the development of this trade the advent of ocean-going transport represented one of the notable early breakthroughs. Since those times there have been many other important milestones determining the fluctuating fortunes of nations and, ironically, the most recent can be directly related back to one of nature's bounties – oil. More correctly, perhaps, it is the way in which mankind has managed that bounty that has brought the nations of the world to a remarkably unbalanced situation in terms of relative international wealth and poverty and created the so-called world debt crisis.

In spite of these contemporary, precarious situations, however, international trade continues to flourish, and one ingredient making a significant contribution to its success is international credit.

This handbook is all about the management of international credit and, whilst concentrating on those aspects normally directly under the control of the international credit manager, it does not neglect the peripheral activities to which he or she is constantly exposed in the course of the day's work.

But from the individual company viewpoint why bother to 'go international' in the first place?

Many reasons are given, all of them sound. Exporting is the only way to expand. It uses up spare production. It's a profitable alternative to domestic trading. It offers a much larger market. And so on.

Overriding all of this is the simple fact that national well-being depends upon international trade. Yet the average company or corporation needs a lot of incentives to get into it.

The great problem, of course, is that until an enterprise has tried going international, it all seems too complicated, particularly the financial aspects. It is much more comforting to withdraw into our domestic shell and focus our commercial acumen upon that familiar home market.

The likelihood, too, is that even in the home market we have credit management problems, so why should we try to run before we can walk and extrapolate our difficulties in the direction of these apparently hostile regions beyond our own shores and borders?

Why? For the reasons given above and because not only does national well-being thrive on world trade, but international progress and understanding grows from it; and I hope it's not too trite to say that, despite all the impediments to world trade and the sometimes undesirable uniformity that stems from it, the world is a better place because of it.

If none of that appeals, then I have one last reason: international credit management can be a lot of fun!

Reverting to the impediments to world trade and particularly its complexity, I have a simple international credit management creed:

I believe fervently in the quest for simplification of the present morass of international trade procedures and the application of automatic processes to that end. Yet deep down, what little I know of human nature leads me to believe that these worthy objectives will not be completely achieved for perhaps a generation or more.

So, whilst striving for these ends alongside those gallant official bodies dedicated to the task, we have to react to the world as it is rather than as we would like it to be. International credit managers must thus be individuals who can be proactive and innovative whilst having constantly to predict and handle situations over which they often have little or no control. They are essentially practitioners.

This handbook is therefore essentially a book for practitioners written by practitioners. Those contributors who are not themselves experienced credit managers represent – and are equally experienced in – the professions which provide so many services to the credit industry. As a result the handbook offers a comprehensive examination of international credit from a variety of viewpoints and opinions. Some overlap of related topics is therefore inevitable and indeed desirable since it enables varying slants to be put on the same subject. For the same reason no attempt has been made to impose an artificial consistency in style or opinion: credit management often offers several solutions to the same problem!

The contributors having now put down their authors' pens and resumed their daily credit management tasks, we all hope this handbook will enable you to improve your international performance toward the realization of those profitable objectives of improved cashflow, prompt payment and reduced risk of bad debts, as well as the ultimate achievement of the lofty ideals expressed above.

Brian W. Clarke
December 1988

Notes on contributors

Brian W Clarke, MICM, editor *(Responsibilities, expertise and resource, Sharing the risk, An outline of settlement methods, Documentary letters of credit, Collecting overdue debts, European and US export finance)* has spent over thirty years in international credit and finance and for a good deal of this time was responsible for the international credit management function of Imperial Chemical Industries, the UK's largest chemical company. In recent years he has also developed a considerable involvement in external corporate training, blending his multinational experience with an understanding of the credit and finance needs of small to medium-sized companies. He is a well known presenter and runs regular training seminars for a number of clients, including the Department of Trade and Industry (British Overseas Trade Board) and Dun & Bradstreet Ltd. He is a member of the British Institute of Credit Management and has served as a European Director of FCIB (Finance, Credit and International Business), the international affiliate of the US National Association of Credit Management. As ICI's representative, he was for many years chairman of FCIB's largest common interest industry group.

Thomas A Auchterlonie *(Organization and policy).* A graduate of the University of Pittsburgh, Tom Auchterlonie began his business career in 1954 after having been an artillery officer. As an employee of Aluminum Company of America, he had assignments in the sales department until 1962 when he joined Alcoa International to do specific sales administrative work as part of a team to install a selling organization in Canada for Alcoa. Assignments with Alcoa International followed in Jamaica and Miami, Florida, dealing with Canadian and Latin American sales administration and credit. His last assignment with Alcoa was as the Financial Manager of Alcoa Inter-America Inc, which is a western hemisphere trading company. In 1977 he joined the corporate staff of PPG Industries Inc as Credit Manager – International to develop PPG's export credit operations. He has since worked also with various PPG overseas affiliates in the development of their credit operations as well as being active as a speaker and participant in International Credit Executives and FCIB-NACM. He has travelled extensively including the People's Republic of China. Tom's uncompleted graduate study was at University of Miami.

Dr Hans P Belcsak *(Country risk assessment, Exchange controls)* is President of S. J. Rundt & Associates Inc in New York City. Born in Austria and educated for the most part in Innsbruck, he majored in Commercial Law and Political Economics and obtained the degree of Doctor of Jurisprudence. His dissertation in Economics was a critical appraisal of Keynesian fiscal policy applied to modern economies. Following his formal education, Dr Belcsak was associated with banks in Germany and Italy. In 1964 he came to the USA to head the World Trade and Transportation Department of the Toledo Area Chamber of Commerce. Dr Belcsak joined the Rundt Organization of consultants on international business in 1967 as research analyst. Soon afterward he became a partner and then a senior partner. Since 1973 he has been President of S. J. Rundt & Associates Inc, as which he is the active principal of that organization.

Dr Belcsak is publisher of *Rundt's Weekly Intelligence Briefs* dealing with global political and economic trends, *Rundt's World Risk Analysis Program* of country risk assessments, and the *Financial Executives Country Risk Alert*. His firm ranks among its clients the top names among multinational corporations and banks in the USA and abroad. He is a regular contributor of articles to international trade and financial journals in North America as well as Europe, and has made contributions to several books on international finance. He has been a frequent lecturer and conference chairman for the American Management Association in the USA, Canada, and Mexico, for the World Trade Institute of New York, and for scores of national and international trade associations, business conferences, bank training programmes and chambers of commerce. He is a member of the Advisory Council of the World Trade Institute, a member of the International Advisory Council of the American Management Association, and on the board of directors of the FCIB-NACM Corporation.

Peter Cecil *(Treasury/cash management)* has worked in an exporting environment for almost the whole of his career. He spent ten years with Ford in Essex during which time he gained practical experience and obtained a business studies qualification that concentrated on economics and international trade. He then joined the Rothmans group with which he spent a further ten years. While with Rothmans he developed a treasury operation for the group UK company, a major exporter to the whole of the world but particularly Africa and the Middle East, and later as Group Treasurer set up a European treasury operation that netted and managed the cash and foreign currency exposures of six major group companies within Europe through a factoring and reinvoicing centre. Peter joined the Export Finance Company (Exfinco) in November 1984 as Treasury Director and is a Foundation Fellow of the Association of Corporate Treasurers.

Paul Dawson *(Credit insurance)*. After a period as a credit manager in industry, he joined the Export Credits Guarantee Department (ECGD), where he remained for ten years. Since that time he has worked in the credit insurance broking market, firstly with Matthews Wrightson and, since 1987, with Jardine Insurance Brokers, where he is responsible for export, political and home trade risks. In June 1988, he was elected Chairman of the UK Credit Insurance Brokers' Committee.

Nick Douch *(Foreign exchange exposure management)* is the senior manager leading the corporate treasury team at Barclays Bank plc in London. He has a wide experience in advising customers on a range of currency problems, having worked in Barclays treasury area for seven years. He believes strongly that the correct specification of the scale of the currency problem is more important than the search for some obscure product derivative which appears to fit the bill.

Herbert Edwards, FICM, FIEx *(The range of risks, Risk management)* is a well-known writer and speaker on credit management topics. He had a long career in credit and treasury management for multinational companies and was European Credit Manager for the ITT group at its Brussels headquarters. Previously, he was with the Singer Corporation, British Steel and Thorn-EMI and in 1983 set up a risk management subsidiary for the Jardine Matheson group in London. Burt is a Fellow and council member of the Institute of Credit Management in the UK and also a Fellow of the Institute of Export. He is on the teaching faculty of Management Centre Europe and trains extensively for several organizations, particularly Dun & Bradstreet and his own company, Capital Business Training. His books include *Credit Management Handbook* and *Export Credit* (both Gower) and *Credit Insurance* (Woodhead-Faulkner) as well as the credit insurance section of *International Financial Management* (Kluwer). His special interest is in analysing credit risks.

Jim Hackett *(Tender and performance guarantees)*. Educated in the UK and Germany, Jim Hackett completed his full-time education in 1965 with a Diploma in Business Studies with special reference to modern languages. His working career has been in capital equipment manufacturing, firstly with Alfred Herbert Limited and Coventry Climax Engines Limited and, since 1974, with Massey-Ferguson Manufacturing Company, where he is currently Contract Administration Manager. His involvement throughout has been in export operations where he has had first-hand experience of export shipping and documentation, export finance, contract administration and control of a multi-million dollar guarantee facility.

Simon Harris *(Countertrade)* is Manager, International Barter and Countertrade at Lloyds Bank plc in London. He is a career banker with a total of seventeen years' experience, primarily centred on corporate and country risk analysis and management and recovery techniques. He has spent the past three years specializing in countertrade and other non-conventional trade finance mechanisms.

Ian Hyslop *(Maritime fraud)* served for fourteen years as a police officer in Kent. He is now employed as Information Officer and Assistant Legal Adviser by the International Chamber of Commerce International Maritime Bureau.

Robert T Lambert *(Operating through subsidiaries and affiliates, Supporting systems)* was educated at the Texas Technological University, Lubbock, Texas, and at the Graduate School of Credit and Financial Management in the USA. In March 1962 he joined the General Foods Corporation in Arlington, Texas, USA as an entry level credit analyst and has progressed through increasingly responsible credit management positions until becoming Director, Corporate Credit in January 1986. He is a Director of the FCIB-NACM Corporation, the international affiliate of the US National Association of Credit Managers.

Jacques P Lardinois *(Bills of exchange, Documentary collections)*. Treasurer of Celanese SA in Brussels, Jacques Lardinois has been actively engaged for more than twenty years in international cash and credit management. Previously he worked in the banking sector where he specialized in credit matters. He has been lecturing for eighteen years at Management Centre Europe (the European division of the American Management Association) where he co-chairs the bi-annual international credit management seminars. He serves as a member of the Advisory Council of the FCIB (an affiliation of the US National Association of Credit Managers) of which he has been a member since 1965. He is a charter member (1966) of the Credit Managers Club of Belgium and holds a university degree in commercial and consular sciences.

Gerd-Peter E Lota *(The role of credit in world trade)* is Executive Vice-President of the FCIB-NACM Corporation, the international arm of the US National Association of Credit Managers, of which he is also a vice-president. He is editor of the FCIB *International Bulletin* and of the international section of the *Credit Manual of Commercial Laws,* and is a regular columnist on world trade in *Business Credit* magazine. Prior to joining the FCIB he was Vice-President of International Sales and Marketing with DDI in New York, and for more than ten years he worked in Paris, where his positions included Export Director of Cozelem SA and Construction Mills-K, and Circulation Director of the international economic magazine *Vision.* During this time he also served as a member of the French Foreign Trade Advisory Council to the French government.

He holds degrees in Economics and International Commerce from the University of Paris, a degree in International Trade and Marketing from the University of Hamburg and is Associate Professor of International Marketing and Finance at the New York City University. He is a committee member of the New York District Export Council and a member of the New York Institute of Credit and the International Fiscal Association.

G Paul Mitchinson *(Customer risk assessment)* joined Dun & Bradstreet Ltd in 1982, having been an officer in the British Merchant Navy. He spent a number of years as part of Dun & Bradstreet's business analysis team before becoming a training officer training analysts. He was instrumental in the design and implementation of Dun & Bradstreet's financial ratio products and credit rating system in the UK. He is now responsible for information sources and systems within Dun & Bradstreet Ltd.

A Don Nelmes *(Agency representation)* is the Credit Manager for ICI Fibres, now part of ICI Chemicals and Polymers Ltd UK, a subsidiary of Imperial Chemical Industries plc. He has held this post for some twenty years, with responsibility for the credit management of sales world wide. Prior to this he held similar posts in the export finance areas of two major UK textile and fibre producing companies. He has experience of international trade with the widest range of countries (some of which no longer exist!), has travelled to many of them and been in constant and close contact with customers, agents and subsidiary companies in all of them. He is a member of FCIB, the international arm of the US National Association of Credit Managers and is currently Chairman of their largest common interest Industry Group.

Roger Pilcher *(UK export finance)*, at one time Managing Director of International Factors, went on to establish Credit Factoring International, a wholly owned subsidiary of National Westminster Bank and Britain's largest factoring company. Subsequently, he was invited to set up the Export Finance Company Limited (Exfinco), a specialist treasury operation which was established to meet exporters' short-term finance and foreign exchange needs. He is a past chairman of the Association of British Factors and a member of various organizations and committees specifically concerned with trade finance and export services.

Michael Rowe *(Legal and regulatory issues)* is a lawyer, journalist and writer, living in France. He qualified as a solicitor (England) in 1969, and holds the degrees of Bachelor of Laws (London School of Economics, 1966) and Master of Laws in European Legal Studies (Exeter University, 1976). He was legal attaché to the International Chamber of Commerce in Paris from 1976 to 1986, and frequently appears as a speaker at international conferences on banking, business and payments topics. His published books include *Letters of Credit* (Euromoney, 1985), *Electronic Trade Payments* (IBC, 1987), and *Guarantees* (Euromoney, 1987). He also writes frequently for the financial press. Journals publishing his articles include *Trade Finance, Banker International, Development Business, ICB, American Banker* and *International Financial Law Review*.

Gray Sinclair *(Terms and conditions for international trade)* is an international cashflow consultant, publisher of the fortnightly *UK International Commerce Commentary* and a writer on a number of subjects associated with trans-border trade. This follows a number of years with responsibility for export banking and documentation in the UK with the General Motors, Morgan Crucible and Beecham groups, prior to which he was in commerce and banking in the Middle East. He is consultant to ICC United Kingdom, the British affiliate of the International Chamber of Commerce, a member of the Payment Procedures Policy Group of the UK quasi-governmental Simpler Trade Procedures Board (SITPRO), and a member of the Institute of Credit Management.

PART I
THE INTERNATIONAL CREDIT MANAGEMENT FUNCTION

1

The role of credit in world trade

Gerd-Peter E Lota

In the early years of our civilization people developed the need for goods that others produced, and which those others were willing to exchange for merchandise that they needed in return. For many years this was the way goods were traded. (So who said countertrade was new?!)

This need for other people's goods took on larger proportions over the decades, and merchants began travelling the world to find new commodities to exchange for or complement their own. Venice and London became famous places for such merchants, and soon every corner of the world was trading with every other. In Germany free trading cities like Hamburg, Bremen and Lübeck quickly established themselves. Holland, Italy, Portugal, Spain and Great Britain became important world trading nations and later the Orient and North Africa joined in.

Out of all this came the idea of exchanging goods for gold and precious metals; and as time went by, traders eventually accepted coins and currencies in return for goods and services. With this worldwide infrastructure in place, many nations became accustomed to buying foreign goods and such goods became part of their everyday life.

From the early days, the realities of economics have played an important part in international trade. Thus it was when buyers could not afford to pay for merchandise immediately, credit extensions began to be granted, allowing the buyer to receive the goods but pay at a later date.

History tells us that wars were started because people did not always pay for merchandise received, but none of this could stop the development of a vast international trade in which credit has become a solid part of the many transactions which take place between merchants in all the countries of the world.

SOME STATISTICS

International commerce has over the last forty years been growing at an accelerated rate, perhaps unprecedented in its history. Total world exports at current prices have increased from US$51 billion in 1947 to US$2475 billion in 1987 – a compounded annual growth of well over 9 per cent. This increase in trade was substantially greater than the growth of world population. By comparison, over a similar period world production of primary products increased by only 2.5 per cent per year, whilst production of manufactured articles increased by about 5.8 per cent per year.

The impetus for the expansion in world trade has slowed down in recent years and thanks only to the increased exchange of goods between the industrialized nations has the volume continued to rise, by roughly 3 per cent in 1985, 4 per cent in 1986 and 5 per cent in 1987. For the developing nations the picture was different. Although a longer-term comparison shows that the developing nations have been able significantly to expand their position in world trade, from 1982 to 1986 their share of the international exchange of merchandise steadily declined and it has only been in 1987 that that share has begun to show a small increase.

Following an upsurge of greater than 8 per cent in real terms in the international exchange of goods overall in 1984, there was a significant slackening in the increase during the following two years. Although during 1985/86 the volume of world trade between industrialized nations rose by the 3 per cent to 4 per cent indicated, the international exchange of merchandise in value terms – due to the dollar decrease and the decline in commodity and oil prices – remained virtually unchanged.

Compared with the 1970s, the industrialized nations' share of world trade has diminished slightly. Whereas in 1973, more than 70 per cent of total world exports and imports were transacted by industrial countries, this share fell to about 68 per cent for imports and 66 per cent for exports in 1985. Whilst participation of Eastern bloc countries in the international exchange of goods has fluctuated only insignificantly since 1973, the developing countries have made an above average contribution to the more than 40 per cent rise in the volume of world trade during this period.

The long-term structural change in favour of the developing nations can mainly be traced to the emergence of the Asian threshold countries, Taiwan, South Korea, Hong Kong and the People's Republic of China,

4

among the world's twenty most important importers and exporters. Taiwan, as a large exporter, South Korea as both importer and exporter, and the People's Republic of China as an importing nation, are now higher in the league table than long-standing industrialized trading nations such as Switzerland and Sweden.

These shifts have become particularly evident in the export of industrial products, with the developing countries' share showing a gradual increase from 7 per cent in 1973 to more than 12 per cent in 1985 and 1986. As far as the importing of industrial goods is concerned, the position of the developing nations, at a 22 per cent share in 1985 alone, is statistically still relatively high, but has declined by 25 per cent since 1981. The reasons behind this decline lie in the increasing indebtedness of the developing countries (see below).

The narrower category of oil-exporting developing countries continued to expand its position in world trade from 1973 to 1986, especially with regard to imports. During this period their share of global trade increased from 3.4 to 5.6 per cent. The oil price collapse at the end of 1985, however, has had a detrimental effect on the trading activities of these countries and this looks set to continue.

Apart from the shifts between the three main blocs – the industrialized nations, the Eastern bloc and the 'Third World' – significant movements among the industrialized nations themselves have also taken place. Although there has been virtually no change in the ranking of the five largest industrial countries since 1973, with the USA now occupying second place behind West Germany and ahead of Japan in respect of exports, there have been significant changes in the respective shares of global imports and exports during the years under review.

Between 1973 and 1985, the United States has registered easily the largest upturn in imports, rising by more than five percentage points, which is equivalent to the total imports of the United Kingdom or France. Conversely, Japan was able to expand its portion of global exports from 6.4 to 9.2 per cent – almost half as much; its share of world imports, on the other hand, has remained constant at 6.5 per cent since 1973. The counter-trend in the USA and Japan's foreign trade is worth special mention considering that, between 1973 and 1986, both countries were able to register higher economic growth than the other OECD countries. The total value of exports of the industrialized nations in 1986 was US$1525.9 billion, comprising North America, Europe, Australasia and Japan.

In the OECD area, from 1973 to 1986, real gross domestic product went up by 2.6 per cent on an annual average; the average growth rate in the USA amounted to 2.8 per cent and in Japan it was as high as 4.1 per cent. As the USA's share of total world exports narrowed considerably during this period, the above average growth of the American economy is obviously the result of a relatively robust domestic economy. This has contributed to economic growth in other countries via a corresponding upturn in import demand, particularly so in Japan, which has been able sharply to increase its exports to the USA. The USA's external trade deficit has of course widened as a result, to many economic observers' consternation.

WORLD UNDERSTANDING THROUGH TRADE AND CREDIT

World trade has enabled different nations to approach one another, most of the time peacefully, and to gain a better understanding of one another's wide array of cultures and ways of life. The importance of international business cannot be over-emphasized. Even countries which do not have formal diplomatic relations due to political differences continue to trade with one another. The extent is sometimes small, but trade exists between all nations.

World leaders readily recognize that in modern times the well-being of most of the world's population depends on a flourishing international trade in goods and services. Credit extensions and financial assistance have emerged as important factors in today's international business environment. It can now fairly be said that world trade depends upon credit – the willingness of suppliers to provide buyers with merchandise and services and wait for payment at a future date. Credit is a present right to a future payment. Credit may also be defined in terms of its functions. As a medium of exchange, it can be referred to as 'future money'. As such, it provides a time element in commercial transactions that makes it possible for buyers to satisfy their needs despite the lack of ready cash.

Unfortunately, even in this enlightened age, far too many exporters do not understand the true cost to their business of the credit periods they are granting to (or which are being taken, over and above the allowed period, by) their customers – or, most serious of all, which are being additionally imposed by their customers' governments. Of this more in the next two sections.

THE WORLD DEBT CRISIS

Overshadowing trade throughout the modern world is the spectre of the 'world debt crisis'. There are several origins to this crisis which is expected to stay with us well into the twenty-first century.

Mostly it was about oil prices, which rocketed sky high, then dropped to dramatic lows, pushing first the non-oil-producing nations, then the oil-producers into difficult economic situations.

When the oil boom came in the late 1970s all too many of the oil producers expanded their economies in total reliance on the continuing high price of oil in the world market place. In anticipation of future income, many of them went on a spending spree and borrowed heavily overseas against future oil revenues which, as time has now shown, never materialized. As these developing nations, with all their oil reserves, tried to improve their domestic economy, they suddenly learned the lesson that after an oil boom can come an oil doom.

Meanwhile, during the boom especially, other developing but non-oil-producing nations had to spend more of their scarce foreign exchange to pay for their energy requirements; and any growth in these countries was achieved only with heavy borrowing from the industrialized nations.

As a result of all this, nations accumulated debts, some higher than others, but in many cases proving too much for the countries themselves to handle. All these debts needed to be serviced and most of the new credit loans and foreign borrowings granted to those unfortunate countries were used to pay for the interest required to service their debts. So the debts kept on growing, and international institutions such as the International Monetary Fund and the World Bank finally achieved stardom as many nations asked them to come to their rescue. Not infrequently, the international agencies discovered mismanagement of economies. Natural catastrophes did not help the situations either in Mexico, Venezuela and other debt ridden nations.

Initially, these difficulties were largely confined to Third World Latin American and African nations, but today many other nations have similar problems. The USA is the largest debtor in the world, with no relief in sight. France owes a fortune to West Germany. Some Asian countries such as the Philippines, India and Pakistan have similar problems. The overall situation has not improved since the beginning of 1986 and many countries have tried to service their debt by borrowing again.

The international credit management function

One of the main problems for the Third World nations is that they do not have sufficient quality products to export. To produce them they urgently need modern equipment and machines. These and other important products can only be delivered from the industrialized nations, but having been burned already over the past ten years, many of those nations' exporters are unwilling to continue to sell to the Third World countries unless they can be guaranteed payment at due date and a reasonable profit margin.

For some Third World debtors the situation now looks hopeless and the First World governments, banks and institutions, to whom this massive debt is owed, have long since realized that some degree of debt forgiveness will be inevitable. Banks and others have in effect begun writing down their debts by setting up provisions out of current profits. Many creditors have begun to cut and run, by selling their debts at large discounts to any entrepreneurs who can find a way of investing their blocked funds in the debtor country. At times those entrepreneurs may be fronting for the debtor government itself – an elegant way of achieving 'debt forgiveness'.

The present world debt crisis, if considered rationally, looks incapable of an absolute solution and the hope seems to be that with a gradual process of debt/equity swaps, interest rate adjustments, debt forgiveness and 'kicking the debt around until it hopefully disappears', the problem will, over a very long period of time, slowly diminish. But it will never just go away.

The more hawkish view says that sooner or later there will have to be a day of reckoning and on that day a lot of banks, institutions and investors are going to get hurt.

Either way, the debtor countries have to go on feeding, housing and clothing their populations and attending to their health care; and, despite the burden of their old debts, they still have to go on trading. Their terms of trade, though, have had to change and present terms must offer a high level of security to suppliers. Trade is thus restricted to what the debtor countries can afford by way of available foreign exchange, but, if the product is right, trade can still be profitable. Overall, international transactions have become more complex and nowadays more detailed work is required before merchandise can be shipped or services rendered. It is here where the skill of the credit manager comes into its own, assessing the degree of risk correctly and, in collaboration with the export sales function, finding the right trading formula to manage and control that risk and win sound business.

Without any doubt, the world debt crisis has highlighted the always present need for corporations to devote first class resources to international credit management.

THE TRUE COST OF EXPORT CREDIT

Companies breaking into exporting, or with only a small export portfolio in relation to their domestic sales, often fail to appreciate the true cost of the overall credit period relating to such exports. More often than not this is because, in their cost accounting systems, they do not separate the costs and profits associated with export trade from those of their home trade. Margins on export trade are traditionally low and are constantly under attack, not simply from the financing cost of the credit period given, but also from that of the quite often substantial periods which customers (or their governments) take in addition.

Being unaware that, in real terms, export sales are being made at a loss (because that loss is masked by hard earned profits on domestic trade) such companies neglect to install good credit management procedures, an omission that they may live to regret if and when the business is eventually unable to sustain its overall net losses.

The remedy is simple: in cost accounting terms treat exports and other international trading as a separate business; *and follow good credit management procedures*. This handbook is all about the latter.

INTERNATIONAL CREDIT MANAGEMENT – PROFESSION OR HOBBY?

The management of debts receivable requires special attention, particularly in economically difficult and tense times. The efficient and constant monitoring of customer credit risks as well as quick and secure collection procedures not only decreases risk, but also facilitates financing efforts and helps to ensure liquidity.

Cashflow is the life-blood of any successful company. Funds often have to be borrowed to start up or expand a business and great skill is required to find the right kind of financing at the cheapest acceptable cost.

In the quest for such finance, however, it tends to be forgotten that a prime source of cash flow should also be the prompt collection of sums rightfully due to the corporate entity. Their ability to achieve this, however, will be in direct proportion to the resource applied to all aspects of credit management.

In the USA, credit management is generally viewed as the management of accounts receivable and is, to a large extent, an integral part of international company organization. The credit executive has a great deal of authority and, as a rule, is also very high up in the company hierarchy. Only in such an influential position is the credit executive in fact able to take the measures that are necessary for the quick and secure regulation of accounts receivable; and to co-ordinate – or to regulate by means of his or her decisions – the divergent opinions of separate departments of the company. With such a set of tasks, it is not surprising that the status of the US credit executive is increasing in importance and responsibility.

In Europe where, ironically, international trade has far wider application, that status is still lacking to some degree, although the appropriate institutes and other common interest bodies are doing their best to put matters right. The key to proper recognition lies in managements' understanding of the real value of the activity to their various businesses and not treating it as a pastime to be indulged only when spare time permits.

Given the right status, the credit manager can contribute far more to the business than simply, say, overseeing the export ledger and chasing debts when they become overdue. There is much solid profitable business to be won provided ways can be found to bring risks down to a manageable level. Corporate systems can be improved with input from the credit executive and, perhaps on a more idealistic level, he or she should be at the forefront of national endeavours to simplify and harmonize world trading procedures.

EXPORTING COMPANIES AND MULTINATIONALS

This handbook may find its way into the libraries of corporations as diverse as the large multinational and the small exporting company employing just a few people. Although the scale is different, the message is still the same: prompt cashflow will help sustain your company; neglect good credit management procedures at your peril.

Of course the multinational has the benefit of large-scale operation; of course it can raise finance cheaply, handle its own foreign exchange dealing and use its muscle to achieve its aims. But it suffers from a number of disadvantages because of its sheer size. Communications can never be as good as in a small company and business activities will tend to be compartmentalized with nobody seeing the overall picture in anything but superficial detail. And then again, some companies are simply better than others, and have a better internal corporate set-up.

In corporations both large and small, however, the international credit management function, by its very nature, looks outward to many other functions and, if properly organized and given the right level of support, understanding and status, can play an important part in the management of the business.

LONG-, MEDIUM- AND SHORT-TERM CREDIT

A corporation's credit management approach will always be conditioned by the nature of its product and the traditional period of credit relating to it.

Manufacturers of capital goods, heavy machinery and equipment are accustomed to selling on medium terms (beyond 360 days) and/or long term (up to ten years) credit. This kind of trade is characterized by being financed by long-term loans (often government syndicated), much giving of tender and performance bonds and much laying off of the credit risk by way of credit insurance, guarantees and forfaiting.

Consumer goods and services, as the name implies, are consumed much more rapidly and should therefore be paid for much more quickly. Short-term credit periods ranging from immediate payment to settlement within ninety days are most common for such exports, although in the more remote and poorer markets up to 180 days or even longer is not unusual. However, as such payment terms approach 360 days, 'short term' begins to sound a little contradictory and exchange delays imposed by overseas exchange control authorities can exacerbate the situation.

By contrast, some consumer products, especially to the poorer countries, are exported under government programmes, enabling exporters to get paid immediately whilst their governments take on the burden of delayed payment.

By its very nature, short-term credit demands a more continuous, varied and detailed credit management activity than long- or medium-term credit and it is inevitable that in all seminars, courses and, indeed,

11

handbooks on international credit management, there will be a bias, as regards quantity of information, towards short-term credit.

COMMENTARY

The world is in crisis. It is not war, but an economic crisis, yet who can say that such a crisis is not as disastrous as a world war? Countries piling up huge debts are first unable to service them, and then face the threat of being unable to import essential products to keep their populations alive and healthy. Statistics clearly show that many countries have had no economic growth for years, with no improvement in sight. Whilst some people still ignore this situation, the more responsible have recognized its severity, and are trying to do something about it. Governments and financial institutions are working together, trying to solve many of the existing problems. Not all can be solved at once, but efforts are being made to calm the situation, and once again encourage world trade to grow. The USA and some other industrialized nations having similar debt burdens are at last doing something about them and working towards a balanced budget and an acceptable trade balance. Relative exchange rates and world stock market values will pass judgement on their success or failure.

History has shown that one country will always be more prosperous than another, but never before has our civilization seen such a great debt burden hanging over so many nations. Nevertheless the world's drive has to aim towards a solid rebound. And that rebound will depend upon improved international trade, selling more goods across borders, and providing more services to other parts of the globe. International business will hopefully expand in the years to come as consumer markets around the world increase in demand.

Credit will be a vital ingredient in any expansion and, in the world trade context, will continue to be a blessing. Whether it will be a blessing or a curse for any individual exporting corporation, however, will depend on that corporation's attitude to international credit management. Many more corporations will join in profitable international business, whilst others, not well prepared, will lose ground or go under. The latter will include those whose managements correctly consider sales and marketing as vital in keeping their company in the market place, but are unable to comprehend that credit management should be right up there at the top as well.

Recommended reading

Edwards, H. (1982) *Export Credit*. Aldershot: Gower. Strong on information sources and export credit management procedures.

2

Responsibilities, expertise and resource

Brian Clarke

For a company to succeed in international trade, it has to recognize the need to fulfil the requirements of the international credit function, no matter how it is organized.

An efficient credit control unit does not have to be an empire builder's dream. Everything is relative and, depending upon the company's size, one or two properly trained people may be all the resource needed to staff the unit. The important thing is that they should not be beset with other jobs, such as posting the ledger, unless they are still left with adequate time to fulfil all credit management requirements as and when they arise.

Equally important is the forging of close links with other departments, notably sales, finance and accounts. The linkage with sales should be reinforced by a similar linkage at senior management level. The international credit manager will normally report to the finance director but should also act as the catalyst for maintaining the link between the finance director and the sales director.

Only with close co-operation and understanding between the sales and credit functions can a company hope to control its international debtors. The company which neglects to collect its overseas debts on time can easily incur devastating losses, cancelling out profits hard-earned on its domestic business.

Sales and credit should thus work together to plan their company's strategy and tactics, measure actual performance against plan, review the shortcomings and agree action to improve their performance.

The important aspects of credit policy, accountability and relationships are discussed in greater detail in Chapter 24 where the various organizational philosophies for the credit function are examined.

14

RESPONSIBILITIES

The international credit function will normally embrace the following responsibilities.

1 Co-operate with sales/marketing to advise the finance director and sales director on the company's credit strategy, having regard to the company's policy, product spread, available markets and overall financial position.

2 Establish operational plans and decide the tactics necessary to achieve the company's strategic plan.

3 Obtain all necessary risk-assessment and creditworthiness information to facilitate the regularly updated categorization of countries and customers and the establishment of credit limits and other credit control criteria.

4 Play a leading role in the development of international credit management and associated systems.

5 Recommend appropriate terms of sale and methods of settlement, in collaboration with sales/marketing department.

6 Regularly research ways of financing and laying off risks (for example forfaiting or credit insurance) and make appropriate recommendations to help win otherwise unacceptable business.

7 Maintain appropriate records on customers in conjunction with the sales ledger section (this may be integrated with the credit management department).

8 Check orders/sales against credit limits or other criteria and action transgressions promptly.

9 Monitor prompt payments by customers and progress overdues energetically. Follow up, without undue delay, with stronger action.

10 Assist with all cash/currency management operations, ensuring all incoming funds are routed as swiftly as possible into the company's bank account(s).

11 For financial accounting and other purposes, regularly revise the bad and doubtful debts provision. Display this and other debtors information to senior management to keep them informed of the value and quality of debtor balances.

12 If involved in operational or line management terms with the sales ledgers, ensure they are maintained properly and kept constantly up to date to facilitate all international credit control operations, as well as meeting statutory and company requirements.

13 Provide a resource to check incoming letters of credit and the documents presented against them, to ensure that the required guarantees of payment are not frustrated by bad documentation.

14 Regularly review the performance of and liaise with the company's overseas branches and representatives (subsidiaries, associates and agents) to ensure their obligations are fulfilled in terms of adherence to policy, assistance in debt recovery, and provision of information.

15 Keep abreast of the company's foreign exchange policy to advise sales/marketing on pricing and invoicing in foreign currencies.

EXPERTISE

Sound, intelligent staff are required for the credit management function, preferably with grasshopper minds, capable of skipping from one problem to another without losing continuity or neglecting priorities. The job is necessarily multi-faceted, often requiring once-off additional effort to fulfil some urgent project whilst keeping the more routine work under control.

The prime objective of the function should be to protect and enhance the company's profits, and the ideal personnel will treat the company's business as if it were their own. They will lean towards proving the management 'Theory Y', which contends that people will work enthusiastically and efficiently if allowed to participate in decision making, rather than 'Theory X', which assumes that people will by their very nature avoid work as much as possible. It follows that those responsible for such staff should not be frugal in the delegation of the decision-making process.

As you read through this handbook you may be struck by the wide variety of disciplines and activities into which the international credit manager must dare to become involved. To do the job properly, he or she must have the following qualities and acquire the knowledge indicated.

Desirable qualities

- Numerate
- Articulate
- Analytical
- Dedicated and responsible

- Persistent yet diplomatic
- Organizational skill
- Ability to work under pressure
- Ability to determine priorities
- Prepared to travel
- Negotiating skill

Necessary direct knowledge

- Interpretation of financial statements
- Basic bookkeeping (or at least record keeping)
- Outline of import and exchange control regulations for countries handled
- Customer relationships
- Corporate organization and policy
- Sources of risk assessment information
- Terms and conditions of international sale
- International settlement methods
- International financial instruments
- International methods of funds transfer
- Availability of credit insurance
- Other ways of securing the risk
- Export finance options

Desirable knowledge

- Computer systems operation
- Foreign exchange management
- Banking operations
- Commercial law
- Treasury management

For many credit managers the 'desirable knowledge' soon becomes 'necessary'. But even where, for instance, in very large multinationals, the treasury, foreign exchange and other functions are separately organized, the credit manager must still have a firm though peripheral knowledge of these matters. He or she is collecting in the cash that requires managing and the currencies that are being dealt in the FX market. He or she is treating with the foreign lawyer progressing that badly overdue debt. And who better than the credit manager to help design the computer system that will improve all aspects of credit control?

It is indeed a multi-faceted job and needs the right calibre of people to do it and the right level of training in the many disciplines represented. Much of this training will be on the job, aided and abetted by the wealth of information which is always available to the curious and persistent (see the Appendix at the end of the book, which describes some of the sources of such information).

RESOURCE

Given the right calibre of people, there is still the question of the right numbers and the right support. No efficient and profitable corporation can afford to over-resource; but it is equally unprofitable to devote too few resources to that most important of functions, protecting the corporation's substantial asset tied up in debtors.

People

Assessment of the human resource requirement, and indeed individual performance measurement, can be *assisted* by a variety of easily established statistics and pointers, but there is no absolute method of assessing either.

A study made by the US National Association of Credit Management towards the end of 1987 offers an interesting example of an attempt to define an initial job standard against which both resource requirement and individual performance might be measured. Some 180 corporations in a common interest industry group were canvassed to compare accounts receivable workload measurements, mainly of a home market nature, along the following lines.

1 How many accounts would the average employee handle?
2 How many transactions, on average, would pass through such accounts?
3 How many debt-progression communications would the average employee initiate per month (by telephone, by letter, by telex and so on)?
4 How much time would the average employee spend per month on account reconciliation problems?
5 How many payments does the average employee handle each month and how many individual transactions do these settle?

Obviously, there was nothing sacrosanct about these questions and their precise range and detail and the weight each would be given would depend upon the particular application being studied. For the large international company, many other aspects of the job would need to be taken into account.

Nevertheless, by gradually building up in any given credit location an average credit assistant's workload and dividing it into the overall workload, the optimum human resource level can be roughly ascertained for the location and a case made for the appropriate resource allocation.

Supporting systems and other resources

Whilst people are the most important resource in credit, they are not the only resource. Suitable equipment, particularly of the electronic variety, and adequate running-cost budgets are also required.

Here again, the optimum level and cost-effectiveness have to be the watchwords and very often these resources are the subject of competition between departments.

Obviously no rules can be laid down as to how a corporation should spend its operating budgets, but suffice it to say, as examples pertinent to the credit function:

(a) it makes no sense investing large sums, say, in constructing a computerized modelling system for treasury management, if collection of the funds they should be managing is not under control because the accounts receivable system is archaic.

(b) an urgent visit to a foreign country to shift hitherto uncollectable large debts should not be postponed simply because there is nothing left in the department's overseas travel budget.

Neither of these situations is uncharacteristic. It all comes down to making the right case to higher management: the credit manager has, as was said above, to be analytical and a skilful negotiator.

Recommended reading

Edwards, H. (1982) *Export Credit*. Aldershot: Gower. Strong on information sources and export credit management procedures.

3

Agency representation

Don Nelmes

Exporting is a skilled, dedicated and sometimes difficult business, which requires that most companies engaging in it establish a professional export department staffed by well-trained and experienced personnel. The credit manager has a significant role to carry out in both this area and that of the activities of the overseas representative.

Finding, developing and servicing an overseas market or customer is the initial task of the export department, with regular visits to that market by the department's personnel. However, the need soon arises for more and in-depth support in the country itself. This is the major and special function of the representative or agent.

The function of agency or 'representation of another's interests' must have existed in one form or another almost as long as mankind and the requirements have not altered much throughout that time.

The requirements begin with a reputation for skill and reliability. They will include a thorough knowledge of the market (though not necessarily of the products), of the customers in the market, their probity, financial status and their place in the market's hierarchy. For the most part they will be nationals or members of the locally accepted trading community. They have to be trusted both by those they represent and those to whom they present themselves.

APPOINTING AN AGENT AND THE AGENCY AGREEMENT

Great care has to be taken in the appointment of an agent, be it an individual or a long-established agency company. Much harm can be done to the exporters' relationship with their customers if their interests are badly or ineptly handled. The commercial attaché or embassy of

20

one's own country present in the market are usually well informed and give good guidance in these matters. Government export trade bureaux, where these exist, are also a good source of information.

The overseas agent that you choose is likely to be with you for many years – it is well that you both choose wisely.

The appointment of an agent, the drawing up of an agency contract and the full legal implications are not for detailed consideration here. They are very much the province and speciality of the contract lawyer. There are, however, many related matters which impinge upon the credit area and with which the credit manager should have at least some knowledge or acquaintance. A useful guide obtainable through offices of the International Chamber of Commerce is the ICC publication No. 410, *Guide for the Drawing up of Contracts – Commercial Agency*.

In choosing an agent for the first time, or a new agent, it is advisable to adopt a 'trial basis'. An arrangement for one, two or three years enables the representative and the represented to determine if they are going to be successful together. During this trial period a letter of agreement should be exchanged between the two parties and not a formal agency agreement. This will follow if the trial proves successful.

Whichever course is followed, either letter of agreement or agency contract, the necessity for one or the other cannot be too strongly stressed. It will avoid misunderstandings, disagreements and worse.

As with most other contracts, the agency contract will normally be concluded in accordance with the law of the principal's country. Many countries, however, have their own laws which can override any external laws and render them inoperable for specific clauses. This is especially so where restriction of trade may arise. Another likely and highly contentious area is that related to termination of an agency or compensation clauses. In the case of agents of long standing a principal may find it obligatory to pay a much higher amount of compensation than that specified in the termination clause of the agency agreement.

It is as necessary to choose a good contract lawyer as it is a good agent.

The credit manager will wish to see written into the agency agreement secure and operable clauses relating to those areas affecting the credit function. Close liaison should be maintained by the credit department with the agent well in advance of an order being placed, right through until the funds have been paid and received in the seller's country.

The relationship between the credit department and the agent is an important one and should be as close as that between the sales department and the agent. Every opportunity should be taken to meet the agent so that he can be made aware of and updated on the criteria and aims of the credit and finance function. In turn, the credit manager can discuss and receive current market and customer intelligence from the agent. The time and effort devoted to these ends will be amply rewarded in the subsequent day-to-day operation of the business.

Agency, as already defined, is the representation by an individual or company for and on behalf of an external principal and for the purpose of that principal selling his products. Agency is not, of course, restricted to 'overseas agency' and very many agencies operate on behalf of domestic manufacturers, particularly in specialist trade areas. The requirements and the operations of both the domestic and overseas agent are common.

DISTRIBUTORSHIP

By comparison with agency, distributorship is the function of a trader who stocks, mostly for his own account, products which are eventually sold or distributed in the foreign country to fulfil orders placed directly with the distributor. Dependent upon the conditions of the supplier, the goods may be on-sold at a mark up price allowing for profit. The stocks held and all risks entailed are those of the distributor, subject to the normal contract of sale conditions as between buyer and seller, and variable by agreement.

Agency and distributorship, at least in common products, are kept quite separate so as to avoid confusion and possible conflict of interests. They are not, however, necessarily mutually exclusive.

The holding by an agent of consignment stocks does not, however, constitute distributorship. The matter of consignment stocks is referred to later in this chapter.

DUTIES AND OBLIGATIONS OF THE AGENT

The duties and obligations of an agent are considerable and in practice go well beyond the narrow definitions covered in the legal agreement. The export business and its practice is organic and subject to continual changes. These include the development of new technologies; the rapidity with which cargoes can be distributed between one country and another, often overtaking the ability to pass documents of title speedily enough (normally where technology or international agreements are lacking); rapid movements in exchange rates; sovereign or political risks; and the availability or otherwise of convertible exchange. These and many others on an ever growing list require an involvement from the agent. They come within the following general definitions.

1   To represent the principal in accordance with the conditions of the agency agreement or contract.
2   To exercise reasonable care in the execution of their duties so as to protect the principal from loss or damage. Negligence in this regard resulting in loss to the principal can be construed as the agent's liability.
3   To seek out and obtain business for the principals, promoting their products to the exclusion of those of any competition.
4   To ensure, in so far as is reasonable or possible, that orders received by the agent and passed to the principal are bona fide and that the customers concerned are solvent, properly established in their business and of known probity.
5   To advise with regard to method of payment, trading terms, names and addresses of bankers, correct legal trading style of each customer and to assist where required in obtaining credit data.
6   To advise the principal of all necessary import regulations of the country and to ensure that these are complied with and kept up to date. Where import licences are required, it is the normal practice of an agent to assist the customer as necessary.
7   Where the terms of payment are against letter of credit, to assist as necessary in its correct and prompt establishment by the customer and their bankers. To assist, so that the credit is raised in such a manner that the principal is able to conform to it and ship within its terms; and to follow through any subsequent amendments.

These are only a few of the duties and obligations which fall under the general heading 'protecting the principal's interests'. Many other duties will suggest themselves in line with the specific trade or industry represented.

AGENCY STATUS

Within the main conditions of the agency agreement there will be a definition as to the actual status of the agent or agency.

A *sole agency* will define the agent as being the only authorized agent or representative for a company's products or interests. This may entitle the agent to commission on products imported into the 'agency territory' by routes other than the agency.

A *limited* or *specific agency* may, however, limit such interests to specific product lines or to exclude products into which the principal's product may also be incorporated in whole or in part.

Equally, where agency is exclusive or sole it is usual for the agreement to stipulate that an agent may not handle the like products of a competitor. It is unusual that an agent acts only for one principal and it is to be assumed that the agent cannot, unless empowered to do so in specific cases, engage, contract, issue guarantees or otherwise confirm orders, delivery or prices. This remains the right of the principal who will normally issue quotations mailed or telexed through the agent to be followed by written order confirmation. Similarly, the agent is not usually empowered to grant credit or to offer credit terms. The same applies to delivery dates and product or quality guarantees, these functions being reserved to the principal.

Whilst the 'exclusions' are not necessarily part of the credit manager's 'over-sight' they are very important parts of the agency agreement which affect the credit and 'risk' area and to which attention must be paid, if future confusion or disagreement is to be avoided.

COMMISSIONS

Commission is the reward, the 'salary' paid to the agent against completed, successful and 'fully paid' business.

The commission payable is a negotiated and agreed percentage of the invoiced or selling price or, as negotiated, on net FOB (that is, excluding freight and insurance), and possibly net of financing costs (in the case of expensive or long-term credit) or on such basis as the parties to the contract agree.

On the basis that a 'sale is not a sale until it is paid for', commission remuneration is not normally paid until after receipt of proceeds in the seller's country. This of course concentrates the mind of the agent wonderfully, to pass the principal good and sound business from customers who can pay, and to encourage the agent to devote adequate time and effort to debt collection, which will be referred to later.

Commission to the agreed percentage and basis is usually generated in the currency of the underlying transaction, credited in accordance with prevailing systems by transaction, by month or whatever period. It is then held in the agent's account in the principal's books, being remitted under agreed procedure and frequency to the agent. Typically this will be monthly or quarterly after receipt of proceeds.

Some exceptions to the general rule can and do apply:

Exporters in countries with exchange control regulations

Exchange control regulations of some exporting countries require that reimbursement of credits of whatever kind can only be made after the proper receipt of the sale proceeds in external exchange, or in an 'approved manner'. Where this applies, the rule is obvious and mandatory.

Countries whose import restrictions or laws require deduction of commission 'at source'

Certain importing countries, in order to conserve precious foreign exchange, specify that commission must be paid by deduction 'at source'. The principals can establish this fact either from the agent or their own knowledge and information of import regulations of the country concerned. In this situation the commission calculation, based on the agreed formula, is shown on the face of the invoice and as an extension of the invoice value. The commission, included in the total invoice price is collected by the collecting bank at due time of payment (where draft or other payment instruments are involved) and the commission element transferred to the agent in the domestic currency. This, if anything, confirms the basis of 'payment of commission after payment for the goods' and obviates the necessity on the part of the exporter to issue credit notes or maintain an agency commission account. Where commission appears on the face of the invoice, it has the disadvantage of showing the customer the remuneration paid to the agent (not always something the agent may wish to have widely known).

Guaranteed minimum or otherwise limited commission

Where a new agent is being appointed in a market or where under-developed markets are being expanded or new products are being introduced, an agent may need to place significant extra effort and resource at the disposal of the principal than would be usual. In such a situation the agent may well be guaranteed a minimum commission. This may be for a given period of time (say the first one or two years) and for a specified amount regardless of actual 'sales produced earnings'. Equally, commission income might be based on a sliding percentage over sales, so as to achieve the same result. On the other hand, where a subsequent rapid growth potential is envisaged, the commission might be limited to a 'maximum' figure on a reducing percentage scale. The reducing scale concept is of course a much more difficult concept to 'sell' to a sales-orientated agent.

AGENCY EXPENSES

In addition to commission payments, and dependent on the nature, size and scope of the agency as well as its generated income, the agreement may well include the payment of specified expenses. Examples of these are telex and telephone costs, travel to the principal's country (where required by the principal), travel to and attendance at international trade fairs or meetings in pursuance of the principal's business and, as will be referred to later, extraordinary expense or activity with regard to debt collection or other assistance to the principal. This category of remuneration may replace the need for 'minimum or introductory commission' referred to above.

DEL CREDERE

Whilst the agent, as specified in his general duties and obligations, is required to protect the interests of the principal and, if a commission income is to be earned, needs credit-worthy and fully paid sales, no legal liability in this regard falls on the agent. This, of course, excludes the possibility of some total act of carelessness, wrong or misleading information – in which wilful neglect might be construed. Clearly the principals have overriding responsibility and duty to establish facts themselves and should never rely implicitly on the views or recommendations of any agent. The financial penalty for an unpaid sale is 'no commission' – and, if there are too many such occurrences, presumably an end to the agent's services.

The agent may, however, for all or specific business, agree or offer to take the '*del credere*'. This is a long-established concept although the phrase itself does not lend to simple translation. What it does mean is that the agent undertakes or underwrites the credit risk and that in the event of non-payment by the customer the agency will reimburse the principal.

Such an underwriting sounds a brilliant idea for the seller and, unless already credit insured, removes the problems associated with payment, or more relevantly non-payment, on the day.

Like most simple or good sounding ideas, *del credere* is not necessarily as good or as easy as it sounds. The negatives are worth listing.

1   A much higher commission will usually be required by the agent – even if the risk is 'first class'. If the exporter determines the need for 'risk cover' or their policy is to credit insure, then the credit insurance market is likely to offer at least competitive rates.
2   Is the agent financially capable of assuming the credit risk – or are the exporters merely exchanging one risk for another? They might need to credit insure the agent!
3   When is 'non-payment' to be determined? Does payment in local currency, with transfer delays, qualify as payment? Is non-payment arising from a disputed or alleged complaint? Was an unacceptable repayment programme proposed to the customer? Against the variable background of all these circumstances, when can the exporter claim under the *del credere* agreement?
4   In the event that problems arise on transfer of the availability of external currency, when is payment deemed to have been made? In most countries payment in local currency, with an undertaking to make good any exchange shortfall, is deemed to have fulfilled the legal requirement. In some countries undertakings to make good exchange losses due to devaluation of the local currency may in fact be proscribed by national law.
5   If an import licence system exists, carrying with it a payment permit, can the agent as a third party effect a transferable payment?
6   In the last resort, would the principal be prepared to invoke the *del credere* agreement and enforce, if necessary, payment by the agent? Many companies and particularly larger companies are reluctant in practice to call on the agent's *del credere*.

These are very serious questions which should be subjected to the closest scrutiny before considering the agent in a *del credere* capacity. It has much the form of a guarantee which itself is notorious and difficult in implementation and which many givers hope will never be called upon.

In spite of this formidable list of negative points there may be good and sufficient reasons to operate a *del credere* agreement. If the value of debts is relatively modest, it may be less costly than other 'risk limiting' actions or credit insurance cover. It should not, however, be seen as a substitute for sound credit control criteria and judgement.

CASE OF NEED

The function or duty of the agent as 'case of need' is associated with documentary collections sent through banks, forwarding agents or others, and for drafts or bills of exchange already lodged with banks for payment at maturity. (Chapters 14 and 15 define and discuss bills of exchange and documentary collections respectively.) It is standard practice that letters of collection carry an instruction reading along the following lines: 'In the event of any difficulty, non-acceptance, discrepancy or failure to pay at maturity, please contact immediately our agent shown as case of need, under telex copy advice to us'.

The case of need is then empowered to act in one of two capacities:

1 In an advisory capacity only: here an agent can only give temporary holding instructions and take minimum actions to limit any damage to the principal, whilst waiting for the principal to issue the necessary instructions or amendments.
2 Empowered to act: where this instruction is given, the agent is able without a formal power of attorney to clear cargo into the bank or other warehouse so as to limit demurrage, to postpone temporarily the 'due date' on a draft or bill and, if given full powers, to vary the amount of the bill. For the most part, a bank will accept such instructions from an agent empowered to act in accordance with the authority designated in the case of need 'box' of the letter of instruction.

It is of course essential that, whatever mandate is given to the agent in the capacity as 'case of need', the actions taken are communicated back to the principal and confirmed in due course by the principal.

DEBT COLLECTIONS – CHASING OVERDUES

The existence of overdue debts, of slowly paid or unpaid bills is a fact of life. (Chapter 18 explains how to collect overdue debts.) When an agent has obtained and passed an order which is duly shipped and invoiced, the agent's duties are not at an end – indeed they are only just beginning.

As mentioned in the earlier section, 'Commissions', no commission payment is normally due or available until payment has been made of the underlying invoice.

Dependent upon whether the transaction is on draft terms or open account, the principal's credit department will have in its ledgers a due date for the transaction, a transfer 'tolerance' where necessary and a signalled 'overdue' category.

Documentary bills transactions

In the case of bills of exchange transactions, customers who have difficulty in meeting the bill on time due to financial reasons or other problems – say a quality claim – would be expected to have contacted the agent for onward transmission of the facts to the principal well beforehand. An extension to due date may then be agreed, a new bill raised or payment suspended pending a resolution of the problem.

Where bills of exchange and their honour are held in high regard and where a customer's administration is well ordered, prior discussion and amendment would be the case. These two factors are of course not universal and unpaid and consequently dishonoured bills of exchange will arise.

The dishonour or non-payment of a bill will be known to the agent and drawer immediately the payment date is passed, by virtue of the fact that the bank where the bill is presented should notify both the drawer and the case of need (agent) on the day and by telex. (Again, refer to Chapters 14 and 15, and the ICC Uniform Rules for Collections in cases where the country concerned is a signatory to them.)

In circumstances of dishonour and in the absence of prior contact, the agent, without first referring to the principal, would be expected to make immediate contact with the customer to establish the reason for non-payment and simultaneously to instruct the collecting bank to 're-present the bill for payment'. In line with the principal's standing instructions and policy, the agent – if so empowered – will instruct the bank to note or protest, or to hold for protest, as the case may be (see Chapters 14 and 15).

Protest may very well be delayed where its effect would do more harm than good and where local circumstances dictate – this is very much a matter of local custom and practice.

Thereafter the procedures followed will be close to those for open account overdues.

Open account transactions

These require slightly different initial procedures to those on bill of exchange or documentary collection terms.

In the first instance, the agent is unlikely to know if a debt has been paid or not. Remittances are normally made directly by the customer or his banker to the supplier's account as instructed on the invoice – by bank telegraphic transfer or, less frequently, mailed by banker's cheque. These remittances are not normally advised to the agent.

Consequently, the first indication will be when the debt goes overdue in the exporter's ledger. However, the agent may well have a good knowledge of the state of the account and of the day-to-day circumstances of the customer – frequent commercial visits are likely to be made if for no other reason than to seek orders. The agent is likely to maintain some form of 'local memorandum ledger' in order to monitor commission earnings and availability. The principal in turn should provide the agent with a detailed monthly print-out for all accounts within the agency territory.

Again, depending upon the exporter's systems, a regular, possibly monthly, statement of account will be sent to each customer, usually through the agent. When a debt falls due or past-due, the exporter's credit department will contact the customer directly asking for payment. A copy of this chaser, as with all correspondence, confirmations of order, invoices and the like should at all times be sent to the agent. The actual debt chasing, be it by letter, telex or telefax, may be routed through the agent or sent direct to the customer. In this area of debt collection the following factors are most important.

1   The information should be as up to date and correct as possible, so that debts for which payment is already in course of transmission are not being chased – this only negates the value of the data and vitiates debt-chasing actions.

2 The communication will benefit from being in the language of the recipient – a good reason to route through the agent.
3 The chaser may carry more weight if it appears to originate from the principal – even though routed through the agent.
4 Additional pressure must be applied by the agent and subsequent payment or payment promises monitored and, if not fulfilled, pursued rigorously.

The agent, as the 'person on the spot' has an invaluable role to play in this phase of the debt collection operation. The agent needs to be fully in line with and to support the principal's philosophy and attitudes towards the maintenance of their terms of payment and contract and to understand the cashflow, risk and cost elements associated with overdue debts.

Some overdue debts will inevitably go sour – companies fail, going into bankruptcy, liquidation, suspension of payments, receivership, Chapter 11 or whatever the insolvency or bankruptcy procedures of the country concerned provide. The agent will be expected to assist the principal and become involved in whatever action is required under these circumstances. Prior to this it may well be necessary to negotiate repayment programmes or to initiate legal action. Unless the principal already has a chosen local lawyer, the advice and recommendations of the agent will be sought and close liaison maintained throughout between lawyer, principal and agent.

It is obvious that the agent may be involved in extraordinary activity, time and cost where these cases arise. These costs and, in the event of the ultimate failure of the debtor, the forfeiture of rights to commission will clearly be taken into account by the principal and, without prejudice to those rights, be reimbursed under the agency expenses category.

The calibre of an agent is proven in the determination and enthusiasm shown not only in obtaining orders in the first place, but also in ensuring that payment terms are followed. There is a fine balance, however, between the prudent business of assessing and taking risk and the over-cautious approach which can turn away good business and lose more profit than the bad debts it avoids. Where this is identified, it is for the principals to advise the agent of their policy with regard to laying off all or part of the risk in the development of business. These options and possibilities are explored in Chapters 9 and 10.

CONSIGNMENT ACCOUNTS

Consignment accounts are 'local stockholdings' and are usually suggested for speciality products or large product ranges, where customer call-offs are in small units which might otherwise be uneconomic to ship individually. A consignment will be shipped on a 'free of charge on consignment' basis and held in the name of and under the title of the principal. It may be held in an agent's warehouse – having been customs cleared, in an independent warehouse or in a 'Free Port' or customs warehouse (duty where applicable unpaid until clearance).

The clearance, storage, warehousing etc. will depend totally on local circumstances and import regulations. Considerable care, however, has to be taken by the exporter, not only to conform to these requirements, but also to clear the tax position in the country concerned. This is a matter for advice from the taxation experts, because the company might otherwise find themselves treated as 'trading' inside a country and become subject to local taxation laws. These might in turn spill back into their domestic trading even where mutual taxation agreements exist.

Given that a consignment account is established, the local agent will then have to operate the day-to-day control of the stock, maintaining full and complete records for onward transmission to the exporter. Transfers out of stock to point of sale may be invoiced direct by the exporter or, not unusually, by the agent, using the exporter's headed notepaper or invoices, transferring accounting copies of these back to the exporter for incorporation into the customer's account.

Because the 'stockholding' is at all times the property of the exporter, all risks are for their account. The exporter therefore directly, or through the agent, must keep the property insured and establish that the warehousing facilities are adequate, securely maintained and meet the requirements of the insurer. All costs in the stock and its warehousing will be for the account of the exporter. The final selling price agreed may differ from the 'free of charge value' mentioned earlier, probably recovering the incurred costs of 'stockholding', and invoiced on shorter credit terms than would be usual for direct indent business. Once invoiced, the transaction becomes part of the standard direct indent procedure.

There is a continual need with consignment stock accounts for the agent and the principal to reconcile holdings and to ensure correct product rotation. Exchange control regulations need equally careful observation so as to ensure that unsold product can be transferred back either to the seller or exported to some other determined destination.

A subsidiary area of consignment account operation may arise where a direct indent sale becomes frustrated for whatever reason – for example, a customer no longer wants the particular product, a credit problem arises so that product is recovered or delivery withheld, or quality problems suggest product is taken back from the customer. In these cases, and with the agreement of the agent, such product is cleared into a local warehouse or into the agent's warehouse, either in the exporter's name or that of the agent. Much the same procedure then follows as that for consignment stock itself, the role of the agent in this case being to endeavour to re-sell the product locally or to arrange shipment back to the principal or to a destination determined by them. All costs will be for the principal's account and it may well be that funds to cover this will be required by the agent 'up-front'.

This is another clear example of the 'extraordinary' duties and obligations assumed by the agent, which will seldom be written into the agency contract.

SUBSIDIARY OR RELATED COMPANIES ACTING AS AGENTS

Most of the comments and subject matter in this section on overseas representation have been addressed to the concept of the 'independent agent', or agency company and have not had regard to the fact that an agency may be established which is either one's own subsidiary, related/associated company or quite simply a 'liaison office', with members of the exporter's own staff operating in an overseas territory.

Subsidiary or related company agencies

The requirements that the parent company has for such an agent are substantially the same as if it were an independent agency, excepting a number of points.

Clearly the parent company's own subsidiary or staff will act under direct instructions and mirror faithfully the philosophy of the parent company (not that all children obey their parents).

The treatment of such an agent with regard to commission will also differ fundamentally. Commission will clearly be based on total running cost reimbursement plus an element of local profit. For the most part such commission will be paid 'up-front' and not after the receipt of, or be contingent upon the receipt of funds from customers in settlement of the underlying sales.

The salaries of a company's subsidiary or associated company staff and the costs of running the office have to be met, whether sales are made or not and regardless of payment being received. A subsidiary similarly often supports many more staff and overheads in the projection of a 'company image' than would be the case of an agency company or individual agent running, as it were, on one officer and a secretary.

The independent agent or agency company is seldom restricted to a single agency and provided the representation is non-competitive, such an agency will represent a wide range of principals from many countries in their portfolio. The subsidiary or associated company will of necessity usually represent a narrower group of interests, as defined within the principal's own group of companies or associates.

Comparison between the function of an agency and a subsidiary company is not strictly valid because their respective purposes are disparate. (Chapter 4 covers the various aspects of operating through subsidiaries.)

It is often the case that a large company with specific local manufacture in a country and a number of home-based subsidiary companies will also have an overseas subsidiary. In such a case it may make for group sense and economics, as well as administration, to use that subsidiary as one's agent. The same might apply where there is an associated company in which the principal has a substantial investment.

Liaison offices

In a very limited number of cases, a company may decide to have a liaison office in a territory. This may suggest itself where a subsidiary company does not exist, or is not warranted; or where it cannot exist because of the country's laws, but where the company believes there is a need for substantial involvement; or equally in those more unusual circumstances where the company wishes to operate outside the local subsidiary company arrangements.

A liaison office staffed by a principal's own direct employees will act in exactly the same manner as an agent, having the same responsibilities but, like their subsidiary company confrères, be totally cost covered 'up front' and funded regardless of sales income generated or payment for sales.

TERMINATION OF AGENCY

As happens from time to time, a principal's business grows or increases through merger or acquisition to the point where the need for a local subsidiary company in a territory is indicated – the principal's interest in the country as it were outgrowing the agent. Company takeover or merger produces the same situation – especially where more than one agency exists in the same market.

In this situation one or both agency agreements may have to be terminated. The problems and the arrangements surrounding termination have been referred to earlier in this chapter. An existing agent or agency company, or part of it, may be incorporated into the new subsidiary company – an arrangement which is often most successful.

These cases have to be dealt with most carefully, observing not only the original agency contract but again referring to the local laws concerning agency termination. Agency is, however, much more than a question of laws and contracts: it is one of relationships, of relationships built up perhaps over many years on a tripartite basis – the principal, the agent and the customer.

Although an agent may have to be replaced for all kinds of good and sufficient reasons, the principal must always be aware that all three will still remain in the market.

Recommended reading

Ezer, Shaul (looseleaf update) *International Exporting Agreements*. Albany, NY: Matthew Bender. Provides precedents and information on US practice.

Schmitthoff, Clive M. (1986) *Schmitthoff's Export Trade*, 8th edn. London: Stevens & Sons. The standard English work on this subject.

4

Operating through subsidiaries and affiliates

Robert T Lambert

From initial entry into the international market place with exports through a broker or representative, many companies became multinationals with world-wide operations. More companies are following this example as the world becomes one market place. Any company which is to remain viable should plan for international expansion as part of their overall growth.

Large multinationals generally have a corporate level international credit officer to oversee the investment in accounts receivable and regularly report on its trend and condition to top management. The degree of control of the credit officer will vary from company to company, based on individual corporate culture.

It is generally preferable for the international credit officer to be free from any domestic credit responsibility. Where the international credit officer has both a domestic and international responsibility, time and energy will invariably be directed to the domestic responsibility. The domestic responsibility has the comfort of familiarity. There are no culture or language difficulties and there is a feeling of more control over the receivable investment.

Operating through a foreign subsidiary or affiliate has all of the problems, risks and opportunities of domestic business, plus the additional problem of operating in an environment where the culture, language and governmental regulations are quite different.

International credit executives need a thorough understanding of each subsidiary's organizational structure and how it functions in its home environment. Although credit management has basic principles which are valid regardless of the country, credit and collection customs and practices do vary from country to country.

ORGANIZATIONAL OPTIONS

There are three basic organizations to be considered in understanding a company's international structure. The subsidiary may act only as a commission agent, or as a national sales company, or may function as a manufacturing subsidiary with administrative, selling and manufacturing capability. Most large multinationals utilize all three organizations as they approach international expansion on a country by country basis. The prelude to forming a subsidiary may be a joint venture or acquisition.

The decision as to which type of organization is utilized by a specific company is driven by numerous factors. They include the amount of international experience, risk tolerance, investment capital, governmental laws and regulations, economic conditions and commitment to the international market place.

The decision on organizational structure is not always the optimum one or the one preferred for a certain region or country. Today's multinational may have wholly-owned subsidiaries, minority interest subsidiaries and joint ventures. In most countries, foreign investment is regulated by the government which may restrict the amount and form of the investment. The governmental factor may force the multinational to compromise on the preferred organizational structure.

Joint ventures

If the multinational is not sure of the reception of its product in a country or does not want to risk a subsidiary investment initially, a joint venture may be negotiated. The risk of the initial investment may be lessened by making the contribution in the form of technology, spare home country equipment or the right to use a well-known trade mark. The home country partner may put up the manufacturing capability (if required) and a sales, distribution and administrative system.

The joint venture agreement should contain a provision for the periodic review of the joint venture by the credit officer and the submission of regular reports on the condition and trend of the accounts receivable. The agreement should also contain authority for the multinational to appoint the chief financial officer of the joint venture.

The astute multinational will also negotiate terms for cancelling the joint venture as well as an option to buy a larger or complete interest if the joint venture is successful.

Acquisitions

Multinationals today expand by acquisition. There is a definite role for the credit officer in the acquisition process. The first step in an acquisition is the signing of a letter of intent, that is, an agreement to negotiate a definitive acquisition agreement.

During the period following the signing of the letter of intent, two major events occur: first, the terms of the definitive acquisition agreement are negotiated; second, the acquiring company performs a due diligence review to verify that the business is as represented by the seller.

The role of the credit officer during the contract negotiations is as follows.

1 To be available for consultation on functional elements of the contract.
2 To provide functional expertise to the negotiating team.
3 To review the contract language through multiple revisions.
4 To provide recommendations to the negotiating team at key points in the process of developing and finalizing the contract.

The role of the credit officer in the due diligence process is discussed next. In evaluating the quality of the purchased accounts receivable and developing an insight into how the new subsidiary operates its credit function, the following checklist will prove helpful.

1 Construct a flow chart of the generation of the accounts receivable.
2 Review an organization chart of the collection function.
3 Review the invoicing procedures from receipt of order to the accounts receivable ledger.
4 Determine who makes credit decisions and the scope of their authority. Do they have sufficient credit and financial data for making the decision?
5 What are the credit terms and what is the procedure for exceptions or changes?
6 How are receivables collected – local deposits, direct deposits, wire transfers, cash, international payment, or other method?
7 Construct a flow chart of the receivables cash collection system.
8 Review accounts receivable systems and interfaces.
9 Review controls for accounts receivable collection.

10 Review how accounts receivable are reconciled with the general ledger.
11 What sources of information are used to post accounts receivable?
12 Is there a cash forecasting system and, if so, how are cash receipts forecasted?
13 Prepare a detailed listing of amounts ninety days or more overdue and determine if they are collectable.

The checklist can be expanded or reduced as needed in evaluating receivables in a specific acquisition.

The credit officer's review will focus on the quality of the receivables purchased. Are they collectable in the normal course of business? Look for amounts which are disputed or skipped over in the normal collection process. If there are significant uncollectables in the accounts receivable, the acquisition price may have to be adjusted.

The purpose of the due diligence review in an acquisition is to verify that the assets purchased have the value represented. The credit officer's review includes a verification of the value of the assets and at the same time establishes a foundation of knowledge for bringing the new subsidiary's credit practices into line with the parent's customs and practices.

SUBSIDIARIES ACTING AS COMMISSION AGENTS

Commission agent companies may be preferred for handling international business if the multinational has a product line which is easily distributed in one country yet is manufactured or processed in another. It requires a smaller investment to establish this type of subsidiary presence in a country.

As profits would often be difficult to remit due to overseas exchange controls, they are normally included in the export price and a separate commission is paid to the subsidiary for the sale. Commissions are sufficient to cover the selling overhead.

In addition to representing the lowest investment, this type of subsidiary can provide a profitable foreign operation where it may not be possible because of exchange shortage to repatriate profits from a manufacturing or national company operation. At the further extreme a really severe shortage of foreign exchange might make imports impractical and force consideration to be given to an alternative form of subsidiary presence in a particular country.

Commission agent companies do not usually maintain their accounts receivable at the local country level. The agent sources product from one or more manufacturing or processing facilities and the credit is managed by the shipper as an export credit sale. Where agents are sourcing from multiple warehouses or plants, credit is usually managed on a regional or centralized basis.

Credit control

Regional or central credit control allows control of both the customer and country risk. Multiple location sourcing to one customer must be controlled on the basis of the total exposure. In the absence of adequate credit control, multiple sourcing can lead to both a large commercial risk and a country risk.

Credit and collection administration may be either regionalized or centralized: the choice between the two alternatives is usually governed by the size of the international business. The multinational may begin with a centralized international credit organization and move to regionalization as the volume of international business grows. Regionalization comes from growth into a geographical unit, such as Western Europe, Eastern Europe, the Far East, North America and South America.

Most multinationals with either a centralized or regional credit organization will carefully evaluate the commercial risk inherent in the sale. Many companies dealing in the export field fail to have a systematic process for evaluating the country or sovereign risk in export credit sales. The country risk must be evaluated as carefully as the commercial risk or the exporter may be faced with lost or blocked funds.

Any company exporting in today's international financial climate must have a system of protection against the country-risk exposure. This system must be either one of systematic evaluation of the country risk or of transferring the risk to a third party through insurance or some other means. Without one of these, rapidly changing international conditions may jeopardize the timely collection of the company's export receivables. Chapters 6 and 8 cover the assessment of country risk and the principles of risk management respectively, and Chapter 9 discusses the means of sharing the risk.

Some suggested steps toward developing a systematic process for examining country risk and using the information gained for the multinational group as a whole, are as follows.

1 Review and develop information on country credit and financial conditions from financial newspapers and periodicals, a major bank or export country risk-rating service, and information obtained through participation in programmes sponsored by export trade groups.
2 Develop and issue a periodic report that tracks exposure by country for all units involved in export credit sales. The report should reflect the short-term economic and political factors which may affect the timely payment of the country's imports. Available risk ranking, payment-trend surveys, and foreign exchange availability should be included.
3 Establish restrictive terms (that is, confirmed irrevocable letter of credit or cash in advance) when a deterioration in country conditions makes itself evident.

The international credit officer will find it advantageous regularly to visit the subsidiaries and develop personal relationships with the branch personnel and major customers. Many credit/sales clashes can be avoided by a personal acquaintance with the other party. Major customers should also be visited to gain first hand knowledge of the customers and the local market place. Active involvement with such customers allows the credit officer to establish firm relationships and effective business practices upon which to build future growth, and to avoid disputes.

Marginal risk business

An active multinational credit manager who is close to the branch personnel and major customers is well positioned to take on marginal customer business. There is a growing trend toward accepting marginal customers and recognizing them as an important business segment. Marginal customers are determined from the credit evaluation, which indicates that selling to the customer represents a higher risk than is usually accepted. (Chapter 7 examines the assessment of customer risk.)

Marginal customers are ones who usually have one or more of the following traits:

(a) payments are usually made beyond terms;

(b) management is weak or inexperienced;

(c) financial statements, if available, indicate a weak balance sheet or a recent trend of operating losses.

Marginal customer business must be handled carefully if it is to be profitable. The credit officer must determine the trend of the marginal customer. Customers who are marginal because of the rapid growth of their business offer an excellent opportunity for the supplier to make profitable sales. A customer who is marginal because of a deteriorating trend in the business will usually lead to an ultimate bad debt loss. With rapid turnover of the receivables and careful control of the credit limit, maximum profits can be extracted from these customers before sustaining the eventual loss. A supplier with excess production capacity may find the marginal customer business a real profit opportunity.

No one can predict how long a marginal customer may be sold successfully. One approach to selling marginal business is to risk one quarter's gross profit. For instance, assume a quarter's gross profit on a marginal account's purchases is $100 000. Establish this amount as the credit *limit* and ship up to the limit. Insist on payment prior to shipping additional goods. Ultimately, the $100 000 will be lost, but good profits can be earned in the interim.

MANUFACTURING SUBSIDIARIES

Manufacturing subsidiaries are usually wholly owned, since they represent the largest type of investment undertaken in the international arena. This type of company functions primarily as a domestic company within its home country. It is responsible for manufacturing, sales, distribution, marketing and credit and collection.

The responsibility of the international credit officer for the manufacturing subsidiary is usually a functional authority over the resident subsidiary credit manager. The subsidiary credit manager will report through the financial management of the subsidiary.

The international credit officer should receive monthly or quarterly reports from the subsidiary which contain at least the following information.

1   Ageing of the accounts receivable, indicating amounts current (within terms) and past due (by number of days: up to thirty; thirty-one to sixty; and over sixty).

2 Days' sales invested (DSI) or days' sales outstanding (DSO) calculation, using whichever methodology is preferred by the company.
(Chapter 8 discusses this calculation and its uses).
3 Summary of the reporting period activity in the reserve for doubtful
accounts (bad and doubtful debts provision), indicating amount
reserved at the beginning of the period, additions to the reserve,
write-offs against the reserve, recovery of prior write-offs and the
closing balance.
4 A listing of the largest customers with an ageing of their individual
account receivable balances and any pertinent comments concerning overdue amounts.

The reports should be reviewed and compared to prior reports to
identify trends. The credit officer should immediately request additional information from the unit credit administrator about any unfavourable trends which are revealed; and should request that specific action
plans be submitted to remedy the situation.

Credit reviews

Many multinationals use a periodic credit review as a way of maintaining uniformly high standards of credit and collection management
among a diverse group of subsidiaries.

The credit review usually takes place annually. It consists of a visit to
the subsidiary by the corporate or international credit officer for an
on-site detailed review of the following matters.

1 Does the subsidiary have an up-to-date credit and collection policy
and procedure which is consistent with corporate policies? Are the
unit personnel adhering to the policy?
2 What is the condition and trend of the investment in accounts
receivable?
3 Is the reserve for doubtful accounts adequate and has it been
administered in a proper manner?
4 Is adequate information contained in the credit files upon which to
assign the level of credit limit required by the customer?
5 Are the credit officer's remuneration and job level adequate to
secure and maintain a competent credit professional?
6 Are there adequate training and educational opportunities for the
credit officer and staff to develop in their function?

At the conclusion of the review, the credit officer discusses the findings with local management and makes recommendations for improving the credit operation, reducing the investment in accounts receivable and avoiding large credit losses.

A report of the findings of the credit review and the actions recommended is prepared and distributed to management. A periodic follow-up is maintained to monitor progress in implementing recommendations.

NATIONAL SELLING COMPANIES

National selling companies are subsidiaries which import the multinational's products and distribute them from a sales branch.

Credit management may be at the branch level if it is sufficiently large for a local credit operation. If the branch's sales and profits are insufficient, a regional or centralized operation may be used. Where there is an off-site credit officer, the gathering of credit and financial information and the collection activity will mainly be done by the local branch personnel, working with the credit officer.

For the international credit officer, management of the credit function for national selling companies will be similar to that of a manufacturing subsidiary. Periodic reports of the status and trend of the accounts receivable investment are required. These reports are particularly important where the credit officer is not based at the branch's location. The periodic credit review can be used to ensure that adequate credit controls and collection follow-up procedures are employed at the branch level.

Sovereign or country risk

Although the branch may be adequately financed and have every desire to remit amounts owed to the parent, a country's foreign exchange situation may cause restrictions of outgoing cashflows back to the parent. (Exchange controls are discussed in their many forms in Chapter 19.)

The experienced multinational has learned to manage the sovereign risk of its own branches in the same way as for its export customers. It may actually become necessary to impose restrictive terms on a subsidiary. The exposure may be controlled by maintaining as much of the profit as possible in the export selling price from the shipping unit, with the branch operating much as a commission agent, since profits are usually more difficult to remit if there are severe exchange controls.

RE-INVOICING AND NETTING

Multinationals can use a variety of re-invoicing and netting techniques to:

(a) enhance local credit management;
(b) centralize or shift foreign exchange exposure; and
(c) reduce bank float and charges.

Re-invoicing via the local group company

Goods shipped from a group company in one country direct to a customer in another country, where the multinational also has a group company, can often be reinvoiced via the latter to the benefit of the group as a whole.

The main objective will be to get the debts into the local subsidiary's books so that they can progress them as if they were in respect of their own supplies.

The technique also increases cash management opportunities through increased inter-company cash flows. In addition, if the customers are to be invoiced in their own currency, the option of carrying (or covering) the exchange risk in either the supplying company or the local company can be simply determined by the currency in which the inter-company invoice is denominated.

The main impediments to local re-invoicing are:

(a) exchange controls or import licensing regulations if they are severe in the customer's country – if this is the case, however, there is probably no subsidiary through which to re-invoice;
(b) suspicions of price rigging – the local company will usually need to inflate the value of the second invoice to reflect its mark-up and this will probably need careful explanation to any price control authorities;
(c) burden of administration – but for most multinationals, computerized order/invoicing systems, electronic transmission and local printing can normally overcome this problem.

Using a centralized re-invoicing centre

In addition to re-invoicing via the group company, and as a prelude to it, multinationals now often use a re-invoicing centre and a system of netting receivables and payables to reduce and centralize their foreign exchange exposure. These systems can also be utilized to provide sources of short-term finance by a process of 'leading' and 'lagging' individual units' payments and receivables (this process is described in the next section: 'Short-term financing').

Structuring a system of re-invoicing and netting receivables and payables requires the assistance of the banks and a careful study of the tax and foreign exchange laws of the country in question.

The re-invoicing centre may be one of the multinational's branches but is usually in a neutral tax country. The centre is an office or address which provides the billing address used by the multinational's participating branches. Each subsidiary invoices the centre in its home currency and establishes a receivable with the centre.

The multinational may also pool the participating subsidiaries buying needs for raw materials and buy at the lowest price based on total quantity. The materials will be invoiced to the centre, which will make payment in the invoiced currency.

The centre thus has payables to and receivables from the units in a variety of currencies, whilst the units have no foreign exchange exposure. Normally the centre will net off the receivables and payables of each participating subsidiary and arrange a monthly settlement of accounts.

The group's exposure risk is reduced substantially because the exposure is limited to the net difference of each national subsidiary's payables and receivables with the re-invoicing centre.

Short-term financing

As mentioned above, some short-term financing capability is available through settling a unit's receivables with the centre using accelerated terms (leading), while delaying settlement of the unit's payables on extended terms (lagging). This form of short-term financing is practical when one or more of the subsidiaries have seasonal cash generation while other units have seasonal cash shortages, or there are cash rich subsidiaries in the system. An appropriate interest charge will normally apply, and the whole activity will be subject to any local exchange control regulations.

COMPUTER SYSTEMS FOR MULTINATIONALS

Credit officers, whether at headquarters or branch level, need up-to-date information on the status of customers' accounts in order to fulfil their responsibility of managing the accounts receivable investment. For large volumes of work, the credit officer has come to depend upon the computer as a partner in identifying customer accounts which require attention and avoiding the review of accounts which do not require attention.

Computers and computer systems have become commonplace in business, virtually world-wide. (Chapter 25 discusses support systems generally, with particular emphasis on computers and the design of computer systems.) Multinationals have the choice of a centralized or decentralized computer configuration. If decentralized, they may also choose whether or not to use common systems.

Centralized computer systems

Computers today have enormous computing capacity and almost unlimited storage capacity. A world-wide communication system can be tied into a centralized data centre for parent and subsidiary on-line computer processing. Regardless of location, the credit officer can have on-line access to the computer from any place with telephone communications.

For some companies, a world-wide centralized computer system and data centre may be cost-effective and meet corporate objectives of control and instant availability of information. A multinational whose business depends on constantly changing commodity prices finds a centralized, on-line and real time system an absolute necessity.

Additional advantages of a centralized computer system are uniform data input and output, uniform reporting and the ability of the international credit officer to review account status on an ongoing basis. The main disadvantage is that a system failure brings the whole system down worldwide.

Whilst capacities are increasing, the physical size and cost of computers are both decreasing. These factors will cause additional companies to consider and implement a centralized computer system. Large multinationals will move in this direction in the future.

Decentralized computer systems

The majority of multinationals operate with decentralized computer systems. Each unit, as well as headquarters, has its own computers and data centres. Part of this is due to corporate moves to decentralization in recent years. Part of it is due to the decentralization decision occurring prior to the availability of computers with sufficient computing power for a centralized operation.

Multinationals with a decentralized system must still resort to paper based reporting of information and results. Whether printed as computer output or typed from other output, it must be either mailed or faxed to headquarters. This inefficiency argues for a centralized computer system and data centre, with networking to all units.

Common systems

Centralized systems run one system which is common to all units. Decentralized computer systems are more efficient if common systems are used in all subsidiaries. One accounts receivable system, whether developed in-house or purchased as a package, can usually be utilized by all subsidiaries. This also applies to other systems – the general ledger, order processing, invoicing, inventory and so on.

Common systems are desirable for the following reasons:

(a) stronger technical support of a common system may be achieved by limiting the number of systems supported by the systems group;
(b) costs may be lower by negotiating significant discounts (in a purchased system) for multiple unit use;
(c) input and output is uniform for all units.

Management of today's multinationals should have a long-term systems plan which will respond to the quickly changing hardware and software environment. The microcomputer is becoming smaller and faster, with more storage capability, and has a place in the systems plan. Lap-top computers with the capabilities and storage capacity of yesterday's microcomputer are now available.

The multinational which stops and waits will be passed by very quickly.

PART II
ASSESSMENT AND MANAGEMENT OF CREDIT RISKS

5

The range of risks

Burt Edwards

The credit management function looks after a company's investment of funds in what is normally its largest, and certainly its riskiest, asset – accounts receivable, or trade debtors as it is sometimes known. Receivables represent perhaps 25 per cent of a company's total assets and 40 per cent or more of current assets. As well as being the asset most vulnerable to erosion from the ravages of time and a panoply of costs, receivables have a fragile position as the source of most if not all of a company's cash. As the intermediate stage between sales and cash, receivables deserve management of the highest calibre and seniority – to make sure that sales do indeed turn into cash.

Technically, receivables are merely book entries to record invoiced sales and, sadly, there are many companies which just sell and keep accounting records. Most of the all-time high insolvencies of recent years have been companies of that kind, which concentrated on product and sales priorities and neglected to manage their assets, so that they became over-borrowed and ran out of liquidity. More astute companies learned long ago of the need to give top-level attention to the generation of cash. Rather than regarding receivables as an accounting chore, successful companies manage them from the point where they are created – the customer's order – or even earlier, at the stage of identifying sales prospects.

THE REAL COST OF CREDIT

Credit management is defined differently in different companies but a general view is that the task is to identify and manage the risks that may arise in selling on credit terms, so that profit is maximized.

Assessment and management of credit risks

Credit risks are the events which may prevent sales turning into cash, either temporarily or forever. Sales are the means to cash but companies need cash, not the sales achievement alone. The means to cash is the profit element of sales and, in between logging sales in the profit and loss account (and counting its profit content from day one) and receiving payment from customers, there is the crucial period of waiting. During that time the balance sheet shows the sale as an actual asset owned by the seller. But it is a weak asset, constantly under pressure and sometimes lost. Compared to retail sales over the counter, or any sales on cash terms, the business decision to allow credit to customers is a decision to expose the bottom line on the income statement to uncertainty.

In an era when credit is taken for granted by customers, when interest rates are high and insolvencies are at record levels, it is necessary for

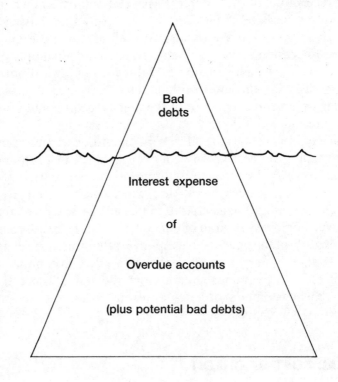

Figure 5.1 The iceberg of credit risk

companies to apply the same adequacy of resource to managing credit as they do to selling and production.

Most companies borrow working funds and in the UK, for example, pay from 10 to 15 per cent per annum for the privilege, when net profits average only between 2 and 5 per cent of sales. Contracts may specify monthly payment terms but the reality is that receivables usually represent between two and three months' sales value and therefore tie up borrowings at expensive interest rates for that length of time.

The 'iceberg' cliché applies very aptly to credit losses. Whereas bad debts attract emotion and noise, because they are specific and visible, they are only the tip of the iceberg. The expense below the surface, possibly ten times greater, is the interest cost of unpaid and overdue accounts. Its less visible mass has the extra menace of hiding the next few insolvencies to hit the business. Figure 5.1 shows this in diagrammatic form.

CUSTOMER RISK

The two key questions to probe credit risk are:

1   Are they going bust?
2   Can they pay our sales value on time?

The information needed to answer these questions will also help sales staff to assess: 'Are they growing or declining in ability to buy from us in the future?'

Thus it is possible to assess solvency, liquidity and growth.

Companies are free to sell or not to any customer, and a seller's available customers have a wide and complex mixture of strengths and weaknesses, so it is worth getting information before risking loss from trade credit.

Commercial credit risks are those which lead to non-payment by trade customers, in both home and export sales. Political risks affect payments by governments or lead to actions by them to hinder payment by trade customers and are found only in international sales.

The general risk in trade credit

In the UK trade credit is between two and three times greater than bank lending in overdrafts. The risk for creditors is higher than that for banks, who have the ability to demand balance sheets, charge interest and take security on assets. Trade debtors average about seventy-two days of sales value in the UK, on terms which mostly require settlement at the end of the month following date of invoice. In any one industry, companies competing with similar products to similar customers vary between 50 and 150 days' sales outstanding (DSO – see Chapter 8 for further discussion of this and other financial ratios)! The national tolerance of slow payments is highly vulnerable to interest expense and bad debts.

A company borrowing at 15 per cent per annum with a net margin of 5 per cent, loses that profit if the customer has not paid after four months. The cost of replacing a totally lost investment – a bad debt – is also very high. A company making 5 per cent net has to sell twenty times the value in new business to recover a lost debt.

> In the ever-changing world of contemporary commerce, it seems to me essential that management should realize the vital importance of employing experienced and skilled credit managers.

It is not surprising that Sir Kenneth Cork, the world's most famous insolvency expert, wrote thus in his foreword to *Credit Management Handbook* (Gower, 1979). His experience in investigating the downfall of so many companies clearly demonstrated to him the need to manage risk better.

Are failed businesses just unlucky? Or did they perhaps make and sell without bothering to check their customers' ability to generate payment? Or perhaps not give senior enough attention to the total credit task?

There is no 'standard customer'. The financial strength of each company is as unique as a fingerprint. A seller's portfolio of customers is a complex mixture of large, medium and small firms, with debts ranging from huge to tiny. Some customers are growing, and others in decline, all at different speeds; some are more liquid than others; some are profitable, others less so; some have more lively managements than others. Yet credit is allowed to all and sundry, so a seller should not be surprised that they cannot all make payment on time.

Even those sellers who check creditworthiness have commercial pressures which lead them to 'oversell', that is, to sell more to a customer than the customer has the capacity to pay for. How much greater the risk for companies that oversell without knowing the status of their customers!

Credit, or the ability to acquire value without payment, has become normal for individuals, firms and nations. The abnormal increase in risk to sellers has not yet been fully realized, but is the sole reason why the job of credit manager is important today, when it didn't even exist fifty years ago.

Bad debt risk increases the longer that accounts remain unpaid. Not only are overdue accounts the ones most likely to fail, but their amounts are greater because further sales have been made in the meantime.

Tables 5.1 and 5.2 illustrate the effect of overdues on profits and the sales needed to replace bad debt losses.

The credit period agreed in a contract is usually regarded as unimportant compared to other obligations such as price and delivery. Many managers seem to believe that anything to do with money is a formality for the 'office', and not part of their commercial responsibility. It may be significant that senior German sales managers would discuss payment terms as earnestly as they pursue price increases. Is it a coincidence that their country enjoys more buoyant trade, cheaper money and a slower development of the credit manager job?

So, trade credit is both a valuable financial donation to a customer, who also enjoys the benefit of the goods, and a risk decision for a seller, whose profit varies with the date of payment.

Profits and credit

The effect of payment delays on margins – not gross margins, but what is left after all expenses are deducted – can be easily measured. For example, a 4 per cent net profit before tax is lost after a four-month payment delay, if money costs 1 per cent per month. A seller's aged debt analysis may show debts twelve months or more overdue. By reference to Table 5.1 it is possible to see the point in time when the profit on debt of any age disappears.

The need to assess creditworthiness

By definition, a seller should trust every credit buyer. Small firms with few credit accounts can possibly know every one closely enough to judge them. But as businesses grow it becomes impossible to know all customers personally, so the trust decision has to be standardized.

Table 5.1
Effect of overdue debts on profit

Number of months overdue after which a loss is caused by interest expense

Annual cost of borrowing (%)	Net profit on sales (%)						
	10	*8*	*7*	*5*	*4*	*2*	*1*
6	20.0	16.0	14.0	10.0	8.0	4.0	2.0
8	15.0	12.0	10.5	7.5	6.0	3.0	1.5
10	12.0	9.6	8.4	6.0	4.8	2.4	1.2
11	10.9	8.7	7.6	5.5	4.4	2.2	1.1
12	10.0	8.0	7.0	5.0	4.0	2.0	1.0
14	8.6	6.8	6.0	4.3	3.4	1.7	0.8
15	8.0	6.4	5.6	4.0	3.2	1.6	0.8
18	6.7	5.3	4.6	3.3	2.6	1.3	0.6

Table 5.2
Extra sales needed to recover bad debts

If you have an actual loss of (£)	And your pre-tax profit is						
	2%	5%	7½%	10%	12½%	20%
	You will require this amount of additional sales to offset your loss (£)						
100	5 000	2 000	1 333	1 000	800	500
500	25 000	10 000	6 666	5 000	4 000	2 500
1 000	50 000	20 000	13 333	10 000	8 000	5 000
2 000	100 000	40 000	26 666	20 000	16 000	10 000
5 000	250 000	100 000	66 666	50 000	40 000	25 000
10 000	500 000	200 000	133 333	100 000	80 000	50 000
50 000	2 500 000	1 000 000	666 666	500 000	400 000	250 000

Assessment and management of credit risks

Credit is expressed in money and time, for example '£5000 can be allowed to customer A on thirty-day terms, but customer B is only good for £500 and we require payment in seven days'. Those different decisions are based on information, which somebody has to obtain and evaluate.

Poor credit granting may include overlooking the limited liability aspect when someone has a personal relationship with the customer. Most credit managers will have heard, at some time, a comment such as: 'Don't worry, they're OK, I've known the owner for years.' Whilst personal friendship is useful in selling, it has little to do with financial ability, and at meetings of creditors, there are usually some people with long faces who have 'known the owner for years'.

Payment behaviour

Commercial credit risks concern, in the end, the buyer's insolvency, because the other main losses – from payment default and repudiation of contract – are caused by actual or near insolvency. There is also considerable breach of contract by companies from day to day. 'Cash management' is often a euphemism for delaying payment for 'as long as we can get away with it', regardless of agreed terms.

The wide range of excuses for delaying payment only exists because companies know they are in the wrong. Credit managers soon get to know the highly improbable excuses, such as:

- 'The cheque is in the post.' – one of the great lies of life!
- 'The computer run is in two weeks' time.' – the tail wags the dog!
- 'Mr [important person] has to approve all payments.' – do we tug forelocks?
- 'One of the signatories is not here.' – is the ship rudderless?
- 'Can you send proof of delivery?' – again!
- 'We've run out of cheques.' – rudderless again?
- 'We have a temporary cashflow problem.' – this particular one has legal implications; and directors know they must never admit that their company cannot meet its liabilities.

There are debtors who refuse to pay until good and ready, stating: 'We pay everyone at sixty days – if you don't like it, we'll buy from someone else.' Such threats are very worrying to smaller businesses, which suffer real damage from slow payments. Other threats include 'we'll cancel the contract unless you agree to . . .', or 'we know other suppliers who are willing to give us longer credit'.

Customers' excuses when asked to pay are an under-used source of credit risk intelligence. The seller cannot be sure when, if ever, payment will be made. Those who continue to play games with no genuine reason are frequently found to be the insolvencies of the near future. A genuine inability to pay is rare. If customers want to pay they will, even if they have to borrow extra from the bank. It is when borrowing powers are fully stretched and the bank takes a closer interest that failure becomes a strong possibility. This critical period is usually unknown to supplier-creditors which is why unreasonable delaying tactics must be taken seriously.

Some sellers create their own problems by being unwilling to ask for payment in case it upsets customers. Not only do such firms fail to take the right collection steps but they also incur larger bad debts. Any sales advantage (which is doubtful anyway) is outweighed by the interest cost and bad debt risk.

The Law of 10:1

This states that: 'The average company incurs ten times more expense in interest on the extra borrowings needed to finance overdue debtors than it loses in bad debts each year.' Any company can work out its own ratio but whatever it is, the general obsession with bad debts should be replaced with closer and more senior attention to collect slow-paying debts. This would, in event, improve bad-debt figures.

Standard or special goods

Credit risks take on more significance when products are specially made for a customer and would be dead stock if credit were restricted. Standard goods can usually be sold elsewhere. This difference helps to decide whether credit needs to be checked at the order stage or only when delivery is due. For example, a manufacturer of garden spades would not suffer unduly if an order were frustrated, because exposure would only occur at delivery. But a manufacturer of parts for a particular customer's machinery would suffer if orders were cancelled because the special goods would not be saleable to others. Where a company is able to deliver immediately orders are received, all credit risks begin at the same point.

Why do companies fail?

In the record insolvency losses of 1984 to 1987, two common factors stood out. First, the failed businesses lacked liquidity, that is, they were unable to repay their creditors, and their banks refused to lend any more because they had no confidence. It is not enough for companies to plead solvency to banks and creditors – they must also prove they are liquid enough to pay back commitments. Insolvency is prevented by liquidity, not solvency alone, or even profit.

The second factor was a lack of management information. Frequent operating data gives warning of problems early enough to correct them. Companies get into trouble when they do not produce timely data or choose to ignore it. Many failed businesses had excellent products and technical skills, but no information structure for managing in their industry environment.

One kind of company at risk is that dominated by an autocrat who always suppresses the views of his or her functional directors. Another is where personal relationships with suppliers have created a false sense of well-being, which amounts to nothing when the bank calls in the overdraft. An even worse risk, because it could be tackled, occurs when large corporations develop too many levels of management. The board of directors becomes isolated from daily decisions and problems are slow to reach them because of all the layers of people protecting their own positions. Even established companies can become inefficient, over-borrowed and vulnerable to acquisition – a more respectable form of failure.

Small firms often rely on outside accountants, auditors, or their bank to warn them of unsatisfactory financial trends. But those parties have no such obligation and when the crash occurs the plaintive cry is heard: 'Why didn't anyone warn me?'

A sobering statistic is that one in two newly formed companies fails to survive their first two years of life. This is why credit managers put a special 'watch' coding for a few months on new accounts which are also recently formed businesses.

Financial analysis of a cross-section of companies in various industries shows that solvency, liquidity and growth ratios either rise or fall gradually over a short period of years. They almost never zig-zag. For companies going downwards, it is the angle of decline which decides whether rescue is possible or not.

Warning signs of insolvency

There is almost always plenty of warning for creditors, but commercial pressures make it difficult sometimes to face up to restricting exposure. Credit analysts have their own favourite ways of spotting impending doom. These can be grouped thus:

(a) account behaviour;
(b) financial ratio trends;
(c) behaviour of key personalities;
(d) computer forecasting services.

John Argenti has written in *Corporate Collapse* (McGraw-Hill, 1976) that the final stages of a company's failure are not reversible. He observed that symptoms show in three phases over a short period. The first is a major imbalance of senior management, which leads to the second phase of mistakes in financing; then, more visibly externally, are the final acts of desperation – creative accounting, cut-backs in operations, resignations and so on, up to the end.

Credit analysts have developed profiles of failed firms and compared them with those that have succeeded over a period of years. The balance sheet features and trends are given scores, and useful comparisons made with existing or new customers. There are insolvency forecasting services available, which establish for each industry sector a vital pass-mark level. Companies scoring above that are expected to survive and below it to fail. There is never a predicted actual date of failure but the general warning may be valuable. Howard Tisshaw of Performance Analysis Services Ltd states confidently 'no company has failed without warning since 1972 and there has usually been three years' notice'.

People managing credit from day to day apply common sense to payment behaviour. Dick Bass in his book *Credit Management* (Business Books, 1979) warns that cheques returned by the bank 'refer to drawer', rather than 'please re-present', are a reliable indicator of near-insolvency. And when salesmen talk to customers about orders and credit staff telephone for payments, both are wonderful opportunities to detect likely insolvency. A customer's employee may say: 'Can you wait a few days, we've got some problems here, I've heard the bank is cracking the whip.' Or: 'We've been told to freeze orders [or payments].' Sales and credit staff should be trained to listen for signals. And use them!

Disputed debts as a risk

True bad debts only arise from insolvent customers. But millions of pounds are written off each year by sellers in respect of old, uncollectable residues of debts due from perfectly solvent customers. These are usually items on which there was a query or dispute at the due date for payment. Customers do not normally wish to pay until mistakes have been rectified. The errors are typically for wrong prices, defective goods, late delivery, shortages, proof of delivery needed, and so on. Many sellers take months to rectify errors and customers have learned that it pays to defer payment as a lever to get action. Customers in financial difficulty are able to play the system and delay payments by alleging faults and defects. The time lapse before their true motive is detected depends on the efficiency of the supplier in handling claims. With luck, the customers do not fail meanwhile.

Apart from the interest cost of supporting receivables inflated by excessive disputed amounts, some suppliers lose more than they need to in insolvencies, if they have been slack in resolving claims so that properly due balances may be collected.

The last throes

When a company borrows significant sums, the lender normally secures the loan by a debenture or charge on the borrower's assets. Legally registered, this carries the right to appoint someone to take charge of the business if the lenders get concerned about the prospect of recovering their investment. When the debtor experiences liquidity problems and is required to repay the loan, frantic activity may be seen to raise capital elsewhere while payment is delayed to other creditors to conserve funds. The directors may sell off plant or stock at a loss, or even the entire business. Any creditor in good contact with their major debtors would soon become aware of the death throes and have the chance to avoid further exposure, press or persuade for payment and possibly take back useful goods not paid for – especially where the creditor has Retention of Title rights.

Summary of commercial risks

Sellers can increase profit performance by avoiding the losses that arise from poor management of credit risks. Whereas revenue could be protected by selling for cash only, or by allowing credit only to govern-ment and 'blue chip' companies, profitability would be adversely hit by low volume effects. Commercial realities dictate that credit must be risked with some firms in the 'poor' category. The major problems are slow payments and bad debts, in that order. Their effects are interest expense and lost revenue respectively.

These risks and losses occur in domestic and export sales, and in exporting there are also significant risks from political or governmental events. These are dealt with next and methods of risk control are covered in Chapter 8.

RISKS IN INTERNATIONAL TRADE

The problems of slow payments and bad debts apply just as much in international trade as in home trade. In addition, export sales profits have been hit in recent years by the inability of nearly two-thirds of the world's governments to remit hard currency after actual customers have paid locally. The delays and, in some cases, the protracted negotiations for rescheduling foreign debts have produced serious losses for ex-porters not carrying credit insurance protection. While the transfer risk is the main worry, there are other actions by governments which prevent intended export deals from being completed.

The differences in export credit

The principal differences involved in granting export credit as compared with domestic credit are as follows:

1 Longer time scales: for delivery, funds transfer and the credit period.
2 Extra time and distance require terms which provide security for the risk perceived.
3 The expectation of local credit terms for each market.
4 Competition from other countries having different money costs and governmental policies.
5 International standard terminology.

Export credit terms

The range of credit terms is very wide. The minimum risk exists with

Assessment and management of credit risks

Cash in advance, or at least before shipment. But that is not very competitive and is only possible in a strong selling position. Letters of credit, in all their variety, have flooded back into use in recent years because of the transfer risk in so many markets. They have always been an option for specifically risky customers in any market. Most foreign business outside of the EEC and North America has been transacted on terms involving documentary bills of exchange, whether payable at sight or on a term basis. This has the advantage of involving the banking system in collecting and provides a certain security in controlling the release of goods. Some European markets, mainly France, Spain and Portugal, work quite normally with bills. And then there is the use of ordinary open account terms, where the customer is trusted to remit direct to the seller after the credit period.

The risks in export terms

Because a seller may have to agree any number of different terms and credit periods it is vital that they are fully understood and operated correctly, with documentation produced to international standards.

An irrevocable letter of credit cannot be revoked or amended without the exporter's agreement, but its 'no risk' value depends on compliance with its conditions and the liquidity of the opening bank. Confirmation by a first class bank in the seller's country removes the latter risk.

In CAD (cash against documents) or sight draft transactions, the seller's continued ownership of the goods, until payment, works with sea shipments because the bill of lading is a document of title. But exports by air, road or rail have no document of title and are simply released by the carrier to the consignee on arrival, so they should be consigned to a bank or a representative of the exporter, to maintain control of the goods until payment.

With term drafts, the security is the same as with sight drafts, except that the bank releases the goods against an acceptance instead of actual payment.

Political credit risks

'If the country risk is not acceptable, there is no point in examining the buyer' (R. Bass, *Credit Management*, Business Books). The best assessment of export customers is pointless if their local payments of pesos, kwachas or other soft currencies cannot be converted into dollars, pounds, or some other hard currency. Nearly half the nations of the world have almost zero hard currency to pay for imports. And they impose restrictions of all kinds to deter importers and frustrate contracts between willing commercial parties. (Chapter 19 discusses exchange controls in their many varieties.)

The two main political risks, therefore, are:

(a) *transfer* risk, where a shortage of foreign exchange delays payment to the UK;
(b) *political events* which prevent payment even if currency exists.

The risks are listed in detail by the OECD state credit insurance agencies as follows:

1 A general moratorium on external debt decreed by the government of the buyer's country or of a third country through which payment must be made.
2 Any other action by the government of the buyer's country which prevents performance of the contract in whole or in part.
3 Political events, economic difficulties, legislative or administrative measures arising outside the exporter's country which prevent or delay the transfer of payments or deposits made in respect of the contract.
4 Legal discharge of a debt (not being legal discharge under the proper law of the contract) in a foreign currency, which results in a shortfall at the date of transfer.
5 War and certain other events preventing performance of the contract, provided that the event is not one normally insured with commercial insurers.
6 Cancellation or non-renewal of an export licence or the prohibition or restriction on export from the exporter's country by law.

Political risks are considered to be outside the control of both exporter and buyer. They exist in most of South America and much of Africa and Asia. In 1987 sixty of the world's 208 countries were talking to the International Monetary Fund about help in rescheduling their existing foreign debt. About two-thirds of the world's countries are net importers from the other one-third on a continuing basis, so they will remain net debtors, but with reducing capability to pay and eventually to import. The prospects of being paid in traditional ways are unclear, and innovative forms of funding will have to be developed in the near future if essential needs are to be met. So it seems unavoidable that exporters will have to compete harder in the few, strong markets still available and also learn the more complicated ways of getting paid from many soft-currency markets. The risk management task is certainly increasing in complexity.

The transfer risk

Hard currency is allocated by poorer nations to lists of products according to national priorities. Defence items, food and medical goods understandably have preference over luxuries and consumer goods, whilst royalties, dividends and profit remittance are low in pecking order. Delays in transfers are also due to bureaucracy of administrations, as well as to the accuracy of the exporter's paperwork. Thus, delays varying from one to twelve months from the same market may be due to different priorities for goods, efforts of local agents, standards of documents or state administrative systems.

Import licences are widely used to control foreign currency. In better-organized countries, priorities are decided before orders can be placed by importers, so that a licence equates to currency allocation and no licence means no payment.

The transfer problem also has the effect of increasing the risk of buyer default and insolvency. Because he is responsible for finding enough local currency to meet the full invoice value at the eventual date of foreign exchange transfer, a buyer may find the burden too great so long after he took in the goods. Many a large-scale importer has for this reason either defaulted on foreign payments or gone right out of business.

If governments reschedule foreign debts during the waiting period before the foreign exchange transfer, uninsured exporters have no option but to wait – up to twelve years has been known.

Other political risk events

Government bodies, outside the control of both exporter and buyer, may act to nullify a contract already signed. They may forbid the import, seize equipment, interrupt shipment or local performance, or simply prevent payment. Usually it is the customer's government which does these things. But it may be the exporter's, by refusing a licence for hi-tech equipment, for example; or it may be the government of a third country, for example refusing to allow goods to be transhipped because of a political stance. Not all events can be foreseen and many contracts suffer from overnight decisions by governments. This risk of the un-expected leads prudent exporters to the credit insurance market if possible losses could be painful.

Risks exist not only in countries short of foreign exchange. There are the East–West trade restrictions, protectionist quotas, various alliances between nations and against others and, in 1988, an estimated seven-teen wars being waged. Various blacklists and embargoes have a limiting effect on free trade between willing parties – and affect the prospects of funds being remitted when deals are agreed.

Large contracts for capital goods usually have 'conditions precedent' to be met after signing but before contracts become effective. The conditions may require an advance payment, ministry approvals, tech-nical tests, sample signatures and cross-guarantees for pre-payments. After the publicity fanfare of a major contract signing there usually follows frantic activity, as subordinates seek to satisfy the preconditions in time. In some cases, especially in Africa at the start of the debt crisis, governments prevented conditions from being met as a means of conserving funds, and exporters were left with much advance expense but no contract.

An impending change of government in a country already in difficulty is usually a signal for prudence by exporters. It is sometimes the case that a new regime announces restrictive measures which prevent in-tended imports or cause orders to be renegotiated on less favourable terms.

The world debt crisis will restrict trade and payments for a long time to come, and more and more official interference in commercial con-tracts will be experienced both before and after they are signed.

SUMMARY

These then are the risks that face the credit manager. Export credit management has always had to assess customers for solvency and liquidity, and the assessment methods are all covered in Chapter 7. Now, however, there is the additional and more complex task of judging country risks which have such critical effects on marketing plans, contract negotiations, cashflow and profit. Chapter 6 examines the way in which these judgements are made.

6

Country risk assessment

Hans Belcsak

It is generally accepted that an international credit manager – aside from having to be thoroughly familiar with the terms and conditions of sale in cross-border goods exchanges, with documentation and with the various methods of settlement and transmission of funds – needs to be well versed in the assessment of customer risk, that is, the judgement that is needed to determine whether a given customer will pay, and will do so on time.

Credit people, particularly when they have just moved from domestic to international operations, are often not nearly as aware of the crucial importance of assessing country or sovereign or transfer risk, although it often is a far more decisive determinant of an exporting company's bottom-line performance than any error that may be made in gauging a particular customer's ability and will to settle bills promptly.

As a concept, country risk has been much disputed, heatedly debated and all too often belittled in the years since World War II. This was true in the 1950s, when full currency convertibility was still comparatively rare. It remained a fact of life through the booming 1960s, during the oil crises of the late 1970s and early 1980s, and more recently, since the onset of the international debt crisis in 1982.

Part of the problem has been that many multinational banks, some of the largest US financial organizations among them, took the attitude that 'there is no such thing as soverign risk,' since countries 'never go bankrupt'.

Maybe so. But this is a question of semantics. Certainly, we have seen numerous cases in the recent past of countries becoming unable to service what they owe, and/or losing their will to carry the interest obligations on their outstanding IOUs. The Perus, the Nigerias and the Zambias of the 1980s have come as close as any nation can come to bankruptcy. The multinational banks, by setting aside large reserves for Less Developed Country (LDC) loans and by selling off LDC debt paper in the secondary market at a fraction of face value, are implicitly conceding that some of the loans in their portfolios will never be repaid.

Just because a country is having difficulties with interest and amortization payments on bank loans does not necessarily mean that exporters to that nation will have serious collection problems as well. There have been a number of instances in recent years when countries declared a unilateral or contractual moratorium on bank debt, but continued to remit payments for imports more or less promptly. Indeed debt reschedulings by banks and foreign creditor governments frequently are intended, inter alia, to give the over-borrowed LDCs breathing room so that they can continue to purchase abroad what they need to keep their economies growing.

But a country's difficulties with bank creditors are usually not without consequence for its trade relationships. They can trigger a tightening or withdrawal of trade financing facilities and impair the ability of suppliers to get export credits confirmed. As a rule, the same policies and trends that lead a nation into inability to service debt to foreign banks also raise the spectre of abrupt changes in foreign exchange policy that may make it difficult or impossible for the importer to pay for goods on the due date, in the currency of the invoice. This, however, is only one aspect of the country risk discussed in this chapter.

THE CONCEPT OF COUNTRY RISK

Sovereign risk in international business is a fairly broad concept that is usefully divided into three categories.

1 Transaction risk: linked to a specific transaction that involves a specific amount and is tied to a specific time frame, such as an export sale on six-month draft terms.
2 Translation risk: which stems from the obligation of multinational companies regularly to translate foreign-currency assets and liabilities into the parent company's accounting currency, a process that can give rise to bookkeeping gains and losses, such as a German firm translating US dollar assets into German marks at times of a falling dollar.
3 Economic risk: which in the broadest sense encompasses all changes

in a company's international operating environment that generate real, economic gains or losses.

The country risk that international credit managers are confronted with overlaps all three of these categories. It is usually a transaction risk, has accounting-exposure implications, and invariably entails economic consequences, good or bad. In simplistic terms, analysing country risk means determining a nation's (as opposed to a customer's) creditworthiness with the focus on the ability and willingness of a foreign government to put at the disposal of local companies, public or private, the foreign exchange necessary to service their foreign-currency-denominated obligations and liabilities to foreign suppliers.

In practice this means that the credit manager must consider political risks, economic risks, social risks, import and export regulations, foreign exchange risks and a variety of other internal and external country conditions and trends as an essential part of the credit approval process.

But 'risk' is not inherently a negative term. It embraces opportunity as much as it does danger. No business would survive long under the onslaught of competitiors if it were single-mindedly focused on the avoidance of risk. In international as in domestic business, risk is not something that should be shunned at all cost, but something that should be carefully managed.

Risk analysis as a tool

Seen against this backdrop, country risk analysis is neither a 'time-wasting exercise in trying to gauge the unmeasurable,' as some business managers tend to think of it, nor the infallible 'decision maker' from which others expect to be provided with 'go/no-go' solutions. It is nothing more and nothing less than an essential management tool for the international credit executive, one that will allow him or her to manage risk without eliminating too many opportunities.

Country risk analysis – the gathering and evaluation of economic intelligence with the objective of prudently managing risk in international business – has gone through a number of ups and downs in Europe as well as in North America. As a formal discipline it entered a flourishing period right after the Shah's fall from power and the subsequent Islamic revolution in Iran, which caught more than just a few traders and investors by surprise with its abruptness and violence. The heyday for country risk analysts came in the late 1970s and early

1980s, and it ended, paradoxically enough, on the day on which Mexico in 1982 informed its creditor banks in no uncertain terms that it was no longer able to service its obligations to them.

One might have expected that the threat of default by one of the heavyweights among the over-borrowed LDCs – which in turn marked the onset of the world debt crisis – would have given country risk analysis a vigorous push. Instead, although the now chronic debt problems of the Third World have made managers acutely aware of the vulnerability of business operations in such lands, many multinational corporations on both sides of the Atlantic have disbanded in-house risks assessment teams or at least cut them to a bare-bones staff.

The profession, which has been practised in the trading nations of the world since the Phoenicians, has had its reputation tarnished. Top managements frequently feel that the 'predictive powers' of the analysts in whom they put their trust has not measured up. But before one draws the conclusion that country risk analysis can be safely dispensed with, perhaps one ought to take a look at what went wrong, and why.

Indeed, if one contemplates the headaches that now confront banks with outstanding loans in Latin America or in Africa, investors seeking to repatriate profits and dividends from problem countries ranging from Algeria to Zaire, or exporters waiting for the settlement of their invoices in so many lands around the globe, one may well ask where the risk analysts were when the troublesome deals were made. Considering the difficulties that manufacturers and financial institutions have with blocked funds, woefully past-due payments and reschedulings imposed upon them, one can hardly fail to see why the profession has suffered a blow to its prestige.

Strengths and weaknesses

Why did banks get caught with some of their heaviest loan exposures in Poland, Mexico, Brazil and Argentina? Why did experienced exporters fail to see the handwriting on the wall? Why did they continue to ship and run up huge receivables in Nigeria and Iraq? The reasons for the errors made are legion.

To begin with, country risk assessment never has been, and never will be an exact science. Analysts in this field must work with a daunting array of interdependent variables where errors made in the projection of one inevitably lead to whole chains of false conclusions. They must attempt to evaluate dynamic forces that frequently are difficult to detect in their early stages, problematic to forecast and virtually impossible to quantify.

Even the so-called 'hard' statistics on which the assessment must rely are almost always incomplete, often less than dependable, and occasionally outright lies. For example, Mexico since the eruption of the debt crisis has not published regular, consistent and comprehensive official reserve statistics. The only current figures on Argentina's hard-currency and precious metals reserves come from private estimates and occasional leaks by lower-echelon bureaucrats. And governments do 'cook books'. One only needs to recall the Philippine Central Bank's deliberate overstatement of its reserves by as much as US$600 million prior to 1983.

The law of averages, in a word, does not favour country risk analysts always being right. It weighs even more heavily against those who are inclined to rely primarily on econometrics – numbers, ratios, and equations that ignore or skim over the often overwhelming importance of political and social influences. Such forces are not easily measured, sorted, put into neat little categories and plugged into the computer. Yet time and again they prove to be more crucial for a country's ability and, above all, willingness to pay its dues than are the 'objective', quantifiable facts.

Then, too, business and banking managers in Europe and North America frequently assign the entire task of country risk assessment to individuals not trained in political analysis. They rely on economists, technical people, overseas representatives, even 'old hands' whose only claim to expertise is that they may have done a stint in foreign territory.

The assumption behind this approach is usually that anyone reading up on current events can do a good job. Unfortunately, this is as wrong as believing that a bright handyman reading medical journals can perform complicated surgery. On the other hand, using 'top-level experts' such as former government officials or diplomatic personnel tends to produce assessments that are often just general surveys without recognition of the corporate decision maker's real needs.

Not much better is reliance on simplistic models that compare countries on a numerical or alphabetic scale, in many cases according to a quite rigid, mechanical system. These models are justifiably criticized as generating far more heat than light as they spew out 'quantitative non-information'. Behind the numbered or lettered ratings is usually a single questionnaire, one set of queries with which the analyst seeks to capture the bewildering intricacies of the world's extraordinary diversity of heterogeneous countries and nationalities.

This, in itself, is an impossibility. One may get some insights from asking 'have there been recent religious tensions' in India or Iran, but the same question is hardly relevant to a judgement of the socio-political stability of South Africa or Taiwan. Besides, what good does it do executives pondering difficult decisions if they are told that a country rates eight on a scale of ten? What they need to know are the powers that could ruin an economy or destabilize a political establishment, the personalities of the people at the helm, the fears that could unleash sudden capital flight, the soft spots in a country's balance of payments likely to lead to a foreign exchange shortage.

This is not to say that numerical risk ratings are meaningless, or worse, misleading. At S.J. Rundt & Associates we use them fairly extensively because of the discipline of thought they force on our analysts. It is one thing to say 'I think the risk of expropriation without adequate compensation' in country X 'is pretty high,' quite another to state that 'on a scale from one to ten, I judge the risk to be a nine'. Also, measured ratings give a quick impression to the reader of a risk report, in a way that words never could. But the 'numericals' cannot stand alone. They must be accompanied by concise explanations and carefully considered qualifications, and they must be adaptable to an individual nation's peculiarities.

A ratio showing that foreign reserves cover barely one month of imports would be a startling warning signal if it came from a country like Venezuela. It would hardly merit a second glance if it described the position of, say, Switzerland with its ample earnings from invisibles (tourism, banking and the like) and its easy access to the international capital and credit markets. The threat of a sudden change in government would have to be a matter of serious concern in Saudi Arabia, but it is less than alarming in Italy, a nation that has averaged roughly one new Administration a year since World War II, and where basic policy does not change just because a new face is in the Palazzo Quirinale.

Good country risk assessment, in short, is not an easy quest. On behalf of the profession it should also be stressed that in all too many instances where corporations and banks are now struggling to cope with irretrievable loans and uncollectible trade payments, managements were cautioned by risk analysts well in advance, but chose to ignore the warnings.

Many of the better-known services in the field, and numerous in-house teams, concluded as early as 1979 or 1980 that Mexico was headed for inescapable external-liquidity problems. But few banks at the time were willing to listen to anything that might have crimped their profitable Mexican loan business. It was entirely predictable a few years ago that South Korea would achieve phenomenal improvements in its foreign trade and current account payments balances, yet many exporters to that nation until recently sought to keep their Korean exposure small, because they were worried about the country's relatively large foreign debt.

The need remains

Still, it would be wrong for managements now to turn away from country risk assessment with the argument that it cannot be wholly reliable and therefore is not useful. The world around us is getting smaller. Thanks to meteoric developments in the means of transportation, technology and communications, it is rapidly becoming an ever more integrated and interdependent market for goods, services, money and information. But while we are increasingly moving toward a true world economy, governments continue to fashion policy in a strictly national sense and interest.

For international business this will always create risks. The subsidiary of a multinational is a hostage of the country in which it is located. In trade, not even letter of credit terms are fail-safe for the exporter in the event there is a discrepancy in the L/C documentation. But, again, business means taking, not evading risk. In international business, as in all other commercial activity, danger is inextricably intertwined with opportunity. To separate the unacceptable degree of danger from the acceptable one and to spot and define opportunities effectively, business has a vital interest in assuring that decisions affecting overseas assets are the best informed possible.

Rather than dismissing country risk analysis as a key input to decision making, greater attention should be paid to making such analysis systematic, objective and relevant. This requires, first of all, a clear vision of the purpose the results will have to serve. It necessitates, further, a consistent methodology. And it means, finally, that country risk evaluations should be built not only into individual, isolated decisions, but into the day-to-day management of exposures.

SOURCES OF INFORMATION

The sources of information from which to gather the needed input are manifold. Their reliability varies greatly, and one of the most important tasks of the country risk analyst is to evaluate them, rate them, and cross-check them regularly to make sure that there has been no change in their quality. The international credit executive has three options:

(a) to marshall information in-house and analyse it internally;
(b) to use the services of an outside consulting firm, for a fee; and
(c) to employ a combination of options (a) and (b).

The third alternative is the one most frequently resorted to by experienced credit managers.

Of the main categories of information sources, six, in particular, stand out.

Governments and their agencies

Governments, through their various ministries, departments and statistical agencies, as a rule provide a wealth of information on such things as domestic financial and economic growth trends, social data, export–import trade, the balance of payments and available foreign exchange reserves.

The figures they provide tend to be the most authoritative obtainable, but this is not always the case. The People's Republic of China, for instance, publishes three different sets of 'official' foreign trade results (through the Customs Office, the Ministry for Foreign Economic Relations and Trade and the Central Bank) which show enormous discrepancies. A number of Latin American nations release exchange reserve figures only sporadically, if at all. There are frequently major disagreements between official and private estimates of inflation in LDCs and, more often than not, the private assessments come closer to the actual rate of monetary erosion.

Governments in less developed countries often delay the unveiling of monthly or quarterly reports if these are unfavourable. And, of course, the COMECON members have developed statistical window-dressing to an art form, with figures that as a rule are limited to percentile increases and decreases minus an absolute base, so that Western researchers find it extremely difficult to check what the regimes choose to announce.

Multinational banks

Banks with long-standing business connections in many lands are excellent sources of country information. They can and do tap their overseas branches, subsidiaries and correspondents, and they are usually very careful with the data they disseminate. Their information is rarely limited to bland statistics. More often than not it includes useful background material on key trends and developments. One big plus is that information from banks is usually available free or at only a nominal cost. Another advantage is that it often is presented along with interpretations, commentary, and forecasts.

Credit executives should keep in mind, however, that at times the very presence abroad that allows a bank to get information quickly and reliably may prevent it from being outspoken about unfavourable country conditions. Host countries do not take kindly to criticism, particularly if it originates from a foreign-owned business or banking establishment on their soil. Executives seeking the advice of banks will thus do well not to rely only on what the financial institutions put out in print, but to consult their account officer and ask for verbal comments from the contacts provided. There are many things bankers know which they will gladly discuss over the telephone – but would never want to appear in black and white.

Multinational agencies

In this category, the International Monetary Fund and the World Bank in Washington are among the most useful sources of information a credit executive can tap, but there are many others, including a number of United Nations agencies, the Basle-based Bank for International Settlements, the OECD in Paris, the Inter-American Development Bank, the Asian Development Bank and various other regional development banks.

The International Monetary Fund publishes the most comprehensive global statistical compilation available. It issues an annual book on foreign exchange restrictions world-wide, regular studies on global export and import trends, and individual country studies (the release of which depends, however, on the consent of the nation under study). The World Bank is best known for its publication of the so-called World Debt Tables (with intermittent addenda and supplements), which give the reader a bird's eye view of countries' overseas indebtedness, public and private, of servicing obligations and of possible difficulties due to an impending bunching of maturities.

Again, though, it should be kept in mind that such organizations can publish only what the countries concerned provide and allow to be exposed to public scrutiny. The information is often quite dated, it has yawning gaps that the uninitiated will find difficult to fill, and any criticism is usually couched in polite bureaucratic terms, so that one has to read between the lines to get a clear picture. This makes it advisable for the credit executives conducting their own research and analysis to develop good personal contacts with country desk officers, so that they can find out in personal conversations what is 'too hot' for the institutions to commit to print.

The FCIB–NACM Corporation

The FCIB is a professional organization of international credit executives in business and banking that is headquartered in New York, but has centres of gravity also in Europe and in the Asia–Pacific region. Its regular Round Table Conferences bring together exporters, importers, credit managers of multinational corporations, bankers, government officials and representatives of official and private credit insurers.

These delegates discuss current country conditions, up-to-date experience with collections, changes in import and exchange control regulations, the availability of insurance cover, and terms and conditions granted. The discussions are carefully recorded and reprinted in minutes that are then sent to the entire membership. Perhaps most important of all, the FCIB offers its members a unique platform that can be used for extensive networking.

Independent economic and political intelligence services

These are private organizations specializing in the gathering and evaluation of country risk information. As a rule, they maintain sizeable country information databanks and staffs of domestic and overseas analysts trained to assist corporate decision making. They provide their services on a fee basis and concentrate on the assessment and projection of economic, political and social factors at work in a country.

As independents, organizations of this kind can afford to be outspoken and to express opinions – in print – that may not sit well with the nations they are discussing. They also frequently have 'inside channels' allowing them to gather data not easily accessible by others. In rating them, a credit executive should seek to determine how long they have been in the business, what sort of reputation they have earned themselves, who the principals are and what sort of 'track record' they have.

Newspapers and magazines

Many newspapers and magazines cover a wide range of topics international credit executives must stay abreast of to handle their difficult profession effectively. Key characteristics of the best are objectivity, global coverage, a clear division between news and editorial content, and independence of reporting. It would far surpass the scope of this chapter to attempt to list all the major publications meeting these criteria, not to mention those with primarily regional or local emphasis. But in terms of usefulness for credit executives in the English-speaking world, the leader (by considerably more than a nose) is the *Financial Times* of London, followed by the *Wall Street Journal* and, increasingly, the *US Journal of Commerce*. Examples of other, more limited, general-purpose publications are:

- *The Economist* (UK)
- *Trade Finance* (Euromoney, UK)
- *Institutional Investor* (USA)
- *Far Eastern Economic Review*
- *Middle East Economic Digest*
- *African Economic Digest*

Personal visits

Whatever else a credit manager may do to gather the information needed for reliable country risk analysis, there is nothing that can fully compensate for the value of a personal visit. Seeing the countries in question first-hand, talking to customers face to face, looking up local branches of foreign banks, talking to the managers of a parent company's own subsidiaries and calling on diplomatic personnel (ambassadors, consuls, commercial attaches) can provide valuable insights.

Selectivity

This, to be sure, is only a rudimentary and fragmentary list of the many, many wells from which country information can be lifted. But already from the few sources mentioned, it must be clear that selectivity is a must if the cost of data gathering is to be kept within reasonable bounds, in terms of both manpower and company cash put on the line. How much information is needed, from how many different sources, will largely be a function of:

(a) the total number of foreign customers;
(b) the total amount of foreign accounts receivable;
(c) the number of countries where customers are located;
(d) the number of customers in each country;
(e) the credit terms that tend to be extended;
(f) the overall strategy of a company in its international dealings.

In general, the more countries a company sells to, the more customers it has in each market; and the larger its accounts receivable are, the more daunting will be the task of marshalling the facts, forecasts and opinions that are a *sine qua non* for effective country risk assessment. But in any event, gathering information is only the first step. Raw information must be 'processed' to become useful. It needs to be sorted, compared and evaluated. And it is here that careful guidelines need to be followed to make sure that nothing important slips between the cracks and nothing inconsequential assumes more weight than it should be accorded.

STRUCTURING INPUT

To structure the variables that need to be collected, rated, forecast and compared for a sound assessment of the dangers and opportunities of doing business in and with a given country, we, in our organization, have taken a leaf out of the book of bank examiners and use the guide-word 'CAMEL' as a rule of thumb. The 'C' stands for Current Earnings, the 'A' for Asset Quality, the 'M' for Management Quality, the 'E' for Earnings Potential, and the 'L' for Liquidity.

Current earnings

In a country context, an analysis of current earnings should encompass past and present exports, imports and invisible trade, in short, the current account balance of payments of a nation. This kind of information is usually the easiest to obtain, if not from the country itself then from supra-national organizations such as the International Monetary Fund.

A nation's current account balance of payments is in many respects similar to a company's profit and loss account. It measures the present state of its financial condition. A negative balance means that the cost of imports surpasses income from exports, leaving a differential that will have to be financed either through foreign borrowing or from reserves. A positive balance means that more is being sold than bought abroad, that foreign reserves are being created, and that debt will be repaid. If a country runs a deficit, it is important to determine how the gap will be bridged. The negative implications are lessened if there is access to official grants or long-term, low-interest-rate loans from organizations such as the World Bank.

Of course, it will not be sufficient merely to look at historical trends and establish what has happened in the most recent past. Risk assessment deals with the future, and there are many forces bearing on a nation's foreign merchandise and invisibles trade. Balance of payments developments need to be projected, and to do this effectively a good analyst must be aware not only of conditions in a given country's main foreign markets, but also of internal and global tendencies likely to affect major positions in the external accounts.

To forecast trends for Argentina one must have insight into world grain trade. For Ghana, a knowledge of the international markets for cocoa is required. An assessment of Saudi Arabia's balance of payments prospects is impossible without concrete ideas about oil price trends. Pakistan has a heavy preponderance of jute in its exports. And in a tourist spot such as Jamaica, a mere hint of political and social unrest can cause the inflow of foreign exchange bearing visitors from abroad to dry up rather abruptly.

The evaluation of current account balance of payments trends, in short, is no easy task. Even more of a challenge is the assessment of the second category of variables, those determining asset quality.

Asset quality

Under this heading, the analyst's concern should be a country's natural, human and general economic resources. Gross domestic product figures are useful as a measure of the size of an economy, and the composition of GDP as an indication of the underlying structure, but good assessors are bound to cast their nets wider.

Ample natural resources such as oil, metals and fertile soil can make an otherwise less-developed nation rich (as has been the case with Saudi Arabia). But there are many examples of countries poor in natural assets that have built thriving economies on their human resources (Japan, Hong Kong, Singapore, Taiwan and Korea come to mind, as does Switzerland) while others with a wealth of resources in the ground have never been able to move from square one because their people and/or economic infrastructures have not been equal to the task (such as Zambia, Zaire, and Bolivia).

Within the field of asset quality, we at Rundt's tend to take a close look also at such things as the ratio between investment and gross domestic product (which is a good indicator of commitment to future economic growth and productivity), the local savings rate (which shows a nation's ability to self-finance progress), the ratio between consumption and investment spending, and the confidence that locals and the international financial community have in the national currency.

Management quality

Such considerations tend to spill over into the third category, that of management quality, which in country-risk terms means the government and its policies. While resources can 'make' a nation, government policy can break it. The strength of the leadership is crucial. So is the direction in which the powers that be wish to take a country and its economy. So is the leverage of the opposition, legal or otherwise.

The analyst needs to take a close look at the degree of social and political unrest, past, present and prospective. He needs to judge the ability of the government to manage the economy, its attitude toward foreign trade and investment and its fortitude in implementing unpopular decisions. The average age of a nation's population can play a significant role. A developing country where more than half the people have not outgrown their teens will perforce be more volatile, socially and politically, than the mature industrial nations of the West with their generally far more conservative, greying populations.

Some of the pertinent variables can be readily quantified and projected numerically, among them government spending (perhaps as a percentage of gross domestic product), money supply growth targets versus actual expansion, the official influence on credit extension, inflation (and the likely effect of state efforts to curtail it), the trend in the tax structure and wage policy. Others are much more intangible, but must be weighed just the same, such as the confidence that local business has in the government's course.

Earnings potential

When it comes to a country's earnings potential, the main focus should be the potential size of the domestic market (population, wealth distribution, consumer preferences, protectionist tendencies and the like) as well as on what the nation could achieve in international business if it had the best possible management (by this is meant a business-favouring, market-oriented and performance-conscious government).

Alongside, the analyst should draw a realistic picture of probable (as opposed to potential) balance of payments prospects, factoring in such considerations as a country's terms of trade (trends in export and import prices), the dependence of its overseas sales on uncontrollable influences (the weather for cash crops, world market conditions for commodities), the exposure of key non-trade sources of foreign exchange to sudden reversals (for instance, the homebound remittances of expatriate workers) and the diversification of foreign markets.

Liquidity

Liquidity, finally, is the hard, convertible currency to which a country has prompt access for the servicing of foreign obligations. Unfortunately, in this all-important area reliable current information is even more difficult to come by than for any other part of the analysis. Especially in the developing countries, those 'in the know' – national Treasuries, Central Banks, exchange control authorities – draw up different balance sheets depending upon whether they talk to an impatient creditor, a prospective lender, or a curious journalist, and some governments have become masters at obfuscation. Yet, foreign exchange cashflow prospects are often the most decisive determinants of suddenly emerging difficulties in international payments.

Organizations such as the International Monetary Fund, the World Bank and the Bank for International Settlements are still lagging considerably in their efforts to collect and compile pertinent data. But they are making progress. And in the interim, one often can get the needed information in a roundabout way, perhaps, through connections that may include a Central Banker whose son one entertained on a visit to New York (and whose birthday one never forgets to note with a telegram or a quick phone call), or a former government member with continued access to the 'inside track', or friends among members of the political opposition seeking to discredit the 'ins'.

We usually work with a number of ratios to get a meaningful picture of a country's international liquidity, present and prospective. These include one that shows the ability of a nation to cut its purchases abroad at times when exchange earnings shrink (import compressibility), one that measures the relationship between official reserves and monthly imports, another one that stacks debt interest and scheduled amortization payments against export earnings, and one that fathoms short-term capital flows across the border.

What the analyst must determine is the probability of a foreign exchange squeeze, in the near future and over a longer term. This kind of danger hinges at least in part on forces lending themselves only to judgemental evaluation. There is no way of reliably quantifying the likelihood of a sudden surge of capital flight, which is surely not always based on rational thinking by the owners of the funds that are being shunted to safe havens abroad. Nor can one always clearly determine the will and the ability of governments to control such a vote of no confidence in their policies.

Indonesia in mid-1987 experienced a severe case of speculative outflows of private funds, although the danger of a sizeable devaluation was minimal at the time (in fact, the Rupiah was subjected to several small revaluations against the US Dollar). The exodus of money stopped only when the Central Bank resorted to draconian steps to tighten liquidity. In Mexico observers were surprised at the determination with which the authorities kept money tight and interest rates in the stratosphere during 1986 and much of 1987, to force the repatriation of flight funds from abroad, even though the credit crunch turned financing into a monumental headache for most private companies on the spot.

EVALUATING DATA

Once the requisite information has been gathered, it must be sorted, sifted and evaluated. In this process, three principles stand out.

First, while we all have a tendency blindly to accept the Einstein theory but feel an urge to test the veracity of a sign that says 'wet paint', we should beware of emulating Nasrudin, the character in a Mid-eastern fable who insisted on looking for his misplaced key in a place where he knew he had not lost it, simply because the light was better there. The early hints of trouble brewing in a country are rarely found in the most obvious places. They have a confounded habit of showing up where one least expects them. Analysts must, therefore, be alert to anything that breaks a pattern or does not seem to fit past conclusions.

Second, although there will be times when the analyst's work must be done in a hurry, there are no missteps surer to lead to disaster than snap judgements on the basis of incomplete information. For sound, solid risk assessment one must make sure that one considers all the facts one can get one's hands on – good, bad, or indifferent. It is enormously tempting to concentrate on a handful of selected indicators because they happen to fit together and because adding the rest would greatly complicate the puzzle. Yet, such short-cuts can lead to worse results than foregoing analysis altogether.

Third, when one feels one does have all the information available, one must still watch out for the trap of preconceived notions that can seriously colour one's judgement. We all have some set ideas about countries and nationalities – the Latin Americans are unreliable, the Germans work harder than anyone else, the Chinese are impossibly tough bargainers, the Japanese strive for nothing more than lifetime employment with a paternalistic company. Such generalizations are invariably false.

Worse, even the kernel of truth they may contain can, and does, change. There is a world of difference between the Japan of the 1980s and that of the 1960s. China over the past few years has gone through a startling metamorphosis that has left an indelible imprint on its people, from the industrial workers in Shenzen and the shopkeepers in Shanghai to the peasants in Shandon Province and the bureaucrats in Beijing. Not all the Swiss are frugal. Not all the Arabs are impassioned hagglers. Preconceived notions are never easy to shed, but they do stand in the way of objective reasoning.

Finally, even the best country risk analysis is of little avail if it is not specifically geared to the user's needs and is not integrated into a company's or bank's overall exposure management. The risk that an exporter faces when he sells to a foreign customer on open account or on the basis of a 180-day sight draft is entirely different from that confronting a bank loan officer who opens a credit line to a foreign-owned shipping concern. The dangers (and opportunities) that await an investor building a manufacturing complex on foreign soil have little in common with those impacting the bottom line of a firm leasing oil-drilling equipment for another nation's offshore wells.

A SYSTEMATIC APPROACH TO RISK MANAGEMENT

To make sure that country risk analysis is performed with the end-user's concerns in mind, is kept as company- and perhaps even transaction-specific as possible, and results in action rather than just awareness, we usually suggest a seven-point procedure guaranteed to IMPROVE risk management. In the proper order of sequence it calls for:

- Identification
- Measurement
- Projection
- Risk assessment
- Options review
- Valuation
- Execution

Identification

At the identification stage, management determines exactly what type of exposure it is dealing with, and what kinds of developments in the host or customer country would have the greatest impact on it. There can be no concrete evaluation of risk without a concrete assessment of the exposure to it. Credit executives usually know that transaction risk has real, economic implications for their companies and banks (that is, it is also an economic risk), but they are not always certain whether a given exposure will also show up as a translation (accounting) risk (meaning that it appears as an exposure in the consolidated balance sheet). They should be conscious of any tax consequences and of the effect on corporate cashflow.

Measurement

Measuring the exposure is important for determining the corporate resources that are to be assigned to risk assessment and management. It should be done country by country, as well as customer by customer. And it should be done in systematic fashion allowing credit managers to put their finger quickly on problem areas.

Company policy will generally say whether bunching large amounts of exposure in high-risk countries is acceptable, or whether management is to play it safe by concentrating big exposures on low-risk areas while allowing only minor exposures elsewhere. Surprisingly, though, many companies do not even keep close track of how their exposures are distributed – and how badly they could be hit if a country in which they have massive exposures (because it was thought to be low risk) suddenly turns bad. Measuring exposure is particularly essential if ongoing business causes its magnitude to fluctuate.

Projection

Since it is future risk that needs to be guarded against, or an upcoming opportunity that is to be taken advantage of, exposure has to be projected. An investor needs yield forecasts, a lender indications of the borrower's future requirements, and an exporter sales projections.

Risk assessment

Only then can the risk assessment be tailored to the task, a *sine qua non* if one considers the vastly differing concerns of, for example, a mining enterprise in Zambia (which will be keenly interested in political and expropriation risk, but need not worry much about inflation and currency changes), a pharmaceuticals manufacturer in Brazil (for whom inflation, credit conditions and regulatory changes are of crucial importance, but who need not be too concerned about political changes and expropriation dangers), and a bank with loan commitments to the Philippines (for which the issue of uppermost concern is exchange availability for debt service payments).

Options review

Once the risk has been determined, management usually finds that it has a variety of options to respond to it. In international trade, these options range from changes in terms, changes in the billing currency, hedging contracts in exchange forward markets, the taking out of insurance and the establishment of special reserves all the way to temporary cut-backs in export sales and perhaps even plans for a long-term retrenchment.

Valuation

Overall corporate goals will frequently favour some alternatives over others. A company policy geared to the achievement of maximum cash flow will mandate steps different from those likely to be taken by managements seeking the best possible per-share earnings; a policy striving to limit exposure will suggest a course quite at odds with that required for maximum market penetration. But each option has a cost, and each yields benefits.

Step six in the risk management process consists of weighing the former against the latter by means of a careful, comprehensive and precise cost–benefits analysis.

Execution

Once this has been done, the final step – translating the risk analysis into action by selecting the best option and implementing it – becomes almost automatic.

If approached in such a systematic and structured way, country risk assessment will not only accomplish the job it is meant to do, but will become an indispensable element of good international business administration. It will not eliminate risk, but will make it manageable. It will also define it clearly, highlighting opportunities as well as dangers.

After all, while banks since early 1987 have been up in arms over a unilaterally declared Brazilian moratorium on interest payments to them, and while there is probably no financial institution with outstanding loans to Brazil that would describe the country as a 'good risk' at this time, many exporters have continued to do business with Brazilian customers on open account, with excellent experience. Conversely, Venezuela has punctiliously remained up to date on its interest and principal obligations to the international banking community, whereas exporters to that country have long been plagued by slow payments, bureaucratic obstacles, customer headaches and frequent changes in regulations.

Good country risk analysis, to be sure, must have the strength of conviction to be truly useful. Analysts must take a clear point of view. They can hardly be effective if they are afraid to disagree with their companies' marketing departments, representatives abroad, or top management. In the tricky business of country risk assessment you gain credibility not by saying what the corporate brass would like to hear, but by sticking your neck out – and being right most of the time.

There is little to be gained from what one wag once called 'participatory forecasting,' in which the analysts confine themselves to pointing out various limbs and leave it up to their superiors or clients to choose the one they feel like climbing out on. Alternative scenarios can have value, but only if the analyst makes his or her personal opinion perfectly clear. Indecisive 'on-the-one-hand, on-the-other-hand' reports convince no one, least of all the people who need practical input for hard decisions.

COUNTRY RISK CONSULTANTS

Withal, it should be obvious that country risk assessment is as difficult as it is essential. There are no real short cuts, and no ready, pat answers. Because of the high cost of gathering the necessary information, the expense involved in setting up a fully-fledged in-house team of analysts, and the danger that the judgement of company employees may be shaded by their desire to please top management, many (particularly small and medium-sized) corporations use the services of consultants in this field. But consultants, too, need to be carefully selected.

To do their job effectively, consultants must have first-rate international connections allowing them to get information that may be unavailable from public sources. They must be thoroughly familiar with the history, the social make-up, the legal frameworks and the political systems of the countries they are instructed to assess. They need to have a good grasp of macro-economics, a well-founded understanding of international commerce and finance, a keen appreciation of geopolitics, and more than just an inkling of psychology.

Good consultants clearly understand the needs of a client, and custom-tailor their advice. They will have a track record strong enough to be shown to prospective clients without any cover-up of (inevitable) intermittent errors. They must use a well-planned, carefully thought-out, structured approach. If they use numerical ratings (as most do), they will offer sufficient verbal explanations and qualifications to permit the reader of a report to see how they arrived at their judgement.

Good consultants – and for that matter, good risk analysts in general – are those who are not afraid to admit mistakes. They are people who prefer to eat their crow while it is still warm, by abandoning erroneous conclusions and immediately informing all concerned the moment they realize they have made a miscalculation. Serious mistakes in this field tend to have grievous consequences – holding on to a view in the face of mounting evidence that it is skewed, simply because one finds it difficult to concede an error, can be disastrous.

7

Customer risk assessment

Paul Mitchinson

In today's economic environment the prime function of credit management is to enable the company to achieve the optimum cashflow and maximum profitability from trading. Credit management is therefore not just the collection of overdue accounts or the avoidance of bad debts. For a company to survive and grow in an increasingly competitive commercial environment it is not usually possible to market solely to low-risk, safe customers. Introduction of such a policy would exclude the significant amount of business to be gained from those customers who are for one reason or another deemed to be only marginally creditworthy. The credit management policy must allow full exploitation of the markets open to the company whilst minimizing the financial risk and consequent bad debts associated with this class of customer.

Debtors, whether home or overseas, are an investment for the company. The investment, in the form of goods or services, is made on the promise of payment at a subsequent date. The value of this investment is not always fully appreciated. However, it is not unusual for a company to have some 25 per cent of its total assets invested in this way. Like any other asset, debtors must be managed to maximize the investment – credit management. Indeed, it can be thought of as part of the marketing operation, aiding sales to target profitable areas for growth.

It is unfortuante that many sales people have problems understanding credit management. Sales managers and representatives are very often measured on the volume of business they bring in without regard to the ultimate collection of cash. So it is hardly surprising that there is an automatic disregard for any procedure which would slow down the taking of new orders. Indeed, many would sell to virtually anyone willing to give them an order. If, however, this was allowed to occur, sales made to poor credit risks and/or late payers would suffer from bad debts. Furthermore, the increase in trade debtors would have to be financed by increased bank interest charges or, at worst, force the business to run out of finance and into possible insolvency and liquidation.

However, good credit management will improve collection periods and reduce trade debtors, increasing the cash available or decreasing the overdraft and/or other bank borrowings, thereby helping to make the company successful, prosperous and financially sound.

It can readily be seen that customer risk assessment is clearly fundamental to credit management and a successful business. Without adequate and regular assessment, selective risk-taking to achieve optimum profitability becomes impossible or fraught with danger and business opportunities will be wasted or go unnoticed. In addition properly evaluated risk allows the setting of terms and timing of shipment to minimize the risk of late or non-payment for goods. Moreover, the initial and subsequent assessments are an integral part of the collection procedure as, without adequate understanding of the risks, it will be difficult to determine the timing and nature of follow up action.

INFORMATION SOURCES AND THEIR RELIABILITY

The first task in determining a customer's risk must be to build up as complete a picture as possible of the customer and their financial condition. In order to achieve this, information from a variety of sources must be obtained and collated. The depth and coverage of information, which it is economically viable to obtain, must be determined by looking at the volume of prospective business with the customer – not just the initial amount of credit to be extended but also whether there is the likelihood of further orders to follow. Without doubt, a small one-off purchase would not be worthy of an in-depth investigation. If, however, it was of reasonable value or likely to be followed by more orders, then a full investigation becomes an economic necessity. In this regard, good relations and communication between the sales and credit departments must be developed.

Equally, the gathering of information should not be treated as a one-off when an account is first opened. The effective monitoring of established customers must be undertaken to identify any changes in the status of the account. Discerning adverse changes will allow the credit manager to take action to minimize the possibility of late or non-payment, whilst positive changes such as growth or expansion of the company can be used by the sales department as a prospect for increased sales.

Referees supplied by the customer

In many companies it is established practice for a prospective customer to be asked to supply details of their bank and two or more trade referees. This practice is clearly advantageous as it gives the prospective customer the opportunity to supply information which will be of value to the credit manager in setting up the account. It is also an ideal opportunity for the credit manager to establish formal contact with the prospective customer. It is better that this contact is made at the start of the business relationship rather than later when the account may be overdue and in need of remedial action.

The basic details required are as follows:

(a) name of contact(s) and their position(s);
(b) full legal name of the business and its registered number;
(c) full trading address and registered office address;
(d) telephone number of the business;
(e) details of your payment terms;
(f) an estimation of the maximum credit expected to be needed;
(g) details of bankers – the branch, its address and account number;
(h) the names and addresses of two or three trade referees who will speak for a credit figure comparable with the maximum expected.

It is also sensible to request a copy of the prospective customer's headed letter paper and to ensure that any order is signed by a principal or an official with the authority to do so.

When these basic details have been supplied you will then be in a position to start gathering the information needed on which to base a credit decision.

The bank reference

It is not uncommon for business concerns to maintain a number of bank accounts, one of which will be kept in credit and used when references

91

are requested, while another or others may be overdrawn and reflect a truer picture of a concern's ability to meet its debts as they fall due.

Care must be taken to ensure that the banker's opinions requested allow for this eventuality.

As a general rule the more information supplied to the bank when asking for the bank's opinion of the customer/prospective customer, the more meaningful will be the reply. It is in order to ask the length of time that the account has been held and whether the bank has secured charges, as well as their opinion as to whether the customer is suitable for a figure of £— per month or over a period of time.

Generally speaking, the opinions of the bank can be trusted. However, it must be remembered that the customer is also their client and the bank is not a disinterested third party.

As an example of this, it is not unheard of for the local bank branch manager to reply stating that the customer is good for the figure you asked about. However, a week later the bank head office, worried about the state of the account, appoints an administrative receiver over the assets – assets which include those goods despatched on the basis of that good bank reference.

The value of the opinion will also depend on the person preparing it and the freshness of the information to hand. This is well illustrated by a letter to the editor of *Creditnews* (Volume 7, No. 7):

Dear Sir,
In any discussion on bank references, I am wont to relate the sorry tale of the day I received two communications from the same bank, in two separate envelopes. One contained a reference for a company in the usual 'Considered good for your figure' vein, the other contained a bounced cheque ('insufficient funds') for £2000 for the same company.

It is just these types of problems that have lent credence to the saying, 'The only good bankers' opinon is a bad opinion'.

However, on the basis that one source of information complements another and a variety of data sources will be utilized before credit is granted, then the bank opinion will be of use. Indeed, since the bank details are often to hand and the opinion can be obtained quickly and relatively cheaply, it should be utilized.

Trade references

Trade references can be one of the most useful sources of credit data. It is important that they should be impartial and that the trade references given are independently assessed as having or not having connections with the customers. It would be unlikely that an uncreditworthy customer would give the name of referees who would give adverse information. It is known that many businesses who generally pay late will always keep two or three suppliers happy by paying more promptly. Indeed, it is probably more common for the important or principal suppliers of goods to a business to be paid more promptly than the smaller, less important suppliers.

This should not invalidate the very useful information which, by using a few simple precautions, can be obtained.

Requests for trade references should be sent to concerns who sell on terms and at a level similar to those which you are contemplating.

Companies which are known to be associated with the customer should not be approached for a reference and steps should therefore be taken to ascertain the level of association of any referee. A careful check will certainly reveal the names of other group companies as well as the businesses of family relatives being given as trade references, which at best can be of very limited value and at worst misleading or fraudulent.

A further source of trade references, other than the customers themselves, are other credit managers in the same line of business as yourself. This can potentially be one of the most valuable sources of information. The time and effort needed to build this range of contacts can be amply rewarded by the information which can be obtained.

Many credit managers will have saved an almost certain bad debt from occurring, by contacting a colleague who revealed that the customer had been refused credit on any further supplies until the account was cleared or substantially reduced. This situation can easily occur in a highly competitive market where a customer will go from one competitor to another, running up debts with first one, then another supplier.

Trade references should not merely be utilized to ascertain that the customer can handle a certain volume of credit and pays reasonably promptly or late. An analysis of payment terms will not only reveal the payment habits of the customer but also of the industry. An analysis of this type will obviously require a large number of references over a period of time but the results can greatly influence the terms you offer, the collection method employed and the generation of new business from current and potential customers.

An analysis of this type may well indicate that the normal payment terms for the industry are sixty days after date of invoice. If your terms were thirty days after invoice date and were strictly enforced, you may well have found yourself in the position of losing sales to your competitors offering sixty-day terms. This kind of information can obviously be used to your advantage, as you know what to expect in the way of payment habits of the industry and your customers. Products can be priced to allow for this and cash management can become more precise. There is also the added bonus of knowing which of your customers should be actively encouraged to buy more and those on which any sales or marketing activity would be wasted.

Newspapers, periodicals and magazines

While bank opinions and trade references can be sought at any time, it would be difficult to pick up today's newspaper or periodical and find out information on the customer in question. However, regular reading of the financial and business press will often reveal information on customers which is of benefit to the credit manager. It will also allow the credit manager to follow trends in the customers' industries and change the credit policy in response to them.

Throughout the world, there are specialist press cutting agencies which will disseminate information, to your criteria, from thousands of newspapers and journals. By selecting information on concerns which are major customers or indeed direct competitors, the credit manager can be kept informed of any changes.

With the increasing use of computer technology, there is now the ability to search databases of press information by key words, such as a company name. This allows information to be gathered on new customers as well as monitoring existing accounts. Generally, this information can be accessed from a terminal located on site so that it is readily and speedily available when needed.

Gazette information

The information found in business gazettes consists of public notices of legal information obtained from official registries and courts. Generally the information is detrimental and concerns business failures or impending failures.

The valuable information in these publications covers judgements, bankruptcies and dissolutions, meetings of creditors, petitions to wind up, notification of appointments of liquidators, administrators and receivers, as well as listings of principal creditors involved in bankruptcies or liquidations. All this can be valuable knowledge if you have extended credit or are thinking of doing so.

Some of this information may be too late to be of use to the credit manager, as the customer's business may already have failed. However, details of judgements made against a concern or of a concern being an unsecured principal creditor of a company in liquidation often indicate further problems in the future, which the credit manager would be wise to keep in mind. There are after all numerous cases where a strong viable business has not survived when one of its principal customers has failed, leaving a substantial debt; and judgements against a business are often a warning of possible insolvency.

Company accounts

These can be obtained from a number of sources, namely the concern itself, an official registry or agent or from the financial press. Those companies which publish accounts in the financial press are generally large concerns quoted on a stock exchange. The format of their accounts as published are generally abridged and further copies are usually available from other sources. These accounts do however serve a useful purpose, whether they are interim or for a full year, in showing overall trends in a company's performance. However, for a credit decision to be made, further accounts may well be required. The best source of full accounts is from an official registry or the like, such as the Companies Registration Office in the UK, or from the subject concern itself. While it is most likely impractical for the credit manager to visit such registries himself, there are always agents who for a fee will readily supply copies of the accounts held. Some of these agents also offer translation services and, although this can be somewhat expensive, it may well be necessary.

If, however, accounts are not available from any of these sources, then this probably leaves the best source of financial information as the customer himself. It would be untrue to say that this does not have its drawbacks. At worst a request may well be treated as an invasion of privacy and lead to the customer taking the business elsewhere. If, however, this happens then it may be likely that the concern wishes to hide something and the credit manager has saved himself the time and effort of dealing with a problem account in the future. If, however, customers or prospective customers need goods or services on credit, they will generally supply a copy of their accounts.

As with all the data sources available to the credit manager, accounts are more meaningful if they are independently assessed or audited. Throughout the world there are different accounting methods and standards as well as audit requirements. Some of these are relatively strict while others are ignored or non-existent. For instance, in one south European country, a request to a company for a copy of its accounts resulted in the director taking pen to paper and asking 'what would you like the assets to be?' The inference was that the company would make up accounts to satisfy the needs of whoever wanted them. While, on the face of it, this may seem to be a rare occurrence, it is practised to a greater or lesser extent all over the world. Even in countries with strict auditing standards, there is scope for manipulating the final accounts, the most common area being the valuation of the stock of raw materials. An illustration of this is the convex or concave accounting principle, that is whether the ground below the heap of coal, ore, or whatever is raised (convex) or a dip (concave). This obviously governs the volume of raw material the heap contains and therefore its value. Depending on what the company actually wants to show in its accounts, it could be a convex or a concave financial year and the value of stock on the balance sheet adjusted accordingly.

If the credit manager is aware of the limitations of accounts and the fact that they are of a historical nature, they can provide a valuable insight into the performance of a customer. For all these drawbacks, accounts are, if properly analysed, one of the credit manager's best sources of business information.

INTERPRETATION OF FINANCIAL STATEMENTS

A study of the accounts can provide a valuable insight into a customer's creditworthiness. The depth of analysis undertaken will no doubt depend on the amount of money at risk. However, even a cursory inspection of the accounts is worthwhile for smaller customers, as in conjunction with other information it will result in a more accurate assessment of the customer. For larger accounts a more in-depth analysis will be required, with ratios being used as part of the analysis.

When interpreting financial statements to ascertain the creditworthiness of a customer, the following are commonly available and of most value:

- the balance sheet
- the profit and loss account
- notes to the accounts
- the auditor's report
- the chairman's statement

These should be reviewed and interpreted by credit managers to enable them to become acquainted with the customer's financial position as well as any items which cause concern. The main points to look out for are listed below. These are not necessarily in order of priority but rather the order in which they appear in financial statements.

1   The chairman's review of the year will give an overall view of the trading condition of the customer concern. Reading it will allow the credit manager quickly to become familiar with the customer as well as indicating the future prospects for the company.

2   Is the auditors' report qualified? If it is, then is the qualification significant? A qualified audit report will generally leave the credit manager in no doubt as to its meaning and the implications on interpreting the financial statement.

   Generally speaking, qualifications of opinion fall into only a few categories:
   (a)   the auditor is unable to express the opinion that the financial statement gives a true and fair view;
   (b)   the auditor's opinion is that the financial statement does not give a true and fair view;
   (c)   the auditor expresses the view that, subject to a particular matter which is not considered fundamental, the financial statement gives a true and fair view;
   (d)   in an 'except for' opinion, an adverse opinion is expressed which is not fundamental.

3   Has the customer been making reasonable profits for its turnover and industry for the past three years?

4   Are the profits increasing regularly and at a rate above inflation? If they are not, then the customer is standing still or losing ground. If

the profits show a declining trend, then that trend could become serious.

5 Do the current assets exceed the current liabilities, that is, is the net working capital positive? If not, then the short-term creditor may not have sufficient cover. As a rough guide, a ratio of 1.5:1 or better is preferable. It should be noted, however, that a ratio of 2.5:1 or more could well indicate that the customer's asset management is weak. This could well indicate weaknesses in other areas and be cause for alarm.

6 The liquid ratio, or acid test, should be calculated. Essentially, this involves taking the liquid or quick assets, that is, those which can be quickly turned into cash, and dividing by the current liabilities. Generally a ratio of 1:1 or more is excellent, whilst a ratio of 0.5:1 or below is weak.

7 Is the tangible net worth substantial enough for the size of the company and industry? A negative tangible net worth is cause for alarm as it indicates insolvency. If the trend of net worth over the past three years is up, this is a good sign; however, a decreasing trend is cause for alarm.

8 What are the fixed assets of the customer? Such intangibles as formation expenses, goodwill, trademarks and patents have little, if any, cash value and should be discounted. Land, buildings, new plant and machinery and the like offer better security as they have real cash value. Also, have fixed assets been recently revalued, thereby showing a higher although realistic value, or have they been depreciated and amortized, and therefore are they now being shown at less than their real value?

9 Are there any secured charges or debentures over the customer's assets? The more severe the charge, the greater cause for alarm for the credit manager, whose organization is more than likely an unsecured creditor.

10 What is the net bank position? If there is a substantial bank overdraft this may be cause for alarm and it may well be secured by a charge over the assets. The long-term bank borrowing is unlikely to represent more than 50 per cent of the tangible net worth. However, if it does, this is also cause for alarm.

11 The value of the stock and work-in-progress should be assessed with regard to the size of the concern and its industry. It is also a good sign if the stock can readily be turned into cash, this being better security than items which are not readily saleable.

12 The Days' Sales Outstanding (DSO) should be calculated, by comparing the trade debtors with sales, remembering to make allowances for any taxes. If the figure seems abnormally high, it could be due to the seasonality of the business; however, it could also indicate that a cash crisis is not far away, especially if it is high compared to the industry.

13 The break-up value of the concern should be calculated to show the true value in the event of business failure and liquidation. All the assets, apart from cash, bank deposits, freehold land and buildings should be heavily discounted. If there is a substantial excess of assets over liabilities less net worth, it means that the creditor is well covered. A deficiency means that the creditor is not well covered and the chances of an unsecured creditor being paid in full are slim.

Ratio analysis

The real value of financial statement analysis lies in comparison: firstly, of the various figures and ratios relative to the business at a particular moment in time; secondly, to compare with previous years to ascertain trends – whether up, down or even; thirdly, to compare with the industry – how does the concern compare with its peers?

A business is dynamic, constantly changing and reacting. It can therefore be dangerously misleading to read too much into a single financial statement or single ratio. For instance, certain industries such as hotels, car and plant rental companies always have a high proportion of their assets as long-term/fixed assets. Their liabilities, however, are not split the same way. The acid test and current ratio will therefore always show superficially weak results. An acid test result of 0.2:1 and current ratio of 0.4:1 are not uncommon for these industries. Neither are they bad results for these industries when you consider their operating requirements.

The ratio is probably the best way of presenting the relationship between one financial aggregate and another, thereby showing its real significance. Ratio analysis places the various financial elements in perspective with one another and enables the credit manager to evaluate the customer's status and performance. Unless measured against a norm, in order to establish whether they are good or bad, the ratios for a single concern are of limited value. There is therefore a substantial need to determine how the performance of the customer compares with others in the same industry. The other companies comprising the industry norm group are in effect competitors to the subject company. The comparison with its peers is therefore an invaluable method of diagnosing and evaluating performances and creditworthiness.

The usefulness of ratio analysis depends vitally on the correct selection of the right ratios and the selection of companies to form the industry norms. Dun & Bradstreet Ltd, for instance, have identified twenty key business ratios and process hundreds of thousands of financial statements to form the industry norms by Standard Industrial Classification (SIC) group.

The number of firms in the sample must be representative or the results will be unduly influenced by irregular figures from relatively few companies. The hundreds of thousands of companies used as a basis for the industry norms by Dun & Bradstreet allow for more than adequate sample size in most cases.

Each of the twenty ratios is calculated individually for every concern in the sample group. These individual figures are then sequenced for each ratio according to condition (best to worst) and the figure that falls in the middle point of this series becomes the median for that ratio. The figure half-way between the median and the best ratio of the series marks the upper quartile, and the figure half-way between the median and the least favourable ratio of the series marks the lower quartile. In a statistical sense, each median is considered the typical ratio value for a concern in a given SIC category.

It should be noted that upper quartile figures are not always the higher numerical values, nor are lower quartile figures always the lower numerical values. The quartile listings reflect judgemental rankings; thus the upper quartile represents the best condition in any given ratio. In some instances, such as total liabilities to net worth, or collection period, a lower value represents a better financial condition.

The twenty business ratios have been categorized into four main groups.

1 *Financial status:* these are also known as solvency or liquidity ratios, and are significant in evaluating a company's ability to meet short- and long-term obligations.
2 *Asset utility:* these ratios indicate how effectively a company uses and controls its assets. This is crucial information for evaluating how a company is managed.
3 *Profitability:* these show how successful a business is at earning a return for its owners.

4 *Employee:* these ratios show the relationship of labour investment to productivity.

Financial status

Acid test

This is computed by dividing cash and equivalents plus trade debtors by total current liabilities. Current liabilities are all the debts that fall due within one year. This ratio reveals the protection afforded short-term creditors in cash or near-cash assets. It shows the number of pounds of liquid assets available to cover each pound of current debt. Any time this ratio is as much as 1:1 (1.0) the business is said to be in a liquid condition. The larger the ratio, the greater the liquidity.

Current ratio

This is total current assets divided by total current liabilities. Current assets include cash, trade and other debtors, stocks and securities. This ratio measures the degree to which current assets cover current liabilities. The higher the ratio the more assurance exists that the payment of liabilities can be made. The current ratio measures the margin of safety available to cover any possible shrinkage in the value of current assets. Normally a ratio of 2:1 (2.0) or better is considered good.

Total liabilities to net worth

This is obtained by dividing total current liabilities plus long-term and deferred liabilities by tangible net worth. The effect of long-term (funded) debt on a business can be determined by comparing this ratio with current liabilities to net worth. The difference will pinpoint the relative size of long-term debt, which, if sizeable, can burden a firm with substantial interest charges. As a rule, total liabilities should not exceed net worth, since creditors then have a greater stake in the company than the owners.

Fixed assets to net worth

This is total fixed assets (land and buildings plus fixtures and equipment) divided by tangible net worth. The proportion of net worth that consists of fixed assets will vary greatly from industry to industry, but generally a smaller proportion is desirable. A high ratio is unfavourable because heavy investment in fixed assets indicates that either the concern has a low net working capital and is overtrading, or it has utilized large funded debt to supplement working capital. Also, the larger the fixed assets, the higher the annual depreciation charge that must be deducted from the income statement. Normally, fixed assets above 75 per cent of tangible net worth indicate possible over-investment and should be examined with care.

Current liabilities to net worth

This is derived by dividing total current liabilities by tangible net worth. This contrasts the funds that creditors are temporarily risking with a concern with the funds permanently invested by the owners. The smaller the net worth and the larger the liabilities, the less security for the creditors. Care should be exercised when selling to any company with current liabilities exceeding two-thirds of net worth.

Current liabilities to stocks

This is calculated by dividing total current liabilities by stocks. This ratio yields another indication of the extent to which the business relies on funds from the disposal of unsold inventory to meet its debts. Combined with stock turnover, it indicates how management controls inventory. It is possible to have decreasing liquidity while maintaining consistent sales:inventory ratios. Large increases in sales with corresponding increases in stock levels can cause an inappropriate rise in current liabilities if growth is not undertaken wisely.

Asset utility

Stock turnover

This is calculated by dividing annual net sales by stocks and work-in-progress. Stock control is a prime management objective, since poor controls allow inventory to become costly to store, obsolete or insufficient to meet demands. This sales-to-stock relationship is a guide to the rapidity with which merchandise is being moved and the effect on the flow of funds into the business. This ratio varies widely between different lines of business, and a company's figure is only meaningful when compared with industry norms. Individual figures should be examined with care. Although low figures are usually the biggest problem, as they indicate excessively high inventories, extremely high turnovers might reflect insufficient merchandise to meet customer demand and result in lost sales.

Collection period

This, otherwise known as *Days' Sales Outstanding* (DSO), is calculated by dividing trade debtors by sales and then multiplying by 365 days. The quality of the receivables of a company can be determined by this relationship when compared with selling terms and industry norms. In some industries where credit sales are not the normal way of doing business, the percentage of cash sales should be taken into consideration. Generally, where most sales are on credit, any collection period more than 30 per cent over normal selling terms is indicative of some slow-turning receivables. When comparing the collection period of one concern with that of another, allowances should be made for possible variations in selling terms.

Asset turnover

Asset turnover, or *asset utilization*, is computed by dividing sales by total assets. This ratio measures how efficient the company's management have been in generating sales from the operating assets at their disposal. The measure can vary considerably from industry to industry and should therefore be judged according to the industry norms. This indicator of resource utilization is most valuable when analysed in conjunction with other measures of efficiency, especially the assets to sales ratio.

Sales to net working capital

This is obtained by dividing net sales by net working capital. (Net working capital is current assets minus current liabilities.) This ratio indicates whether a company is overtrading (handling an excessive volume of sales in relation to investment) or undertrading (not generating sufficient sales to warrant the assets invested). Each industry can vary substantially and it is necessary to compare a company with its peers to see if it is either overtrading on its available funds or being overly conservative. Companies with substantial sales gains often reach a level where their working capital becomes strained. Even if they maintain an adequate total investment for the volume being generated (assets to sales) that investment may be so centred in fixed assets or other non-current items that it will be difficult to continue meeting all current obligations without investment. A ratio falling into either an extremely high or low position may indicate potential problems.

Assets to sales

This is calculated by dividing total assets by net sales. This ratio ties in sales and total investment that is used to generate those sales. While figures vary greatly from industry to industry, by comparing a company's ratio with industry norms it can be determined whether the business is overtrading or, conversely, carrying more liquid assets than needed for its sales volume. Abnormally low percentages (in the upper quartile) can indicate overtrading, which may lead to financial difficulties if not corrected. Extremely high percentages (in the lower quartile) can be the result of overly-conservative or poor sales management, indicating that a more aggressive sales policy may need to be followed.

Creditors to sales

This is computed by dividing trade creditors by annual net sales and then multiplying by 365 (days). This ratio measures how the company is paying its suppliers in relation to the volume of sales being transacted. A high number, or one higher than the industry norm, indicates that the firm may be using suppliers to help finance operations. This ratio is especially important to short-term creditors since a high number could indicate potential problems in paying vendors.

Profitability

Profit margin *(return on sales)*

This is obtained by dividing profit before taxes by net sales. This reveals the profits earned per pound of sales and therefore measures the efficiency of the operation. Return must be adequate for the company to be able to achieve satisfactory profits for its owners. This ratio is an indicator of the business's ability to withstand adverse conditions such as falling prices, rising costs or declining sales.

Shareholders' return *(return on equity)*

This is obtained by dividing profit before taxes by tangible net worth. This ratio is used to analyse the ability of the company's management to realize an adequate return on the capital invested by the owners of the business. There is a tendency to look increasingly to this ratio as a final measure of profitability. Generally, a relationship of at least 10 per cent is regarded as a desirable objective for providing dividends plus funds for future growth.

Return on capital

This is obtained by dividing profit before taxes by net capital employed. This ratio is a key measure of managerial performance by relating pre-tax profit to the long-term investment in a company. It is a good guide as to whether sufficient return is being generated on the long-term funds employed by the business. If a low return is being earned for any length of time, liquidity problems are likely to develop.

Return on assets

This is profit before tax, divided by total assets. This ratio is the key indicator of profitability for a firm. It matches operational profits with the assets available to earn a return. Companies efficiently using their assets will have a relatively high return; while less well-run businesses will be relatively low.

Employee ratios

Capital employed per employee

This is obtained by dividing total capital employed (or net assets) by the number of employees. This ratio shows the value of the assets employed per employee. The higher the ratio, the greater the capital intensity.

Sales per employee

This is derived by dividing turnover by the number of employees. This gives an indication of the efficiency of the labour force. This ratio will vary considerably from industry to industry.

Net profit per employee

This is profit before tax divided by total number of employees. This ratio gives a guide as to how effectively the labour force is utilized and is the best way to measure the productivity of labour investment.

Average wage per employee

This is calculated by dividing total employee remuneration by number of employees. This is a useful measure for comparing wage levels within a sector, and indicates how effectively labour costs are controlled. Allowance must be made for the possible presence of part-time employees' wages in the accounts.

Definitions and calculations

The terms and ratios discussed in the preceding section are summarized below.

Tangible net worth:

Shareholders' equity − Intangible assets

Net assets or *Capital employed:*

Total assets − Total current liabilities

or:

Shareholders' equity + Long-term and deferred liabilities

Net working capital:

Total current assets − Total current liabilities

Operating cash flow:

Net profit (loss) plus depreciation

Financial status ratios

Acid test (X:X):

$$\frac{\text{Cash} + \text{Trade debtors}}{\text{Total current liabilities}}$$

Current ratio (X:X):

$$\frac{\text{Total current assets}}{\text{Total current liabilities}}$$

Total liabilities to net worth (%):

$$\frac{\text{Total current + deferred + long-term liabilities}}{\text{Tangible net worth}} \times 100$$

Fixed assets to net worth (%):

$$\frac{\text{Total fixed assets}}{\text{Tangible net worth}} \times 100$$

Current liabilities to net worth (%):

$$\frac{\text{Total current liabilities}}{\text{Tangible net worth}} \times 100$$

Current liabilities to stocks (%):

$$\frac{\text{Total current liabilities}}{\text{Stocks + Work-in-progress}} \times 100$$

Asset utility ratios

Stock turnover (X:X):

$$\frac{\text{Turnover}}{\text{Stocks + Work-in-progress}}$$

Collection period (days):

$$\frac{\text{Trade debtors}}{\text{Turnover}} \times 365$$

Asset turnover (%):

$$\frac{\text{Turnover}}{\text{Total assets}} \times 100$$

Sales to net working capital (X:X):

$$\frac{\text{Turnover}}{\text{Net working capital}}$$

Assessment and management of credit risks

Assets to sales (%):

$$\frac{\text{Total assets}}{\text{Turnover}} \times 100$$

Creditors to sales (days):

$$\frac{\text{Trade creditors}}{\text{Turnover}} \times 365$$

Profitability ratios

Profit margin (%):

$$\frac{\text{Profit before tax}}{\text{Turnover}} \times 100$$

Shareholders' return (%):

$$\frac{\text{Profit before tax}}{\text{Tangible net worth}} \times 100$$

Return on capital (%):

$$\frac{\text{Profit before tax}}{\text{Capital employed}} \times 100$$

Return on assets (%):

$$\frac{\text{Profit before tax}}{\text{Total assets}} \times 100$$

Employee ratios (000s)

Capital employed per employee (£):

$$\frac{\text{Capital employed}}{\text{Employees}} \div 1000$$

Sales per employee (£):

$$\frac{\text{Turnover}}{\text{Employees}} \div 1000$$

Profit per employee (£):

$$\frac{\text{Profit before tax}}{\text{Employees}} \div 1000$$

Average wage per employee (£):

$$\frac{\text{Employee remuneration}}{\text{Employees}} \div 1000$$

Uses of business ratios

Recent research for Dun & Bradstreet's financial products such as *Duns Financial Profile, Profile Plus, Industry Norm Report* and *Key Business Ratios* has revealed that the use of financial ratio analysis via industry norms is very useful in areas other than credit management.

Some of the more widely used applications which the credit manager can integrate into his or her own company, thereby increasing its overall performance, are described below.

Credit

The industry norm data has proven to be an invaluable tool in determining minimum acceptable standards for risk. The creditworthiness of an existing or potential account is immediately visible by ranking its solvency status against that of the industry. Short-term solvency gauges, such as the acid test and current ratios, are ideal indicators when evaluating an account. Balance sheet comparisons supplement this qualification by allowing the make-up of current asset and liability items to be compared. Moreover, gearing ratios such as current liabilities to net worth and total liabilities to net worth provide valuable benchmarks to spot potential problem accounts, while profitability and collection period figures provide cashflow comparisons for an overall evaluation of accounts.

In addition to evaluating accounts against industry standards, internal credit policies also benefit from key business ratio data. Are receivables growing at an excessive rate as compared to the industry? If so, how do your firm's collections compare to those of the industry?

Finance

Ratios provide a unique opportunity for financial executives to rank their company or the company's subsidiaries and divisions, against peers. The efficiency of management can be determined via ratio quartile breakdowns which provide a company with the opportunity to pinpoint its profitability position versus the industry. For example, are returns on sales comparatively low, thereby indicating that pricing per unit may be too low?

Comparing growth and efficiency trends to those of the industry reveals conditions which prove to be vital in projecting budgets. If asset expansion exceeds the industry standard while asset utilization is below par, should growth be slowed?

Investment executives have also used this diverse information when identifying optimal investment opportunities. By uncovering which industries exhibit the strongest sales growth while maintaining adequate returns, risk is minimized.

Corporate planning

Corporate plans, competitive strategies and merger/acquisition decisions dictate a comprehensive analysis of the industry in question. Industry norm data provides invaluable information when scrutinizing the performance of today's highly competitive, and sometimes unstable, markets. Does the liquidity of an industry provide a sufficient cushion to endure the recent record-high interest levels or is it too volatile to risk an entry? Are the profitability and equity statuses of an acquisition candidate among the best in the industry, thereby qualifying it as an ideal acquisition target? (The section in Chapter 4 headed 'Acquisitions' discusses the role of the credit manager during a takeover.)

Key business ratios data provides these all-important benchmarks for setting strategic goals and measuring overall corporate performance.

Marketing and sales

Attaining an in-depth knowledge of a potential or existing customer base is a key factor when developing successful strategies and sales projections. Key business ratios provide a competitive edge when determining market potential and market candidates. Those industries that meet or exceed your qualifications can be identified by isolating the industries which experience the strongest growth trends in sales and inventory turnover.

You can use this information from a different perspective by examining the industries on existing accounts. If an account's industry shows signs of faltering profitability and stagnating sales, should precautionary measures be taken? Will the next sale be profitable for your company or will it be written off? Industry norm data assists in answering these and many other important questions.

CATEGORIES AND CREDIT LIMITS

When all the available information on a customer has been compiled and assessed, decisions as to whether to allow credit, the amount of credit and the terms will have to be made. This is normally the responsibility of the credit manager although, below a certain monetary limit, it will possibly be delegated to junior members of the credit department. Each company will, depending on the credit manager, size of company, number of accounts, industry, operating conditions, and credit policy, assign credit limits as well as categorize customers in its own way. It would be difficult to say which of these is right or wrong as the final measure of their effectiveness is the success of the company. After all, credit management is an art rather than a science.

Customer categories

Unlike many business concerns throughout the world, which have hundreds or thousands of accounts, Dun & Bradstreet make decisions on millions of accounts who are customers for someone. These millions of customers must be assessed and categorized, bearing in mind the different conditions and information available from diverse countries and industries. In order to categorize any given customer successfully, two factors are of prime importance. These are:

1 confidence in the customer's ability and intention to meet their obligations, and
2 the volume of credit on whatever payment terms will have to be extended, in order to satisfy the orders to be made.

These factors are not mutually exclusive and will at times conflict. It therefore makes sense to categorize each customer into a condition category, reflecting possible risk as well as independently assessing the volume of credit to be extended.

For any categorization system to be effective, there must be sufficient categories to allow an adequate grading of the overall condition of a customer. However, there should not be so many that the distinction between one level and another becomes indistinct. Research by Dun &

Bradstreet showed that there should not be fewer than three or more than five. Dun & Bradstreet generally uses the five described below.

Very good condition

This would be assigned to companies of undoubted credit standing and financial strength. The risk associated with being a creditor of these concerns would be negligible or zero, the concern paying its bills promptly perhaps with a cash discount. A concern should not be placed in this category purely because it is a publicly quoted company. They must be selected with care and with full knowledge of their financial and trading capacity. After all, recent years have shown many household name companies failing or coming very close to foundering.

Good condition

This would be assigned to financially sound concerns, having no known record of bad payments and paying suppliers reasonably promptly. The risk associated with being a creditor of these concerns would be low and they would be classified as an ordinary trade risk. This category is likely to be the most populous, with customers placed in a worse category moving to this one when they have established their creditworthiness and ability.

Fair condition

This would be assigned to concerns believed to be basically financially sound, but with a history of slow payments, some losses, working capital deficit or other causes for alarm. The risk associated with being a creditor of these concerns is higher and they would be classified as potentially slow payers or fair trade risk. The overall condition of a customer assigned to this may seem similar to one assigned the second category. However, any customer with a financial weakness, no matter how slight, may well let his account become overdue if allowed to do so.

In the event of the customer running into financial difficulties less money would be at stake, as category three customers must be strenuously encouraged to pay in a prompt manner.

When dealing with concerns in countries known to have a high level of political or economic risk, category three should be assigned even if the customer is sound. This is because payment may be subject to delays in transit as well as delayed due to political or economic pressures.

Poor condition

This would be assigned to concerns of known or suspected financial weakness, a number of years' losses, higher than normal working capital deficit, a negative tangible net worth which is worsening, court judgments, bad payments etc, that is in poor condition. The risk of being a creditor of these concerns is high or significant and consequently the majority of bad debts would occur from customers in this category. As such, they need special attention and it is not uncommon to find businesses in this category potentially more profitable, if handled correctly, than less risky customers.

Early identification of customers in this category, or current customers falling into this category, is extremely important, if effective credit procedures to control the level are to be usefully implemented.

Undetermined condition

This would be assigned to companies where there is insufficient information available to express any opinion on the condition, financial soundness or payment history of the concern. Concerns in this category may later progress to other categories as they become established and many new business concerns with no past history will be initially assigned to this category. This is not to say that there is not profit in dealing with these customers. However, like those in category four, there may well be the need to impose prepayment terms and credit control procedures such that no goods are despatched until payment has been received.

Further to this indication of the overall condition of the customer, there is a need to know the size of the customer. Due to the international nature of business this must be common to all concerns independent of country, currency and industry. For these reasons and others, Dun and Bradstreet also use an indicator of the financial strength of a customer. This puts the categorization of condition into perspective by reflecting the size and trading ability of the customer business.

Credit limits

A credit limit or line is the level of finance that the credit manager is willing to extend as a result of credit sales to a customer. There are many varied ways of setting credit limits, some relying on experience; others are fractions of financial figures or are calculated by a formula using certain financial ratios. While any of these methods may suit particular circumstances at a certain point in time, none of them takes into account all the data available in such a way as to be generally recommended. For instance, limits equal to 5 per cent of current assets, 10 per cent of net worth, 1 per cent of cost of raw materials or 20 per cent of trade creditors are all based on the customer's financial statements and can ignore the customer's ability to handle such amounts. For the same customer a principal supplier will allow more credit than a minor supplier supplying goods irregularly. Indeed, the size of the customer, the industry, the type of goods you are supplying and your own credit policy will all impact on the credit level that is set.

The credit manager should never overlook the reason for granting credit. This is deliberately to encourage customers to purchase your goods and services and by doing so maximize your profitable sales and cashflow. For this reason, fixed methods of assigning credit limits should not be allowed unreasonably to inhibit business.

VISITS AND ON-THE-SPOT ASSESSMENT

A visit to a customer's premises can prove to be valuable in assessing creditworthiness, particularly where there is a large volume of business at stake and relevant facts have not yet been ascertained or the information to hand needs further clarification. Just as important is the opportunity to meet the customers and build a lasting business relationship with them. An on-the-spot visit offers the opportunity to view the reality of the business and determine details of stock, assets and other suppliers which are useful in evaluation.

The credit manager's visit to customers for assessment purposes should be arranged with the sales manager. In fact, the sales manager should be encouraged to accompany the credit manager as often as possible. This has a number of advantages in that it shows the customer that the sales and credit departments are working together to facilitate the sale of goods. It also demonstrates to the sales manager the criteria used for assessment which will lead to a better understanding and working relationship between the sales and credit departments. If, following the analysis and visit to the customer, credit cannot be given, it is much better that the sales manager was part of the discussions and appreciates the reason for the refusal.

When visiting a customer for assessment purposes, the credit manager should see as much of the company as possible. Most business concerns will respond warmly to people taking an interest in their business and show off their premises. Much useful information would be lost if all the credit manager saw was the inside of a director's or manager's office. A tour of the site will allow the credit manager to assess the scale of the operation and its future prospects.

It is vital that any appraisal of this type is realistic and objective. With this in mind the following matters should be assessed.

1 Are the premises well situated to meet the customer's needs? For instance, if it is a shop, is it in a high street location or, if it is a warehouse, is it well situated for deliveries?

2 Are the premises in a state of good repair and are they new or old, prestigious or dilapidated?

3 Do the premises have good access for customers and deliveries? Are they well situated for main roads, motorways, railways and airports?

4 Are the premises fully utilized, cramped, or is there room for expansion?

5 Are the site and premises owned, leased or rented?

6 What impression is given by the reception area?

7 Are the reception staff helpful and courteous? Are visitors attended to expeditiously?

8 Is the administrative office area well organized and efficiently run?

9 Is the office well equipped and pleasant to work in?

10 Are the operation areas well equipped? If there is machinery, is it modern or old and how well is it looked after?

11 Is the work place large enough or is it small and cramped?

12 How do the staff appear to be? Are they busy, competent and well motivated?

13 Are the goods quality items, or of inferior quality?

14 Are the goods readily saleable?

15 Are the goods supplied to one principal customer, or do the customers represent a broad cross-section?

16 Is the stock of materials effectively managed or are there signs of old obsolete stock?

17 What other goods are being supplied to them and by whom? This can be a valuable source of trade references.

18 Is the despatch area well organized and full of goods?

19   Do the customers have their own transport? If so, is it owned, leased or rented, and from whom?
20   Are couriers or despatch companies used? If so, are they reputable? Again, this can be a valuable trade reference.
21   Are the management offices suitable and pleasant? Is there a substantial difference between these and the administrative office areas?
22   What are the principal people in the business like? Are they knowledgeable, professional and efficient? Are they autocratic in the way they deal with staff? If so, this can be a cause for worry.
23   Is the top management well balanced in its make-up or are there significant areas of weakness?
24   What are the ages of the principals? Is there an even split between old and young? If there is a preponderance of older people, the business may be reluctant to change with the times. If they are all young and possibly inexperienced, they may tend to be rash and make wrong business decisions.

This list is not meant to be exhaustive. However, it does indicate the main areas to be assessed.

As an indication of how important these visits can be in gathering information not otherwise available, it is worth drawing attention to the following scenario, which has been seen to occur over and over again.

A new company trades successfully and grows for two or three years and becomes reasonably established. It then obtains a large, important order, a government or regional grant for expansion or an award such as the Queen's Award for Industry in the UK. When this happens, the company directors think they have made the big time and to reward themselves they order the flag pole for the front of the offices, a Rolls Royce car for the directors and a company helicopter. Of course, the business cannot support these expenses and the business fails with catastrophic consequences for many of those concerned. Signs of this happening only become readily apparent on visits to the customer.

As a final note on this topic it should always be remembered that any business is about people. The customer may be a proprietorship, a partnership, a limited company or a large corporation, but it is only as strong as its directors, principles, managers and staff. Unless confidence in them is established, the credit manager may do well to be hesitant to invest substantial credit, irrespective of favourable comments from other parties.

Recommended reading

Bathory, A. (1987) *The Analysis of Credit*. London: McGraw-Hill. Covers traditional and modern analysis techniques for credit assessment.

Dun & Bradstreet Ltd (1988) *Key Business Ratios*, 2nd edn. London: Dun & Bradstreet.

Holmes, G. and Sugden, A. (1986) *Interpreting Company Reports and Accounts*, 3rd edn. Cambridge: Woodhead Faulkner.

8

Risk management

Burt Edwards

Let us remind ourselves that the main credit risks, described in Chapter 5, are the insolvency and non-liquidity of customers and political actions of countries, especially the non-transfer of hard currency. Interwoven with all of these is the risk to marketing activity and company progress which is directly related to the financial condition of a seller's customers and the markets in which it operates.

The risks and credit problems should always be viewed in terms of

- Can we take the business profitably?
- For how long might sales remain uncashed?
- What can we do to protect the profit and cashflow?

Credit management means responsibility for the company's riskiest asset and is without doubt one of the most difficult jobs in any company, regardless of size. Both the long-term planning and the daily hurly-burly are full of conflicting priorities, since there is no value for the company in being too cautious or too liberal. The business world is constantly changing its shape, trends, priorities and, most of all, its risks. It can be no coincidence that credit managers in the larger corporations tend to 'burn out' or move on earlier than their peers. The task is fascinating but constant, rewarding but wearing. Success in achieving the right control systems and company-wide understanding of good credit practices is always transitory; it is only as good as the next commercial panic or change of sales strategy. 'Eternal vigilance' could well be the motto of the mature credit manager.

Credit managers are faced with the general mission of finding a way to solve all credit problems so that orders can proceed. They have to have a positive approach to succeed, yet the natural reaction to seeing clearly awful information as well as a poor payment record is to refuse the risk.

118

On the basis that all problems in life are really opportunities, the credit manager's door receives an abundance of knocks.

When companies take a close look at how they might manage their credit risks better, they realize the complex nature of the job. It cannot be too junior, because of the need for daily decisions at an effective level, and the person has to influence other managers he or she does not control. The job has a genuine conflict of loyalties – the need to control risky sales yet increase total sales. To do all that, this remarkable person has to be a man or woman for all seasons: partly salesman/analyst/ accountant/lawyer/economist/psychologist/trouble-shooter and per-suader – Oh yes, and also the normal good manager of staff and resources.

RISK CONTROL IN SALES CREDIT

The basis of good risk control is information, which is then used objectively and quickly to make a useful decision: yes or no, how much credit, what terms, and any special conditions which may be needed.

Most well-organized companies these days apply credit limits to customer accounts – although they may call them credit lines or credit ratings, which do not sound as negative as 'limits'. We shall use the term 'credit limit' as it is the most common at present.

Credit limits are, in fact, corporate investment decisions – 'We will lend £n of our money to XYZ Company Ltd, based on what we know, in the belief that they will pay us back. If they do so at the agreed date, we shall make a profit.' Several different kinds of information are used by companies to assist in the decisions and it is hard to see how sellers can allow their own funds to be tied up in sales credit without a good view of the 'borrower'.

Every seller should periodically test the controls applied before and after a sale, to see what approach is used to assess the worth of customers and whether collection methods are good enough.

Treasurers of large corporations spend a lot of their time and expertise in getting funding from banks at fractionally better rates to fund operations, while tolerating millions of pounds of excessive debtors caused by inadequate credit management. If the senior skills applied to borrowing money were expended instead on credit and collection techniques to bring in the company's own money faster, the borrowings would not be needed anyway. A company with sales of £300 million a year and a DSO of 72 (the UK national average) and paying 12 per cent for its borrowings, can reduce the overdraft by £6 million and add £720 000 to the profit and loss account by reducing the collection period by 10 per cent. After all, no major company should have a DSO anything like as high as the national average, or even its industry average. And companies without the luxury of a treasurer should expect the same approach from the top financial man.

RECEIVABLES STATISTICS

The quality of the debtors asset cannot be assessed from its total. If debtors used to be £3 million but are now £2 million or £4 million, we cannot know if they are being collected faster or slower without comparing the total to the most recent sales recorded.

The most widely used ratio is the DSO, or days' sales outstanding, also called the debtor days or the collection period. It shows the debtors total as the equivalent of all sales made for a certain number of days.

An average DSO can be calculated if only the total sales and the period and total debtors are known. For example, if annual sales were £10 million and year-end debtors £1.8 million, the DSO could be assumed to be roughly 66 days, calculated as follows:

$$\frac{1\ 800\ 000}{10\ 000\ 000} \times 365 = 66$$

These days it is usual to calculate the ratio each month-end by counting back through the most recent sales, as being the most likely to have influenced performance. Table 8.1 illustrates this, and the example shows that sales turn into cash every 63 days! A DSO usually varies only slightly from month to month, unless payment terms change significantly. Sales fluctuations have little effect, since debtors move in sympathy.

Within industries, DSO varies considerably between companies, indicating different corporate attitudes to the importance of cash. Companies allowing customers to take too long to pay (judged by the shorter DSO achieved by competitors) generally incur more and larger bad debts – and certainly much more interest on the extra borrowings needed.

As well as the DSO for showing the turnover rate of receivables, an analysis of the debts by age, from the current month to, say, six months old, is also in wide use as a basis for deciding action priorities.

Table 8.1
Days' sales outstanding using the 'count-back' method

		£	
September debtors' total		6 250 000	
Equivalent to sales for:	September	2 950 000	30 days
	leaving	3 300 000	
	August	3 050 000	31 days
	leaving	250 000	
	July (part – £3 875 000 = 31)	250 000	2 days
		–	63 days

ORGANIZATION OF CREDIT MANAGEMENT

(Readers are referred to Chapter 24, for a full discussion of this topic.)

Every company, regardless of size, should decide at board level how to manage its risk investment – who should do it, at what authority level, whether to adopt a cautious or liberal approach, what level of debtors in relation to sales, and so on: in other words, a policy in fact, although that sounds too grand a term for the average company. A credit policy is nothing more than a set of conscious decisions – usually more efficient than a 'Topsy' evolution – in respect of any major company activity, and surely the planning of the company's valuable, large and risky means to produce cash, is sufficiently important to deserve a policy! So, a few items of policy decision:

1 A sales or a finance function? Financial control of credit is essential as a check to the ability of sales to commit the company. Credit managers must anyway behave commercially and try to accept all possible orders. There is some evidence of a trend toward credit jobs reporting to sales people who have a defined financial responsibility. This also makes sense, as does reporting to a third force such as a treasurer or a managing director.
2 The priority of front-end risk assessment, compared to collections. Too many companies start credit management (or credit control, as such companies usually call it) with the ledger and collections. Thus, the unknown mix of risks taken on will need extra collection resources to achieve good cash inflow. At the other extreme,

excessive credit checking of orders to make accounts more collectable may frustrate sales efforts by rejecting risky but still profitable business. The right mix is essential.

3   Procedures? Decisions are needed on how customers should be evaluated, how credit limits and risk categories should be used; which techniques to employ for collecting debts of different age, size and importance; when to demand security; and how management reports can give visibility of exposures to people who need to know.

4   Resources? Decisions are needed on people and systems needed to achieve DSO levels; what involvement in sales planning; how many letters, faxes, telexes, telephone calls and visits; how best to get fast clearance of claims and disputes; and controls which are not top-heavy.

5   Involvement with others. Collaboration with sales to identify and tackle priorities; special arrangements for risky customers; a combined sales/credit team for problem-solving visits to customers and meeting them when they visit; high visibility in company gatherings; and frequent contact with other departments.

Credit department duties

The duties of the credit department would include those listed below. (Chapter 2 elaborates on these and describes the expertise and resources required to achieve them.)

- Planning, budgeting, forecasting and reporting receivables
- Planning, budgeting, forecasting and reporting expense levels
- Maintaining the customer data file
- Opening new customer accounts
- Assessment of customer risk
- Setting credit limits
- Deciding credit risk categories for daily use
- Checking daily orders and shipments
- Handling over limit situations
- Dealing with orders from unsatisfactory accounts
- Administration of credit insurance
- Taking action on bad debts
- Processing selective legal action
- Meetings with customers
- Collecting accounts**

- Inputting cash to the computer system
- Resolving customer claims and disputes.

(** the job clearly has a few more things to do than just collect debts **.)

CREDIT RISK ASSESSMENT

The risk in granting credit depends on the financial worth of the customer, the profit margin and the business need. The order may be a one-off or part of a continuing purchase. The margin may or may not be able to afford a delay or a loss. A sale of obsolete stock may be a special priority. The seller may have a high-volume scatter of low-value accounts; or there may be a good company reason why the order should be taken regardless of risk. What matters is that credit decisions should be conscious ones, not just automatic nods.

We can return to the three standard credit questions:

1 Will the customer 'go bust' before payment is due?
2 If not, can the customer generate the cash needed to pay us in time?

and if both answers are favourable:

3 Is it viable to spend time and money on this customer for the future?

Assessments may have to be restricted to customers above a certain value, for reasons of time or expense. Ways of assessing risk vary from a 'finger in the wind' through to the latest computerized forecasts. A sales manager may say, 'push that order through, I've known the owner for years'. On the other hand, some systems are so bureaucratic as not to be cost-effective.

Salesmen acquire useful data on the state of customers but may lack a structure for channelling it into decision makers. Information could be captured by using a checklist of items such as the state of premises, whether owned or leased, employee morale, condition of plant, names of other suppliers, key contacts and so on. Latest sales figures and sometimes an interim balance sheet can also be obtained.

The sales ledger is much more useable than for its basic purpose of recording debits and credits. Usually, as well as listing all customers, with sales codes, regions, and categories such as major, government and the like, it shows sales by single item, account total monthly, annually or any other period, and by trend. Also visible are payment habits, responses to contacts and tendencies to be difficult, and quality control is assisted by showing invoice and product errors and deductions.

External information varies from the free of charge to the expensive, so data should be obtained according to the value of the business, not on a standard basis such as 'we always get a credit report, a bank report and two trade references'. Good credit managers select data from:

- banks
- trade references
- industry contacts
- balance sheet analysis
- trade journals
- the financial press
- customer meetings
- credit registers
- credit agency reports

Risk assessment matters for many reasons. If it were possible for a seller to have reports on all, say, 1000 customers, there would be a useful profile of their varying creditworthiness, that is, their ability to buy and pay. As these are the outlets on which the sellers depend, they would probably be depressed to find that only ten were 'undoubted' or no-risk accounts. Perhaps 300 would be very risky indeed and the other 690 a moving mixture of average status. It would be possible to answer the three key questions on each one, so that appropriate credit limits, payment terms, collection methods and sales expense could be available. However, such full and instant visibility is not available. Even companies with good credit control have imperfect systems making the most of data which is up to date in varying degrees and then for only a selection of customers. The limitations can be compensated for by a combination of experience and a good system of evaluation. For key accounts, credit dossiers should certainly be kept. Even with imperfect data, all accounts can be allocated a credit limit and even a risk category, as long as the codings are understood.

Credit limits

A credit limit should be the maximum a customer will be allowed to owe. It can be assessed from an array of opinions such as bank and trade references, or can be calculated from balance sheet data according to accepted formulae, or a rating can be purchased by taking the one shown on credit agency reports. All three approaches are in wide use.

It is not very wise to set a credit limit equal to current sales needs, because it will bear no relevance to the customer's ability to pay, which could be higher or lower. And it may need frequent updating when it could have been higher in the first place.

A rule of thumb method used by some credit managers is a maximum of 20 per cent of working capital or 10 per cent of net worth. This approach says: 'We know the customer's total worth and we are willing to risk a certain proportion of it.' Not many sellers would want to be owed more than, say, 25 per cent of a customer's total creditor figure, another rule of thumb adopted by some analysts. The debtor's own DSO period will indicate how much cash they can generate and at what intervals, and the same ratio applied to their purchases shows how, on average, they pay others.

Credit limits can never be 'correct' but are useful as general guide-lines. If a customer's indicated limit is about £1000 and they are sold £10 000, it is obvious that not enough cash can be found to pay promptly. Such a seller would incur a self-inflicting overdue account; but no credit manager would quibble over delivering £2000 of goods or services to a £1000-limit account if payments have been good to date.

In the UK Companies House provide microfiches of filed accounts. Even if a customer is delinquent in lodging accounts, ratios and trends over the previous three years can still be a good guide. The ratios most useful for risk assessment are probably:

(a) liquidity, that is, the coverage of current liabilities by cash and debtors;
(b) DSO, that is, how quickly the *customers* collect their own receivables;
(c) stocks:sales, that is, how long the customers takes to sell their output;
(d) debt:equity, that is, the burden of interest to be met from profits;
(e) net worth:current liabilities, that is, how much the customers have invested in their business compared to outside creditors.

Net profits should keep pace with sales growth, as a percentage, any decline being a warning to check further. Looking at three-year trends allows a reasonable indication of the status of customers and gives more confidence in risking credit.

Credit risk categories

Risk can be assessed as a general view of solvency, that is 'how likely are they to go bust?', from the information gathered. As with all general views, it is a good idea to codify the impression by allocating a category of A, B or C where, for example, A = no risk, B = average risk and C = high risk.

Using credit limits and risk categories

Having done all the work of assessing information to set limits and categories, companies should record the amounts and codings on whatever computer or manual systems are used for decisions and reviews. It should not be necessary, except in special cases, to look into papers and files after the assessments have been made. The combination of the customer's aged account balance with the credit and risk codes is an excellent and powerful tool for good credit management.

The codings can be used for priorities in sales and credit work. For example, 'C £500' accounts deserve less sales attention than 'A £20 000' accounts. Stop-lists should operate earlier for slow-paying 'C' accounts than for 'B' types. Urgent orders from 'A' accounts should be serviced before those of 'B' and 'C' risks. Many sellers have order backlogs and quote fairly standard delivery periods to customers on a 'first come, first served' basis. Where delivery is quoted to all at, say, six weeks, it would make more sense to quote three weeks to 'A' and 'B' customers and eight weeks to 'Cs'. In systems for collecting cash, there may not be enough time to tackle all overdue accounts properly in a given period. It makes sense, therefore, to send reminders first to all the risky accounts, assuming that all really large debts of whatever risk category have been obtained. Rather than a standard A to Z approach for all collections, there are distinct advantages in setting out a timetable which combines size, age and risk coding of accounts.

Credit risk codings can be used imaginatively to improve customer service and cost-effectiveness in many areas. A prime objective of good credit management, after all, is to cultivate and increase the proportion of good, growing customers and to discourage, if not improve, the more risky ones.

Salesmen are forever under pressure to make more customer calls and to increase the ratio of orders to calls made. It makes no sense for them to expend equal time and money, on all customers when they have differing power to purchase. Some of them will not even be in business in the future period being discussed. If credit assessments are fairly accurate, they should be extremely valuable in directing sales efforts towards more worthwhile firms and away from the hopeless cases.

Customer awareness of assessments

There is no reason why an assessment should not be discussed openly with a customer. Credit limits can be shown on monthly statements and credit letters, and brought up at the right moment in meetings. A customer who does not agree may well offer later information to justify an increase. But customers who get upset at the mere principle of an external comment on their worth should be reminded that banks and analysts also assess companies, so a supplier/creditor is certainly entitled to.

Some customers have little or no analysis of their own business, relying on outside accountants or auditors to 'do their books'. Far from objecting to a stated credit rating, some owners who never seem to have the time to stand back and look objectively at their results actually welcome an assessment of their progress. There are credit managers with a few customers who annually send them their latest balance sheet, asking: 'How are we doing?'

Day-to-day risk control

A small 'faststart' credit rating can be allocated to all new customers without any checking at all, except for pausing to think whether anything obviously adverse is known. The standard 'faststart' amount should be one which would not hurt the business if it were lost. A full assessment can then be made in an orderly way if a second order is expected, without holding up the vital first one.

Where there are long delivery dates, credit limits need apply only at the despatch stage. Computers enable a system easily to add the value of a proposed delivery to the account balance and compare the total with the credit limit. If the answer is negative, delivery can be held until the over-exposure is solved. Perhaps the limit can be increased or a payment obtained; otherwise it may be possible to split the order into acceptably valued phases to fit the risk.

OPENING A CREDIT ACCOUNT

Customers should be required to complete a standard application for credit facilities so that there is no undue customer dominance at the important start of a relationship. The application process tends to correct any assumption, by sales staff as well as customers, that credit terms are an automatic right.

Whatever the style of the credit application, it should call for precisely accurate details of the customer's name and address, with the name of a contact and telephone number. The customer should be asked to estimate the amount of credit required and should sign a confirmation that the seller's payment terms are understood. At this point (or on receipt in the sales office if sent through the post) the salesman should validate the amount of credit required, by multiplying the value of business being discussed by the payment terms. For example, expected purchases of £5000 per month on monthly account terms would require credit of £10 000.

The application should call for the customer's bank details, in order to obtain a reference, and whilst it is standard practice to ask for two trade references who can speak for the required amount, it is better if the salesman has to obtain the names of two suppliers, since a naughty customer may supply names cultivated specially for references.

DOING BUSINESS WITH MARGINAL RISK ACCOUNTS

The whole subject of analysing credit data and turning it into credit limits and categories of risk has been amply covered in Chapters 6 and 7, and has been mentioned in Chapter 5 and this chapter. At this point we should consider that sellers have a reasonable feel for the degree of risk in their customer portfolio, which is the vital ingredient in looking for ways to maximize sales, with some profit, from the worst end of the risk spectrum. The high-risk customers are still currently in business; they need to purchase goods and services; there are sales and profit to be had from them before they go under. The task is to watch the risks so that there is not too much unpaid debt when the worst happens, with the added complication that collections will probably be difficult – a typical prelude to insolvency.

A company's customers and potential ones should all be regarded as potential sources of income, regardless of their financial condition.

What matters is the period of time that business is available, which is governed by creditworthiness. This highlights how credit management can help increase profitable sales, viz, 'Let's consider every order, but check out potential problems. Then we can sell to risky accounts with an agreed control on how much we might lose and we can get some useful profit before things turn sour.'

Marginal customers can be defined as accounts with:

(a) a high probability of going out of business (insolvent); or
(b) excessive slowness in meeting agreed payment dates (illiquid).

The approach which appeals most to sales colleagues is to build customer information, communicate with sales staff about the risky ones and encourage them to sell up to the limits set; but get them to support the controls because of the chances being taken.

An indirect advantage of segregating marginal accounts is that orders from the other, less risky accounts can flow through quickly. Instead of being accused of losing orders through credit stringency, a marginal risk policy allows credit managers to demonstrate the extra sales and profit obtained. The board should agree the value or percentage of high-risk business that the debtors may contain, accepting the consequence that most will pay slowly, some will go bust, and extra cost and 'noise' will occur. A typical policy would be for 20 per cent of the asset to be high-risk 'C' accounts. The essential proviso must be to limit high-risk sales input to that level of debtors. The policy must not be an open door to uncontrolled credit.

Controls for risky accounts

There are three separate stages when control should be exercised on high-risk business: before delivery; in collection work; and at any time as prudence directs the need for risk reduction.

1 *Pre-shipment:* control requires referral of all incoming orders to make individual authorizations following a scrutiny of existing debts, current payment performance and the credit rating. Information on file should be updated at short intervals.
2 *Collection:* the degree of control depends on size and needs telephone or quick sales contact. After any one unsuccessful collection effort, further deliveries must be held until the account is paid.
3 *Risk reduction:* the available controls include:

- prepayment of all or part of an invoice
- shorter payment terms, such as seven or fourteen days
- cash discount, recovered in price
- third-party guarantee
- letter of credit terms
- bills of exchange, collected via a bank
- offset of payables, by written agreement
- retention of title clause, if product is identifiable
- credit insurance.

Credit insurance

This is described in detail in Chapter 10 but it is relevant to mention here that insolvency and default can be insured against in both domestic and foreign trade, with a choice of either all sales or selected accounts only. It follows that the premium rate is higher for selectivity but the overall cost may well be lower. Any seller looking at insurance protection should always use a specialist broker. It will cost the sellers nothing and they will have the benefit of the broker's experience of other cases when arguing for more cover and the settlement of claims. The golden rule of credit insurance is that it complements credit management – it does not substitute for it.

Bad debt reserve policies

Categorizing risky accounts increases profits by reducing the provisions taken out of net income, as it is only necessary to cover debts on high-risk accounts. The three most common methods are:

1 100 per cent: a monthly reserve of all 'C' balances.
2 According to age: a percentage of 'C' accounts for each column on the aged debt analysis, for example 25 per cent for one month overdue, 50 per cent for two months and 100 per cent for three months. This approach recognizes the risk in slow payers.
3 Annual write-off experience: instead of the traditional general provision of, say, 1 per cent of all debtors, a seller who knows that all bad debts occur in the 'C' accounts can more economically cover a higher percentage, say 5 per cent of only those.

Where credit insurance is held, expense on provisions can be much reduced, as it only has to cover the uninsured part of 'C' debts.

RISK CONTROL ON OVERSEAS ACCOUNTS

Even when export risks have been assessed and payment terms properly arranged, there are still exceptional problems which can significantly delay payment, that is, to the point where all profit has been used up in financing the wait, and sometimes cause insolvency.

These are:

- shipping delays;
- a change in economic circumstances by the time the goods arrive;
- bills of exchange not accepted;
- deliberate default at due date;
- delays in transfer of funds by banks;
- shortage of hard currency at central bank;
- actual or near-insolvency of the buyer.

The effects of these situations can be minimized by:

- applying terms to suit customer and country risk situations;
- processing orders accurately from quotation to shipment;
- getting documentation right first time;
- using rapid (telephone or telex) means of contact;
- making full use of local action by agent or representative;
- using third-party services when appropriate;
- keeping well informed by established information sources.

Foreign losses and delays usually result from poor handling of non-standard situations. The credit manager should check export documents for accuracy immediately prior to sending them to customers or banks. He or she has the motivation for getting paid quickly. On letter of credit shipments the documents are stipulated precisely; for bills of exchange there will be standards for each market plus those items specified in the customer's order. With open account terms, a copy of every invoice should always be sent to the local agent to use in clearing disputes and chasing up slow payments.

Shortfalls in local currency payments

Bills of exchange are paid by customers in their own currency. If that currency devalues before the bank transfers the hard currency equivalent, the exporters will be short-paid unless they have instructed the bank only to release documents to the customers if they provide an undertaking to put up enough local currency to meet the full invoice value at the time of transfer.

Collection of export debts

There are two golden rules: *immediacy* and *local contact*. Taken together, these mean that traditional customer contact by elegant letter through the vagaries of international postal systems is too slow for today's foreign debts problems. Immediacy requires the use of telephone or telex from the seller's desk, with enough awareness to deal with problems the moment they arise. Local contact means that it is far better for an agent or representative to visit or call the customer or bank on the spot. An expensive telephone call, cable or even a plane fare is invariably cheaper than the interest cost of slow payments or bad debts. (Chapter 18 discusses procedures for the collection of overseas debts.)

A checklist for good export risk control

1   Is recent credit information held on all foreign customers and markets, or at least the few that provide 80 per cent of sales?
2   Have credit limits and risk categories been applied to all customers and countries?
3   Has credit insurance been arranged for all identified risks?
4   Are orders acknowledged, showing all key terms and conditions?
5   Have letter of credit details been given to the customer?
6   Does the customer know where to send payments – bank code and other details?
7   Is there an agent or associate in place in each market?
8   For letter of credit terms, is the L/C received before shipment and checked?
9   Where an import licence is essential, has it been issued before shipment?
10   Is the customer/market still creditworthy at shipment date?
11   Has the credit department checked the shipping documents?
12   If open account terms, is a copy invoice sent to the agent?
13   Has the bank used for collections been reviewed for speed and competence?
14   Has the bank been instructed on protest, interest, case of need and exchange clauses?

15 Are problem accounts always contacted by telephone, cable or visit?

16 Are funds always cabled or sent by telegraphic transfer, even at own expense?

17 Have you made sure that nobody regards legal action abroad as an easy option, and therefore everything possible is being done to avoid it?

SUMMARY

The management of credit risks is a key part of a progressive sales policy. The benefits to the profit and loss account and cashflow are obvious when delays and losses are reduced. The less obvious benefit of a specific approach to managing risks is that sales attitudes tend to become profit attitudes. Until that transformation is achieved, all the credit slogans in the world, such as the need for lower DSO and the importance of the credit job, will remain just rhetoric and the great sales/credit divide will stay as frustrating as ever. The message is clear – somebody has to be responsible for identifying and then plugging the profit leaks which sprinkle costs and losses all about, whenever a company decides to trust customers to pay later.

PART III
LAYING OFF THE RISK

9

Sharing the risk

Brian Clarke

For any potential international business opportunity, when all necessary risk assessment work has been completed and it is decided that a risk or range of risks is unacceptable, it may be possible to lay off all or part of those risks to a third party and still win profitable business.

Obviously, whoever takes on the risk is going to do so only if in their turn, they consider the risk to be acceptable in *their* line of business; and if so they are going to charge a price for doing so. This price needs to be weighed carefully by the supplier against the expected benefits and profit margin.

Several of the more common ways of laying off the risks can also be categorized as methods of settlement or ways of raising the money to finance international trade. This short chapter summarizes them all and, where more extensive explanations or cross-references are necessary, points the reader towards the appropriate chapters.

GUARANTEES AND AVALS

Guarantees from a third party can be an appropriate tool of international trade in the following circumstances:

(a) to protect a purchaser of goods or services against frivolous tendering;
(b) to ensure that a successful tenderer will be able and willing to carry out the contract in all its aspects satisfactorily;
(c) to ensure payment of a debt is made at the contracted time or later when difficulties arise.

Such guarantees would normally be given by a bank or a surety company. Those designed to meet the requirements of (a) and (b) are known as tender/bid bonds and performance bonds, and are dealt with in Chapter 12.

Payment guarantees

Payment guarantees can take a variety of forms and bestow different degrees of security. The most common will be issued by banks on behalf of and at the expense of the debtor or the debtor's parent company.

Another form of guarantee might be given personally by a proprietor, on behalf of his or her separate business persona, or by the parent (multinational or otherwise) on behalf of its subsidiary. In both cases the quality of the guarantee and the assets behind it would require close scrutiny. And with all forms of foreign payment guarantee, it should always be remembered that, no matter how willing the guarantors may be to fulfil their commitments, if their government is short of foreign currency there could be a very long delay before the beneficiaries under the guarantee finally get their money.

Avals

Special kinds of payment guarantees, known as avals, can be added to bills of exchange. These are fully described in Chapter 14. They are often given by state or other major banks in forfaiting operations (see below).

CONFIRMING HOUSES

The role of confirming house is just one of the roles played by export houses (see also Chapter 21).

Confirming houses developed in the UK, largely as agents for overseas buyers, particularly from the British Commonwealth countries. Over the years, buyers in other countries have also become their principals.

The confirming house's traditional role has been to find suitable suppliers for eager overseas buyers and in this context they have always received their commission from the buyer. As time has gone by, however, their services have been extended to offering exporting suppliers the opportunity to receive payment for approved sales in advance of the due date and without recourse. Naturally there is a cost for this service, made up of an interest charge commensurate with overdraft rates, plus an appropriate proportion of the premium paid by the confirming house for its credit insurance, suitably loaded to cover administration.

The advantage of using a confirming house lies in the fact that the customer can enjoy long-term credit in excess of that which the exporter might be prepared to offer. Additionally, the confirming house will probably be expert in a range of particular markets and may have a lot of good advice and business opportunities to offer the exporter.

In the UK advice on confirming house services can be obtained from the British Exporters Association, incorporating BEHA – the British Export Houses Association, at 16 Dartmouth Street, London SW1H 9BL (telephone 01-222-5419).

FACTORING

Factoring is covered in detail from the export finance viewpoint in Chapter 21 and will also be seen to be an effective way of transferring the credit risk from supplier to factoring house.

For approved sales, under a non-recourse 'maturity' agreement, the factor will, for an appropriate fee, give 100 per cent credit risk cover. The arrangement usually forms part of a whole package in which the factor also provides a complete sales ledger and collection service as well as up-front financing.

The service can relieve small to medium-sized exporters of considerable administrative burdens. The larger companies, however, usually find they can run their own accounts receivable, credit and collections departments at considerably less cost than the relatively substantial percentage of sales charged by the factoring house for such services.

FORFAITING

The term 'forfaiting' derives from the French *à forfait*, which means to give up the right to something. A forfaiting operation involves the sellers in giving up their right to claim payment for goods or services from their customers, in return for the forfaiter paying the sellers for such goods or services, immediately upon shipment, on a discounted basis.

The evolution of forfaiting can be traced back to the period following the Second World War when it became popular as a way of financing capital equipment and industrial plant sold from West Germany to Eastern Europe. As a result, the forfaiting market developed initially in financial centres near to the Comecon countries, mainly in Zürich and Vienna. The centre of gravity has now shifted to London.

Forfaiters are specialist finance houses, mainly owned by banks. Their business still accounts for less than 1 per cent of world trade – the OECD estimate for 1987 was of the order of US$20 billion – but it is thought to be growing in popularity.

Although essentially a medium-term financing method, forfaiting also enables the credit risk, and the exchange risk after shipment date, to be transferred to the forfaiter. The latter can, for approved sales, provide up to 100 per cent finance at a fixed interest rate *without recourse* (so long as, of course, the sellers have fulfilled all their commercial obligations). As their own form of security, however, the forfaiters will require trade bills of exchange or promissory notes relating to the transaction to be avalized irrevocably by a state bank, or in certain cases some other major bank, in the importer's country (see Chapter 14 – 'Avals' – for a detailed discussion of this procedure). The forfaiter thus needs to be actively involved in the early stages of negotiating and setting up the deal.

Whilst the technique still tends to be mainly applicable to medium-term and some long-term deals for the sale of capital goods, forfaiting has gradually been extended to short-term consumer goods transactions and terms of 180 days are now not uncommon.

As with any other method of financing and laying off the risk, there is a price to be paid for the benefits of a forfaiting operation. The forfaiter's discount will vary according to the period of credit being allowed to the buyer, the degree of credit risk – both country and customer – and the prevailing rate of interest relative to the currency in which the deal is being made.

CREDIT INSURANCE

The classic way of laying off any risk is to take insurance, and international credit risks are no exception. Credit insurance being such an important subject for the international credit executive, a complete Chapter, 10, is devoted to it.

LETTERS OF CREDIT

The types of letters of credit used in international trade have evolved to a point where they have become a popular method of settlement, can offer financing opportunities, and above all can relieve the seller of all credit risk – provided they are set up properly in the first place and provided all their terms and conditions are rigidly adhered to.

Letters of credit represent another topic which warrants a detailed examination and this is given in Chapter 16.

DEL CREDERE

Not very popular these days, because of the difficulties explained in Chapter 3, a *del credere* arrangement can be built into an agency agreement to provide for the agents to pick up the tab for any debts arising under their agency, where the customer is unable (not unwilling) to pay. The agent's consideration for taking on this responsibility will usually be an additional commission.

For most agents, however, if their *del credere* commitment is at any time invoked, there is always the likelihood that, to fulfil their obligation, they would probably have to go out of business. This threat in turn causes them to become extremely cautious when seeking customers and the chance of profitable marginal business can accordingly be lost.

If, however, it is possible for the agent to insure locally and relatively cheaply against the likelihood of this kind of commitment being invoked, then there may still be some merit in attempting to build a *del credere* arrangement into the agency agreement.

Recommended reading

Crédit Suisse *Documentary credits, Documentary collections, Bank Guarantees*, Publication Vol. 69. Crédit Suisse. One of many excellent free booklets published by the major banks.

Edwards, H. (1982) *Export Credit*. Aldershot: Gower. Strong on information sources and export credit management procedures.

Guild, Ian and Harris, Rhodri (1985) *Forfaiting*. Cambridge: Woodhead-Faulkner.

Laying off the risk

Rowe, Michael (1987) *Guarantees*. Milton Keynes: Euromoney. Looks at all the uses of bank guarantees and other security devices in international business. Includes chapters on practical procedures and key country studies.

10

Credit insurance

Paul Dawson

'Insurance protection against non-payment for trade-related debt' is the simplest definition that can be given of credit insurance. Other financial methods and means exist to transfer or lay off the risk and these are dealt with in Chapter 9. Most organizations supply goods or services on credit terms and therefore have an exposure to the risks of non-payment: these are just the circumstances that cause companies to insure against the risk.

Although in an international context credit insurance relates mainly to exports, it must also be remembered that many multinationals control subsidiaries in other countries whose sales and credit insurance requirements are of a domestic nature.

GENERAL PRINCIPLES

The general principles of export credit insurance may be summarized as follows.

1 Both insured and insurer must share in the risk. Therefore credit insurance policies usually cover between 75 and 95 per cent of the loss according to the type of policy.
2 Cover is restricted to agreed debts and disputes must be resolved before a claim under the policy can be paid.
3 Insolvency losses must be admitted by the liquidator or receiver to rank in the debtor's estate.
4 The terms of payment must be appropriate to the goods or services concerned.
5 Cover will be restricted to debts arising in the ordinary course of the

business of both the buyer and seller, thus excluding retail sales to private individuals.

6 Credit insurance does not guarantee payment at due date and is not, therefore, a financial guarantee.

7 Cover is not usually available on purely financial transactions.

8 Where commitments or deliveries have already been made prior to inception of the policy, cover is seldom available.

9 Transfer losses must be registered with the overseas central bank.

It would be impossible for any underwriter to exist if it only offered cover in respect of buyers or countries which were known to be in difficulty. Claims would undoubtedly arise and the underwriting company would not be able to continue in business. Frequently companies wish to offer for cover contracts with customers or countries where problems may not yet exist, but where they believe there will be payment difficulties. They seem surprised when the underwriter declines to quote for the business.

This should not be surprising. The very same information, be it financial, economic or status, that caused the company to be concerned is also available to the underwriting company. Credit insurance does not cover bad risks, rather it covers good or reasonable business. Should that business run into difficulties because of insolvency or political causes, then credit insurance fulfils its basic *raison d'être* and replaces capital quickly and restores the cashflow. It covers good or reasonable risks which become bad. In the same way that it would be difficult for a sick person to obtain life or health insurance, so it is difficult for a contract with a sick company or country to be credit insured.

The very simple device that has enabled credit insurance to grow and to survive, notwithstanding the fact that claims are paid out year on year, is the emphasis on a spread of business being offered to the underwriter. Known as 'whole-turnover' or 'comprehensive', this arrangement, whereby all or most of the business is covered, has given the underwriters sufficient premium income for them to offer cover on a wide basis. The fact that claims are paid out each and every year is proof that this arrangement is not unduly restrictive and that underwriters do take risks.

Of course, some businesses are not able to offer a spread of risk – those involved in manufacturing or selling capital equipment where only one or two units are produced every year, for example. In these instances it has been recognized that the spread of risk cannot be offered. Single-name policies or single-country policies, sometimes only covering one single contract, have been used to insure these risks. The premium rate will vary according to the underwriter's perception of the risk but, as a general rule, these single or specific policies will attract a higher premium than the whole-turnover type. It must be emphasized that, in these single or specific policies, the underwriter will examine in close detail the underlying contract and especially the creditworthiness of the buyer. In all instances, whether single risk or spread risk, the underwriter and the credit manager will normally view the information available on the buyer in a similar way. So, just as the company will wish to avoid bad debts, the underwriter will feel the same. The activity of the underwriter and the credit manager should not be seen as conflicting, but rather their relationship should be a harmonious partnership.

The exchange of information is, for many companies and their credit managers, one of the major benefits that credit insurance brings. The underwriter is as anxious to earn premium income as the sales manager is to make a sale. Yet at the same time the underwriter is keen to avoid a bad debt, which is after all the view of the credit manager. The dialogue between the underwriter and the credit manager is a real advantage which provides not only a source of informed advice but assurance that if they are both wrong, then a claim will be paid. This teamwork is vital and is not understood by many credit managers as being one of the main advantages of a credit insurance policy.

DISCRETIONARY LIMIT

Most companies with active sales ledgers find the Pareto ratio applies to their business, that is, that 80 per cent by value of sales are with 20 per cent of the customers in number. This frequently occurring rule governs the way that credit insurance operates, as it provides either a basis for a split in the responsibilities of the underwriter and the credit manager, or else it clearly demonstrates where the real risk lies and how the credit insurance should be organized.

A company with most of its sales being made to a handful of customers is exposed to the risk that, if one of these customers fails to pay, then the impact of the loss caused by a bad debt would be very great. If the customer is a 'blue chip' name then the risk is a good risk, but it remains a risk and credit insurance should be used to transfer the risk or part of it to the underwriter. Primarily companies do not exist to take risks: they exist to trade. Credit insurance companies exist to take risks. The discretionary limit is used by underwriters to recognize the skill of the credit manager and to build on the detailed knowledge of the business that the credit manager has. Thus, if a company wishes to insure most of its sales ledger, the underwriter will allow the credit manager to decide how much credit to grant a potential customer or an existing customer. This is done at the middle and lower end of the sales ledger, so that the underwriter will only take formal credit limit decisions for the larger exposures. Depending on the perceived skill of the credit manager, as evidenced by the amount of bad debts written off in the past, the underwriter will vary the level of discretion given to the credit manager.

The bands of value vary from company to company but are really in three parts.

1 *Major exposures* – underwritten by the credit insurance underwriter. These will be the few names that account for a large amount of the turnover.
2 *Smaller risks* – underwritten by the credit manager after examination of status and financial information. These will include many names and may be confined to the customers who account for 20 per cent of the turnover.
3 *Insignificant amounts* – quite normally small losses arise when customers do not pay for trial orders and the like. These show a pattern year upon year and can either be included in the credit insurance or, as is normally the case, be excluded.

The advantage of the discretionary limit to the company is that it allows freedom of action regarding the credit manager's role, provided that proper credit control and assessment is exercised. To the underwriter it is a division of labour which delegates part of the work back to the company and at the same time allows the underwriter to concentrate on the major names and risks.

The regular bad debt write-offs can be absorbed by most companies and are sufficiently small not to impact on the overall profitability.

Examples of this division of labour and of the trust and respect given by the underwriter to the credit manager will be seen later in this chapter under 'Types of credit insurance' where, particularly in forms of home trade credit insurance, the delegated responsibility to the credit manager is most clearly shown in the annual aggregate form of cover.

CREDIT TERMS

Credit terms for trade between companies is now considered normal and most selling is transacted on terms of payment between thirty and 180 days. Longer terms of payment are given for capital goods. Whilst credit insurance may support overseas sales on terms of payment over 180 days, home trade sales – those between a buyer and seller in the same country – involving over 180 days, are seldom covered by home trade credit insurance (sometimes also described as 'domestic' credit insurance). The reason for this is that finance is frequently sought whenever longer terms of payment are involved; in export transactions this will link with bankers and financing techniques which may transfer the risk but will certainly replace working capital. These financing schemes may well work in conjunction with the government-linked export credit underwriter. Home trade transactions on longer terms are more usually the subject of hire-purchase or leasing contracts and therefore not credit insured as the risk has been transferred.

Terms for goods

It is important to note that there exists a firm intention on the part of all credit insurers that the terms of credit extended for a contract should be governed by the nature of the goods and the size of the contract. Thus perishable goods will not be covered if sold on lengthy credit terms; and consumer goods would not warrant extended payment terms, irrespective of the value or size of the contract.

This understanding on the part of credit insurers, and the export credit insurers in particular, is in spirit with the GATT guidelines established in the 1940s and 1950s to prevent an escalation of the length of the credit terms. Their main concern is that neither unduly long terms of payment nor oversubsidized interest rates for financing should be provided, and that all sellers should compete on equal terms.

CONSENSUS

Following the oil crisis of 1973 and 1974 many governments feared the effects of a credit war. As a result the Arrangement on Guidelines for Officially Supported Export Credits in 1976 sought to limit export credit subsidies particularly in the area of preferential rates of interest charged to overseas purchasers. The system works on the basis that there is a table of minimum interest rates and signatories to the consensus are prevented from subsidizing export credit at lower rates than the minimum. The rules also cover 'terms for goods' as described above, setting a maximum period, and deal with the quantum of any down-payment required wherever terms of payment extend beyond two years.

In essence, the consensus recognizes the classifications of countries into three bands depending on their gross national product:

(a)   relatively rich;
(b)   intermediate;
(c)   relatively poor.

This classification determines the minimum rates of interest to be allowed, with the relatively poor countries being charged at the lowest rate. The interest rates are influenced by a number of considerations, not least of all being the exchange rate for foreign currency.

BERNE UNION

In the same way as the consensus has prevented an escalation in financing terms, so the International Union of Credit and Investment Insurers, known as the Berne Union, has operated to stop any credit war arising.

This body has one or two members per country, one of whom will be linked in some way to the government and will offer a measure of protection against risks of a political nature preventing payment. Governments have become involved in export credits from the very beginning, as it became necessary to encourage companies to sell overseas and thereby earn foreign currency. As some of the causes of loss that need to be covered are outside the control of anyone except the government, it has become usual for there to be a link between the underwriting company and the government. In some cases the underwriter is a government department, in others the government assumes the political risks whilst the underwriter covers the credit risks. But not all overseas business necessarily requires protection against political risks and this is why, in some countries, there is more than one underwriter as a member of the Berne Union. Most export credit insurance originated with a close link with the government and it has become the norm that the provision of export credit insurance is restricted to the nationals of a particular country. Thus, in the UK, ECGD is only allowed to offer cover to companies registered in the UK. Therefore the members of the Berne Union have not tended to compete with each other for business, each one dealing primarily in its own country. In recent years there have been signs of this changing and the events within the EEC in 1992 will undoubtedly lead to real competition.

THE INTERNATIONAL CREDIT INSURANCE ASSOCIATION (ICIA)

The real competition for business may well come from those Berne Union members who have remote links or even no links with their governments. These companies tend to be members of the International Credit Insurance Association. As such they have concentrated on providing cover for home trade credit insurance. They are therefore practised in providing cover against insolvency and protracted default in their own countries. To provide the same cover in respect of business involving purchasers or buyers in other overseas territories has become a logical development. The real competition, now beginning to show, is that members of ICIA may even provide cover to sellers who are outside their country. Thus Trade Indemnity, one of the two UK ICIA members, now offers export credit cover to UK companies and will offer this also to companies based outside the UK. This trend will continue, particularly as other insurers, not members of either Berne Union or ICIA, are also offering cover irrespective of the nationality of the selling company.

In the past there has been a marked distinction between export credit and home trade cover. Whilst this is changing and insurers may be prepared to offer cover for both home trade and export business, sometimes under the same policy, the distinction between the two main classes is fundamental.

Home trade

The international credit manager will appreciate that sales made by overseas subsidiaries to their local customers constitute home trade. The possible solution to the group's credit insurance requirements may

149

not, however, be just one large export credit policy run by the centre but may be locally placed home trade policies run by the various subsidiaries.

The vast majority of home trade policies cover both insolvency, as defined by the law of the land, and protracted default. Some only cover insolvency. The reason for this is that in most developed countries any errant debtors who have failed to pay for a number of months after the due date will find a writ issued against them to commence insolvency proceedings. Therefore the number of instances where claims are paid for protracted default, in countries where the legal system is able to cope with the volume of work, is very small indeed.

The two risks of protracted default (usually defined as six months after the due date) and insolvency are both covered by the description '*del credere*'. These are the only risks covered by home trade credit insurance policies.

Export

Trade with buyers in other countries involves the seller in a number of other risks. Whilst the *del credere* risks will be included in any export credit insurance policy, the cover will also include risks known as 'political risks' which can also prevent the seller from receiving payment. Depending on the underwriter used, it may be possible to insure exports so that sales to certain countries will only be covered against *del credere* risks at an agreed premium whilst sales to other countries will be at an increased premium because the cover will additionally include political risks.

The political risks generally included in export credit insurance are the following.

1 War, in varying forms, including civil war, riots and other events which prevent the contract being performed.
2 Political events, administrative or legal measures, economic difficulties, all arising outside the seller's country which delay, completely or temporarily, or even prevent the transfer of payments made by the buyer. This means that the buyer has paid the money into the bank, has completed all the import documentation required, and yet the payment has not been remitted overseas. Usually this is the result of economic problems in the buyer's country which cause foreign exchange delays.

3   A moratorium on all external debt declared by the government of the buyer's country.
4   Any action by the government of the buyer's country which prevents either part or all of the contract being performed.
5   Shortfall in payment when received, where this is caused by a law in the buyer's country which prevents the payment being topped up. This is frequently caused by excessive currency fluctuation or even devaluation.
6   Public buyer cover. This recognizes that government agencies and nationalized bodies cannot be made insolvent and that public buyers are sometimes capable of acting above the law, and that the seller would find it impossible to sue for the debt effectively.

THE PRIVATE INSURANCE MARKET

Most members of the ICIA are not government departments or agencies. They are increasingly offering not only their traditional home trade cover but are also able to insure export credit. Additionally, as they are in the private sector, they are not constrained by the need to act in support of their national government in only supporting the export sales made by companies established in their own country.

This ability to insure not only third country goods but also sales made by overseas-based companies has opened up the market for credit insurance, so that cover can be placed with different underwriters from those who were the traditional credit insurers. Most of this activity remains in the conventional mode of covering all or most of a company's trade.

One development that must be recorded in this chapter relates to the growth in the 1980s of the political risk markets.

With many of the world's export credit insurers suffering disastrous underwriting results and huge losses, a need arose for many companies to be able to continue to trade with some of their customers in long-established markets. With the export credit agencies retrenching, the demand for cover for countries which were not altogether stable but nonetheless needed goods was provided by a number of specialist underwriting organizations in the private sector.

These were able to assess the risks on an individual basis and to tailor the policy to cover just the causes of losses or risks required by the seller. In the main these policies offered cover against non-transfer.

They were able to provide cover on a select basis and to give cover to those companies in which they had most trust to complete the transactions. The cover was usually offered to companies that had a good track record of trading in the overseas country, had some infrastructure in the buyer's country to handle problems and were involved in selling goods or services that were given high priority by the government in the overseas country.

As these risks are covered singly and therefore the underwriter is selected against, the rates of premium are high. Some companies prefer to use this type of private insurance rather than to hold a policy covering all of their sales, many of which may be with buyers or countries they consider to be too safe to warrant expenditure on insurance premiums. A small number of companies offer political risk insurance and these vary from country to country. Undoubtedly the most well known and recognized is Lloyd's of London.

TYPES OF CREDIT INSURANCE

Home trade

Whole turnover

A whole-turnover policy is written on a comprehensive basis, normally for a twelve-month period, to cover all the company's business.

It normally excludes sales to subsidiary and associated companies, nationalized undertakings, government departments, public authorities, public authority buyers, cash sales and VAT and so on.

The policy normally indemnifies the insured against 75 to 95 per cent of losses incurred.

Subject to mutual agreement between the insured and underwriter, the insured is allowed to grant credit up to a limit of discretion. Larger approvals require specific vetting by underwriters with a subsequent credit limit being issued.

Premium is normally charged as a percentage of turnover.

Specific account (fixed or adjustable basis)

This is applied to revolving business with one or more named buyers and the premium is calculated at a percentage rate on the amount outstanding at one time. The premium calculation is based on the outstanding debts declared usually at the end of each month. If the terms of payment are shorter (adjustable time basis), declarations may be required more frequently. However, if the amount at risk is fairly constant then a fixed premium is usually charged and is based on the maximum limit covered by the policy (fixed time basis).

Specific account (turnover basis)

This is applied to a single contract or series of transactions with one or more named buyers, generally for a period of twelve months. The premium is calculated at a percentage rate on the amount of a contract or on the volume of turnover during the policy period.

Specific account policies can cover up to 100 per cent indemnity. The policy type can be more readily adapted to cover work-in-progress, retentions and extended terms of payment in excess of 180 days.

Annual aggregate first loss

The insured agree to take for their own account a predetermined amount of bad debt losses in any one year. This sum is normally calculated to be above the normal level of expected bad debts experienced by the insured; it normally excludes small losses altogether by the use of a non-qualifying loss excess.

All other losses count towards the policy, once the losses exceed the agreed first loss figure; all subsequent losses are reimbursed by the underwriter 100 per cent up to an agreed ceiling.

Premium is normally charged as a percentage of the slice of cover purchased.

An annual aggregate can be issued with or without credit limit approvals, the client's own credit control forming the base of the policy document.

Each and every loss

This is a whole-turnover policy type where the insured agree to take for their own account a pre-agreed excess of each and every bad debt loss suffered. Once this level has been breached, the remainder of the loss is reimbursed by a 100 per cent indemnity.

Premium is charged as a percentage of whole turnover.

153

Minimum retention

Minimum retention is the most common form of excess employed on whole-turnover policies. The insured agree to take for their own account the minimum retention excess or the uninsured percentage, whichever is the greater, not both.

For example, if the minimum retention were £500 and the uninsured percentage 80 per cent, any bad debt loss up to £2500 would be subject to a £500 deduction. Larger losses would be reimbursed 80 per cent.

Threshold

A threshold policy is a type of whole-turnover policy where the bad debt loss itself has to be in excess of the agreed figure (the threshold) for a claim to be valid under the policy.

The policy excludes any loss falling below the 'threshold'. Above the threshold level, full indemnity is given.

Premium is charged on total turnover, even that which is generated by buyers which fall below threshold level.

Datum line

Datum line is similar to whole-turnover threshold although it is, in fact, a type of specific account policy. Buyers are eligible for inclusion within the policy scope only when the debt owed has exceeded the datum line level.

Bad debt loss under the datum line level may also result in a valid claim if the insured can demonstrate that the buyer had a balance in excess of datum line figure in the previous twelve-month trading period.

Not all credit insurance relates to covering sales of goods or services on credit terms. Other adaptations have been made by underwriters to meet certain requirements.

1 *Work-in-progress*: some form of cover against pre-delivery risks may be included within a whole-turnover policy or, more usually, as part of a policy to cover a specific transaction where the 'pre-' and 'post-delivery' risks are clearly definable.
2 *Supplier default*: issued to cover against consequential loss arising from the insolvency of a supplier.

3 *Credit guarantee*: this helps a purchaser to improve his negotiating ability by providing the seller with a specific credit insurance on that purchaser. Full consultation between insurer and purchaser is necessary.

4 *Breach of contract*: specific cover taken by a company to protect another company against loss arising from the proposer's failure to complete contractual obligations of a financial nature.

5 *Anticipatory credit*: this is a frequently overlooked form of credit insurance which is used to protect stage/advanced payments made before delivery, usually on placing the order. In these instances it is possible to protect against the insolvency of the supplier. Such cover is known as 'anticipatory credit' and is available from many credit insurance underwriters. Increasingly, purchasers who make down-payments or deposits before receipt of goods or services have resorted to the protection available through the use of performance bonds to cover themselves against loss. Use of bonding requires that the supplier arranges for an underwriter to provide a bond to the purchaser whereas anticipatory credit cover is bought and arranged by the purchaser. It therefore provides closer control of the negotiation with the underwriter of any resultant claim. Bonds are described in Chapter 12.

Anticipatory credit insurance is by no means close to most people's idea of what credit insurance covers. It does, nonetheless, draw attention to the basic fact that, unless the supply of goods or services and payment take place simultaneously, then there is a risk that one or other party to the contract will not fulfil their obligations. Anticipatory credit is unusual also in that, unlike most other forms of credit insurance which cover the seller against non-payment or performance, it does not mirror the activities of the credit manager by protecting against the impact of bad debts.

Export credit

As has been mentioned earlier the traditional provider of export credit cover has been linked in some way to government. This has meant that diplomatic difficulties have resulted in changes or cancellations in the cover granted for certain countries. The export credit underwriter has sometimes been prevented from offering cover if relationships between the two countries have deteriorated. Competition for the government-linked export credit insurers has come from home trade underwriters in their own countries. These have been attracted by the business transacted with territories where there is no perceived political risk. A good example of this has been within the EEC where competition from underwriters for this type of business has been keen. In addition, a small number of general insurance companies have offered export credit cover. They have been selective and have tended to operate on a basis of annual aggregate cover. As with the home trade underwriters who also cover export business, these are not constrained by the requirements to insure only their own nationals or only goods manufactured in their own country. There is a great deal of flexibility in their approach.

Short-term credit

Choosing to cover either from date of order (pre-credit) or date of despatch, companies may insure all or part of their export business. Where they choose to select, this is generally only allowed if the selection is on the basis of sales to certain countries. Selection for just a few named buyers is not usually acceptable to the underwriter. Terms of payment covered are up to 180 days. Sales to associated or subsidiary companies overseas may be covered against political events preventing payment.

Increasingly, as a result of competition, variations in the way in which the risk is shared between underwriter and the company have been introduced. These have been adopted from the range of credit insurance products provided by the home trade underwriter, so that a 'datum and threshold' basis of cover can now be offered as well as annual aggregate cover.

Extended credit

Companies selling on terms over 180 days invariably need to seek external financing. Separate credit insurance is available for such business. This may either be written on a whole turnover basis or else may be specific. Because of the need for financing and the consensus rules, a number of variations have been introduced whereby the risk can be transferred.

Since the 1960s and 1970s much of the business transacted on terms of payment over 180 days was covered by means of buyer credit, leasing or forfaiting. In the case of buyer credit the buyer is lent money by bankers to pay for goods on cash terms. This is not credit insurance as such, although the device has been utilized by a number of the government linked export credit underwriters.

A number of specially devised variations exist to cover situations where goods are sent overseas unsold, perhaps for a trade fair or exhibition or even for trial and demonstration. Cover is available to recognize the risk that the goods may not be sold and need to be returned to the would-be seller. The cover is against seizure or inability to re-export the goods.

SELF-INSURANCE

Apart from simply bearing the risk themselves, companies can use a captive company to handle a number of different classes of insurance. This solution has grown in the 1980s. Properly used they can be useful in providing cover in respect of credit insurance.

In essence the captive company provides the insured company (which is generally an associate) with similar cover to that which is available from the established credit insurers. The captive then buys reinsurance from the credit insurance underwriters to protect against the impact of very large losses.

Credit insurance has been found to be very suitable for inclusion in a captive as it provides good cashflow and at the same time is a very tax-efficient method of providing for bad debts.

BROKERS

Credit insurance broking is highly specialized, and it is clear that increased competition between underwriters will give much greater scope for alternative quotations to be obtained. Apart from this fact there is the advantage available from a broker that similar problems will have arisen with other clients and the solution has already been found.

It has always been the credit insurance broker's role to tailor the policy to the company's needs. What is now possible is that a number of acceptable variations can be put together so that the company can choose the cover that is ideal for its own purpose.

Not all insurance brokers have specialists to handle this class of risk; the same must be said of captive insurance arrangements. It is therefore now usual for the broking company used to place credit insurance risks to be different from the broker used to place more conventional insurances.

SUMMARY

Bad debts are never welcome; they occur no matter how carefully vetting or control procedures are implemented. Use of credit insurance to transfer the risk to an underwriter should be considered whenever the exposures with customers are such that a single loss or a series of losses would impact on the balance sheet.

The breadth of cover now available and the increased competition from underwriters for the business should enable all credit managers to buy the cover which dovetails with their needs and protects what is almost certainly the largest of the company's current assets.

PART IV
TERMS AND CONDITIONS OF SALE

11

Terms and conditions for international trade

Gray Sinclair

Should it be said that the contents of this chapter are relevant to the marketing function, that would be wholly correct, and moreover, that is why the material appears in the book. It can perhaps be regarded as the 'nuts and bolts' of international trading, without which no policies no matter how carefully defined, could work in practice.

The idea of the 'total export concept', equally applicable to importing, is probably used around the world in slightly different contexts, but the first official usage seems to have been in the UK in 1978. Then, the title of a working party report, *Through Transport and the Total Export Concept*, relating to the developing trade with Europe, defined it as implying 'integrated production, selling, transport, distribution, payment and customer servicing'. No specific mention of credit management as such at that time, but its importance in linking the selling and payment roles which were referred to, is now well and fully recognized, and, thus, an integral function of any total export concept today.

There has been considerable antagonism in the past; some but considerably less exists today, and there probably will still be an element in the future (yet hopefully diminishing) on the part of marketing people toward credit management, which, in the eyes of the former, carries the stigma of 'control'.

That is a quite natural human reaction anywhere, but it can be kept not only within normal working bounds, but even developed into a harmonious and mutually respectful working relationship. How? – by reaching a situation where marketing executives and staff in any individual organization have come to appreciate that their credit management colleagues are not just going by the rule book, but have an adequate background knowledge of the problems which marketing comes up against in trying to increase the company's sales – and that need not be at all difficult.

A most effective way will be to let your marketing colleagues have a look through the comprehensive contents of this book. That cannot fail to convince them that there is a great deal more to effective credit management than meets the eye, in the interests of the company's overall success.

THE INTERNATIONAL SALES CONTRACT

Selling, or for that matter buying, on an international basis differs from domestic or internal sales, in having additional involvement with the associated contracts covering the shipment by sea, air, rail, road or even post by which the goods are exported or imported, the contract of insurance and, where a letter of credit is involved, the banking contract. Also, delivery of the shipping documents themselves to the buyers or their agent may be an important factor in fulfilling the contract of sale.

The credit manager cannot be concerned with the intricacies of the laws governing international sales. With the exception of the Soviet bloc, the legal framework within which most of the world's trade takes place is fundamentally the same, and varies little as between public and private sector buyers. But there are some important individual differences in application as between the countries of seller and buyer, though to look ahead, many of the problems arising from those differences will be removed by the widest possible adoption of the UN Convention on Contracts for the International Sale of Goods (Vienna, 1980). What does concern the credit manager is that the actual marketing agreement to sell to the buyer establishes a valid and collectable debt for purposes of forecasting cashflow.

Thus one sees a further extension to the total export concept of particular importance to marketing in the first place, by integrating the company's legal/secretarial department whose advice will need to be obtained, not only in the case of direct sales to buyers overseas but in drawing up any agency or distributorship agreements.

Amount owing

Where credit insurance is held, there is an important point to be watched in drawing up the contract which is often forgotten. There must always be an 'amount owing' at any time of performance of the contract, as otherwise the exporters, as the insured, may find themselves unable to make a claim on the insurer. An example could well be that payment is due on delivery of the goods on-site overseas – not an unusual phrasing perhaps – but something happens before that point, and the insurance company will require proof of what was owing. The answer is probably, from the technical insurance viewpoint, nothing owing – so no claim settlement.

Offer and acceptance

The fundamental aspect of the sale is the offer and its acceptance, which has foundered on so many occasions when the sellers have quoted their terms, possibly embodied in preprinted wording on the quotation, and the buyers have accepted according to their own preprinted terms which contain a basic difference, possibly unacceptable to the seller – but the latter does nothing about it and thereby creates a potential problem.

Technically, the sellers have to 'accept' the buyer's acceptance if they so wish, failing which there is deemed to be no contract. But there are other approaches in practice, such as assuming a contract has been concluded unless the seller objects formally. Or perhaps by regarding the contract as consisting of a combination of the sets of preprinted conditions which are either the same or do not contradict each other. The compromise solution offered by the UN 1980 Convention is that a conditional acceptance will be treated as a counter-offer – except that any material differences will be assumed to be acceptable to the other party unless an objection by that party is registered.

TERMS OF DELIVERY

It is very poor workmanship commercially, and certainly very naïve, to be imprecise about the terms of delivery (sometimes referred to as trade terms) for each and every sales contract, thereby failing to establish the exact responsibilities of seller and buyer in the event that something goes wrong along the line.

As far back as 1920, at one of the very early meetings of the International Chamber of Commerce (ICC), attention was drawn to the inconvenience arising from the fact that the practical interpretations of trade terms such as 'FOB', 'C & F' and 'CIF' varied from country to country. It was also felt that although the exporter/importer might ascertain the local interpretation in the country of the importer/exporter, where it was different from their own, the exporter/importer was no better off unless there was an agreement as to which interpretation would apply for the contract.

INCOTERMS

Thus the ICC put together the International Rules for the Interpretation of Trade Terms (INCOTERMS), first published in 1936, expanded in 1953 and now current in their 1980 revision. As the title implies, the object was to make the most suitable of those rules applicable to individual contracts, so establishing a basis for interpretation of any dispute; the 1980 revision explains fourteen different INCOTERMS, being reduced to twelve in the planned 1989 revision.

AFTD

While INCOTERMS are by far the most widely used terms in international trade, they are not the only standard. A US committee, established for that purpose, published the American Foreign Trade Definitions (AFTD) in 1923, which were revised in 1941 and are still in force today. It was, however, agreed at the time of drafting INCOTERMS 1980, that the AFTD would be phased out in favour of INCOTERMS for US international trade, although that is proving a gradual process in practice.

Warsaw & Oxford

The Warsaw & Oxford Rules of 1932 are not widely known, and are not really relevant to the general use of trade terms. Prepared by the International Law Association in conjunction with the ICC, they define a number of specific aspects relating to basic CIF contracts only.

COMECON

1965 saw the introduction of the General Conditions for the Delivery of Merchandise by the Council for Mutual Economic Assistance (COMECON), for internal trade between the Soviet bloc countries, but INCOTERMS have always been acceptable for the bloc's external trade.

COMBITERMS

A Swedish system, COMBITERMS, introduced in 1969 and revised in 1982 to be compatible with INCOTERMS 1980, was developed primarily as a means for standardization of Scandinavian trade. This has a comprehensive system for distribution of the various cost elements between seller and buyer, also adaptable (already looking to the future some twenty years ago) to the introduction of data processing to international trade, of which more later.

INCOTERMS update

An ICC working party started an examination of INCOTERMS 1980 at the end of 1987, to see what alterations and additions might now be desirable. It is expected that a revised 1989 edition will become available by the end of the year or early in 1990 – the 1980 revision remains operational meanwhile. The revision is aimed at the most positive presentation possible of the individual terms, giving a clear indication of the correct term for the mode of transport.

Where the credit manager has the opportunity to comment on sales contracts, quotations, pro forma invoices and sales invoices, the point to be watched is that not only should INCOTERMS be used wherever possible, but they must then be shown as part of the term, such as 'CIF INCOTERMS'. It is no use whatsoever having the intention to apply an INCOTERM but then omitting if from the designation. Should a resultant dispute finish in court, it is very, very unlikely that favourable consideration would be given to claimed 'intent', in the absence of factual evidence of the agreed responsibilities of the INCOTERM. Useful explanatory information can be found in the ICC *Guide to INCOTERMS*.

TERMS AND METHODS OF PAYMENT

In order of reducing security for the exporter, the basic terms of payment (which are expanded on in Chapter 13) have normally been shown as:

(a) cash with order/prior to delivery;

165

(b) confirmed irrevocable letter of credit (CILC);
(c) irrevocable letter of credit;
(d) documentary bank collection;
(e) clean bank collection;
(f) open account;

but trading today includes three other categories, on the borderline of whether they should properly be regarded as terms or methods:

(g) cash on shipment;
(h) countertrade;
(i) forfaiting.

Neither factoring nor leasing is included above as, in general, the paying agent is a domestic bank, finance house or leasing company in the seller's country. But there might be exceptions in any of those in specific circumstances.

Cash with order/prior to shipment

There is not much to say, except that the credit manager may sometimes have to explain to a marketing representative, who comes back waving a cheque following a meeting with the buyer, often in a hotel just before the representative leaves for home, that 'cash' means cleared funds in the company's bank account, nothing less. So there should be no real hope of honouring any promise like 'the goods will be at the airport tomorrow', against the cheque.

Many countries will only release foreign currency to pay for imports against proof of shipment, as a means of avoiding irregular or illegal currency transfers. Offers to pay in advance in the seller's country, may mean the buyers have access to funds outside their own exchange control system, and such offers should be thought over carefully before acceptance.

Confirmed irrevocable letter of credit

The strength of a CILC is that it represents two quite separate banking contracts – the original irrevocable undertaking of the overseas bank opening the credit, and the firm commitment of the confirming bank (usually in the seller's country) to pay without recourse, against presentation of the documents required, if in order and within the period

166

allowed. The risk to the credit manager is only the strength of the confirmer – there should be no need to be concerned with the opening bank.

In no way is this to be confused with a credit issued by a bank overseas, on which is inscribed 'We hereby issue our confirmed and irrevocable letter of credit etc. etc.', which is best regarded as a load of rubbish, even though the original intention may be perfectly honourable – basically, no bank can confirm its own paper in that way.

Irrevocable letter of credit

The use of 'irrevocable' means that the terms can only be changed with agreement of the buyer, the issuing bank and seller, and provided documents are presented in order and within the period allowed, the bank will pay. A revocable credit (defined and discussed in Chapter 16) will not normally be of any trading interest.

Documentary bank collection

The documentary bank collection usually relies on the accompanying bill of exchange, a full explanation of the mechanism being given in Chapter 14.

Within the system and as an opportunity for some extra implied security, the credit manager may consider the use of the 'protest' facility with bills of exchange – but a word of warning. For practical reasons, the instructions to the overseas bank to use the procedure have to be given at the time the collection is initiated by the seller, and be known to the buyer from the outset. The buyers might well take the view that the exporter has no faith in their ability or intention to pay, which is not the best way to establish a business relationship!

Clean bank collection

Here, with the documents enabling them to take possession of the goods having gone to the buyer direct, the supplier is virtually relying on the buyer's knowledge that a local bank is involved in obtaining settlement, to persuade the buyer to pay on time. This is often 'cash against documents' (CAD), not to be confused with CAD done direct with the buyer.

This method may nevertheless have to be used even when there is no established history available on the buyer, to avoid possible demurrage charges for the seller, which might arise if all the documents were to be sent via the banking system as above.

Open account

A considerable percentage of world trade is transacted on an open account basis, but the credit manager has to live with the fact there is no security beyond the honesty of the individual buyer. Here, 'CAD' merely means that the buyer agrees to pay against receipt of the documents with which he can clear the goods, possibly representing thirty days' credit time in practice.

Cash on shipment

Quite different from cash following shipment paid through an export house in the seller's country – that probably being regarded as a domestic sale – cash against proof of shipment is a facility offered by banks and specialist finance houses in many parts of the world. In some cases the facility involves actual purchase of the goods, rather than purchase of the amount receivable; and possibly in discussion with the company's auditors, the credit manager has to decide if there is a contingent liability against whatever recourse to the company the facility may include.

A point to be watched where any such finance scheme is under consideration or has been adopted, is to make sure that there is a word-by-word explanation of the lender's exact possibilities of recourse, and how and when they may be applied. Writing an extended survey of some thirty such schemes in the UK at the end of 1987, brought to light that the interpretation of the same term varied substantially within the banks and finance houses involved.

Countertrade

Now very far removed from the original idea of more or less simple 'barter', the field of countertrade involves a number of quite separate possibilities, each requiring a different approach to the terms and methods of payment. It is usual to find information available from the government trade department of the seller's country, which will reflect the official attitude towards any such arrangements. (Countertrade is considered separately in Chapter 17.)

Forfaiting

Again, forfaiting now bears little resemblance to the original application of the facility for certain specialized applications in the medium-term (five to eight years) credit range. It is now being suggested in applications for as little as ninety-day credit terms in amounts as low as £50 000 or the currency equivalent, although anything less than an annual total of £500 000 minimum on that basis would probably not be practical.

Basically, forfaiting involves payment without recourse to the seller by the forfaiter, against purchase of a piece of paper normally called an 'aval', being a signed acceptance from the buyer to pay for the goods, guaranteed (avalized) by a bank or finance house acceptable to the forfaiter. Thus the buyer may have to sign a promissory note even prior to shipment of the goods, in order to give the seller the security he requires. (Forfaiting is also considered in Chapter 9.)

INTEREST AND DISCOUNT

There are no specific considerations in terms of interest or discounts, and each case will necessarily be treated as it occurs in the light of current circumstances, that is, on a one-off basis.

The credit manager will require payment to be made according to the agreed terms, and would reasonably expect to collect interest beyond that time at least to cover the cost of any additional overdraft, or to compensate for any loss caused by being unable to use the expected funds. But one needs to be aware to what extent, if any, the exchange control authorities in the buyer's country will allow accumulated interest to be transferred to a seller – at best it may be limited to the central bank's own basic borrowing rate or, possibly, to the basic lending rate in the seller's country. Also, the credit manager may wish to consider extending forward currency protection, where interest amounts are likely to be appreciable.

Again, the credit manager may wish to encourage early payment by the buyer, possibly as a means of ensuring that the cashflow forecast is kept to schedule, by offering a discount based on some relationship to the cost of any company overdraft or to the return on the funds used elsewhere. But unless the buyers have been successful in selling the goods either ahead of schedule or more expensively, they will not be keen to incur additional borrowing charges themselves – the position will depend on the situation at the time and on the relative rates of interest/discount applicable. There is also the possibility that, in some countries, requests for payments for abroad are fed into a pipeline in order of basic due date – requests for earlier payment may thus go unheeded.

LOCAL CURRENCY EXCHANGE RISK

The credit manager should have examined the position at the time business in a new country was first proposed – even ahead of examining the creditworthiness of a new buyer – on any delay likely in the transmission of funds, once local currency in settlement of invoices – irrespective of the currency in which they are drawn – has been lodged with the local authorities for transfer. Officially, some countries refuse to admit there is any 'currency pipeline' or delay, so it is advisable to take care with the checking.

The second risk element to be catered for when the invoice is not in the buyer's currency, is an exchange rate movement against the buyer between the time payment becomes due and the time when the required foreign currency becomes available, so that the buyer will need to deposit more local currency as the invoice equivalent. It is normal for any such local currency shortfall to be made the responsibility of the buyer, although some exchange control authorities are reluctant to accept the proviso.

RETENTION OF TITLE

Retention of title is not always as easy as it sounds, but every credit manager should try to have a retention of title clause included in the company's general terms of business, on the lines of:

1 The seller retaining the legal property in the goods until the price is fully paid, along with the right to enter the buyer's premises at any time, without notice, to repossess them.
2 The buyer being unable to on-sell the goods in the meantime except as agent of the seller, and then only to a bona fide on-buyer in the buyer's normal course of business. Any proceeds from such sales should also be kept separate in the name of the seller.

These combine 'simple retention' in (1) and 'extended retention' in (2), but there may well be difficulties over the application of the latter in a number of countries. The so-called *Romalpa* case has been widely quoted as an example of an extended retention being effective, reporting the case of a Dutch company which went into liquidation after purchasing aluminium from a UK company, some of which remained in stock and some on-sold – the UK company was judged to have a retained interest in the goods and in the proceeds.

A 'double-extended' retention, for want of a better phrase, attempts to exercise retention, in the event of non-payment by the original buyer, over the products into which the goods have been incorporated by an on-buyer. It has been established, under English law at least, that the clause is ineffective where the final product has a different commercial identity from the material as sold originally, and against which retention was claimed. In point of fact, the claim which failed referred to an original sale of resin, which was on-sold and incorporated into chipboard.

It is evident that any question of a retention clause is in the first place, one for consideration by the company's legal/secretarial department.

GOODS v. SERVICES

Primarily, and as evidenced by the requirements of certain export credit insurers, there is a difference between what can be called 'associated' services and 'whole' services.

The former are those which will normally be shown on the commercial invoice for the goods, such as directly associated installation charges.

The second can cover a very wide range of both visible and less visible services, from the repair of jet aircraft engines to the provision of training facilities for a country's agricultural programme, and a host of others.

From the credit manager's standpoint, the first sets no problem at all, being part of a formal invoice in the normal manner. With the second, however, there is always the problem of what constitutes acceptance of part or whole of the service by the buyer, such as to constitute a valid debt and, particularly where a letter of credit is involved, sufficient proof of acceptance of the debt by the buyer.

There may also be the angle of local exchange control in the buyer's country, where an intended import has to obtain specific clearance before an import/payment licence can be issued. Such clearance will often involve some form of 'pre-shipment inspection' (see below) and price comparison, before payment can be claimed in the seller's country. Experience has shown that in such circumstances the credit manager should try to arrange for separate 'inspections' of goods and services, as otherwise the inspection agency may take time to try to find out if there has been an attempt at being paid twice!

PRE-SHIPMENT AND PRICE COMPARISON

The question of pre-shipment and price comparison has been the subject of much contention, and of complaints from exporters in a number of countries of undue interference with their legitimate trading activities by the several inspection agencies, of which the Swiss Compagnie Générale de Surveillance (SGS) is by far the largest on an international scale. This led to ICC headquarters, Paris, jointly with its British affiliate ICC United Kingdom, organizing the first international symposium on the subject, in March 1988, where the ICC draft rules for the operation of inspection agency activities on a suggested international basis were first discussed.

The credit manager is unlikely to be involved with or bothered by pre-shipment inspection per se. In fact, this is generally accepted as a means for ensuring that what has been ordered is what is being shipped, as to quality and quantity. Indeed the International Maritime Bureau (IMB) associate of the ICC recommends it as a means of fraud prevention. The use of pre-shipment inspection may be made either on an individual buyer basis, or as a general requirement of an importing country.

The problems, and there have been many allegations of frustration, harassment and almost anything else, arise from the associated 'price comparison', which is now required as an adjunct to the inspection routine by nearly thirty countries, before the branch of the inspection agency in the seller's country will issue its 'clean report of findings' (CRF), which is required before payment can be made; it may also be known as pre-shipment verification (PSV).

Situation continues

This is not the place for a long dissertation on the merits and demerits of the requirement, beyond perhaps noting that price comparison was also introduced to minimize the activities of international fraudsters, not to hinder the activities of legitimate traders.

But from the credit manager's viewpoint, it is quite clear that for the foreseeable future, where the company intends to continue or enter into business with buyers in a country which requires PSV, then the receivable is not going to be cleared unless and until a CRF is issued by the specified branch of the quoted inspection agency.

A practical suggestion which may save endless trouble, nevertheless, involves the fact that under normal procedure the agency will not commence the CRF formalities until they have seen a copy of the document proving shipment. It is likely that the agency offices will be some distance from the seller's location, and there will already have been the delay in getting the transport document to them after shipment. While obviously not his or her immediate responsibility, the credit manager would do well to ensure that the fastest available means are used to deliver the document and have it returned along with the CRF, most particularly when the time factor of expiry of a letter of credit is involved.

THE IMPORTANCE OF GOOD DOCUMENTATION

Good documentation is an issue paramount, one might say, for any export/import operation which hopes to be successful. Taking letters of credit in particular, which account for some 20 per cent of world trade, surveys carried out in the UK in 1974 and again in 1987 indicate that, on average, around half of all documents submitted to banks by exporters for payment are rejected on first presentation for one or more reasons. Unofficial reports from the USA suggest the figure there is even higher, and many believe that the particular UK figure is optimistically low!

Big losses

There are occasions where discrepancies cannot be corrected in time, such as vessels sailing late, credits having expired or documents being presented late, but the failure rate for commercial invoices increased in the UK in 1987 compared with the first survey, which is quite inexcusable. Suffice it to say that the UK Simpler Trade Procedures Board (SITPRO), which instigated the surveys, estimates that in respect of letters of credit alòne, UK exporters are wasting some £70 million annually, through loss of interest due to late payments resulting from discrepancies.

This is an obvious area where credit managers should watch for payment delays with credits and, at the same time, they should be interested in seeing that documentation with other methods of payment is completely correct when issued. Again one can only quote UK figures, but that £70 million wasted soars to £120 million according to SITPRO, taking into account the further loss of interest on bank collections and open account methods. And if the USA has a worse average than the UK on letter of credit failures, then it is just as likely to have the same high wastage on the other methods as well. Human nature being what it is, there is no reason to doubt that failures elsewhere in the major trading nations are just as awful!

Status reports

Although a matter of completing a document rather than of getting it right, the credit manager is directly involved with the wording of requests for bank credit information on overseas buyers. Surprisingly though, many seem to be satisfied with a report akin to 'A properly constituted company considered good for its normal obligations', which is the usual result of an insufficiently completed questionnaire in the first place and, technically, not worth even the cost of the paper it is written on.

Given details of the type of goods or services, the proposed terms of payment, the intended currency and the amount which might be outstanding at any time, the reply should be much more informative, and anything on the lines of 'We have no experience in the amount quoted' should be warning enough.

Customs

Credit managers in Europe, in particular, have been affected by introduction of the new single administrative document (SAD) as from 1 January 1988, which replaced nearly a hundred previous customs documents and forms within the European Community. That may seem odd, but the fact was that failure in the completion of the new documents commenced at some 50–60 per cent according to UK Customs, who considered that their colleagues elsewhere in the EEC would have faced similar problems. The outcome of course, was that shipments were delayed, with more than a strong probability that delays in payment would result, leading to disruption of normally 'reliable' cashflow forecast items.

'Customs 88', as the whole procedure is known, also involved a massive changeover to a new 'harmonized system' for customs classification. By the end of January 1988 nearly thirty countries had notified their adoption of this system, but there is growing concern that in the developing countries of Africa and South America in particular, there will be a number of conditional adoptions, leaving those countries to apply local variations to the system. What that will mean in terms of any eventual slowing-down in the handling of exports and imports is impossible to judge at this stage. But there is no doubt this is yet another example of the need for overall correctness and completeness of trade documentation, and the active credit manager should take an interest with colleagues in the shipping and export departments, to do what can be done to keep documentation errors, along with resultant delays in payment, to a minimum.

THE TREND TOWARD ELECTRONIC DATA INTERCHANGE

It follows from the interest which the credit manager must have in documents and documentation, that such interest will spread within the worldwide development and growth of electronic data interchange (EDI).

Europe is the front-runner towards development of EDI on a global basis, and the UN European Commission for Europe (ECE) committee has been receiving a growing number of requests from countries wishing to become associated with its work, since the acceptance of universal standards in September 1987. That agreement opened the way for replacing paper-based communications with electronic versions, and in view of the demand, three *rapporteurs* are responsible for co-ordinating the setting-up of consultative machinery and providing a framework for development work. Representatives from the USA and Poland are looking after the North American and Eastern trading blocs respectively, and one from the UK is responsible for the European role.

UNCID

No credit manager wishing to have a basic knowledge of what is going on, what the future is likely to bring of interest, and of the basic rules of procedure which have been drafted by a special international joint committee, should fail to read ICC publication No. 452, with the short title *UNCID*.

These Uniform Rules for Conduct for Interchange of Trade Data by Teletransmission (UNCID) are intended as an interim solution to the many legal shortcomings in our paper-oriented commercial usage and trade law, which have become apparent with the rapid development of EDI. Such shortcomings call for relevant adaptation of both trade usage and law which can only come slowly. But, by the same yardstick, trade cannot wait.

Already adopted by the ICC and the UN/ECE, the UNCID rules are already in use for international trade projects. But there is no suggestion that UNCID is the end of the story, although there is now a sound foundation for the future. The ICC publication outlines the need for specific communication agreements, with certain elements that should be considered in addition to UNCID, and discusses them.

PROGRESS

In the UK alone, 'paperless trade' is growing at 200 per cent per annum, with more than 1,000 user companies including over sixty of the 'Top 100'. Credit managers will have an increasing interest in the activities of the EDI Association, with over 200 members in the UK at the end of 1988, and similar organizations will doubtless be formed elsewhere, as the application of EDI is fundamental to exports. Not only is there a positive saving in the cost of producing the necessary documentation, but the removal of a very high percentage of potential human errors means there will be less chance of such events delaying payment – a very important factor in achieving maximum positive cash flow.

Internationally, there was a major step forward in 1988, with UN approval of a common EDI standard for eventual global usage, known as Electronic Data Interchange for Administration, Commerce and Transport (EDIFACT). Coupled with the availability of more powerful small computers, specialized export/import software and a large increase in networking facilities, the current annual increase of 200 per cent in EDI usage seems likely not only to be the basis for continuing growth, but possibly even a pessimistic estimate – and to the eventual benefit of the credit manager.

Recommended reading

Cecchini, Paolo (1988) *The European Challenge – 1992: The Benefits of a Single Market*. Aldershot: Gower.

Ezer, Shaul (looseleaf update) *International Exporting Agreements*. Albany, NY: Matthew Bender. Provides precedents and information on US practice.

International Chamber of Commerce (1980) *Guide to INCOTERMS*, ICC Publication No. 354. Paris: ICC.

Pelkmans, J. and Winters, A. (1988) *Europe's Domestic Market*. London: Chatham House. A preview of the 1992 Single European Market in broad perspective.

Rowe, Michael (1987) *Electronic Trade Payments*. IBC Financial Publishing, Byfleet, Surrey, UK. Describes how computerized techniques are beginning to link export/import documentation and related payment procedures, and analyses the issues involved.

Schmitthoff, Clive M. (1986) *Schmitthoff's Export Trade*, 8th edn. London: Stevens & Sons. The standard English work on this subject.

12

Tender and performance guarantees

Jim Hackett

For many credit managers, particularly those with 'international' in their job title, their responsibilities should include not only credit control but also what we might appropriately call 'debit control'. In other words, while concentrating on the prompt receipt of funds due to the corporation, they should also ensure that funds are not unnecessarily paid away.

One of the most difficult areas to control in this regard is the management of bonds or guarantees provided in the pursuance of overseas contracts.

These most frequently take the form of tender (bid) or performance bonds. Other forms ensure that a buyer's advance payment will be returned if the conditions justifying it are not fulfilled; or that retention monies not withheld will be paid back to the buyer in appropriate circumstances; or that a buyer is compensated if the contractors fail to meet their obligations to maintain a construction project for a period following completion.

This chapter reviews the nature, sources and forms of such guarantees, considers the risk to sellers in providing them and recommends methods of minimizing those risks. It concludes with a brief examination of current efforts to produce an internationally acceptable code of practice.

TERMINOLOGY AND BACKGROUND

The terms 'bond', 'guarantee' and indeed 'undertaking' tend to be used

178

interchangeably in the loose jargon of international business and there has so far been no consensus as to which term is the standard. For the purposes of this chapter we will generally use 'guarantees'. Similarly, our generic term 'seller' may be taken to incorporate all those suppliers, contractors and exporters who are called upon to provide such guarantees.

The above allusion to lack of a standard name reflects the fact that, although the need for sellers to provide guarantees has been steadily growing since the early 1970s, this is still an area where there is no internationally accepted standard of practice.

In 1978 the International Chamber of Commerce (ICC) published its first edition of Uniform Rules for Contract Guarantees (ICC Publication No. 325) in an effort to bring some uniformity to the treatment of guarantees. This document was widely perceived as seeking to recognize only conditional guarantees, a development welcomed by sellers, but which led to its being disregarded by buyers who saw it as restricting their freedom to make claims.

Despite the lack of any internationally agreed code of practice there is, nevertheless, much that the seller can do to ensure that guarantees are:

(a)   issued only where absolutely necessary;
(b)   drafted so as to provide the maximum security possible against unfair or malicious callings.

Guarantee costs can be considerable and the value of guarantees is usually debited (until cancelled) against sellers' borrowing facilities. Guarantees are also usually shown as contingent liabilities on, and thus weaken, company balance sheets.

Unfortunately, one of the first, and often the most costly mistake sellers make when negotiating contracts, is not to discuss guarantee requirements with the buyer and agree mutually acceptable terms. Too often the salesman will return with a contract and mention, almost as an aside: 'Oh, by the way, we've got to put up a performance bond valid to the end of the warranty period.' Equally, the cost of providing guarantees may not be taken into consideration when costing contracts, with the result that profitability becomes unnecessarily diluted.

There is thus every incentive for the implications of guarantee commitments to be recognized and for the quality of those commitments to be maximized.

THE NATURE OF GUARANTEES

Guarantees are regarded as undertakings given to buyers by guarantors (usually banks or surety companies) acting on behalf of sellers. Such undertakings may be required by buyers for a variety of purposes, the principal ones being to indemnify themselves against losses incurred in respect of:

(a) sellers withdrawing bids or failing to take up contracts awarded within bid terms and validities (tender guarantees, bid securities, tender deposits);

(b) sellers failing to meet obligations contained in accepted contracts (performance bonds);

(c) sellers' failure to provide contractually agreed goods or services for which advance payments have been made by buyers (advance payments guarantees).

Relationships between buyers, sellers and guarantors

As is the case with letters of credit, guarantees are separate from the underlying contracts to which they relate. Indeed, in certain circumstances there may be no valid contractual relationship in existence at the time of the issue of the guarantee. For example, tender guarantees by their very nature precede the existence of any contractual relationship. It may also sometimes be a condition precedent to the issue of a letter of credit or even the contract itself that a performance guarantee be issued.

Three separate relationships should thus be recognized.

1 The contract, between the seller and the buyer.
2 The guarantee, between the guarantor and the buyer.
3 The counter-indemnity, between the seller and the guarantor.

In instances where a bank in the seller's country instructs a bank in the buyer's country to issue a guarantee, there is of course also a bank-to-bank counter-indemnity relationship to be recognized. Many countries, particularly in the Arab world, insist that guarantees be issued this way. The issue of guarantees through banks in the buyer's country adds a further level of cost and risk to the seller, of which more later.

Recognizing that at least three, and possibly four parties will be involved in the establishment of a guarantee, one soon becomes aware that this provides good potential for conflicts of interest between:

1 The seller, who wishes to place a burden of proof on the buyer to evidence that the seller has failed to meet his contractual commitments.

    Such evidence could take the form of, for example, an arbitration award or a court judgment in favour of the buyers (conditional guarantee).

2 The buyer, who wishes to maintain his freedom to call the guarantee without any necessity of evidencing contractual default and in spite of any objections made by the sellers (unconditional demand guarantee).

3 The guarantor, who generally (although not always – see 'Surety company guarantees' below) stands aloof from the underlying contract and has neither the desire nor the means to arbitrate on the validity of a claim. The guarantor requires only that the clearly defined and simply stated requirements of the guarantee be fulfilled before it will meet a claim from the buyer.

Given the buyer's preference for unconditional demand guarantees and the guarantor's desire for simplicity and detachment from the underlying contract, it is little wonder that most guarantees given are unconditional.

THE FORMS AND SOURCES OF GUARANTEES

Typically, sellers are given the option of providing guarantees in the form of:

- cash
- certified cheques
- bank guarantees
- standby letters of credit
- surety company guarantees.

Cash and certified cheques

Cash and certified cheques will clearly be the least favoured option since they involve actual debits to the seller's bank account, with the consequent loss of interest-earning capacity and negative impact on cashflow. A cash deposit lodged in a buyer's bank account could also become vulnerable to being used as part of the buyer's cashflow and then not be readily available for return following the expiry of the guarantee commitment. At worst, if the guarantee value is large enough and the buyer unscrupulous enough, neither may ever be seen again!

Bank guarantees

Bank guarantees are the most widely used form of guarantee and are easily and quickly established at relatively modest cost. Requests to issue guarantees may be negotiated on a one-by-one basis between the seller and his bank or, if the level of business requiring guarantee support demands it, a guarantee facility may be arranged permitting the seller to issue guarantees up to an agreed facility ceiling. In certain countries, notably the USA, banks are not permitted to issue guarantees and standby letters of credit are more commonly used.

Standby letters of credit

A special form of letter of credit, known as a standby letter of credit, can be used in place of a guarantee. Standby letters of credit may be revocable or irrevocable, confirmed or unconfirmed, subject to the requirements of the contract as agreed between buyer and seller. Standby letters of credit should always state that they are issued in accordance with the latest issue of the ICC's Uniform Customs and Practice for Documentary Credits (UCP) for reasons that are dealt with more thoroughly in Chapter 16. Within the framework of the letter of credit, the guarantee commitment may be conditional or unconditional and payable on demand, as is the case with bank guarantees. The use of a standby letter of credit issued subject to UCP ensures that a clearly defined expiry date will be honoured by banks in both the buyer's and the seller's country. However, the seller is still not protected against demands to extend the period of validity of the letter of credit under threat from the buyer that he will otherwise call it ('extend or pay' demands).

Surety company guarantees

Surety company guarantees may sometimes be acceptable to buyers, particularly where major supply or construction contracts are undertaken and where the buyer is perhaps more interested in ensuring satisfactory contract completion than in the punitive aspect of receiving recompense for unsatisfactory performance and then having to contract separately for the work to be completed. Since surety companies do not usually have the same quality of counter-indemnity secured against the seller's balance sheet that is available to banks issuing bank guarantees, they will consider more closely the seller's past experience and ability to perform the type of contract proposed, the quality of the buyer and the political and financial stability of the buyer's country. They will also typically examine the contract in detail and specify precisely the terms under which they would be prepared to meet claims.

Thus, from the seller's point of view, surety company guarantees bestow considerable benefits in that they:

(a)   are almost invariably conditional;
(b)   are normally issued in and become payable in the seller's country and are consequently subject to the laws and customs of the seller's country;
(c)   define expiry dates beyond which claims will not be considered;
(d)   are less susceptible to 'extend or pay' demands;
(e)   do not usually restrict the seller's borrowing facilities as is typically the case with bank guarantees and letters of credit.

All this sounds too good to be true. Needless to say, there are drawbacks, notably that the option of surety company gurantees is not often available to sellers contracting in those countries where unconditional demand guarantees are the usual requirement. Conversely, most surety companies would in any case not be willing to offer guarantees to buyers in such countries. Because of the close involvement with the seller needed to formulate surety company guarantees, they do take more time to establish and tend to be more costly to maintain than bank guarantees.

RISKS TO THE SELLER AND MEANS OF MINIMIZING THEM

It will already be apparent that the provision of guarantees carries varying degrees of risk and always adds to the seller's costs. There is a school of thought which suggests that guarantee commitments should be regarded as a cash discount available to the buyer on demand which should be fully provided for in contract pricing. In the fiercely competitive environment in which sellers usually find themselves, few can afford this luxury. More realistically, sellers must make themselves aware of the risks they are accepting and take whatever measures they can to minimize them. The following comments will, it is hoped, provide food for thought.

Pre-contract considerations

Consideration of guarantee commitments should be just as much a part of contract negotiation as price, specification, delivery and payment terms. It is at this stage, before contractual commitments are made, that the quality of guarantees may be negotiable. This can come as somewhat of a surprise to some sellers who believe that the buyer's guarantee terms are carved in stone and sacrosanct. This is certainly not always the case. Attention to the terms of guarantees at this stage can significantly reduce the seller's risks and costs.

It is also at the pre-contract stage that sellers can question the necessity of providing some guarantees at all. For example, it is often the case, particularly for capital equipment purchases, that only a proportion, typically up to 90 per cent, of the value of goods supplied becomes payable at the time of shipment. The retained balance may be withheld until the goods arrive on site at the buyer's premises, complete and in working order. In such circumstances, the seller could arguably question the necessity of providing a 10 per cent supply performance guarantee at all, whilst the buyer is still withholding an equivalent amount by way of a payment retention. Conversely, the seller may argue that a payment retention is not appropriate if a performance guarantee is to be provided. The latter approach does, of course, have significant cost and cashflow advantages for the seller.

Having accepted that guarantee commitments are the unavoidable price of doing business, the seller's first step should be to review and reassure themselves of the quality of the buyer and the political and financial security of the buyer's country in accordance with the risk assessment procedures recommended in Chapters 5 to 8. If the seller has taken out insurance cover against unfair guarantee callings, then evidence of proper risk assessment would have to be presented to the insurers when lodging a claim.

Tender (demand) guarantees

The seller will then turn to look at the buyer's guarantee requirements in detail. The first requirement is usually for a tender guarantee.

184

Because at the time of tendering there is no contract in existence and rarely any opportunity to enter into discussion with the buyer on the form of guarantee, it is difficult to write into the guarantee a requirement for external confirmation of the seller's default as a precondition for the guarantor to meet the buyer's claims. The circumstances under which a buyer may call a tender guarantee are usually that:

(a) the seller has withdrawn his offer within the validity of such offer;

(b) the seller, having been awarded a contract within the validity of the offer, has failed to accept such contract.

(c) the seller, having been awarded and accepted a contract, has failed to provide a performance guarantee (usually within a specified number of days from receipt of contract or advice of contract award).

Under any of the above circumstances the guarantor would be required to pay out on first demand of the buyer without reference to, or approval of, the seller against no more than presentation of evidence of the buyer's identity together with a statement from the buyer that one of these circumstances had occurred. Fortunately, the incidence of unfair callings against tender guarantees is very low.

Conditioning of guarantees

A greater degree of protection is usually available to the seller in the case of performance guarantees, advance payment guarantees, retention monies guarantees, and others. The terms under which the guarantor may be permitted to meet guarantee callings can vary considerably and will afford the seller varying degrees of security. Such terms could comprise any of the following.

1 Receipt from the seller of confirmation that grounds for a calling have occurred and that a claim from the buyer is justified.

2 The presentation of, for example, documentary evidence from an independent arbitrator or results of a court award in favour of the buyer.

3 A signed statement from the buyer indicating the nature of contractual default on behalf of the seller which has given rise to the claim.

4 An unsubstantiated claim received from the buyer.

It will readily be appreciated that the first two sets of circumstances listed represent conditional guarantees and provide the seller with some degree of certainty that the guarantee will not be called unfairly by the buyer. The third circumstance does not represent a secure conditioning of the guarantee, but will generate a statement of alleged default which could subsequently be used by the seller as the basis of a legal action against the buyer for breach of the underlying contract. The fourth circumstance is the weakest of all from the seller's point of view, since it permits the guarantee to be called on demand and unconditionally.

Whether guarantees are given conditionally or unconditionally, their construction should be concise and precise. Some of the key areas for attention are as follows.

Expiry dates

The expiry date of the guarantee and the latest date for receipt of claims should be clearly stated. Often buyers' forms of words will indicate that guarantees will expire 'within thirty days of the date of expiry of the bid validity', or 'at the end of the warranty period'. In the case of tender guarantees, the actual date of expiry should be stated and must correspond with, for example, whatever date thirty days after the date of expiry of the bid validity happens to be. In the case of warranty periods, definition of the expiry date may be further confused if an item is replaced under, say, a twelve-month warranty and the buyer then argues that the guarantee validity should be extended to the end of the further period of warranty applicable to the item replaced. Guarantors must not be placed in a position of having to arbitrate on when ill-defined expiry dates will occur.

Expiry events

In certain instances, it may be appropriate for guarantee commitments to expire upon the occurrence of events such as works completion or completion of deliveries. Guarantees may then be written so as to expire upon presentation to the guarantor of documents evidencing contract completion such as acceptance or installation certificates issued by the buyer or bills of lading evidencing shipment. In addition to expiry events, expiry dates should always be stated and the guarantee should be worded to expire upon expiry event or expiry date, whichever occurs first.

Extension of validity

Extension of validity should be controlled by the seller. Giving authority to the buyer unilaterally to demand an extension should be avoided. Equally, sellers should avoid giving guarantees that are automatically extendable until such time as the buyer indicates that the need for the guarantee commitment no longer exists and that the guarantee may therefore be cancelled.

Commencement of guarantee validity

The time of commencement of guarantee validity should also be clearly defined. It is often the case that contracts will not be signed until a performance guarantee has been issued. Under such circumstances, the seller's guarantee could be issued but claused to become operative only upon receipt by the seller of a signed contract accompanied by, if applicable, an acceptable letter of credit in the seller's favour. Similarly, in the case of advance payment guarantees, they could be claused to become operative only upon receipt by the seller of the advance payment.

Reduction clauses

Reduction clauses can also be worked into guarantee wordings. For example, where guarantees are issued in respect of supply performance or progressive works completion, they can be claused to reduce in value pro rata with deliveries of goods, as evidenced by presentation of bills of lading, or with each stage of works completion, as evidenced by presentation of completion certificates issued by the buyer.

Topping-up clauses

Topping-up clauses provide for guarantee values to be reinstated to their original value following a calling made by a buyer. Needless to say this represents an open-ended value commitment and should be avoided wherever possible.

Place of issue

The place of guarantee issue is of crucial importance. It is generally

187

accepted that the legal basis of the guarantee will be that of the country in which it is issued. Thus, when a bank in the seller's country counter-indemnifies a bank in the buyer's country to issue a guarantee to the buyer, then the laws and customs of the buyer's country will apply to the treatment of that guarantee. Many countries, particularly in the Arab world, insist that guarantees be issued in this way. Such arrangements will not favour the seller since:

(a) expiry provisions may be overridden;
(b) the seller's bank will not normally release the seller from his counter-indemnity until such time as the issuing bank in the buyer's country confirms that the guarantee has been returned by the buyer and may be considered cancelled;
(c) the seller has to meet the costs not only of his own bank but also those of the foreign issuing bank together with any taxes, stamp duties and other costs that may be applicable in the buyer's country.

Choice of issuing bank

The choice of foreign issuing bank should be left to the seller's bank unless a particular bank is nominated by the buyer, since this places on the seller's bank an onus of responsibility to ensure the competence of the issuing bank.

Applicable law

The law applicable to the guarantee should be that of the seller's country wherever possible and should be so indicated in the guarantee wording.

Extend or pay demands

'Extend or pay' demands are an all too frequent concomitant of simple demand guarantees. Such demands are often made in the case of tender guarantees when the buyer is not ready to award contracts within the validity period of the seller's offer or, in the case of performance guarantees, when the buyer is not satisfied that all contractual commitments have been adequately met by the seller. 'Extend or pay' demands made against tender guarantees are, by definition, unfair and the seller will be justified in arguing with the guarantor that such demands should be resisted. This may be possible if the guarantee is issued in the seller's country but will prove more difficult if issued through a bank in the buyer's country. If the buyer has insured himself against unfair callings, he must discuss the situation with his insurer before refusing to agree to an extension and thereby possibly provoking a calling, albeit unfairly made.

Standard forms

Standard forms of guarantee are available from banks and trade organizations in most countries as well as from the International Chamber of Commerce. They may prove useful, suitably modified to the requirements of the contract concerned, as a basis for the issue of a guarantee, always provided of course that no other predetermined form of words is imposed by the buyer.

Insurance

Finally, the seller may wish to consider insuring against unfair callings. A variety of insurance schemes are available from private sector insurers as well as from government backed credit insurance authorities (see Chapter 10 for a full discussion of credit insurance). The scope of cover can vary greatly and the relative advantages of schemes must be weighed. In the case of high value guarantees, unfair calling cover may be a prerequisite demanded by the guarantors, without which they would not be prepared to issue a guarantee. The following are some of the questions a seller should be asking when considering insurance.

- Is cover available for individual contracts or only available on a risk-spreading whole turnover basis?
- Is basic credit risk insurance a prerequisite of guarantee unfair calling cover?
- Is cover available for contracts with private as well as public sector buyers?
- Is cover available for commercial as well as political risk?
- Are minimum or maximum guarantee values prescribed?
- What are the preconditions for making a claim?
- What is the waiting period before claims will be paid?
- Are maximum guarantee periods specified?

- Is cover available for contracts in the range of countries with which the seller is doing business?

Sellers would be well advised to review their requirements in detail with insurers or brokers with expert knowledge in this very specialized area.

CONCLUSION

Looking to the future, it is hoped that a code of practice, similar to that which exists for letters of credit, will be formulated and receive international acceptance.

Of greatest hope to the international trading community is the work currently being done by the International Chamber of Commerce's Commission on International Commercial Practice towards developing a universally acceptable set of rules covering conditional and unconditional (contractual and demand) guarantees.

The two documents providing input to the deliberations at present are the ICC's own Publication No. 325, Uniform Rules for Contract Guarantees which have never found universal acceptance, and a draft code of practice for issuing banks recently drawn up by the British Bankers Association and the Committee of London and Scottish Bankers.

Given the success of their Uniform Customs and Practice for Documentary Credits, the ICC must be the body most likely to succeed in introducing an acceptable code for this most contentious area of guarantees.

Meanwhile, awareness of potential problems and the application of simple and commonsense measures, such as – but not limited to – those outlined above, can certainly improve the quality and security of a seller's guarantee commitments.

Recommended reading

Confederation of British Industry (1987) *Contract Bonds and Guarantees*, 3rd edn. London: CBI.

International Chamber of Commerce (1988) *Rules for the ICC Court of Arbitration*, ICC Publication No. 447. Paris: ICC.

International Chamber of Commerce (1978) *Uniform Rules for Contract Guarantees*, ICC Publication No. 325. Paris: ICC.

International Chamber of Commerce (1983) *Uniform Customs and Practice for Documentary Credits*, ICC Publication No. 400. Paris: ICC.

International Chamber of Commerce (1982) *Model Forms for Issuing Contract Guarantees*, ICC Publication No. 406. Paris: ICC.

Schmitthoff, Clive M. (1986) *Schmitthoff's Export Trade*, 8th edn. London: Stevens & Sons. The standard English work on this subject.

PART V
SETTLEMENT METHODS

13

An outline of settlement methods

Brian Clarke

This brief chapter introduces Part V of the handbook, which picks up the variety of terms and methods of payment described in Chapter 11 and, under the main method categories, discusses in detail their operation and the ways in which they may be used to best advantage.

THE MAIN SETTLEMENT METHODS

The five main ways in which settlement of international trading transactions can be arranged are:

- Open account
- Documentary collection
- Documentary letter of credit
- Cash with order
- Countertrade.

Documentary collections, letters of credit and countertrade are major subjects in themselves and are examined in detail in Chapters 15 to 17.

Bills of exchange

Bills of exchange are often erroneously regarded as a separate method of settlement. In reality, they are instruments which may be used as part of one or other of the main settlement methods listed above. Their multiplicity of usages is explained in detail in Chapter 14.

Open account

Open account is the riskiest method of settlement.

Settlement methods

There is no security for the seller, since both the goods and the documents of title are sent to the customer, who is thus under no pressure to pay other than through fear of losing the seller's goodwill or eventually of some form of legal action.

The method is nevertheless widely used for North American, West European and other business where ongoing trade has created conditions of trust.

Even with such a risky method, however, there are ways of improving the chances of prompt payment. Above all, get the documentation right! Can customers really be blamed if they receive an invoice with a marginally wrong value and decline to pay it until the error has been put right?

'Clean' bank collection

To achieve a little security and make their cash flow more predictable, when despatching the documents to the customer some exporters also send a clean bill of exchange to the customer's bank for acceptance/ collection. Until, however, the bill has been accepted, the open account transaction is totally at risk and, as with a documentary collection, after acceptance there is still a considerable degree of risk until the bill has been paid.

Documentary collection

A documentary collection essentially involves the use of a third party, almost invariably a collecting bank, to act as an intermediary and for a fee to exchange documents of sale for payment or a promise to pay. With sea shipments the documents will include the bill of lading. This, amongst the different transport documents, is the only one which controls title and in such cases the customers should (in theory, but not always in practice) only be able to take possession of the goods after they have paid the bank or made a formal promise to pay.

The promise to pay normally takes the form of a bill of exchange or occasionally a promissory note (both are covered in detail in Chapter 14).

In a documentary collection operation the banks do *not* have a responsibility to check the documents and any deficiencies can cause considerable delay in payment, especially where eventual remittance of funds to the seller depends upon exchange control approval.

The many and varied facets of this popular method of settlement are described in Chapter 15.

Documentary letters of credit

Twenty or so years ago, letters of credit were thought by many to be 'old hat', a method of settlement likely to become outdated as the world modernized and international trade moved towards better technologies. Then came the world debt crisis!

So today letters of credit are a very popular method of securing payment of international debts. But they have to be used with great care and precision and this will be neither the first nor the last time in this book that it will be said, *for the best possible security, the right form of credit must be used and the documentation presented against it must be 100 per cent accurate and delivered on time.*

Chapter 16 develops this theme.

Cash with order

A credit manager's dream – unless his or her customers *all* agreed to it, in which case there would be no credit to manage!

But that is unlikely to happen: international business thrives on credit and only in extreme cases of dubious risk, in a seller's market, can customers occasionally be persuaded to pay up front, and then only if their exchange control authorities will allow it.

Countertrade

Whether we like it or not, countertrade is a currently well-established method of settlement, often embodying in its wide array of variants the need to apply some of the other methods summarized above.

A significant proportion of world trade now involves some form of countertrade and, from the credit management viewpoint, the most important axiom is to ensure that the credit function is involved at the outset. Many credit managers have come close to apoplexy when presented with a *fait accompli* countertrade deal by a well-meaning but ill-informed sales executive.

Countertrade is discussed in detail in Chapter 17.

TRANSMISSION OF FUNDS

So, the point is reached where the customer is willing to pay, the bank is poised to remit and even the local exchange control authority is willing to let the money out of the country. (Reading some of the necessarily more cautionary parts of this book, you may wonder whether these happy events are achievable all that often, but they really do happen with most international transactions.)

But because that point has been reached, it is no time to relax.

Studies carried out in the UK recently indicated that many exporters wait for the use of their money for up to several additional weeks, simply because they do not use the fastest appropriate method of funds transmission and – even more remarkable – do not give correct instructions as to precisely where the funds should be sent.

The need for correct remittance instructions

International credit managers should ensure that all documents which provoke payments – invoices, documentary collections, remittance letters and the like – all bear precise details of how payment is to be made and where it is to be sent: which bank, their full address, the account number and exact name of account holder.

To some readers this advice may seem so basic as hardly to warrant inclusion in this handbook, but current facts demonstrate that, basic as it is, the advice is not being heeded and as a result companies are incurring great additional costs on account of totally avoidable transfer delays.

Ways of transmitting the funds

The choice of the right method of funds transmission can greatly enhance working capital by substantially reducing bank float (a comprehensive explanation of which is given in Chapter 23).

Suppliers should not only give clear instructions, but should monitor that they are being carried out and take appropriate action when they are not.

Telegraphic transfer

For the vast majority of international transactions, this is the only method of funds transfer which should be recommended. It ensures immediate transfer from bank to bank. The cost of the cable or telex is not large and, to encourage use of the method, suppliers may have to offer to bear that particular cost themselves. The modest expense is invariably justified by the substantial saving in float time, when compared with other methods.

The detail required to identify and allocate such funds in an export sales ledger may, however, be too expensive to transmit telegraphically and arrangements are normally made for a separate advice to be delivered by other fast means to facilitate the beneficiaries' administrative procedures.

Airmail transfer

This is another way of transferring funds from bank to bank but the airmail medium is comparatively slow.

Cheques

The slowest of all the ways to transfer cash, cheques have to be sent by mail and are then subject to considerable delay (especially if in a foreign currency) before they can be cleared and the funds finally credited to the beneficiary's account. Cheques do, however, have the merit of usually being accompanied by an advice, giving comprehensive detail as to exactly what is being paid. So, whilst definitely out of favour with cash managers, they do find affection amongst sales ledger keepers.

Banker's drafts

These offer a faster method than cheques, since clearance procedures are normally restricted to two days. They still have to be sent by mail, however, and like cheques find more favour with ledger keepers than with cash managers.

Direct debit

Although proving, in certain circumstances, to be a practicable way of arranging payments in a home market, direct debit is unlikely to be countenanced internationally for obvious reasons of mistrust, exchange controls and so on.

Settlement methods

Exporters of small lots of goods, such as publications, may however find their customers will accept a direct charge to a credit card account, thereby obviating considerable administrative effort in the collection of small amounts.

Recommended reading

Rowe, Michael (1987) *Electronic Trade Payments*. Byfleet: IBC Financial Technology Publishing. Describes how computerized techniques are beginning to link export/import documentation and related payment procedures, and analyses the issues involved.

14

Bills of exchange

Jacques P Lardinois

At present, a difficult aspect of the operation of bills of exchange in international trade is the division of countries into two coalitions.

On the one hand we have the Anglo-Saxon laws based on the English Bills of Exchange Act 1882, which influenced the drafting of the US Uniform Negotiable Instruments Law 1896. On the other, there is the Geneva Convention group of countries which signed the 1930 'Uniform Law on Bills of Exchange' mainly inspired by the German and French laws. This group unifies nearly thirty countries, of which twenty-one have ratified the convention and harmonized to various degrees their own legislation: Austria, Belgium, Brazil, East Germany, Denmark, Finland, France, West Germany, Greece, Hungary, Italy, Japan, Luxembourg, Monaco, the Netherlands, Norway, Poland, Portugal, Sweden, Switzerland and the USSR.

In addition, the following have signed the convention but not ratified it: Czechoslovakia, Colombia, Ecuador, Peru, Spain, Turkey and Yugoslavia.

The world is roughly divided into two leagues:

Geneva Convention	*Anglo-Saxon legal system*
Continental Europe	United Kingdom
East European countries	USA
Ex-colonies of European countries	Commonwealth countries
	Ireland, Israel
Iraq, Syria	Other Latin American countries
Brazil, Columbia, Ecuador	

Table 14.1 compares the key points in the UK, US and Geneva Convention legal systems.

Table 14.1
Bills of exchange: comparison of key points under three systems

	Uniform Commercial Code, article 3 (USA)	Uniform Law on Bills of Exchange and Promissory Notes 1930 (Geneva Convention)	Bills of Exchange Act 1882, as amended (UK)
Formal requirements	In writing; signed by drawer; unconditional order to pay a sum certain in money; payable on demand or at a definite time; payable to order or to bearer.	The term 'bill of exchange' in the language of the instrument; an unconditional order to pay a determinate sum of money; the name of the drawee; the time of payment (or if not indicated the bill is payable at sight); place of payment; name of the person to whom or to whose order the bill is to be paid; date and place of issue; signature of the drawer.	Unconditional order in writing, addressed by one person to another, signed by the person giving it, requiring the person to whom it is addressed to pay on demand or at a fixed or determinable future time a sum certain in money to or to the order of a specified person, or to bearer.
How negotiated	By endorsement and delivery if made out to order; by delivery alone for a bearer instrument.	By endorsement, even if the bill is not expressly drawn to order. If the bill expressly indicates that it is not drawn to order, it cannot be negotiated, but can only be assigned (an assignee can receive no better right to the instrument than the assignor has to convey).	By endorsement and delivery if made out to order; by delivery alone for a bearer instrument.
How does the drawee become bound by the bill?	By acceptance.	By acceptance.	By acceptance.
Guaranteeing payment	A party can indicate on the bill that he or she will pay if the primary party liable dishonours it.	Payment may be guarenteed by an 'aval' on the bill itself or on an 'allonge' (a separate piece of paper). A simple signature on the face of the bill, if not that of the drawer, is assumed to be an 'aval'.	The Act does not specifically refer to guarantees, but parties frequently guarantee payment by signature on the back of the bill. The Act provides that where a person signs a bill otherwise than as drawer or acceptor he or she thereby incurs the liabilities of an endorser to a holder in due course.

Procedure on dishonour (non-payment or non-acceptance).	Notice of dishonour is required to charge the drawer and endorsees. Protest is necessary only if the draft appears to be drawn or payable outside the USA.	Formal protest required. In addition the holder must give notice to his or her endorsee and to the drawer.	Normally, notice must be given to each drawer and endorser. Protest is required only for foreign bills.
Types of endorsement	Special – in favour of a particular endorsee; or general – in blank. The latter makes the draft payable to bearer. It can then be negotiated by delivery.	Special or in blank. To show title the possessor of the bill has to establish that he or she received it through an uninterrupted series of endorsements. Accordingly an endorsement in blank does not turn the instrument into a bearer bill. An endorsement 'to bearer' is regarded as equivalent to an endorsement in blank.	Special – in favour of a particular endorsee; or general – in blank. The latter makes the draft payable to bearer. It can then be negotiated by delivery.
Can drawer exclude rights of recourse against him or herself?	Yes	Drawer may release him or herself from guaranteeing acceptance but not from guaranteeing payment.	Yes
Protection of holder against defects in title	A holder in due course is entitled to look to prior parties for payment despite defects in title. A holder in due course is one who takes the draft for value in good faith and without notice of defects in the title. Other holders can obtain no better title than the transferor.	Persons sued on a bill cannot set up against the holder defences founded on their personal relations with the drawer or with previous holders, unless the holder, in acquiring the bill, has knowingly acted to the detriment of the debtor. There is no requirement for the holder to have given value.	A holder in due course is entitled to look to prior parties for payment despite defects in title. A holder in due course is one who takes the draft for value in good faith and without notice of defects in the title. Other holders can obtain no better title than the transferor.
Effect of fraud	Holders, including holders in due course, cannot normally enforce the instrument against a party whose signature was forged or is otherwise ineffective.	A forged or otherwise ineffective signature does not bind the person whose signature it is or purports to be, but the obligations of the other persons who signed it are nonetheless valid.	Where a signature is forged or is otherwise of no legal effect a subsequent holder in due course has no rights against those who were parties to the bill prior to the ineffective signature.

Source: Michael Rowe, *Letters of Credit* (1985). Reproduced by kind permission of Euromoney Publications Ltd.

Although there are contradictory aspects between the two groups and despite the specific regulations inserted in their local laws by the countries which have accepted the Geneva Convention, there is a common understanding in international trade as to what bills of exchange (also called drafts) are and how they should be used.

DEFINITIONS

The following simple and clear definitions given by the UK Bills of Exchange Act is quite compatible – except for the last three words – with most other national definitions:

> An unconditional order in writing, addressed by one person to another, signed by the person giving it, requiring the person to whom it is addressed to pay on demand or at a fixed or determinable future time a sum certain in money to or to the order of a specified person, *or to bearer* [emphasis added].

Local laws naturally differ in detail from one country to another but, venturing that they are 'average' on prominent issues, the following two average and functional definitions are suggested.

1 An unconditional order written in the form determined by the law applicable, addressed by a person (the drawer) to another (the drawee) to pay a certain amount of money at a determined or determinable time and place to anyone, the drawer or a third party, who is or will become the lawful beneficiary (the holder).
2 An instrument which, transmitted by the drawer to the beneficiary, gives to the latter or to the person to whom it has been endorsed, the right to be paid by the drawee at a determined or determinable date a certain amount of money.

SALIENT FORMAL FEATURES

The following are the normal features of a bill of exchange, those marked with an asterisk being essential as per the 1930 Uniform Law.

1 The place where it is issued.
2 The date at which it is issued.*
3 The signature of the drawer.*

4   The unconditional order to pay.* The instruction to pay cannot be
    subject to any qualification. An order to pay out of a particular
    fund, for instance, is not unconditional.
5   The amount to be paid,* which is generally written both in words
    and in figures. When there is a discrepancy between the two, the
    amount denoted by words is the sum payable.
6   The name of the person to whom the order to pay is addressed (the
    drawee).*
7   The name of the person to whom or to whose order payment is to be
    made (the beneficiary or payee).*

In the Geneva Convention countries – and contrary to the UK
and the US laws – the bill of exchange cannot be established
payable to bearer. It must be established payable to a specified
person or to his or her order, but may in practice become an
instrument payable to bearer when blank endorsed by a beneficiary.

In international trade practice, the draft usually names the
sellers (or the bank handling the collection for their account) as the
beneficiary.

8   The period allowed for payment (maturity). Under the Geneva
    Convention, if this is not specified the bill is deemed to be payable
    at sight.
9   The place where payment is to be made.
10 The denomination of 'bill of exchange', expressed in the language
    employed in drawing up the instrument ('*lettre de change*', '*Wech-
    sel*', '*Wisselbrief*', '*cambiale tratta*', '*girado*' or whatever).* This
    requirement does not exist under Anglo-Saxon laws.

All ten salient features are indicated on the bill of exchange in Figure
14.1.

Bills drawn in a set

While domestic bills are generally drawn singly (the sole bill being
referred to as a sola of exchange) it is common practice in international
trade to draw bills in a set of two or three. This is particularly applicable
to collections relating to goods shipped by sea. In such cases, each part
of the set will be sent separately, attached to a separate original bill of
lading, to ensure that in case of loss or accidental destruction in the
transmission, at least one copy will arrive at the collecting bank (see
Chapter 15 for documentary collection procedures). The payment of

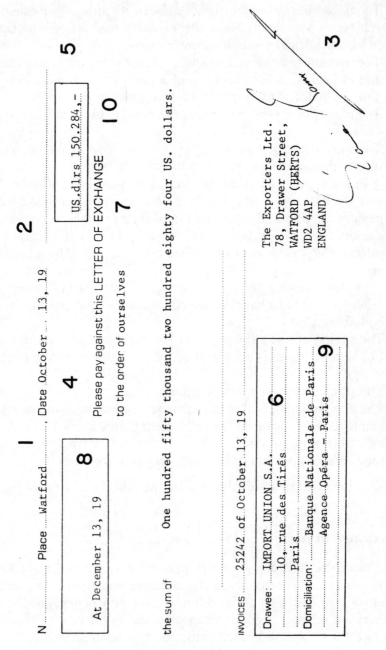

N .... Place ...Watford........ , Date October ... 13, ..19.

At December 13, 19 **8**

Please pay against this LETTER OF EXCHANGE **7**

to the order of ourselves

the sum of .... One hundred fifty thousand two hundred eighty four US. dollars.

US..dlrs..150..284.- **10**

2

5

INVOICES ...25242. of October 13, 19.

Drawee: ..IMPORT..UNION..S.A. **6**
........10,.rue..des..Tirés.
........Paris.
Domiciliation: ....Banque..Nationale.de.Paris.
...........Agence..Opéra.-.Paris. **9**

The Exporters Ltd.
78, Drawer Street,
WATFORD (HERTS)
WD2 4AP
ENGLAND

3

4

1

ACCEPTANCE (AND AVAL)

206

Figure 14.1 Ten features of a bill of exchange

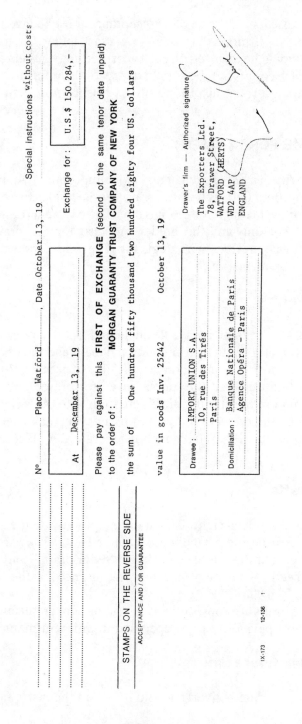

Figure 14.2 Bill drawn in a set

one copy discharges the whole. Acceptance must be given on one copy only because, if more than one copy is accepted, the liability of the acceptor would be engaged on each accepted copy. When a bill is drawn in a set, each copy is numbered ('first', 'second' or 'third') on its face and must contain a reference to the others as shown in Figure 14.2.

THE TIME FOR PAYMENT

The maturity of a bill of exchange is more important than the due date of an open account debt as it is necessary for the holder to present it to the drawee for payment on the day it is due. The payment (or non-payment) is crucial not only for the holder but also for the drawer and any endorsers who may be guaranteeing it. They must know the fate of the draft as soon as possible.

Sight drafts

A draft drawn 'at sight' is payable on demand, at first presentation to the drawee. It is strictly an instrument of payment and the drawer is free to choose the date of payment, that is, the date of presentation. Local laws in some countries limit the time allowed for presentation to a certain number of months after the draft's creation date. As a sight draft is not accepted by the drawee, it does not in any way make certain the debt that it represents. By itself it does not generate any added safeguards for the drawer.

Time drafts

When not payable at sight, bills of exchange indicate the agreed period of credit by ordering payment at a deferred date. They are called 'time drafts', 'term drafts', 'usance drafts' or 'tenor drafts', and the period of time allowed for payment is called the 'usance' or the 'tenor' of the draft.

Usance drafts are consecutively instruments of credit and of payment. The date of payment can be specified in different manners:

At a fixed future date

The maturity date is fixed and stipulated on the instrument when it is

208

drawn, without any possible ambiguity as to the due date: 'On 28 February, 19—.'

Such drafts are often called 'date drafts' or 'dated drafts'.

At a fixed period after sight

At time of issuance of a draft specified payable at thirty, sixty or ninety days after sight, its maturity is not known. It is only a 'determinable future time'. The usance begins to run from the date of presentation of the draft to the drawee, which is normally also the date of acceptance if the bill is accepted, or the date of protest if the draft is protested for non-acceptance. Such drafts are very commonly used in overseas business and often permit the foreign buyer to enjoy the full period of credit granted by matching acceptance and the release of the controlling documents by the collecting bank with the arrival of goods. Until this event takes place – and in certain cases it can be far beyond the normal time – the exporter misses a fixed date of maturity.

At a fixed period after date

To avoid the ambiguity resulting from drafts not being presented to and/or accepted by the drawee in a timely manner, exporters should resist drawing 'from sight' drafts and endeavour to negotiate instead a tenor starting from a definite known date, such as the date of drawing of the draft, the date of the shipment or the estimated time of arrival of the vessel. They thereby tighten up credit by ensuring a definite maturity regardless of the date of acceptance.

On or at a fixed period after the occurrence of a specific event

The event must be certain to happen, though the time of happening may be uncertain. (An instrument expressed to be payable on a contingency is not a bill and the happening of the event does not cure the defect. To illustrate this point, a bill could be made payable upon the death of a specified person but not upon the marriage of that person.)

This method of fixing a maturity is practically unknown in international trade and is not provided for in the Geneva Convention.

Wherever possible it is to the exporter's advantage to set a fixed maturity date on the draft, even at the cost if necessary of allowing a time factor for the voyage period of the goods. It is always preferable to pre-calculate the maturity date of a draft based upon the period of credit agreed in the contract. For instance, the due date on a sight draft could be set in accordance with the estimated time of arrival, so reverting to a simple 'dated draft' and allowing no question about maturity.

ACCEPTANCE

Acceptance is the signification by the drawees of their assent to the order of the drawers.

The only legal obligation of the drawee to accept a bill is that arising out of the underlying trade transaction and the drawee who does not accept the bill is not liable on it per se.

Form

The acceptance (see Figure 14.3) is written on the bill of exchange and normally expressed by the word 'accepted', signed by the drawee; but the mere signature of the drawee *on the face* of the bill is sufficient to constitute an acceptance.

Character

Under most local laws the acceptance is unconditional and cannot be qualified. The drawee may, however, restrict it to part of the payable sum. For instance, a bill for $2000 can be 'accepted for one thousand five hundred dollars'. By accepting, the drawees formally incur the obligation to pay a definite amount at a definite date (the tenor of their acceptance) and become the primary obligators on the bill. This obligation is absolute and, through its acceptance, the bill of exchange becomes the customer's formal promise to pay. An accepted bill of exchange is often referred to as an 'acceptance' and it is correct to regard it as the vehicle whereby payment will be coming in at due date.

Points on acceptance

Sight drafts are not accepted since their payment should take place immediately upon presentation.

Drafts issued payable at a fixed period after sight acquire their

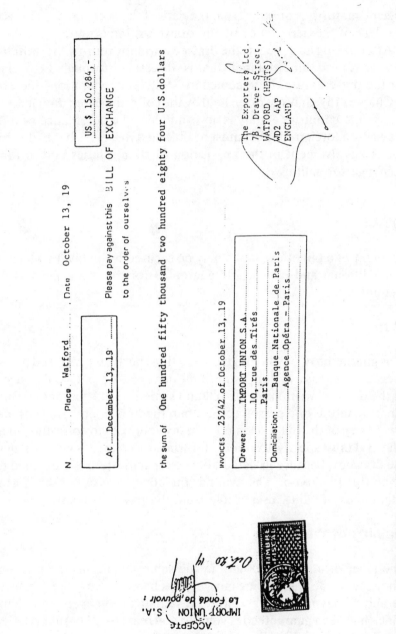

Figure 14.3 Acceptance of bill of exchange

211

specific maturity, counting from the date of the acceptance. This is why the date of the acceptance by the drawee is important.

After having accepted it, the drawee normally returns the draft to the drawer via the same channel (that is, directly or through a bank) used for the presentation. In documentary collection operations (described in Chapter 15), they are often held by the collecting bank until maturity.

In some countries – Italy is an example – the acceptance of a draft drawn by a foreign supplier must be obtained through a bank, due to the banks' involvement in the imposition of stamp duties and in foreign exchange formalities.

AVALS

Payment of a bill of exchange may be secured by an 'aval', which is an unconditional and irrevocable guarantee for the whole or part of its amount.

Form

This guarantee of payment, given by a third party, is expressed by words such as 'Good as aval for [*name of the drawee*]', or 'per aval for account of the drawee' written on the bill and signed by the guarantor. But the mere signature of a person (other than the drawer and drawee) placed *on the face* of the bill is deemed in many countries to constitute an aval. The aval must specify absolutely for whose account it is given (generally the drawee), because in default of such specification it is deemed to be given for *the drawer*. The aval has the advantage over other forms of guarantees of being inseparable from the payment instrument.

Liability of the surety

The giver of an aval is bound in the same manner as the drawee for whom he or she has become guarantor. The aval guarantees against any default of payment by the buyer. It remains valid even if the liability which has been guaranteed is void for any reason (other than a defect in the form of the bill) as it is an abstract obligation not dependent upon the performance of the underlying trade contract. A guarantor who pays the bill of exchange acquires the right to claim payment from the guaranteed person (usually the drawee).

Practical use of aval

It is not unusual in international trade for the exporter to require the buyers abroad to pre-arrange to accept the bill and have it avalized by their bank or by the owner of the company or by the parent company.

Once the aval is properly written and signed by the bank, the owner or the parent company, the obligation of the prime obligator, the drawees to pay the draft at maturity as incurred by their acceptance is absolutely guaranteed by the bank, the owner or the parent company.

In the case of forfaiting (discounting of a draft or promissory note on a totally without recourse basis) the seller's bank will often require the aval of the foreign buyer's bank, unless the buyer is of such financial standing and international repute that a guarantee is considered unnecessary (see Chapter 9 for further reference to forfaiting).

Points on avals

The enforceability of an aval in some jurisdictions must be checked. It is important to ensure that the aval is given by the guarantor exactly in conformity with the rules applying in the particular country where it is given, not only as to its form but also with regard to the foreign exchange regulations.

In some countries the term 'aval' has no legal significance and in these instances the guarantee must be given on the drafts in a more explicit manner, such as:

> For consideration received, we irrevocably and unconditionally guarantee payment of this bill of exchange in the maximum amount of [*amount and currency*] drawn by [*drawer*]. If [*the drawee*] does not pay for any reason, exchange restrictions included, we will pay at first demand even without the bill having been protested, at [office designated to receive payment].

It can also take the form of an appended document.

The added security for the drawer (and other parties to the bill) of an avalized draft is only measurable, as with any guarantee, by the quality of the surety.

By virtue of the nearly universal principle of novation (substitution of a new obligation for the existing one) the beneficiaries of an 'avalized' draft usually lose the benefit of the aval if they agree to modify the terms of the bill, for example by extending its maturity, without the prior written assent of the guarantor.

NEGOTIATION

Negotiation means transferring ownership to another person in such a manner as to constitute the transferee the holder.

A bill of exchange is by definition a negotiable instrument and, even if not expressly drawn 'to order', may be negotiated very simply by means of endorsement and without the drawee having to be notified of the transfer of the debt.

Form

Negotiation is normally achieved by the beneficiary writing on the back of the bill the words 'Pay to . . .' and signing beneath (see Figure 14.4); but the signature of the endorser without additional words is sufficient.

The draft can be endorsed to a person, to the order of a person, to bearer, or 'in blank' – that is, signature only. If endorsed to bearer or in blank, the instrument simply becomes payable to the person who physically possesses it, but the holder may reconvert the blank endorsement into a special (nominal) endorsement. The person to whom the bill has been endorsed may re-endorse it and there is no limit to the number of subsequent re-endorsements, unless the last endorsement expressly prohibits any further negotiation.

Title

In legislations codifying bills payable to bearer, such bills are simply transferred by delivery of the instrument. Otherwise, the endorsement is the normal way to transfer the ownership of a bill of exchange.

Its holder is deemed to be the lawful beneficiary if he or she establishes title through an uninterrupted series of endorsements, even if the last endorsement is in blank.

In some countries domestic drafts are the object of a large circulation, passing as a means of payment from holders to their own creditors. It can so happen that the acceptors receive their own acceptance from one of their debtors who received it from a previous endorser.

An endorsement cannot be conditional: it transfers all the rights of the endorser.

214

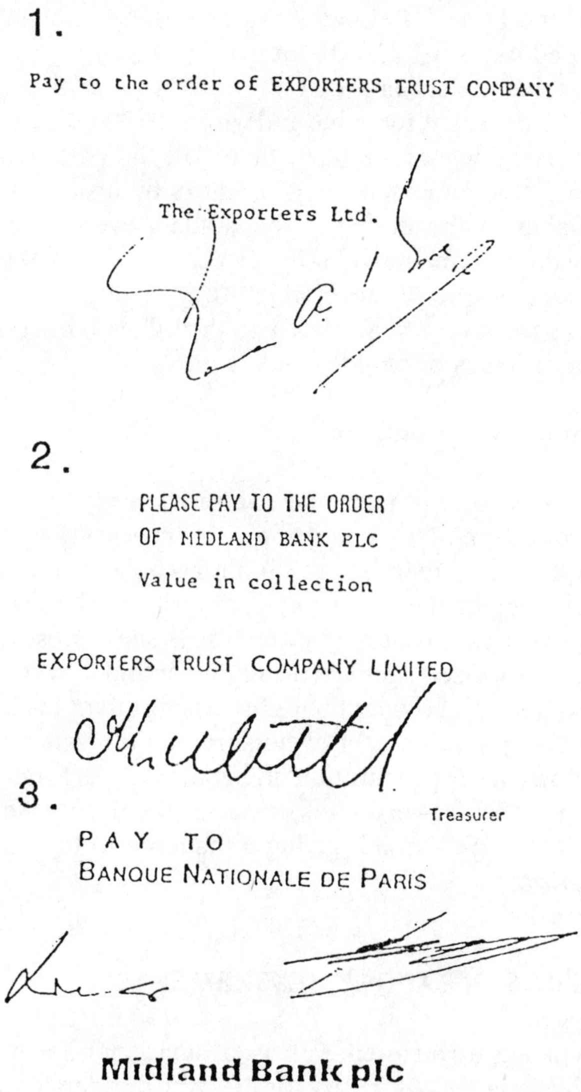

1.

Pay to the order of EXPORTERS TRUST COMPANY

The Exporters Ltd.

2.

PLEASE PAY TO THE ORDER
OF MIDLAND BANK PLC

Value in collection

EXPORTERS TRUST COMPANY LIMITED

Treasurer

3.

P A Y   T O
BANQUE NATIONALE DE PARIS

Midland Bank plc

Figure 14.4   Negotiation by endorsement of bill of exchange

Right of recourse

The endorser guarantees payment to the person to whom the bill is endorsed so that, in case of non-payment at maturity by the drawee and guarantors, the bona fide holder has a recourse against all previous successive endorsers back to the drawer.

So long as the holders have taken the bill in good faith, complete and regular on the face of it, for value and without notice of any defect in the title of the party negotiating it to them, all the parties to the draft – drawer, acceptor, endorsers or guarantors by aval – are jointly and severally liable to the holders. The holders even have the right to proceed against them individually or collectively, without being required to observe the order in which they have become bound. The same rights pass in turn to any party to the bill who has taken it up and paid it to a previous bona fide holder.

Endorsement 'by procuration'

Very commonly, bills of exchange are restrictively endorsed to banks 'value in collection', 'for collection', 'by procuration' or by similar phrases expressing a mandate to obtain acceptance and/or to collect.

The endorsement then is a mere authority to deal with the bill as directed and is not a transfer of ownership. In such cases, the holder (the bank) is the authorized agent of the endorser and may only exercise on his behalf and for his account the rights arising out of the bill. He has no power for example to transfer ownership by endorsement; he can only further endorse it 'by procuration' in his capacity as agent. This is what happens when the drawer's bank endorses the draft to the order of its correspondent bank abroad, giving a mandate to the latter to collect from the drawee.

USE OF BILLS IN EXPORT SETTLEMENTS

Bills of exchange are an intensively used device of trade payment which offer varying degrees of security for the exporter depending upon their being clean or documentary, payable at sight or at a future time, accepted or non-accepted.

Whatever the degree of security it should be kept in mind that trade drafts are not a guarantee of payment. They offer an edge, not a guarantee. A guarantee of payment is only acquired with letter of credit bills or when a bank aval is given.

Trade bills

Clean bills

The exporter draws a bill of exchange for the value of an open account invoice on a foreign customer, who may already have received the goods. Such drafts are essentially a collection instrument. They are called 'clean' or 'simple' as opposed to 'documentary' drafts.

Once accepted, the drafts provide an incentive for punctual payment which does not exist on ordinary open account terms. They also give the exporter an opportunity better to monitor cash receipts based upon definite dates for payment.

In addition, accepted drafts are an attractive financing instrument as banks are prepared to discount them at lower interest rates than those applying to overdrafts or loans which are not backed by a second signature.

The use of clean drafts is so popular in certain countries that some buyers often initiate the making out of an accepted draft and send it to the seller.

Documentary bills

To ensure greater control of the goods, the exporter can attach the shipping documents to a draft in such a manner that they cannot be released to the foreign buyer until the draft is paid or accepted. This is described in Chapter 15.

Letters of credit bills

Acceptance letters of credit and negotiation letters of credit are a specific area for the use of bills of exchange as they require that a draft be drawn and presented by the beneficiary together with the other documents.

If the credit provides for acceptance, a time bill is accepted by the confirming, advising or issuing bank or at times by the customer. It may be returned to the beneficiary of the credit who can usually easily discount it because a bank's acceptance substantially minimizes the risk of non-payment at maturity.

If the credit provides for negotiation, a sight or time bill of exchange drawn on the applicant or on any other stipulated drawee may be paid immediately by the bank to the beneficiary of the credit.

Accommodation bills

The laws of the Geneva Convention countries mention the 'provision' of the bill of exchange. They so refer to the value received by the drawee, that is the consideration given for the bill, the debt owed by the drawee to the drawer. In international trade this is generally for goods delivered or services rendered while in bank acceptances (acceptance letters of credit) it is for the credit facility, that is the bank's commitment to pay the face value at maturity.

If there is no such 'provision', the draft is an accommodation bill. An accommodation party is a person signing the bill as drawer, acceptor or endorser without receiving value and for the purpose of lending his or her name to another. The accommodation party is liable on the bill to the holder for value even though, when such holder took the bill, he or she knew it to be an accommodation bill.

In most countries accommodation bills can acquire an illegal and even punishable character if they are:

fictitious bills drawn upon a person who has no debt to the drawer and has not authorized the drawing, or fraudulent bills drawn up by virtue of a deceitful agreement between drawer and drawee in order to permit one of the signers to obtain funds to the detriment of a third party (generally through discounting the bill at a bank).

PAYMENT

Payment from the drawee is required at maturity by the holder of the bill. The holder can be:

(a) the drawers, if the draft issued at their order has not been transmitted by endorsement;
(b) the original beneficiaries, if they have not endorsed the draft;
(c) the last beneficiary, the 'holder in due course', if the draft has changed hands by endorsement(s).

In practice, however, the payee is normally the drawer's or beneficiary's bank to which the bill has been endorsed 'value in collection'. The payment upon presentation (sight drafts), on the date of maturity (time drafts) or, in many countries, on one of the two business days which follow, constitutes the natural end of a bill of exchange. By payment in due course the bill is discharged.

Place of payment

If not specified, the place of payment is deemed to be the address of the drawee or acceptor.

In international trade the place at which payment is to be made is generally one of the drawee's banks, as indicated on the bill by the drawee (or by the drawer with the agreement of the drawee).

As bills of exchange are usually collected through the banking network, their payment often takes place in clearing houses.

Proof of payment

The drawee who pays a bill receives it from the holder, who usually signs it for discharge of the amount payable. In the case of partial payment – which the holder may not refuse in the countries of the Geneva Convention group – a note of this payment is made on the bill and the drawee may require that a receipt be issued for the amount paid.

PROTEST

Default of acceptance or of payment is evidenced in most countries by respectively, a protest for non-acceptance or a protest for non-payment.

Definition

The protest is an authentic act, a formal declaration, established by a notary public or similarly qualified officer, recording the drawee's refusal or inability to accept or to pay. The form of protest usually states that the bill has been presented and records the answer, if any, given by the drawee (see Figure 14.5 for an example of the English form). It is attached to the unaccepted or unpaid draft.

The protesting procedure, its effectiveness and its legal ramifications vary from country to country, but its prime objective is the same: to

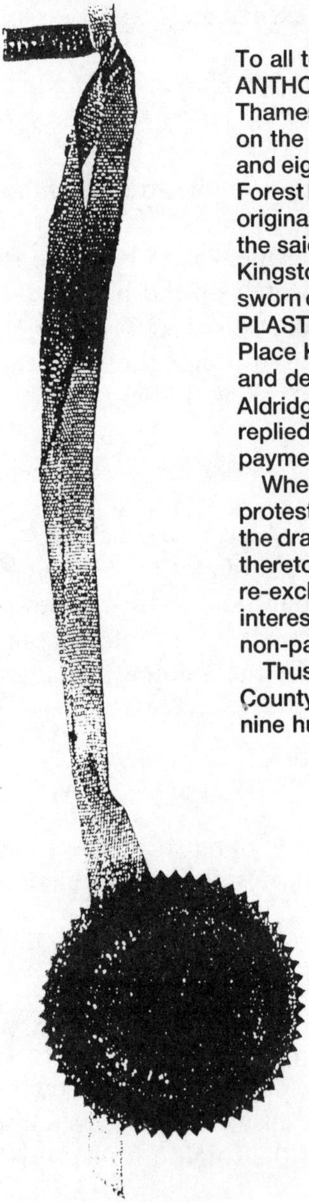

To all to whom these presents shall come I JAMES ALAN
ANTHONY PHILIPSON of 29 Meadow Street Kingston upon
Thames in the County of Surrey England Solicitor do state
on the Third day of October One thousand nine hundred
and eighty-seven at the request of Import Bank Limited 23
Forest Place Kingston upon Thames Surrey and holder of the
original Bill of Exchange a copy of which is affixed hereto I
the said James Alan Anthony Philipson a Notary Public of
Kingston upon Thames duly authorized admitted and
sworn caused due presentment of the said Bill to be made to
PLASTILEX LIMITED at Import Bank Limited 23 Forest
Place Kingston upon Thames for its acceptance payment
and demand to be made therefor to which the said John
Aldridge a Clerk in the employment of Import Bank Limited
replied "No we won't. We have been instructed to withhold
payment."

Wherefore I, the said Notary, at the request aforesaid did
protest and by these presents do solemnly protest against
the drawer of the said Bill of Exchange and all other parties
thereto and all others who it may concern for exchange,
re-exchange and all other costs, damages, charges and
interests already and hereafter incurred by reason of the
non-payment of the said Bill.

Thus done and protested at Kingston upon Thames in the
County of Surrey this Third day of October One thousand
nine hundred and eighty-seven.

Quod Attestor

. . . .

Notary Public

Figure 14.5 An English act of protest

enable a disinterested party to establish the actual fact of non-acceptance or non-payment.

Protesting what and what for?

The protest for non-acceptance of a time draft has no detrimental consequence for the drawee since the non-acceptance is not necessarily a dishonour. This protest is nothing else but a record that a draft was presented but acceptance refused. Protests for non-acceptance are rarely carried out.

Similarly, the protest for non-payment of a non-accepted draft (usually either a sight draft or a matured time draft) does not result in any adverse consequence for the drawees, because they did not enter into any obligation by reference to the bill of exchange. The obligation to pay has to be established based upon the underlying contract. Such protests are very rarely drawn up (Finland is an exception).

The situation is different once the drawees have expressed their willingness to pay the bill; protests for non-payment of duly accepted drafts are a rather common step in international trade.

The significance of protest and the effect it has on the drawees varies all over the map, but it is certainly, in many countries, a very serious measure against them. Not only is it an official record of default, but it can be a public notice, duly registered in an official gazette that they did not honour their signature. It can then have devastating effects on their business standing and creditworthiness.

Noting

Countries of the Geneva Convention group ignore the procedure of 'noting' an unpaid bill before eventually protesting it, as is provided by the law in the USA and in the UK. According to this system, the holders, if they think fit, ask the notary public merely to 'note' the fact that the bill was presented and payment refused. The dishonoured bill is 'noted' with a slip containing the answer obtained on presentation. It is a legal proof of presentation, subject to no publicity, which nevertheless maintains the holder's rights arising out of the bill. The system of 'noting' allows time for negotiation of the settlement of the debt. Once 'noted', a draft can be protested any time afterwards, if necessary, for better security against the drawer (and endorsers, if any).

Protesting procedure

In many of those countries where noting is unknown (and generally in accordance with the Geneva Convention), the protest must be drawn up on one of the two business days following the day on which the bill is payable. This short time limit is imposed on the holders, who also have to exercise their right of recourse against the guarantor by aval, the endorser, if any, and the drawer by giving them notice of non-payment within the four business days which follow the day for protest.

The time allowed for protesting or for exercising recourses may be shorter or longer in some countries than, respectively, two days and four days.

Effects of protest

The situation of the beneficiary depends entirely on the local law but, generally speaking, protesting accomplishes two things: it gives publicity to non-payment and it holds third parties to their liabilities in the bill. It is thus clear that while the protesting of an accepted bill of exchange generally has grave adverse consequences for the drawee, failure to protest has an adverse consequence for the holders if they wish to exercise their right of recourse.

When no other party has an interest in the accepted bill other than the drawer and drawee (in which case there is not any recourse for the drawer to exercise), the only adverse consequence of non-protesting for the drawers is that they lose the advantages provided by local laws in terms of simplified judgment procedure based upon recognized prima facie evidence of a defaulted debt.

Insolvency

In the event of suspension of payments by, or receivership or bankruptcy of the drawee, protests for non-payment do not in most countries give any specific privilege to the beneficiaries in terms of preference over the other creditors. They remain unsecured creditors and the only benefit deriving from the act of protest is that they do not need to prove the drawee's liability through other evidence.

Costs

In practically all countries, protesting entails notarial fees and can be an expensive process.

Clause 'without costs'

In consideration of the cost of protesting, the drawer or any subsequent endorser can insert in the draft the clause 'without costs' or a similar clause such as 'without advice' or 'without protest'. By so doing they express their willingness to remain responsible *vis-à-vis* the beneficiary in case of non-payment even if no protest has been drawn up.

Such a clause simply waives the obligation for the beneficiary to have the unpaid bill of exchange protested while maintaining the right of recourse against the drawer and other endorsers, if any.

If the clause is inserted in the draft by the drawer, it will retain its effects *vis-à-vis* all other parties. If it is added by an endorser (or a giver of aval) its effectiveness is limited to them and further endorsers only. Its backward effect ends at the author of the clause.

The clause does not bar the beneficiary from protesting the unpaid draft if he or she prefers to, but the costs would then be at his or her charge with little or no chance to recover them from the other parties to the draft. It is just a question of who will pay the costs of the protest.

It is a fallacy to believe – as so many people do – that a bill marked 'without protest' cannot be protested. A drawee adding a clause 'without protest' when accepting a draft would be wrong to believe that he is so sheltered from the threat of being protested in case of non-payment.

Extended drafts

In a number of countries, when an accepted bill has been extended it cannot be protested for non-payment at the new due date. In other countries it can only be protested if it has been re-accepted by the drawee for payment at the new maturity.

As the local rules vary widely on the issue, it is advisable, when in doubt, to obtain a new acceptance from the drawee against cancellation of the original one.

PROMISSORY NOTES

Promissory notes are credit and payment instruments generally governed by the same laws and regulations (including the 1930 Geneva Convention) as bills of exchange.

223

Definition

A promissory note (see Figure 14.6) is an unconditional promise in writing (in the language employed in making the instrument: *'billet à ordre/promesse'*, *'Eigenwechsel/Solawechsel'*, *'orderbriefje/promesse'*, *'Vaglia cambiaro/paghero'*, *'pagare'*) to pay a certain amount of money at a determined or determinable time and place to or to the order of a specified person (the payee or beneficiary). Contrary to the Geneva Convention group of countries, UK and US laws also permit them to be made out payable to bearer.

Comparison with bills of exchange

Main differences

The principal differences between bills of exchange and promissory notes are that the latter:

(a) are made out by the debtor (the maker), while bills are drawn by the creditor (the drawer);

(b) are a promise to pay, while bills are an order to pay;

(c) do not require to be accepted – indeed the very concept of acceptance is irrelevant since the maker, through his or her signature, is legally equivalent to an acceptor and bound in the same manner.

Main similarities

Like an acceptance, a signed promissory note is a public acknowledgement of debt. Like a bill of exchange it can be made payable at sight or at a future date, it can be transmitted by endorsement, guaranteed by aval and, in many countries, protested for non-payment.

If the maker defaults, the rights of recourse to the endorsers, if any, are the same.

Like the bill of exchange, the promissory note is a trade paper submitted to strict and formalistic legal provisions which may vary from country to country.

Comments on promissory notes

In many countries promissory notes have a rather restrictive connotation as financial rather than trade instruments. They are used in

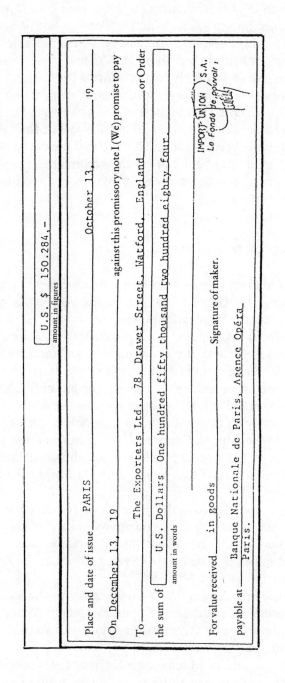

Figure 14.6 Example of a promissory note

225

connection with overdue accounts payable, with compositions for re-payment by instalments of a defaulted debt or with bank loans. In international trade, however, promissory notes may also be encountered as a simple substitute for bills of exchange (Greece is an example), although their use is definitely less common.

A promissory note being, at least in normal practice, a one signature paper, while an accepted bill of exchange is a two signatures paper, the beneficiary's bank will be more willing to discount the latter for two reasons: the built-in recourse to the drawer and the better eligibility for rediscounting at central banks or on the secondary discount market.

The point at issue is the number of parties involved in a recourse arrangement.

APPLICABLE LAW

To minimize conflicts of law – without eliminating them – many national laws (including the UK Bills of Exchange Act 1882) and a complementary Geneva International Convention (1931) have broadly adopted the '*locus regit actum*' principle whereby the applicable law is that of the country where the event under consideration took place.

For instance, the law of the country where the draft is issued governs the form and the essentials of the drawing; the law of the country where the draft is presented for acceptance governs the form of the acceptance; and similarly for the endorsement, the obligation for the holder to accept partial payment, the notice of dishonour and the protest. The determination of the due date when a bill drawn in one country is payable in another is made according to the law of the place where the bill is payable.

A practical consequence of the principle is, for example, that a draft issued in the USA, accepted by a company in England, avalized by its parent company in Germany and intended to be paid at a bank in Switzerland can be governed respectively by the US, English, German and Swiss laws.

Although the principle of 'the local law governs the local act' is well accepted internationally, there are countries which do not subscribe to it. Thus it is important for the exporter to be aware of the regulations in the intervening parties' countries.

As an example, the word 'pay' on a draft, or the words 'I promise to pay' on a note, do not constitute respectively a bill of exchange or a promissory note according to most laws in continental Western Europe. The required wording – 'pay against this bill of exchange' or 'I promise to pay against this promissory note' – is essential for the instrument to be governed by the specific law on bills of exchange and promissory notes in the country of issue.

UNIFORM LAW ON INTERNATIONAL BILLS OF EXCHANGE

UNCITRAL, the United Nations Commission on International Trade Law, has adopted as a priority the drafting of a law on negotiable instruments which would unify the two predominant legal systems: the Geneva Convention Uniform Law and the Anglo-American laws.

A sub-commission has been working on the ambitious project since 1954 and has produced a draft Convention on International Bills of Exchange and International Promissory Notes, which is still under discussion. It is so far a theoretical set of rules, but is certainly susceptible of becoming at a later date a worldwide recognized new convention.

In addition, UNCITRAL offers specimens of both a bill of exchange and a promissory note (Figures 14.7 and 14.8) which are covered by both groups of countries.

Here, as in many other areas, lies hope for the simplification of international trade procedures.

Recommended reading

Hedley, William. (1986) *Bills of Exchange and Bankers' Documentary Credits*. London: Lloyd's of London Press.

Hoyle, Mark S.W. (1985) *The Law of International Trade*. Bicester: CCH Editions Ltd.

National Association of Credit Management. *Digest of Commercial Laws of the World*. New York: Oceana Publications Inc., New York.

Vis, Willem C. (1985) *Unification of International Trade Law*. With special reference to negotiable instruments and commercial arbitration. In *World Trade and Finance*, Joseph Jude Norton (editor), Albany, NY: Matthew Bender.

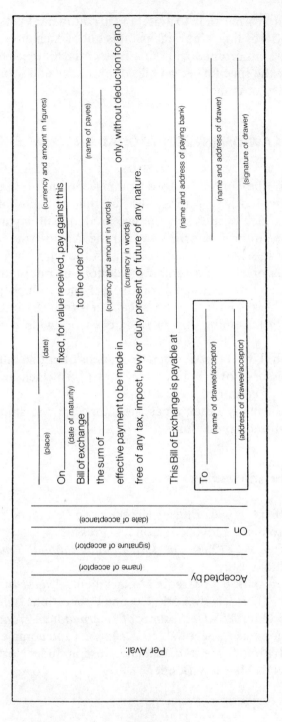

Figure 14.7 UNCITRAL bill of exchange

228

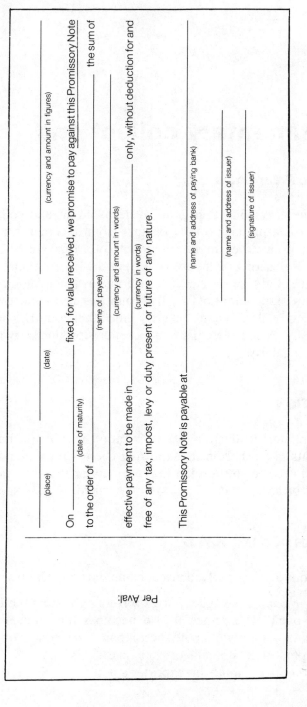

Figure 14.8 UNCITRAL promissory note

15

Documentary collections

Jacques P Lardinois

A documentary collection is an overseas credit and collection bank device. It is a practice totally distinct from documentary credits and governed by a different international code of conduct, namely the Uniform Rules for Collections (URC) of the International Chamber of Commerce, Publication No. 322, in force as from January 1st 1979.

Bankers' associations of fifty-five countries have collectively adhered to the URC while 275 banks in sixty-nine other countries have adhered individually. A complete list of adherents is produced by the ICC and updated regularly.

DEFINITION

A documentary collection is an operation in which a bank receives documents in trust from its exporting client with a mandate to have them remitted to the foreign importer under the conditions (usually payment or acceptance of a draft) prescribed by the exporter.

THE PARTIES INVOLVED

The various parties involved in a documentary collection are as follows.

1   The *principal*: the sellers or exporters entrusting the operation to their bank. The principal also becomes the 'drawer' if a bill of exchange is drawn up to accompany the collection documents (Chapter 14 covers bills of exchange).
2   The *remitting bank*: the exporter's bank receiving the documents,

with a mandate to have them collected, and forwarding them together with adequate instructions to the collecting bank.

3   The *collecting bank* which is the correspondent bank in the buyer's country, chosen by the remitting bank (usually when the latter has no relation with the importer's bank) to be entrusted with the remittance, but acting for the principal and at his risk.

4   The *presenting bank* which usually is the bank suggested by the importer, making the presentation of the documents and collecting the payment. It happens that the presenting bank and collecting bank are invariably the same establishment, so avoiding one link in the chain of transmission.

5   The *drawee*, the buyer, the importer to whom the documents are finally presented according to the terms of payment.

THE MAIN TYPES OF DOCUMENTARY COLLECTION

Depending upon the conditions for the release of the documents as laid down in the contract of sale, there are three main types of documentary collection.

Documents against payment (D/P)

The exporter instructs the bank to release the documents to the foreign importer only against payment of a sight draft (see Figure 15.1).

Procedure

'The presenting bank must make presentation for payment without delay' (URC Art. 9), but in practice banks in many countries withhold presentation until the arrival of the goods. If the principals do not want such a delay, the instructions must stipulate 'payment at first presentation of documents'. If they specifically want to give the buyer the privilege of waiting for the arrival of the goods before paying, they must stipulate in the instructions 'hold for arrival of shipment'.

Degree of protection

The presenting bank will retain the documents and is not authorized to surrender them unless and until payment is made. If goods are being transported by sea, the seller can normally control physical possession of the cargo until the sight draft is paid, because the bill of lading withheld by the bank constitutes title. Bills of lading are, however, the only transport documents which bestow title (see 'The documents' later in this chapter).

Comments on D/P

The following points should be noted.

1   The control of the cargo is independent from the terms of sale, FOB, C & F or CIF, which govern passing of title.
2   The bank is not allowed to deliver the bill of lading without payment even if it is written to the order of the importer.
3   The exporter is not secured against the risk of the importer refusing to pay against the documents (which he may, if he so wishes, examine at the bank's office) or being unable to pay.
4   There is no security against political, economic and transfer risks.
5   For control of physical possession, the goods may be consigned in the first instance to the bank, if transport is by air or parcel post.

Cash against documents (CAD)

The CAD procedure is exactly the same as D/P except that no financial documents, no sight bill of exchange is presented for payment. The importer must simply pay at sight the integral value of the collection to receive the documents. The view taken in CAD is that the bill of exchange is superfluous. It is obvious that a sight draft does not actuate anything except, in case of non-payment, the protesting of a non-accepted bill. This does not add any measure of commercial safety. In case of payment, it does not add anything to the set of documents since it is, by definition, remitted to the drawee immediately upon payment. A sight draft signed for discharge would only be equivalent to taking a receipt from the bank.

In the CAD process, the avoidance of the draft may save a stamp duty or tax in the exporter's or importer's countries. Overseas authorities which impose such duties, however, often stipulate that all documentary collections must have bills of exchange attached simply to raise revenue. In such cases, D/P applies.

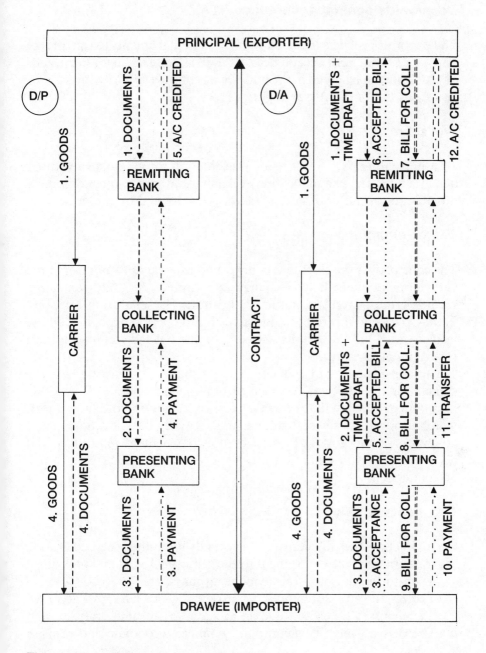

Figure 15.1 Documentary collections

Documents against acceptance (D/A)

The exporter instructs the bank to release the documents to the foreign importer only against acceptance of a time bill of exchange, the usance of which has been agreed in the underlying contract (x days from sight or at a fixed future date) (see Figure 15.1).

Procedure

'The presenting bank must make presentation for acceptance without delay' (UCR Art. 9) and the drawee will have to accept unconditionally the amount of the draft and its maturity as defined by the drawer.

Degree of protection

The control over the shipment being relinquished to the importer at the very moment the bill of exchange is accepted, the only remaining security is the drawee's signature on the draft. The seller from that point in time is extending credit to the buyer for the period expressed by the usance of the bill. He will have to rely on the buyer's creditworthiness for payment at maturity.

The consequences of a documentary time bill non-acceptance are similar for the exporter to those of non-payment of a D/P or CAD remittance: they are limited to the costs of freight (in both directions), warehousing, insurance, banking and, maybe, deterioration in the condition of the goods. In case of non payment at maturity of an accepted draft, they may be much more substantial, as in an open account sale.

Comments on D/A

- In practice, the collecting bank normally holds the accepted draft in trust (rather than returning it to the remitting bank) and presents it again to the drawee, for payment, at maturity.
- There is no difference whatsoever between an accepted documentary time draft and an accepted clean time draft.
- There is no security against the political, economic and transfer risks.

Other terms of collection

Although much less common than D/P and D/A, there may be other conditions imposed by the principal for the release of the documents to the drawee. They are not specifically mentioned by the URC.

Release of documents against payment in local currency

The collecting bank may be authorized to release the documents against provisional payment in the national currency of the buyer, although the respective draft calls for payment in the seller's currency or in a third currency. This method (sometimes and inadequately called 'cash against goods') is generally applied to countries where foreign exchange is not immediately available due to scarcity of foreign reserves. The exporter should request in addition a written commitment by the importer to assume the exchange risk until the invoiced currency is allocated by the central bank. The importer is then bound to put up the additional funds in local currency needed to satisfy the exchange value of the draft in case of any depreciation of the national currency in the meantime.

Release of documents against signature of a promissory note

Such a clause is similar to a D/A arrangement but a time promissory note is signed instead of a time bill accepted.

Release of documents against acceptance plus aval by a third party

The documents will only be released to the importer after the draft has been signed by both the drawee for acceptance and the guarantor 'for aval in favour of the drawee'.

Release of documents against receipt

The receipt to be signed by the drawee will acknowledge only that the documents covering the ordered goods have been delivered. The receipt is not a negotiable instrument.

Release of documents against written undertaking to pay at due date

The documents will be released against the drawee's signature on a letter of undertaking to pay the seller or the presenting bank at a fixed future date.

This procedure is mainly used to save charges on the part of the importer in countries where the stamp tax on the draft may represent a material additional cost (Italy is an example). The undertaking to pay is not a negotiable instrument.

Release of documents against payment subsequent to acceptance of a time draft

The presenting bank will 'present' (not release!) the documents to the drawee and obtain acceptance of a time draft. Both the acceptance and the documents are kept by the bank, which will release them to the drawee at any time but only against payment of the accepted draft. The payment will usually take place before the established maturity (normally when the carrying vessel has arrived) but the drawee is bound to pay at maturity even if the documents have not been withdrawn in the meantime, even if the vessel has not arrived by that date. In any event, the documents may not be released until the accepted draft has been paid.

This procedure, also called 'acceptance with documents against payment' is quite specific to some Far East countries.

Release of documents against 'trust receipt'

The documents will be released against signature of a 'trust receipt', whereby the drawee (usually a dealer or distributor) agrees to receive the documents and to hold the goods 'in trust' on a consignment basis, and promises to pay from time to time or otherwise the proceeds of sales and/or to return the unsold goods after a certain period of time, according to the provisions detailed in the contract.

For the principal (the entruster) the 'trust receipt' is a security title in the property of the goods entrusted for sale to the drawee (trustee). In many European countries such security would be jeopardized by local laws imposing the physical dispossession of pledged chattels.

THE ROLE OF THE BANKS

Banks involved in the documentary collection process merely act as authorized collecting agents on behalf of the principal. They are intermediaries between exporter and importer.

By accepting documents for collection they do not in any manner guarantee payment and they assume no responsibility in case the drawee defaults. They have no obligation to pay before the drawee has paid.

Uniform Rules for Collections

It should be remembered that not all countries/banks adhere to these rules. For those that do, the URC define their liabilities and responsibilities. Key provisions are:

1 'Banks will act in good faith and exercise reasonable care' (Art. 1).

As regards the documents in a collection, 'banks must verify that they appear to be as listed in the collecting order' but 'have no further obligation to examine them' (Art. 2).

The bank's task is merely to pass on the documents and to have them delivered to the drawee in the proper manner. Contrary to the quite separate rules governing documentary credits, it is up to the buyer only, not to the banks, to examine the documents presented and to make the decision to accept them against payment or against acceptance of a time bill of exchange.

2 Article 6 states that goods should not be despatched directly to a bank or consigned bank without its prior agreement. If they are, 'the bank has no obligation to take delivery of the goods which remain at the risk and responsibility of the despatching party'. Its sole obligation in the event of non-payment or non-acceptance by the drawee is to give immediate notification to the remitting bank. The warehousing, sale or return of the goods is then the responsibility of the principal.

Although in practice goods are not despatched to the collecting banks abroad, they are sometimes consigned to them especially when transported by air freight, in which case they are stored under the control of the banks who will issue an 'air release' (delivery order) after payment or acceptance is obtained.

To use the services of a bank as a consignee, it is essential to enquire first whether the bank will allow it, because many banks will not (in some countries the consignee is responsible for duties). If they do, prior arrangements in writing must be entered into.

3 'Banks assume no responsibility for the consequences arising out of delay or loss in transit of any messages, letters or documents' (Art. 4). Remitting banks usually despatch the document within twenty-four hours of receipt.

Once the bank has correctly sent over the documents, it is not responsible for their arrival at their destination; it is the responsibility of the postal system. If bills of lading are to be sent, banks will normally despatch documents by two separate registered posts to guard against loss.

4 For D/P remittances, Articles 11, 12 and 13 of the URC clearly establish that, unless otherwise instructed in the collection order, the presenting bank must only release documents against full payment: in local currency in the case of documents payable in the currency of the country of payment and in the relative foreign currency in cases where they are payable in another currency.

5 'Banks are only permitted to act upon the instructions given in the collection order' (general provision C).

Banks are thus responsible for following through these instructions, unless contrary to the provisions of a national, state or local law and/or regulation which cannot be departed from. This is why it is essential that the principal takes local rules into consideration: the collecting banks hold themselves responsible under their country's regulations which may supersede the instructions received from the remitting bank. Also, the principal should know whether the importing country's banking association or the collecting bank have subscribed or not to the URC, which are still a long way from achieving universal adherence.

6 As regards acceptance of bills, 'the presenting bank is not responsible for the genuineness of any signature or for the authority of any signatory to sign the acceptance' (Art. 15).

7 Banks have no obligation to have the bill of exchange protested (for non-acceptance or for non-payment) in the absence of specific instructions regarding protest (Art. 17).

General points on the role of banks

It sometimes happens that the importer gets control of the goods without having complied with the terms of payment (D/P or D/A). This does not mean that the collecting bank has released the bill of lading improperly, but is generally due to the importers being able to get possession of the goods by presenting a letter of indemnity from their own bank in lieu of the bill of lading. The importer gets hold of the goods, not of the documents, and the remitting bank is not involved. The responsibility is that of the bank that issued the bond for the release of the cargo and the exporter's recourse is against the shipping company which has delivered the goods without the original bill of lading being presented.

The fact that the bill of lading is to the order of the importer does not modify the remitting bank's obligation to remit documents only against payment or acceptance as instructed.

The collecting bank is not responsible for delays in the transfer of the proceeds caused by lack of foreign exchange in the drawee's country. Only after the foreign exchange has been allocated and the transfer authorized must the bank immediately remit in accordance with the instructions given in the collection order.

In a number of countries where the importers are government institutions, foreign trade public organizations or nationalized bodies, they can easily withdraw documents 'in trust' from the banks (also government owned) and clear goods without effecting payment (or acceptance) as required in the collection order.

Sales contracts based upon documentary terms of payment should expressly be drawn up subject to the ICC's Uniform Rules for Collections, Publication No. 322, wherever they are adhered to, in order to avoid disputes in the future.

COSTS

Collection charges

Both the remitting bank and the presenting bank naturally charge fees and expenses based on the servicing and processing of the documents. There is no international uniform tariff and each bank publishes its own listing of conditions and fees (often standardized country by country).

The usual charge comprises the documentary collection commission (as opposed to clean bills collection commission). Additional charges are usually made for:

(a) urgent advices on transactions requiring special treatment by cable, telex, fax or telephone;
(b) postages and other out-of-pocket expenses;
(c) amendments, such as extensions of bills maturing, requiring special or additional correspondence;
(d) holding fees for bills unpaid after three months;
(e) holding fees for bills paid in local currency awaiting foreign exchange allocation;
(f) return of unpaid documents;
(g) protesting.

Collection charges are not negligible; depending upon circumstances they can be as high as 1.5 per cent of the invoice value.

The question that may arise, if the matter has not been clarified in a prior agreement, is whether the buyer or seller (drawee or drawer) should bear these charges. Several scenarios are possible.

1 The drawer absorbs the charges of both banks.
2 The drawer absorbs the charges of the remitting bank but instructs that the collecting bank's charges are for the drawee, although they can be waived.
3 Same split of charges as (2), but those of collecting bank cannot be waived, in which case and under the express instructions of the drawer, documents cannot be released to the drawees even if they are prepared to pay (D/P) or to accept the draft (D/A).
4 Both banks' charges are collectable from the drawee but can be waived.
5 Both charges are collectable from the drawee and cannot be waived, in which case and under the express instructions of the drawer, documents cannot be released to that drawees even if they are prepared to pay (D/P) or to accept the draft (D/A).

Article 22 of the Uniform Rules for Collections is very clear on the issue:

If the collection order includes an instruction that collection charges and/or expenses are to be for account of the drawee and the drawee refuses to pay them, the presenting bank may deliver the document(s) against payment or acceptance as the case may be without collecting charges and/or expenses unless the collection order expressly states that such charges and/or expenses may not be waived.

When payment of collection charges and/or expenses has been refused, the presenting bank must inform the bank from which the collection order was received accordingly. Whenever collection charges and/or expenses are so waived, they will be for the account of the principal, and may be deducted from the proceeds.

Should a collection order specifically prohibit the waiving of collection charges and/or expenses, then neither the remitting nor collecting nor presenting bank shall be responsible for any costs or delays resulting from this prohibition.

There is no set practice as to who should pay the charges, but a most reasonable arrangement is that the exporters absorb their bank's charges and the importers those of the local bank. The principals of a sight collection will appreciate that the payment of the remittance itself can be jeopardized and additional costs (such as demurrage) on the exported goods incurred if bank charges are not waived. They may prefer, considering what they are going to lose, to bear the costs themselves after all. They may also consider adding such costs when setting the price level for the next sale and give the waiver clause. For the exporter, it is a matter of policy: either pricing it to cover the expense or bearing it as a service to the customer.

Stamp taxes

In many countries local regulations prescribe stamp taxes on drafts. Their cost varies widely and they can be either a fixed duty or a percentage of the amount of the bill. Where they are relatively heavy, such taxes explain the importers' reluctance to contract on the basis of bills of exchange (Italy's 1.2 per cent is an example), while a very low fixed rate might partly account for their extensive utilization in other countries (France's fixed FF 0.25 is an example).

There is no established rule as to who – drawer or drawee – should absorb the charge but the implicit consensus would be that each party pays the stamps of its own country.

To avoid their own country's stamp duties, exporters may use the procedure of documents against signature of a promissory note (rather than acceptance of a draft), as the note is established and payable abroad, or of documents against a written undertaking to pay at due date (but remember this is not a negotiable or a protestable document).

It is also the avoidance of stamp duties that explains the tendency to replace sight draft D/P collections by CAD remittances. As there is no draft attached, the two parties get away from the stamp duty obligation.

INTEREST

Article 21 of the URC clearly sets out the course of action presenting banks should follow when the collection order requires the payment of interest but the drawee refuses to pay. The following distinction made by the uniform rules was necessary because some countries do not allow the addition of interest in the body of the draft.

1 *If interest is not embodied in the draft*, that is, when the principal's collection order instructs the bank to collect interest but the bill of exchange or promissory note does not bear an interest clause,

> the presenting bank may deliver the documents against payment or acceptance as the case may be without collecting such interest, unless the collection order expressly states that such interest may not be waived. Where such interest is to be collected, the collection order must bear an indication of the rate of interest and the period covered.

> (e.g. 'interest at x per cent per annum to begin from sailing date' or 'from date of presentation for acceptance'.

2 *If the draft contains an unconditional and definitive interest clause:*

> the interest amount is deemed to form part of the amount of the documents to be collected. Accordingly, the interest amount is payable in addition to the principal amount shown in the financial document and may not be waived unless the collection order so authorizes.

THE COLLECTION ORDER

In their general provisions, the URC specify that: 'All documents sent for collection must be accompanied by a collection order giving complete and precise instructions.'

242

To

MORGAN GUARANTY TRUST COMPANY
        OF NEW YORK

Date: August 29, 19..

DRAWEE'S BANKER

KENYA COMMERCIAL BANK LTD.
P. O. BOX 48400
NAIROBI, KENYA

APPLICATION FOR DOCUMENTARY REMITTANCE

FROM:
THE EXPORTERS LTD.
78, Drawer Street
WATFORD (HERTS) WD2 4AP - ENGLAND

DRAWEE: PLASTIC IMPORT LTD.
Kenyatta House
32, Loita Street
P.O. BOX 511021
NAIROBI - KENYA

OUR REFERENCE: Inv. 362.948

We enclose for acceptance and/or collection the following documents:

Draft Nº	Bill of lading Originals	Bill of lading Copies	A.W.B.	F.C.R.	Commercial invoice	Consular invoice	Packing list	Certificate of origin	Insurance documents	Other documents
B 289	2/3	3			1 x 5	1	1	1		1 certificate of qua-lity, 1 clean report
	Dated Aug. 16									of findings

CURR.	AMOUNT	MATURITY	AFTER COLLECTION, PLEASE CREDIT OUR ACCOUNT	MGT REF. ONLY
US.$	102,368.54	Nov.29th., 19.. Day/Month/Year	US.$ 38650300	

PLEASE FOLLOW INSTRUCTIONS MARKED ‹X›

Deliver documents against	acceptance	X	Do not protest for	non-acceptance		Your collection charges	for our account	X
	‛payment			non-payment			for drawee's account	
Protest for	non-acceptance		Cable advise for	non-acceptance	X	Foreign bank's charges	for our account	
	non-payment			non-payment	X		for drawee's account	X
Waive charges if refused		X	Advise acceptance and due date		X	Do not waive charges		

[X] Special instructions:
. Remit proceeds by cable
. Dispatch the documents by courier
  at our expenses.

[X] In case of need refer to: COMAIP LTD.
                      POB 26334
                      Tel. : 339541
Who is empowered by us: Nairobi

[X] To act fully on our behalf i.e., authorize reductions, extensions, free delivery, waiving of protest, etc.

[ ] To assist in obtaining acceptance or payment of draft as drawn but not altering its terms in any way.

SUBJECT TO THE UNIFORM RULES FOR   COLLECTIONS   (I.C.C. Nº 322)

THE EXPORTERS LIMITED

Figure 15.2 Form of application for documentary remittance

Form

Most banks supply collection application letters for use by exporters when presenting documents. They often consist of a fanfold system for sending the documents, the acknowledgement, and the forwarding letter to the collecting banks. Although not uniform, they provide the same data necessary to the banks (see example in Figure 15.2).

Exporters may prefer to use only uniform letters of their own creation that better fit their particular purpose, such as sending copies to their agents and/or their customers or to a corporate co-ordination centre. These forms generally contain the same information to be filled in as the bank application letters.

Contents

Whatever the design, both systems are suitable as long as the collection order forms contain clear, full and precise information or instructions which will govern the processing of the transaction by the remitting and collecting banks.

The most important points to be unambiguously covered in the instruction form are:

(a) full name and address of the drawee;
(b) detailed listing of all documents (original and number of copies) enclosed with the collection, and divided into first and second mailings if necessary;
(c) exact name and address of the presenting bank (generally the drawee's bank) if known by the exporters, or of the particular bank abroad which they want to be entrusted with the collection;
(d) instructions for the release of documents to the drawee (D/P, D/A or others) as per terms of payment agreed upon;
(e) instructions concerning presentation to the drawee for payment or acceptance only upon arrival of the goods, or not;
(f) instructions as to advices of receipt, acceptance or non-acceptance, fate, payment or non-payment of the collection;
(g) instructions for the collecting bank to return (for example for discount reasons) or retain the time draft after its acceptance by the drawee;
(h) information and instructions regarding the principal's local agent or representative – the 'case of need' – to be contacted in the event

244

of non-payment (D/P) or non-acceptance (D/A) or of any other difficulty, in order to assist the bank abroad;

(i) instructions for protesting or not, claiming from the drawee commissions and other charges incidental to the collection, and for transferring the proceeds in the desired manner.

Depending upon the circumstances, other particular instructions may refer to:

(a) the despatching of the documents by courier at the principal's expense;

(b) the manner (mail or telephone) in which the collecting bank should make the drawee aware of the collection;

(c) the drawee being permitted, or not, to inspect or sample the goods before payment or acceptance;

(d) the cash discount allowed in the event of payment made before tenor;

(e) the collection of interest from the drawee, either by virtue of the draft bearing an interest clause, or as an independent instruction;

(f) the payment of a commission to the local agent to be deducted from the transferable proceeds (sometimes an exchange control requirement);

(g) the enforcement of a foreign exchange clause whereby the drawee remains liable for the full face value of the collection (expressed in the drawer's currency or in another currency) in case the local currency deposited has depreciated during the period imposed by the central bank for the allocation of the foreign exchange.

DIRECT COLLECTION FORMS

The usual method is for the exporters to present the documentary remittance to their bank, who in turn airmail it to the collecting bank or directly to the presenting bank. Slowness in international post is a critical problem, especially on short hauls, where the carrying vessel may well arrive days ahead of the documents, creating difficulties in unloading and clearing the cargo and causing warehouse costs. To speed things up, banks have developed systems to reduce the cycle of time of the operation. These are referred to as 'direct collecting forms' or 'direct collection letters' (DCLs – see example in Figure 15.3).

Settlement methods

Direct Collection Letter

Mail To:

The Chase Manhattan Bank, N.A.
Woolgate House, Coleman Street
London, EC2P 2HD
Tel: 01-600 6141 Telex: 8954681 CMB G
Cables: Chamanbank London EC2
SWIFT: CHAS GB 2L

CHASE

CMB Reference

DIROC 4749

Address all communications to Chase London Quoting DIROC and No

Date August 29, 19 . .

Collecting/Reimbursing Bank

KENYA COMMERCIAL BANK LTD.
P.O. BOX 48400
NAIROBI, KENYA

Drawer Name and Address

THE EXPORTERS LTD.
78, Drawer Street
WATFORD (HERTS) WD2 4AP - ENGLAND

Drawee Name and Address

PLASTIC IMPORT LTD.
Kenyatta House, 32, Loita Street,   P.O. BOX 511021
NAIROBI - KENYA

This collection is subject to the uniform rules for collections (1979 revision) ICC Brochure No. 322

We enclose the within listed draft and documents for collection and remittance of proceeds as instructed. Chase Manhattan Bank requests that you handle this item as if received direct from themselves and will confirm these instructions by following mail. If you have not received the confirmation within 10 days from above date telex Chase at their expense.

Documents	Draft	Invoice	Legalized Inv.	Cert. of Origin	Air Waybill	Bills of Lading	Packing List	Spec.	CRF	INS	CERT quality	
Originals Enclosed	1/2	1 x 4	1	1		2/3	1		1		1	
Duplicates To Follow	1/2	1 x 1		1		1/3	1					

Currency And Amount	Drawer Reference No	Tenor	Date of Draft	Documents Against
U.S.$ 102,368.54	B 289	Nov. 29th, 19. .	Aug.29th19. .	Acceptance

Shipped Per s/s Pritzwald	B/L-AWB Date 435 Aug. 16	Commodity Plastic Resins H.D.P.	[X] Collect XXXXXXXXXX XXXX all other charges

Instructions covering this item are marked "X"

X	Advise by	X	Cable		Airmail	X	Drawee expense		Our expense
X	Remit proceeds by	X	Cable		Airmail		Drawee expense	X	Our expense
	Protest		Non acceptance		Non payment	X	Waive chgs if refused		Do not waive charges
X	Do not Protest	X	If necessary warehouse and insure			X	Re present on arrival of goods		
	Collect interest at		% from		to				

X   If necessary accept deposit for local currency equivalent together with drawees written undertaking to make good any loss in exchange advising us you have done so. Also whether exchange control documentation is complete/not complete

In case of need refer to

COMAIP LTD.
POB 26334
Tel : 339541 - Nairobi

[ ] Who may assist only in obtaining acceptance/payment of the draft documents as drawn

[X] Who has full powers and his instructions may be accepted in any regard as if they had come from us. Please advise us of any action taken

Special Instructions

Payment Instructions (see also reverse)
Two Alternative instructions are provided overleaf covering Cable/airmail remittance. Kindly select our preferred Nostro for the currency of this item and follow the appropriate format from the reverse hereof paying by cable/airmail as instructed above. Payment instructions will be specifically confirmed by Chase in following mail

Instructions To Chase—Payment to be made to drawer by

[X] Credit account number US.$ 26424511   [ ] Credit account number   with
[ ] Other instructions

THE EXPORTERS LIMITED

Incorporated with limited liability under the Laws of the United States of America

FORWARD TO CHASE MANHATTAN

Figure 15.3   Form of direct collection letter

246

Procedure

The exporters (or their freight forwarder) mail the instructions, the draft and/or shipping documents for collection directly to the collecting bank abroad, under cover of a prenumbered instruction form established on the letterhead of and furnished by their home bank. The latter only receive a copy of it to enter the collection on their records and from that point on they follow it up with the collecting bank as if it were their own direct collection. The collecting bank acknowledge receipt to the home bank and will come back to them on any forthcoming event. The home bank can easily identify the collection thanks to the reference number taken from a block of numbers it had specifically assigned to the exporter.

Characteristics

This kind of operation remains a bank collection process. It is actually the bank's form and references that the exporter uses. It is only the initial bank step that is skipped to gain time when time is of the essence, but the exporter's bank remains involved. The exporter is provided with the same service as though the remittance had been entirely handled through his bank. The advantage is to get the documents overseas faster as time is saved on mail and the bank's work.

Comments on direct collections

The 'direct collection form' system should not be confused with the procedures adopted by some of the larger exporters who send their documentary collections direct to foreign banks, using a collection form of their own design and completely bypassing their home bank. In such cases it is the foreign bank which acknowledges receipt of the collection to the exporters, sends them and their local agents status reports and transfers the proceeds by cheque or telegraphic transfer to the designated account.

This more hazardous practice can save time and collection costs, but for any but the largest, well-represented multinational it may prove to be 'penny wise and pound foolish'.

Among the many pitfalls in eliminating the home bank are:

1   The exporter is not able to assess the foreign bank's standing while

remitting banks are quite selective in working with correspondents abroad.

2 There may be reluctance on the part of the foreign banks to act on instructions received from unknown exporters. They might be more inclined anyhow to give special consideration to the handling of a collection received from another bank than direct from an exporter. In case the exporter wants to alter the original instructions (particularly a release of value), the likelihood is that the foreign bank will hesitate to accept cable instructions not authenticated by a test key.

3 The foreign banks would be more willing to incur expenses (storage, insurance, legal) if acting on instructions from a bank rather than for account of the exporter, unless specific relationships have been established.

4 The exporter may receive requests from the buyer to send the collection to a designated bank where the buyers may obtain co-operation which they are not entitled to under the collection instructions. It could be a local branch, that normally does not handle international commercial transactions. The exporter, before acceding to the request, however, would be prudent to check the reliability of the suggested presenting bank.

5 It is a 'do it yourself' program and problems may arise when the exporter or the freight forwarder is not fully trained in presenting all the relevant facts correctly on the remittance letter. Straightening out communication errors, without intervention of the domestic bank when the collection has already gone forward, can be arduous.

6 The exporter does not enjoy the benefit of the remitting bank's expertise and privileged facilities, which could be crucial when a serious problem arises.

7 The only leverage that the exporters have on the local banks is to go through their home banks and 'have the backing of the banking fraternity'.

As a counter-argument to the above, large multinationals who are well represented in overseas markets by local agents – or even their own subsidiaries – will put forward the following points in favour of sending documentary collections direct to a bank in the market.

1 The transmission time for sending documents and money is reduced and some bank charges are saved.

2 Local agents are more effective at progressing overdue amounts than banks.

3   Even if one uses a 'home' bank in the first instance, such a remitting bank would not be liable for any shortcomings on the part of the present/collecting bank (URC, Art. 3).

COLLECTION TRACING

Banks normally keep the principal advised of the progress of collections. Article 20 of the URC details the manner in which banks must advise on the fate of collections.

Timing

No strict tracing cycle is defined for these 'advices of fate' but the key phases in the rules are:

The collecting bank must send without delay:
— advice of payment
— advice of acceptance,
— advice of non-payment or non-acceptance.

In the case of non-payment or non-acceptance: 'The presenting bank should endeavour to ascertain the reasons for such non-payment or non-acceptance' and 'The remitting bank must, within a reasonable time, give appropriate instructions as to the further handling of the documents'.

Sequence of advices

In the case, for example, of a documentary draft (D/A) drawn at a fixed period from sight, and assuming that the operation faces no difficulties at all, the principal would normally receive three advices:

(a)   an acknowledgement that the draft and the documents have been received at the remitting bank;
(b)   notice of acceptance of the draft by the foreign drawee and of the maturity date;
(c)   notice of payment of the matured draft, taking usually the form of an advice of credit to the principal's account.

Procedures

Most banks have a normal tracing procedure, activated at regular intervals. The remitting bank normally sends tracers to the collecting bank if notice of fate is not received within the expected time limit. Experience has shown that, the word 'delay' not being defined in the URC, some collecting/presenting banks may be slower than would be expected in their tracing and reporting on the fate of collections. In some cases, the remitting bank, in order to communicate with the principal, will send him a copy of the tracers but this is not a general practice and the Credit Department of the exporting company should exert its own control over the banks' actions.

Means of communication

The letter of instruction should specify whether advices of fate must be given by cable/telex, otherwise airmail is likely to be used. If the documentary collection is paid (D/P) or accepted (D/A) and everything is all right, the consequences of routine reporting are not important, but in the case of non-payment/non-acceptance, time is of the essence and the information should be sent to the attention of the principal as quickly as possible so that he can promptly take appropriate action.

Responsibility

It is important to know that Article 3 of the URC provides that 'banks utilizing the services of other banks for the purpose of giving effect to the instructions of the principal do so for the account and at the risk of the latter'. The remitting banks are therefore detached from any liability which would arise from inaccurate follow-up by the presenting bank or by the collecting bank.

TRANSMITTING PROCEEDS

Amounts collected (less charges, disbursements, expenses where applicable) must be made available without delay to the bank from which the collection order was received in accordance with the instructions given (Art. 14).

The funds go all the way back to the credit of the principal's account specified in the remitting letter.

If the collection is in a currency other than that of the principal's country, the remitting bank should be instructed as to how credit is to be applied:

- sale of the foreign currency on the spot exchange market
- application against a foreign exchange forward contract
- credit to an account held in the foreign currency.

Means of transmission

The exporter may give instructions that the proceeds of the remittance be sent to the remitting bank by cable/telex to gain days in the use of the funds. The cable/telex costs will normally be for his charge but they are usually more than offset by the earlier use of the funds resulting from the reduced 'float' of the transfer. The SWIFT (Society for Worldwide Interbank Financial Telecommunication) system provides rapid movements of funds between banks through electronic transmission.

THE DOCUMENTS

The Uniform Rules for Collections, in their general provisions and definitions, make a distinction between 'financial documents, meaning bills of exchange, promissory notes, cheques, payment receipts or other similar instruments used for obtaining the payment of money', and 'commercial documents, meaning invoices, shipping documents, documents of title or other similar documents, or any other documents whatsoever, not being financial documents'.

The usual commercial documents

These comprise:

- commercial invoice
- transport documents (see below)
- insurance policy or certificate
- consular invoice
- certificate of origin
- packing lists
- certificate of quality or analysis
- certificate of manufacture.

The transport documents

There is a marked difference in the degree of safety offered by documentary collections as instruments of payment, depending upon which transport document is remitted, consistent with the mode of shipment used.

The supreme transport document is the *ocean bill of lading*, a recognized document of title and a negotiable document *par excellence*. It may be consigned to order and transferred by endorsement to transmit title to the goods. It evidences control of the goods.

The legal status of the bill of lading is really unique and does not apply in any way to any other transport documents, which are simply not negotiable documents, but only evidence shipment of goods directly to the consignee and do not represent the goods to which they relate.

Consequently, when goods are despatched by air, road or rail, the security offered by a normal D/P or D/A procedure is generally illusory, in any case much diminished or even non-existent; the consignee is able to obtain possession of the goods without showing up at the bank and satisfying the terms of the remittance, D/P or D/A. Normally, the only way to prevent the importer from taking possession of the goods is to consign them to the bank. (See 'Treatment of non-negotiable documents', below.)

For air transport

The document used is the 'air waybill', formerly referred to as an 'air consignment note'. It is the contract of carriage and the copy for the shipper is his receipt for the goods remitted to the airline. The third copy made out for the consignee travels with the cargo and its presentation is thus not required at destination for the addressee to take delivery of the goods.

As long as the original air waybill is retained by the exporter, he or she has control of the goods and can modify their destination if they have not yet been despatched by the carrier.

For rail transport

The document used is a 'rail through international consignment note' (also referred to as a rail bill, railroad bill or railway receipt). It is to a certain extent evidence of the contract of carriage. The shipper receives a duplicate. The consignee does not need to present a copy to the railway to take delivery of the goods.

For road transport

The document used is a 'road consignment note', in triplicate, signed by the shipper and the carrier. The shipper receives one copy and the third travels with the cargo. The consignee does not need to present a copy to take delivery of the goods.

For combined transport methods

There is a 'combined transport document', as created by the International Federation of Freight Forwarders Associations, which again is essentially evidence of contract and receipt for the shipper. This new-style document, although not a document of title, 'may be just as useful to the parties and, if issued by a sea carrier, can be treated as an ordinary bill of lading'. (Mark S.W. Hoyle, (1981) *The Law of International Trade*. UK: P. Laureate.)

Treatment of non-negotiable documents

The exporter's reluctance to ship cargo by air, rail or truck to marginal accounts on a so-called CAD basis is because of the possibility of release of the goods directly to the customer without a bank controlled document of title. It has even been suggested that importers short of cash prefer to pay the higher air freight rates in order to get the goods released to them before picking up the documents at the bank, thus gaining abused credit time.

Alternative safeguarding solutions exist, and are described below, but they are not fully satisfactory.

Consigning the cargo to the collecting bank

This requires the bank's prior consent as per URC, Art. 6. The bank, being named as consignee and receiving a copy of the air waybill or consignment note, would release the goods to the buyer after payment (D/P) or acceptance (D/A) by means of an 'air release' authorization.

Banks in many countries would not care to have shipments consigned to them directly, because they would become an importer on official records and might thereby be contravening local regulations. In addition they would be liable for demurrage if the shipment were not cleared and picked up within a given period of time.

A delivery order for truck shipments

For truck shipments, a 'delivery order', addressed to the trucking company, may be sent to the collecting bank with instructions to release it to the drawee against payment (D/P) or acceptance (D/A). At the same time, the trucking company would be instructed to release the cargo to the customer only on presentation of the original delivery order.

This procedure is not much used and is not quite adequate because the goods would generally arrive before the delivery order could materially be in the hands of the customer, thus occasioning demurrage/warehousing charges. In addition, it is administratively cumbersome and vexatious to the customer. It can furthermore be in conflict with import/exchange control regulations.

Warehouse-keeper's warrant

A local warehouse will issue a warehouse-keeper's warrant that gives official title to the goods and can be mailed to the collecting bank to be delivered to the customer against payment (D/P) or acceptance of a time draft or signature of a promissory note (D/A). Once in possession of the warehouse-keeper's warrant, the customer can present it to the warehouse and get hold of the merchandise. This procedure has the same characteristics as the preceding one. It is not often used in international trade.

Forwarding agent or broker in drawee's country

It is usually possible to employ a first class forwarding agent or customs broker in the drawee's country, to whom the air waybill or consignment note would be consigned. The agent's role would be to take possession, hold the shipment and release it to the customer against confirmation by the collecting bank that payment has been made (D/P) or acceptance given (D/A). In other words, the forwarding agent would hold the goods at the collecting bank's disposal.

The goods can also be consigned to the forwarding agents in the buyer's country, mandating them to release the goods after receiving payment or acceptance without any bank intervention. Such a procedure is no longer a bank documentary collection process, since it takes course outside the banking channel of control and transmission. It may also conflict with local import or foreign exchange regulations.

Cash on delivery

With a 'cash on delivery' (COD) shipment, the carrier collects the full invoice value from the consignee and remits it back after deducting freight and fees. The shipment is consigned to the importer with instructions to the carrier to deliver it against payment. However, not all airlines and railways are prepared to act as collecting agent and handle COD shipments (because they are not quite compatible with the straight consignment nature of the air waybill or rail consignment note), and there are many countries where import or exchange control regulations make it impossible. Such a procedure, like the preceding one, is no longer a bank-controlled collection process. The seller incurs a credit risk on the airline, railway or trucking company after the customer risk has been removed by their payment.

Clean draft before shipment

For deferred payment shipments, a clean draft (no documents attached) can be accepted and returned by the drawee prior to shipment. Obviously, this is no longer a bank documentary collection process although the clean draft acceptance and, at maturity, its payment can be handled through bank-to-bank transmission.

UNPAID OR UNACCEPTED DOCUMENTARY COLLECTIONS

In the event that the importers withdraw from their contractual undertaking to pay (D/P and CAD) or to accept (D/A), the collecting bank will be unable to hand over the documents of title to the drawee.

The cargo then remains the legal property of the sellers but, not being picked up fast enough, it may be warehoused at their risk and cost.

Quick action is then required because, after a period of time depending upon the habits and regulations of the importing country, the goods will possibly be subject to confiscation and public auction by the local customs authority.

Drawee's reasons for refusing the documents

The presenting bank should endeavour to ascertain the reasons for non-payment or non-acceptance and advise the bank from which the collection order was received accordingly (Art. 20(c)).

The reasons most often given are:

- the carrying vessel has not yet arrived
- the condition to release the document is not that which was contractually agreed (for example D/P versus D/A)
- the usance of the bill or its fixed maturity is not as agreed
- the amount invoiced is higher than agreed
- the goods were not ordered
- the description of the goods is not in conformity with the order
- the shipment took place before the agreed date
- the shipment took place too late or was delayed on the voyage
- some documents are missing and the goods cannot be customs cleared
- the import licence has not yet been released.

The refusal of documents however can be due to less ethical reasons, such as a fall in the market price of the merchandise concerned between order and time of arrival.

Bank's obligation

Banks have no obligation to take any action in respect of the goods to which an unaccepted or unpaid documentary collection relates (Art. 19).

The collecting bank, however, must advise the remitting bank of the situation without delay and the remitting bank must, within a reasonable time, give appropriate instructions as to the further handling of the documents (Art. 20c).

In practice the collecting bank may take conservatory measures for the protection of the cargo, whether instructed or not, but when so doing they assume no liability or responsibility with regard to its fate and/or condition. The related charges incurred, which may be substantial (warehousing, insurance etc.) will be for the account of the principal (Art. 19).

The ordinary action that the bank may take would be:

1 If the vessel has not yet arrived, keep track of where the shipment is and advise the remitting bank of the expected time of arrival of the goods covered by the unpaid or unaccepted draft. This information will prompt the principal to make decisions as to the action to be taken *vis-à-vis* the drawee as well as the cargo.
2 If the vessel has arrived and the goods are sitting at the port, release the bill of lading to a customs broker with instructions to have them properly stored under customs and properly insured.
3 At a later date, the collecting bank may intervene again to release the refused cargo as instructed by the principal or his local representative.

Principal's representative

It is obviously a major advantage for the exporters to have the local assistance of an agent or a broker, acting as their representative, upon whom they can rely and whom the collecting bank will consult in dealing with the problem, who will care for the cargo and possibly salvage it in the event that the drawees renege on their contractual obligation to pay or to accept.

If the principal nominates a representative to act as 'case-of-need', the collection order should clearly and fully indicate their powers (Art. 18).

The remittance letter usually expresses the extent to which the representative has authority to act on behalf of the exporter along lines such as the following.

● 'authorized to give instructions which may be followed in any respect'
● 'authorized to act fully on our behalf, i.e. authorize reductions, extensions, free delivery, waive of protest, and so on'
● 'authorized to assist only, but not to alter the terms of the collection in any way'.

The principal remains solely responsible for the possible consequences of the actions taken by the case-of-need regarding either alteration of terms and conditions of the remittance or disposal of documents and goods.

Course of action

Whatever measures are taken to save the shipment, the practical options left to the principal (besides taking legal action against the buyer) may be restricted because of the manner in which the bill of lading has been issued (if, for example, it is to the order of the importer, the latter is the only one who can endorse it), because of local regulations (for example, if the importer's country has very strict import licence laws, the documents may not be allowed to be transferred to another party) or even because of the physical conditions of the port of discharge.

Such restrictions and potential difficulties being kept in mind, the options left to the principal are very few and the very act of detailing them illustrates the risks inherent in documentary collections, which the exporter must beware.

Call the shipment back

The repatriation of the shipment will cost the exporter the return freight and insurance in addition to already incurred expenses.

Resell the shipment to another buyer in the same city or the same territory

In this case the bank will be authorized to transfer the documents to the new buyer. The seller will probably stand a loss on both the new price and the costs incurred but this can be the most economical way to dispose of the entire matter.

Move the shipment into another local market

In this case, arrangements have to be made to have the goods transshipped with the intervention of a local transit agent.

Consignee

The exporter will always be wise to ship goods to the order of the shipper, blank endorsed so that, in the event of non-acceptance or non-payment, the bill of lading can be transmitted by the collecting bank to a third party such as the case-of-need or even a broker who can then claim the cargo and take adequate action.

PROTESTING

(Readers are referred to Chapter 14 for a detailed description of protesting a bill of exchange.)

The collection order should contain instructions regarding protest. In the absence of instructions, the bank has no obligation to have the collection protested for non-acceptance or non-payment (Art. 17).

To adopt a blanket policy to protest all drafts if not paid may prove to be a hazardous course of action for the seller. Indeed in some countries, protesting is not permitted (see below). It is wiser to treat each case individually in deciding whether or not to protest.

Arguments in favour of protesting

1 The protest is a natural consequence of a bill of exchange; it derives from it. There may be some inconsistency between drawing a time draft on a customer and not having the intention to use the right of protest. To some extent, the main reason for issuing a bill is the notice of intent to the customer that it implies. The acceptor of a trade draft knows very well that the steps implied by the law on bills of exchange should not be expected to be waived.
2 The instruction to protest is an effective lever, a means to step up pressure on the customer to obtain prompt payment.

Arguments against protesting

1 In export trade, and unless an aval has been given, there is in most cases no third party contingently liable by virtue of an endorsement and there is no previous bearer, from whom the instrument was received and against whom recourse is to be retained, to be held liable. Therefore, one of the useful purposes of a protest is generally not served.
2 The act of protest is usually published in an official gazette and, by other creditors becoming alarmed, the protest can have quite a

damaging effect on the customer which the exporter may not want.

3 Protesting within the time limitation locally applied, generally within the two days following maturity, is equivalent to taking very definite action on an item which is only two or three days overdue. Such a drastic decision should rather be taken as a last resort.

4 The bad impact of a protest on the creditworthiness of the customer can have a boomerang effect on the seller's chances actually to collect the debt.

5 The legal fees to be paid may be disproportionate to the amount of the bill. Protesting can be very expensive in some countries.

6 If the seller considers it necessary to resort to protest in the instructions to the banks, due to the ascertained financial weakness or lack of creditworthiness of the importer, it would be wiser instead to ship on a fully secure basis, such as irrevocable documentary credit.

7 The seller may have contributed to the non-payment; the customer, although bound by the acceptance of the bill, may refuse to pay on valid commercial grounds and may not be to blame. In such a case, a protest instruction would probably mean the termination of the customer relationship and the credit manager's lack of consideration for the customer's reasons would be criticized, especially if previous payment experience was good.

8 Protest being the first stage of a possible legal action, the debt is at that time reconstituted in local currency equivalent. If that currency is not the currency of the bill of exchange, the eventual judgment or settlement may be considerably reduced by virtue of any erosion of the local currency's value.

Other considerations in relation to protesting

In most countries very little is added by an act of protest for non-acceptance of a time draft or for non-payment of a sight draft, because the instrument does not bear the signature of the drawee.

The clauses 'no costs', 'no protest' or similar in the body of the bill of exchange are independent of the instruction to protest in the collection order, and a draft marked 'no costs', or 'no protest' remains protestable. The instruction to protest does not show on the face of the draft as it does not belong to the instrument. It is part of the collection order.

The time allowed for protesting (two or three days in most cases) is in relation to the rights of exercising recourse against other parties to the bill, but in many countries a protest can be drawn up at a later date. It is then too late to exercise recourses in the normal way; it may also be too late to have the protest published in an official gazette, but the late protest remains valid for legally evidencing the non-payment of the instrument.

Regardless of country, if the collecting bank has the buyer as a general customer, they may not be inclined to enforce protesting instructions unless the drawee's payment record is bad. They would probably rather persuade the drawee to find ways and means of settling the bill or to obtain an extension of the due date while requiring confirmation of the protest instruction, given the drawee's reasons for non-payment.

It also happens that the presenting bank will alert the remitting bank right away that they will not protest as a matter of policy.

Conclusion

Exporters should always be careful when filling out the collection order in respect of protesting instructions. They should consider whether protesting is warranted in terms of the various factors to be weighed: the purpose of protesting, its legal aspects, its consequences, its costs, the past experience with the customer and, hopefully, the future relationship.

If an instruction to protest is given, the principal may still exercise flexibility: it is one thing to ask a bank to protest; it is another thing to protest. In countries where the procedure of 'noting' is recognized, instructions merely to 'note' for non-payment should be sufficient.

In some countries protest facilities are unavailable (Bahrain, Bulgaria, China, Oman, Quatar, United Arab Emirates) or complicated and/or very expensive (Algeria, El Salvador, Ethiopia, Indonesia, Iran, Israel, Kuwait, Saudi Arabia, South Korea) or simply not advisable due to serious consequences (Brazil, Dominican Republic, Puerto Rico, Sweden, Venezuela).

Recommended reading

Credit Suisse, *Documentary credits, Documentary collections, Bank Guarantees, Publication Vol. 69.* One of many excellent free booklets published by the major banks.

Settlement methods

International Chamber of Commerce, (1978) *Uniform rules for Collections*. ICC Publication No. 322. Paris: ICC.

FCIB–NACM, New York, *Minutes of round table conferences, USA and Europe*, 1967–1987.

16

Documentary letters of credit

Brian Clarke

Let's start off with a basic statement. If you don't get your documentation absolutely consistent with the conditions of the letter of credit and if
you don't present your documents within the time limits laid down, you
are not going to get your money!

It's not quite as stark or as simple as that, but let's keep that general
statement foremost in our minds as we go through this chapter.

DEFINITION

In the Uniform Customs and Practice described below, a documentary
credit is formally defined in Article 2 as:

> any arrangement, however named or described, whereby a bank (the
> issuing bank), acting at the request and on the instructions of a
> customer (the applicant for the credit),
> (i) is to make a payment to or to the order of a third party (the
> beneficiary), or is to pay or accept bills of exchange (drafts)
> drawn by the beneficiary, or
> (ii) authorizes another bank to effect such payment, or to pay,
> accept or negotiate such bills of exchange (drafts), against
> stipulated documents, provided that the terms and conditions of
> the credit are complied with.

What's in a name?

In the first few lines of this chapter we've referred to both letters
of credit and documentary credits. In international trade you will

alternatively come across L/C, documentary letters of credit, documentary L/Cs, banker's documentary credits, commercial credits or, simply, credits. It all seems very confusing but that's the way it is!

The Uniform Customs and Practice calls them 'documentary credits' up to the definition of Article 2 and thereafter 'credits'. Whatever the instrument is called, however, of far more importance is *what it provides* – and that is all wrapped up in the conditions expressed in, or implied by, each particular credit.

So no one credit is exactly the same as another. The variations are legion, and it should not be surprising that there are several names for the same genre of instrument.

FORMS AND TYPES OF CREDIT

There are basically three forms of credit and each can provide the basis for several different types, depending upon the specific purpose.

The different forms

Different forms of credit bestow different levels of security, always provided the documentation presented against them is in order.

A *revocable credit* is an undertaking given by the issuing bank which can be withdrawn at any time up to payment at the whim of the customer who requested it to be opened. It thus offers little security to the beneficiary and in practice is rarely used.

Remember however that, if a credit does not specifically indicate that it is irrevocable (see below), then it is deemed to be revocable.

For real security an *irrevocable credit* is required. Here the issuing bank in effect gives its guarantee that, however inclined or otherwise the customer may be to pay for the exporter's goods or services, they (the bank) will honour their obligations upon presentation of the documents stipulated by the credit. Customer risk is thereby covered, but not country risk. The issuing bank will be situate in the same country as the customer and, if that country has no foreign exchange available for the currency of the invoice, no matter how willing the issuing bank may be to pay, the exporters will have to wait an indefinite time for their money. An irrevocable credit, per se, is thus only secure when opened in an economically stable country.

To counter unacceptable country risk as well as customer risk, an *irrevocable credit confirmed by a bank outside the country of risk* will be required (and it follows that the confirming bank should not itself be in another bad-risk country!)

Here, over and above the undertaking given by the issuing bank, the second bank gives its own and separate guarantee that it will pay, come what may – so long as the documentation is all in order when presented.

The usual parties to the credit

Credits are opened or issued by the *issuing bank* normally situate in the same country as the *customer* (*importer*) who requests or instructs them.

Once opened, the credit is sent to a bank, usually in the exporter's country, known as the *advising bank* which, as the name implies, advises the *beneficiary* (*exporter*) that the credit is available for utilization.

If the issuing bank indicates that a confirmation is required, this is normally provided by the advising bank which thus also becomes the *confirming bank*. A different bank may, however, provide the confirmation.

The beneficiary should thoroughly check the credit and, only when totally satisfied with it, should then ship the goods or render the service, ensuring that all stipulated documents are gathered together and presented within the prescribed time scale to the advising/confirming bank.

Provided the documents are all in order, the advising/confirming bank will then pay or formally promise to pay the beneficiary depending upon whether sight, acceptance or deferred credits are involved (see below).

These procedures are covered in more detail later in this chapter.

The different types of credit

As an added dimension to the three forms of credit, there are several different types.

Credits allowing prompt payment

If the customer is not being given any time to pay, a *sight credit* is opened providing for immediate payment upon presentation of the documents stipulated.

Credits allowing time to pay

If a period of time is to elapse between presentation of documents and payment, this can be handled in two ways.

1 By the issue of an *acceptance credit*. This will stipulate that a usance bill of exchange, drawn on the confirming/advising bank or customer, should be presented along with all other specified documents. If these are all in order the bill will be accepted for payment at the appropriate maturity date. Such accepted bills are normally readily discountable to raise export finance, often without recourse if they relate to confirmed credits.

2 By the issue of a *deferred credit*. This will itself indicate that payment is to be made at a time certain in the future. It dispenses with the necessity for a bill of exchange to be raised, and any undertaking to pay will normally be evidenced in writing by the bank accepting the documents. Deferred credits are often used to avoid situations where the bill of exchange under an acceptance credit would have to be drawn on the issuing bank or the customer and would attract high local stamp duties.

Negotiation credits

If, for any reason, it is required that the credit is to be paid by a bank other than the advising bank, then a *negotiation credit* will be issued, permitting the beneficiary to present documents to any bank, or perhaps any one of a number of specified banks, for payment or acceptance of a bill of exchange.

The only guarantees of payment rest with the issuing/confirming banks, which undertake to pay on condition the documents presented by the beneficiary are found to be in order.

Credits used for special purposes

The special credits known as transferable, back-to-back, red clause, revolving and standby credits are really variations on the more usual types of credit. They are described later in this chapter.

DOCUMENTARY CREDIT FAILURES: THE CORE PROBLEM

No treatise or seminar on documentary credits will fail to include a reference to the alarming rate of rejection of documents on first presentation to the advising/confirming bank.

Surveys carried out in the UK by the Midland Bank, in conjunction with the Simpler Trade Procedures Board (SITPRO), repeatedly reveal that some 50 per cent of sets of documents are in one way or another discrepant upon first presentation, the underlying transactions thereby often failing to achieve prompt payment and even losing the underlying security of the letter of credit.

Based on the author's own experience, if a survey were made across the broad spectrum of UK exporters and banks, the failure rate would be even higher, perhaps as much as 65 to 70 per cent. Either way there is an almost incredible irony in a situation in which, using the only export payment method (other than cash in advance) which can bestow almost complete security, exporters prejudice that security largely through their own shortcomings and lack of attention to detail.

All manner of reasons are given for such failures and all manner of remedies prescribed. The core problem lies, however, in *getting the letter of credit set up correctly in the first place*.

Many exporters overlook the fact, or perhaps do not appreciate, that it is their customer who has to give the issuing bank precise instructions as to how the credit should be worded. Many customers, in their own turn, believe it is their bank's job to get the credit right – after all they are the experts, they understand the systems and the rules, per Uniform Customs and Practice, which govern the operation of letters of credit.

But how can the issuing bank possibly know whether very precise conditions, which appear perfectly reasonable to them from their perspective, are capable or not of being met by the exporter?

Of course exporters should check credits meticulously when they arrive; of course they should check all the documents equally meticulously before presentation (and this is all covered in detail later). But above all, they should ensure that the credit is opened 100 per cent correctly in the first place, in such a way that it echoes the terms of the sales contract, and that they will be able to perform against all its conditions, both stated and implied.

THE UNIFORM CUSTOMS AND PRACTICE (UCP)

'Conditions, both stated and implied', it says at the end of the last sentence. This is because, as we shall see, it is advantageous for credits to be issued subject to UCP. Once the UCP are made to apply, however, their whole range of default terms and conditions are implicit unless specifically overridden by written conditions in the credits. UCP are thus often referred to as the hidden rules. If, for instance, a credit is silent on whether or not part shipments are allowed, UCP says they are (Article 44). So, if the customer wants part shipments prohibited, the credit must contain a specific clause to that effect.

UCP, or to give them their proper title, the Uniform Customs and Practice for Documentary Credits, International Chamber of Commerce Publication No. 400, in the current 1983 Revision, are a set of rules which have evolved over the years, since the time when it first became apparent that documentary credit trading was here to stay, that the credits themselves were becoming very complicated and that an internationally acceptable set of standards was required to govern their usage.

The first edition of UCP was adopted by the International Chamber of Commerce in 1933 and, over the subsequent fifty years, they were refined and updated to produce, in the latest edition, one of the finest and universally acceptable set of rules for the facilitation of international trade.

Virtually all banks in every country in the world, except the Chinese People's Republic, operate in accordance with UCP; and it is said that even in China credits are checked and processed with UCP as a firm business guide.

Technically UCP only come into force if the credit specifically says that they apply. A clause worded something like 'Subject to Uniform Customs and Practice for Documentary Credits, ICC Publication No. 400' will therefore be included as the last condition or a marginal note of the credit. UCP of themselves have no legal standing but they are recognized in the jurisdictions and courts of a large number of countries to the extent of being accepted as the definitive international 'rules' for the handling of letters of credit.

It also has to be remembered that, in the final analysis, UCP are 'just words' and in any dispute grey areas of interpretation emerge, despite the great care to detail which has gone into the framing of the rules. This does not in any way detract from them; indeed, except in very rare instances it is unlikely that the words themselves could be bettered in order to make the grey areas more black and white. It merely points to the necessity for exporters to take counsel from their own bankers' documentary credits departments when difficult disputes over the interpretation of UCP arise.

In extreme cases, such disputes can be referred to the ICC Banking Commission and from time to time their opinions as to the proper interpretation are published. These publications, like UCP 400 and the Guide to Documentary Credit Operations (ICC Publication No. 415), are invaluable to any credit manager involved with documentary credits.

THE OPERATION OF THE CREDIT

This section runs through the practical processing of a documentary credit through all its stages.

Establishing credits

This is where success or failure in a documentary credit operation is seeded.

The issuing bank formalizes the terms and conditions of the credit, having regard to the customer's instructions and UCP. So it is the customer who has the greatest influence over the way the credit is opened.

It is the exporter, however, as beneficiary under the credit, who has to comply with the credit's conditions. So it makes sense for the exporter to offer guidance to the customer and, after agreeing the negotiable conditions, set down the precise terms of the credit to form the basis of the customer's instruction to the issuing bank.

The areas which particularly need addressing are listed below. (Reference should also be made to the purpose-written ICC Publication No. 416A, Guidance Notes for Credit Applicants.)

Guidance to customers – Points to be agreed when arranging for the issue of letters of credit

1 Ensure the credit is irrevocable.
2 Is it to be confirmed?
3 Precisely what name is to be shown as the beneficiary? (There may be more than one company in the exporter's group, but that to be shown in the invoice header must be the same as shown in the credit.)
4 What are the precise terms of sale – FOB, CIF or whatever?

5   How much is the credit to be issued for and in what currency? The amount should be sufficient to cover goods, packaging and all other costs to be charged to the customer. The addition of the words 'about' or '*circa*' in front of the amount will permit a tolerance of 10 per cent, more or less.

6   What are the precise terms of payment – not just the number of days, but the point from which they begin to run: from date of bill of lading, date of arrival of goods, or what? The start point should be as specific as possible.

7   For how many days beyond shipment date should the credit remain valid for presentation of documents? If the credit is silent on this subject, UCP sets the period at twenty-one days. But even twenty-one days may not be enough to allow for gathering all the documents and having them presented (for example where a consular certificate is required), so a more realistic time may have to be stipulated. At the other extreme, without proper prior consultation, customers and issuing banks may set this number of days ridiculously low, so that the credit becomes unworkable or has to be amended to effect an extension.

8   When should the credit itself expire? A reasonable date should be set here. Remember, documents will have to be presented before the bank closes for business on the expiry date, or within the number of days specified (see (7) above) beyond date of shipment, *whichever is the earlier*.

9   Which documents should the credit call for? These should be limited to those documents absolutely essential to the performance of the transaction covered by the credit. The fewer the documents and the simpler the detail required, the easier it will be to meet the terms and conditions of the credit.

10 How are goods and packaging to be described? The credit should anticipate the exact way they will be described in the commercial invoice. If quantities have to be shown, it is advisable to show them as 'about' or 'approx.', to allow a margin not exceeding 10 per cent, more or less. It follows that a somewhat similar tolerance will have to be allowed for the value as per (5) above.

11 If the goods are going by sea, how is the port of despatch to be described? It gives more flexibility if it can be shown as 'any UK [or European or US] port' rather than naming a specific port.

12 Likewise the port of destination. It is better to be general rather than specific, but the customer may have other ideas. In any event,

the destination details shown must be consistent with the basis of delivery indicated in the contract of sale and as they will be shown on the bill of lading.

13 Are part shipments to be permitted? Allowing them will overcome any problems which may arise, for example, with goods damaged during loading (but the customers will separately want to be reassured by the supplier that they are not going to have to take delivery piecemeal).

14 Is transhipment to be allowed? This again will afford greater flexibility and will often be necessary in any case, where multi-modal or through transport is involved.

15 Where and by whom is insurance to be arranged? Some importers' countries insist that it be arranged by their own national insurers. But the degree of cover and, depending upon the terms of sale, the point at which the risk in the goods changes hands, should be clearly understood by all parties.

16 Is there a possibility that the goods will be stowed on deck? If so, the credit must specifically permit such stowage and the associated risks must be properly insured.

17 Who bears the bank charges? Both parties should be absolutely clear as to which charges are for whose account. One approach might be for the customers to bear those costs arising in their country in opening the credit and for the exporter to bear the local costs of having the credit advised and confirmed.

18 Should the credit be issued subject to UCP? The answer is a definite Yes. UCP gives protection to all parties involved and is applied by virtually all banks except those in the Chinese People's Republic.

Many of the matters in the checklist and indeed the question which precedes them all – Is it really necessary to issue a letter of credit? – will be the subject of negotiation between buyer and seller and it should be borne in mind that the interests of those parties are often diametrically opposed. Table 16.1 illustrates some of these negotiating points.

The quality of a confirmation

This is a rather grey area in the handling of letters of credit.

If, say, you are a UK exporter and you have received a genuine letter of credit, subject to UCP 400 and confirmed by a UK bank, does it matter which bank is confirming, from a security point of view?

Table 16.1
Seller v. buyer: their opposing interests

Question	Seller	Buyer
Do we need an irrevocable L/C?	Yes, for security against customer risk.	No, it ties up part of my bank financing facility as collateral.
Do we need a confirmation?	Yes, for security against country risk.	No, there will be an extra cost which one way or another I will bear.
When should the credit expire?	Late enough to allow for all despatch procedures.	As soon as possible, to release my bank financing facilities.
What period should be allowed for payment?	Prefer immediate payment on presentation.	Can I have 120 days or even longer?
Should part shipment, transhipment and any ports be allowed?	Yes, I want flexibility.	No, I want my goods quickly and in one lot.
Can approximate measures and values be allowed?	Yes, if certain loose products are involved, for flexibility of production and despatch.	No, I want to know what I'm getting and how much it's going to cost.

At first glance the answer ought to be No. In the UK all banks, whatever their parentage, operate under an appropriate Bank of England licence and if they were to renege on the obligation implied by their confirmation, then surely that licence would be withdrawn? In most circumstances it probably would, but (a) can we rely on such an extreme step being taken and (b) in any case what consolation, in that event, would there be for the exporter?

To take the second question first: if, say, the London branch of a foreign bank were unable to honour its confirmation because funds were no longer available from its parent, it would for the time being be 'hard luck' for the exporter, whatever action the Bank of England were to take. In practice this has happened only very rarely but the possibility is there.

And supposing there *were* grounds for the Bank of England to withdraw the licence. With a foreign bank there might be severe diplomatic implications, sufficient perhaps, despite all the unsatisfactory circumstances, for the licence *not* to be withdrawn. Not much consolation for the exporter there either!

So the conclusion has to be that the quality of an L/C confirmation does depend upon the standing of the bank and the financial backing behind it; and where that backing emanates from a high-risk country, then in terms of security the quality of the confirmation cannot be as good as that from a well-established bank such as, say, the clearing banks in the UK.

Checking the credit

As soon as a credit is received it should be checked to see whether its terms and conditions are as originally agreed with the buyer.

In the meantime, things may have changed. The country to which the sale is being made may suddenly have run into severe economic difficulties and become short of foreign exchange; so whereas an irrevocable letter of credit had seemed adequate, now it probably needs a confirmation for added security. Manufacturing or delivery time scales may have changed and the expiry or latest shipment dates stated in or implied by the credit may no longer be realistic.

In the light of current trading conditions, therefore, the questions to be asked are:

1 Can all the terms of the credit be met, especially the shipping requirements and time constraints?
2 Does the credit give a level of security consistent with *today*'s assessment of country as well as customer risk?
3 Can the descriptions of goods and packaging and associated codes quoted in the credit be matched in the documents to be presented against it?

If the credit is unsatisfactory in any of these respects, then an amendment may be necessary and shipment should of course be withheld in the meantime.

Amendments to the credit

Getting a letter of credit amended costs time and money and it is always worth testing the risk of *not* amending it.

If, for instance, a goods description has been misspelt, it may be simpler, rather than to amend the credit, to ensure that the misspelt version, as well as the correct spelling, is shown on the invoice. This is usually acceptable to the banks, but it is worthwhile checking with them beforehand.

Settlement methods

If a term of payment is shown, say, as thirty days from date of delivery, rather than as a required thirty days from date of shipment, what is the effective difference in the time being granted for settlement? And is the difference sufficient to go to the trouble and risk of having the credit amended? Better perhaps, on this occasion only, to allow the longer effective period of credit and show thirty days from delivery on the invoice.

Where, however, a credit has to be amended, time is of the essence.

All necessary amendments should be notified in one operation to the customer, who should be asked to ensure rapid processing of the changes. In especially important cases, it is often worth progressing the amendments from the advising bank end as well (although advising banks have no formal obligation in this area). Such a two-pronged attack at least apprises all concerned, and it is to be hoped will ensure speedy transmission of the amendments. All slow responses should be followed up.

When the amendments are forthcoming, provided they are not rejected within a reasonable time by the beneficiary, they are deemed to be part of the credit; and the relevant documents should then be presented as soon as they are complete.

On occasions, exporters have been known to receive unsolicited amendments to irrevocable letters of credit. There is no obligation to accept such amendments and failure to acknowledge one should not be taken by the advising bank as the exporter's tacit acceptance of it. The Uniform Customs and Practice (Article 10d) makes it very clear that irrevocable letters of credit can only be cancelled or amended with the agreement of all the parties – the issuing bank, the confirming bank (if there is one) and the beneficiary.

The same article also makes it clear, however, that partial acceptance of amendments contained in one and the same advice of amendment is not effective without the agreement of all those parties.

Sometimes the exact meaning of a credit may not be absolutely clear and an amendment might be avoided by the exporters checking out their own written interpretation of it with the advising bank and asking the latter if they will accept documents on the basis of that interpretation.

Presenting the documents

At this point far too many exporters come to grief. They quite simply do not understand the importance of getting their documentation absolutely correct and consistent with the conditions of the credit; nor, it often seems, the importance of meeting *both* deadlines for presentation.

The documents themselves fall into two categories – those raised by the exporters and those raised by external parties.

Documents raised by the exporters

These can be controlled by the exporters and they should have no excuses for not producing them accurately and on time. Quite often, whilst the invoice is being raised in one department, the bill of exchange may be being prepared in another and so on. The credit management function may not have responsibility for raising any of the documents, but it should, within the scheme of organization, have the power to urge their production and co-ordinate the timely assembly of each complete set.

Documents raised externally

Exporters often complain that, when it comes to presenting documents against a letter of credit, they are in the hands of shipping companies, insurance companies, inspection agencies and others such as consulates. The security offered by a letter of credit operation, however, is such that it is not unreasonable to devote considerable time and resource to ensuring that such outside bodies produce the documentation as quickly as possible to meet the time constraints of the credit.

This may, for instance, dictate that information required *by* an inspection company, to enable them to issue a required certificate, be given a high priority rating amongst an array of competing tasks. The establishment of good personal relationships with these outside bodies, upon whom the exporter is so reliant, will also help to keep the documentation coming through in a timely fashion. Other ways can also often be found to avoid delays – insurance companies, for instance, will often allow certificates to be raised on their behalf under a blanket policy.

Unusual certificates

Credits will sometimes call for some unusual requirement, perhaps beyond the previous experience of the exporter. Advice should be sought from the exporter's bank, but when no specific source is stipulated, very often it will be sufficient to make the required statement in the form of a simple certificate signed by an official of the exporting company. At first glance, the following special condition in a credit might seem formidable: 'The beneficiary of the Letter of Credit is obligated and responsible to arrange in such a manner to make possible the inspections by the surveyor to be conducted orderly and efficiently.'

Not altogether clear what is required, is it? But if the exporter simply issues a document certifying that all this will be done, that should be sufficient for the bank to which documents are presented. The bank, remember, is dealing in documents at their face value, *not* goods or intentions. That said, it does of course behove the exporter to make it possible for the inspection agency surveyor to carry out his duties in an orderly and efficient fashion!

Checking the documents

In this part of the operation exporters should be trying to 'outsmart' the banks, by spotting the very discrepancies which, if left as they are, will assuredly be found by the banks and possibly lead to a delay in payment or even the failure of the credit.

It should be remembered that it is not only a question of checking documents against the credit. Each document must be consistent with every other document.

Like the banks, the exporter should work to a disciplined system using a custom-designed form to ensure that everything that should be checked is checked. In many areas it is just a question of matching detail on the credit with detail on one or more of the documents. Where, however, the credit is silent on a particular topic, the underlying rule per UCP needs to be established and understood.

Checklists

Most banks and export-related organizations produce very comprehensive checklists of points to be considered when checking documents, one with another and against the letter of credit, prior to presentation, and exporters concerned with credits should make full use of these. The list of pitfalls which follows has been distilled from several exporters' practical and often bitter experience.

276

Letters of credit – documentation pitfalls

Invoice

- Value exceeds amount of credit with no tolerance allowed.
- Unit prices not as indicated in credit.
- Description of goods differs from description in credit.
- Description of packing differs from description in credit.
- Omission of price/delivery basis and shipment terms (FOB, CIF, C & F or whatever).
- Inclusion of charges not specifically allowed in the credit.
- Not certified, legalized, notarized, signed or witnessed as stipulated in the credit.
- Buyer's name and address is not exactly as shown in the credit.
- Does not include wording such as 'as per pro forma . . .' when it has been included in the goods description in the credit.
- Import licence number not shown, although the credit specifies this should be done.

Bill of lading (B/L)

- Not presented in full sets when requested – if a credit calls for a set of, say, three originals, then this number must be provided, properly signed and all signed negotiable copies must be submitted unless the credit states otherwise.
- Not taken out in the name of the party specified in the credit.
- Alterations and obvious additions not correctly authenticated by the shipping company or their agents.
- Not a 'clean' B/L, that is, it bears a 'clause', not permitted by the credit, indicating that the condition or packaging of the merchandise is defective.
- Credit calls for a Shipped on Board B/L, whereas the 'received for shipment' bill of lading presented does not bear a 'shipped on board' notation, which would need to be dated and signed by the carrier or agent.
- Not 'blank' endorsed when drawn to order, as specified by the credit. (This endorsement can only be made by the party indicated as the shipper on the bill of lading.)
- Not endorsed over to bank or buyer when the credit so specifies. (This endorsement can only be made by the party indicated as the shipper on the bill of lading.)

- Specified notify parties not shown (carriers or agents will not normally show more than two 'notify parties').
- Not marked 'freight paid' or 'freight prepaid' in cases of CIF/C & F shipments (the words 'freight payable at . . .' or 'freight to be pre-paid' do not constitute evidence of the actual payment of freight).
- Freight amount not shown, although credit specifies it should be. (Some shipping lines refuse to show such detail anyway for legal reasons – in which case an amendment to the credit will be necessary.)
- Dated later than the latest shipment date specified in the credit (NB the date of the 'on board' notation will be the date of shipment in the case of a converted 'received for shipment' bill of lading).
- Shipping mark not identical to that shown in other documents and/or does not include the port of discharge.
- Shipment made from a port or to a destination other than that allowed by the credit.
- Weights differ from those shown in other documents.
- 'To his or their assigns' has not been deleted and initialled by the carrier or agent, when credit specifies a 'straight consigned' bill of lading.
- Claused 'shipped on deck' but not specifically authorized by the credit.
- Other types of bill of lading presented, although not specifically authorized, for example charter party and forwarding agents' bills would not be acceptable unless expressly allowed in the credit. However, unless otherwise specified in the credit, bills of lading of the following nature *are* acceptable, provided they fulfil all the relevant requirements of UCP.
  - A through bill of lading issued by a shipping company or their agents even though it covers several modes of transport.
  - A short-form bill of lading (that is, a bill of lading issued by a shipping company or their agents which indicates some or all of the conditions of carriage by reference to a source or document other than the bill of lading).
  - A bill of lading issued by a shipping company or their agents covering unitized cargoes, eg those on pallets or in containers.

Air waybill

- The description of the goods, though only in general terms, is clearly not consistent with that shown in the credit. (Under UCP a general description is allowed even though that in the credit may be detailed: Article 41c.)

- The date of the flight does not comply with the latest date of despatch stipulated in the credit.
- Not signed by the issuing carriers or their agent.
- Absence of authenticated 'flight date' stamp where required.

Insurance certificate or policy

Note: When a policy is called for under a credit, a certificate is not acceptable. However, a policy is generally acceptable when a certificate is called for.

- The amount of cover is insufficient or does not include all the risks stipulated in the credit.
- Not issued in the same currency as the credit.
- Not endorsed correctly in accordance with the credit terms or not signed.
- Certificate or policy bears a date later than date of shipment (unless the shipment date is separately specified in the insurance document).
- Goods are not correctly described.
- Alterations are not authenticated.
- Does not cover transhipment when the bill of lading indicates that transhipment will occur.
- Does not specifically cover 'on deck', including jettison and washing overboard, when bills of lading bear the 'on deck' clause.

Certificate of origin

- Insufficient time allowed for legalization where this is called for. (Delays in chambers of commerce and consular offices can be considerable.)

Clean report of findings/inspection certificate

One or both of these documents are a common requirement for a number of countries. When shipments are planned it is important to take into account the delays that frequently occur in arranging inspection and obtaining these documents from the inspection company.

Other documents

Numerous other documents can be called for in credits. Wherever they are required in the form of a certificate, then they must be signed.

Assembling the documents for presentation

When satisfied with the content of the documents, exporters should collect them up, in the number and in the sequence specified by the credit, and despatch them by the fastest appropriate means to the bank. This may mean using a courier or messenger and it is important to obtain a receipt, evidencing the date and time of delivery at the bank.

Remember, if documents are delivered as late as the expiry date of the credit, or on the last day specified as the allowed number of days from date of shipment, they must be into the bank before it shuts its doors for the day to the public.

When the bank finds discrepancies

No matter how diligently the exporter checks the credit and the documents, banks will still spot discrepancies and withhold payment whilst they wait for them to be corrected.

The first question the exporter has to ask is: 'Is it really a discrepancy?'

At times it may not be. According to value, documents presented against letters of credit may be checked by one or maybe two bank checkers of varying seniority. The more junior checkers may err too far on the side of caution – and there are inevitably 'grey areas' open to interpretation in the UCP.

If an exporter feels that a perfectly reasonable documentation feature is being misrepresented as discrepant, they should challenge it – quickly! Quite often, dubious discrepancies are notified by foreign bank branches and, in cases of difficulty it is worth taking counsel from the exporter's own, established bankers. Most such established banks have strong documentary credit units, who may be able to persuade their foreign bank colleagues that their interpretation is too stringent.

Most times, however, discrepancies discovered by the banks are genuine and for the exporter time is then of the essence. The discrepancies must be put right as quickly as possible! If, however, they cannot be put right within the prescribed time limit from date of shipment or before the expiry of the credit, then the exporter is at risk. The very security which the credit was supposed to have bestowed can well be lost.

There may be ways to salvage the situation, depending upon the co-operation of the customers and their country's foreign exchange availability, but most letters of credit have their origins in the unreliable state of one or other of those factors. The choices available in this situation are:

(a) the advising/confirming bank may telex the issuing bank for their or their customer's agreement to accept the discrepant documents before the limitation dates;

(b) the documents may be sent out 'in trust' after the limitation dates and, if all parties agree that the transaction may be completed, then appropriate aspects of UCP will still apply;

(c) the documents may be sent out 'on collection', the status of the transaction thereby taking on the mantle of a documentary collection (see Chapter 15).

Whilst all this is going on, arrangements might be made for the bank to pay the value of the exporter's invoice under indemnity, or in the case of larger corporations, under reserve. Either way, if things go wrong, the bank can claw its money back, plus interest!

The moral in all this might be best illustrated by the case of the uninformed exporter who shipped goods to Tanzania in 1981 in the belief that the corresponding L/C confirmation gave him absolute security. It would have done, if he had got his documentation right. He didn't. Seven years later he was still waiting for his money!

SPECIAL TYPES OF CREDIT

Variants of all the different types and forms of credit described above arise when special trading circumstances dictate.

Transferable credits

A credit specifically designated as 'transferable' can be used by traders, standing between supplier and buyer, to avoid using more than a limited amount of their own funds in the transaction.

The overseas buyer arranges for the credit to be issued in favour of the traders, who then request their bank to transfer it to the supplier, the 'second beneficiary'. A transfer fee is payable at the time of the request. The supplier's documents are then presented for payment.

Thereafter the traders present their documents to the transferring bank and in effect receive settlement of their invoice less the value of the supplier's invoice. Thus the traders get their profit on the deal.

All this is not, however, as easy as it sounds. For a start, advising banks are not obliged to transfer a credit even though it is clearly stated to be transferable. The terms and conditions of the credit applicable to both the traders and the supplier must be identical except for the amount of the credit, the unit price, latest shipment date and expiry date.

For credits from some countries, beset by strict exchange control and import regulations, transfer can often prove impracticable. Nevertheless, for merchanting trade transferable credits can prove to be a particularly valuable instrument.

Back-to-back credits

As an alternative to transferring a credit, traders may choose to receive a credit from their buyer, and themselves have a second credit issued in favour of the supplier.

The two credits are linked, inasmuch as the trader's bank issuing the second credit will take the first credit as its security; and as with transferable credits only a few specified terms and conditions may differ.

These kinds of operations can however be very complex and banks are becoming increasingly reluctant to handle them, especially when a transferable credit will normally achieve the required result.

Counter credits

Counter credits work like back-to-back credits as far as the terms and conditions being the same, except for amount, unit price, latest shipment date and expiry date. But the ultimate buyer's credit is not regarded as security for the bank which issues the second credit on behalf of the traders in favour of their supplier. The traders must therefore provide separate collateral to their bankers to support the issue of their credit. As we have seen earlier, this will normally be by way of utilizing part of whatever financing facility the traders already enjoy from their bankers.

Assignment of proceeds

As a much simpler method of passing on the proceeds of a buyer's letter of credit, a trader can request the bank, either when presenting documents or when payment is due, to assign all or part of the proceeds to a third party.

The banks are not obliged to comply with such a request and may do so only on certain conditions. In addition, under such an assignment arrangement there is no security for the supplier who at best may receive a letter of comfort from the bank.

Where, however, there is a high degree of trust between trader and supplier, assignment can help the trader to operate profitably on a minimum of working capital.

Red clause credits

Red clause credits can be used by the beneficiary of a credit to obtain an advance, before the credit is properly utilized, to finance manufacture or purchase of the goods to be supplied. The consent of all parties to the credit is required.

This particular kind of credit gets its name from the way in which the appropriate clause permitting the advance used to be inscribed or highlighted in red ink.

A rarely encountered variant is the green clause credit, which also caters for an advance to cover storage costs at the port of shipment.

Revolving credits

The act of having a credit opened uses up part of the financing facilities available to a customer from their bankers. Customers are therefore naturally reluctant to have credits opened for too large a value or for too long a time.

If a contract provides for, say, twelve monthly shipments of equal value over the next year, it is thus in the customer's interest to arrange for a revolving credit to be opened for a value equivalent to one shipment. So long as each shipment is paid promptly, the credit can revolve on to the next one and so on.

Revolving credits can be cumulative or non-cumulative. The former enables unused amounts from, say, the month one shipment to be carried forward into month two. Such accumulation is not available with non-cumulative revolving credits.

Standby credits

Standby credits are used in the main as a substitute for guarantees. This application originated in the USA, where most states forbid the issue of bank guarantees, but standby credits are now common in Europe and elsewhere. They are in effect 'on demand' credits which can only be activated by the beneficiary if certain conditions are not met, for example, if settlement of a sale is not properly made under an open account arrangement backed by the standby guarantee.

Clearly a great deal of trust is required in the buyer/seller relationship before a buyer will be persuaded to open a standby letter of credit.

FRAUDULENT CREDITS

There has been some increase in the last few years in the number of credits which have been found to be fraudulent. Some are so juvenile in their construction as to be laughable; others represent very sophisticated frauds, based on stolen authentic forms and considerable research.

Chapter 27 gives several examples of documentary fraud. Suffice it to say here, from a credit manager's viewpoint:

(a) the Uniform Customs and Practice (Art. 8) states that the advising bank 'shall take reasonable care to check the apparent authenticity of the credit which it advises' and in the view of many experts this does not exonerate exporters from being on their guard;
(b) any credit received other than through a bona fide advising bank, or on occasions direct from the issuing bank, should be viewed with the utmost suspicion;
(c) equally suspicious would be a credit (except from the Chinese People's Republic) which does not state that it is issued subject to UCP 400.

FUTURE DEVELOPMENTS

Talk about the future for letters of credit with the idealists and the discussion will turn naturally to standardization and simplification of procedures and electronic data processing and transmission.

Just pipe dreams or reality?

Many credit managers are both hopeful and cynical about these concepts. Hopeful because we are full of admiration for those who strive to harmonize and simplify the many L/C processes and we know we have to start somewhere. Cynical, because we equally know that the increase in the use of documentary credits has been mainly caused by the world debt crisis and a lack of trust in both countries and customers. The very factors that make credits necessary are regrettably the same factors that for some time will militate against the ideals we would all like to achieve.

In point of fact a few test cases with some large oil business credits have pointed the way ahead to electronic data processing and transmission. Documents have been produced electronically, guaranteed consistent one with the other, and with much greater speed than is normal for the kind of transaction involved. But the trials required priority attention at the correct time by all concerned, and powers of attorney for the bank to print all necessary documents on behalf of the exporter, the insurance company and the shipping company – and finally there was still no alternative but to check the consistent documents against the letter of credit manually.

To extrapolate all that to the scale and variety of documentary credit transactions we all encounter would need immense resource. Nevertheless, it has to be a laudable step in the right direction.

FINALE

To sum up this chapter, the documentary credit melodrama is full of difficulties, threats and pitfalls, but the real villain of the piece is nearly always bad documentation. Improve it and you improve export profitability.

Recommended reading

Davis, M.A. (1988) *The Documentary Credits Handbook*. Cambridge: Woodhead-Faulkner.

Hedley, William. (1986) *Bills of Exchange and Bankers' Documentary Credits*. London: Lloyd's of London Press.

McCullough, Burton V. (Looseleaf update, March 1987.) *Letters of Credit*. Albany, NY: Matthew Bender.

Rowe, Michael. (1985) *Letters of Credit*. Milton Keynes: Euromoney. Looks at the uses of documentary credits and letters of credit in general on international operations, and places these instruments in the context of the overall commercial deal.

Schmitthoff, Clive M. (1986) *Schmitthoff's Export Trade*. 8th edn. London: Stevens & Sons. The standard English work on this subject.

Crédit Suisse, *Documentary credits, Documentary collections, Bank Guarantees, Publication Vol. 69*. One of many excellent free booklets published by the major banks.

International Chamber of Commerce, (1983) *Uniform Customs and Practice for Documentary Credits*. ICC Publication No. 400. Paris: ICC.

International Chamber of Commerce, (1983) *Guide to Documentary Credit Operations*. ICC Publication No. 415. Paris: ICC.

17

Countertrade

Simon Harris

There is no universally accepted definition of countertrade. All countertraders have their own ideas. What is clear is that countertrade is used as an inclusive term for all forms of trading mechanisms involving an element of reciprocity. The sale of goods (tangible or intangible) to an export market is made conditional upon the importing country receiving a reciprocal benefit through a link being made, directly or indirectly, with purchases of its own products and resources.

The element of reciprocity is orientated around the importing country's desire to protect and stimulate its economy, primarily by balancing, at least partially, foreign exchange expenditures.

As an example, countertrade often occurs where a country does not have convertible currency to pay for a priority import. Instead, export products are made available in settlement. These generate the necessary convertible currency to pay for the import.

Countertrade is therefore not necessarily trade without money, the exception being the few remaining cases of classic barter, involving the straight exchange of goods. All other forms of countertrade involve the use of money in some way.

The boundaries of what constitutes countertrade are forever widening as more and more complex and innovative transactions are contemplated. In particular, the ability to link countertrade with financial products and mechanisms enhances the ability to formulate non-conventional solutions to trade-related problems that would otherwise go unresolved.

WHY COUNTERTRADE?

Trade in its earliest form was based on countertrade. The exchange of goods for other goods under barter transactions formed the foundation of commerce as we know it and, arguably, the very survival of the human race.

Over many centuries barter was gradually overshadowed by the widespread use of money as the primary medium for exchange and valuation. Today, money continues to offer unequalled trading flexibility and liquidity, for those countries that can generate it in sufficient quantities.

The imperfections in the distribution of the world's resources and in its economic and monetary systems restrict and sometimes stifle the rate of growth and development of many less fortunate nations. In recent years many economies have been dominated by inflation, liquidity problems, huge balance of trade deficits, foreign exchange shortages, massive foreign indebtedness and, consequently, new financial regulations. As a result, a more subjective commercial environment has been created with financial institutions adopting a more conservative lending policy, both on an individual corporate and country risk basis.

Restrictions in the availability of traditional forms of trade financing, acute shortages of foreign exchange, wild fluctuations in commodity pricing and over-supply have caused many countries to turn to alternative methods of financing their trade, whilst at the same time attempting to achieve their economic objectives. Countertrade can obviate, ease or at least help contain such problems. The expertise and worldwide networks of a new breed of countertraders can be instrumental in the expansion of markets and enable importers and exporters alike to be brought together easily and with the minimum of risk.

Advantages to a nation of a countertrade policy

1 To implement a selective import programme in spite of foreign exchange shortages and credit restrictions.
2 To help balance overseas trade and achieve other economic objectives.
3 To clear surpluses of products at times of market over-supply.
4 To establish incremental sales of traditional products and/or to expand exports of non-traditional goods.
5 To exploit a buyer's market (in respect of the import) to negotiate the best terms and/or generate additional benefit for the economy.
6 To increase employment and generate prosperity.

WHO COUNTERTRADES AND WHO DOESN'T

Less developed countries (LDCs)

More and more countries are turning to countertrade to help relieve economic pressures and most LDCs fall into this group. It largely comprises the LDCs in Africa, parts of the Middle East, Asia, and Central and South America.

These are the countries with limited resources, with infrastructure and industry in the early stages of development and, therefore, a restricted capacity to generate convertible currency to sustain ever increasing import requirements and service possibly huge foreign indebtedness. They are the poorest and often the hardest hit when recession and unease shake the world markets and when demand and pricing fall in respect of their few staple products, which are their lifeline.

Countertrade is used to obtain priority imports, to clear surpluses of traditional products, create new export markets and balance foreign exchange expenditures. But the volume of business transacted in this way is often restricted by the limited availability of exportable products of an acceptable quality.

More and more LDCs are formulating specific countertrade policies, which should outline 1) the parameters within which countertrade is acceptable, and 2) how a transaction should be progressed. For the countertrader, this should help lessen the often extensive organizational and bureaucratic delays experienced in obtaining the ministerial and central bank authorities which are usually required for countertrade transactions to proceed.

Semi-industrialized countries (SICs)

SICs are vulnerable economies, mainly in the southern hemisphere, with a relatively young and growing industrial presence, probably dependent on massive foreign debt and the import of large volumes of raw materials. They are hungry for new export markets, but their products face stiff competition from established foreign manufacturers.

Countertrade is used to develop new markets for industrial products (export-led countertrade) and/or for the procurement of raw materials (import-led countertrade) or to help balance foreign trade in an overall sense.

Settlement methods

SICs engage in countertrade with Western industrialized countries in the northern hemisphere (north/south countertrade), but the development of business with LDCs is becoming increasingly important (south/south countertrade). The LDCs, with their limited industrial development, offer both new and less demanding markets for industrial products and ready sources of raw materials.

East European countries

Exporters interested in East European markets should be aware that countertrade has played an important role in the development of these nations ever since the end of the Second World War. It is commonly used in trade between East European countries and is becoming increasingly important in trade with the West.

Countertrade with Western industrialized countries is largely based on the concept of counterpurchase obligations – 'if we buy some of your goods, you must buy some of ours'. An East European country's foreign trade, including countertrade, is handled by a number of foreign trade organizations (FTOs) each of which has its own product sector to look after. The limiting factor here is that the FTO handling the import of the Western products will usually also supply the counterpurchase goods for export (that is, within the same product sector). This means a restriction on the products that the country will provide to enable the foreign exporter to fulfil the counterpurchase obligation. It is not usual for more than one FTO to be involved in a single countertrade transaction. Co-operation between FTOs under countertrade transactions is infrequent, the few exceptions relating to high value, high priority transactions.

In common with so many nations throughout the world, the East European countries have felt the pressure of international recession and the FTOs are placed under increasing pressure to balance their foreign trade books. Thus higher levels of counterpurchase result.

Viennese banks and trading houses have historically played an important role in East European countertrade. They have been instrumental in finding markets (often in LDCs) for the growing volume of East European industrial products supplied by way of countertrade.

These nations also transact an increasing proportion of foreign trade by way of bilateral trading agreements with SICs (notably Brazil and India) and LDCs throughout the world. These provide East European nations with regular supplies of raw materials and other manufactured products as well as ready markets for their exports. Imbalances in trade under bilateral arrangements sometimes result from a deficiency in the demand for East European products from the overseas partners. These imbalances give rise to a further form of countertrade called 'switch trading', whereby a third party Western nation can fill the gap by exporting its preferred products to an overseas partner instead. Once again, the Viennese have built up considerable expertise in this specialist form of countertrade.

Western industrialized countries

This group is based closely on the countries that belong to the Organisation for Economic Cooperation and Development (OECD), notably the USA, Canada and European countries in the northern hemisphere and Japan, Australia and New Zealand in the southern hemisphere.

These are the more fortunate nations with the resources to generate sufficient convertible currency and the ready ability to raise and service credit to allow their foreign trade to proceed generally without a need to countertrade.

Countertrade is often not promoted and is sometimes actively discouraged because it is regarded as a threat to the multilateral trading system which is characterized by competition, free bargaining, openness and convertible currency.

The system is not perfect and some nations, including the USA and the UK, have adopted a middle of the road attitude towards countertrade. This is generally for the following reasons.

1 They acknowledge that countertrade is playing an increasingly important role in trade with LDCs, SICs and East European countries. They realize that in order to remain competitive, maintain and increase market share and create new markets, exporting companies must become more actively involved in countertrade and the more dynamic among them will even be adopting a proactive (as opposed to reactive) stance towards it. Many governments now provide support and assistance on countertrade to exporters. In the UK the Department of Trade and Industry (DTI), through its Project and Export Policy Division, provides an advisory service in relation to countertrade matters.

2 Export credit agencies, such as the UK's Export Credits Guarantee Department (ECGD), have in general been opposed to counter-

trade. They would only consider a financing proposal incorporating an element of reciprocity, provided the credit risk could stand alone, independent of the countertrade even if in practice it would provide the primary source of repayment.

Some export credit agencies are beginning to take a more pragmatic view of countertrade, both as a source of repayment for new credits and as a means of getting at least some of their money back under recovery situations.

3   Large, usually high-technology contracts between industrialized nations, particularly in the defence and aerospace industries, often include an element of offset (described later). This can offer the buying nation various reciprocal benefits including the generation of orders for its own products, increased employment, transfers of technology and the chance, at least partially, to balance foreign exchange expenditures.

4   Australia and New Zealand have both set in place specific countertrade policies, primarily based on offset. An element of reciprocity is called for in bids from overseas companies for public sector contracts. The policy is designed to promote technology and skills transfer to make the countries more self-sufficient and to increase export capacity.

5   Some countries, such as Greece, Portugal and Spain, recognize how countertrade can stimulate an economy, particularly through the preservation of foreign exchange resources, additionality and increased employment. Consequently, they are opening their doors to countertrade on a selective basis.

TYPES OF COUNTERTRADE

There are six widely discussed countertrade mechanisms.

1   Barter and evidence account transactions.
2   Counterpurchase and counterpurchase obligations.
3   Compensation or 'buy-back'.
4   Offset.
5   Bilateral trade agreements.
6   Switch trade.

Although countertrade is a specialized, non-conventional trading medium, in practice it uses conventional banking services and trading

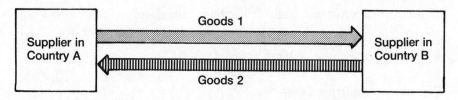

Figure 17.1   Barter

tools, such as documentary letters of credit (L/Cs), bills for collection, international payment mechanisms and guarantees, to achieve its objectives and this should be borne in mind in considering the following detailed reviews.

Barter and evidence account transactions

It is a common misconception for the word 'barter' to be used as the generic term for all forms of reciprocal trade. This is incorrect. Barter is itself a form of countertrade.

It is the oldest, but now the least used countertrade mechanism – a simultaneous exchange of goods (tangible or intangible) for other goods without the involvement of money; often a once-only transaction bound by a single commercial contract.

In practice the Western supplier in country A (Figure 17.1) might delay shipment of its products until it is sure that country B's goods have been shipped first.

A more complex structure can be used to record the two-way flow of goods between commercial parties in countries A and B up to a specific total value (for example US$5 million each way) and over a fixed period of time (say twelve months). The two-way flow of trade would be recorded over notional *evidence accounts* maintained and mirrored by a bank in each country. It would be pre-agreed that imbalances in the value of goods shipped in either direction would be cleared periodically (each quarter perhaps) or within a stated period (ninety days for instance) following the end of the term of the arrangement, by settlement in convertible currency or by a balancing shipment of goods. This overall structure is similar in concept to government-to-government bilateral trade agreements.

Counterpurchase

Counterpurchase is the most extensively used form of countertrade.

293

Settlement methods

There are two distinct counterpurchase concepts:

- Classic counterpurchase
- Counterpurchase obligations.

Classic counterpurchase

Classic counterpurchase is often used in countertrade with LDCs and SICs.

An LDC lacks readily available convertible currency to pay for a priority import. Instead, the country makes available its own goods for export (the counterpurchase or offtake goods), the hard currency proceeds of which are specifically used to pay for the import (the principal products).

There are normally two separate underlying commercial contracts involved:

(a) one between the exporter of the LDC's counterpurchase goods and an overseas buyer;
(b) one between the foreign supplier and the LDC importer in respect of the principal products.

Both contracts would probably be concluded between unrelated parties, that is, separate importers and exporters within the LDC and separate foreign buyers and suppliers.

The parties would be linked together by countertrade documentation which would outline the purpose of the overall countertrade transaction, the responsibilities of the various parties involved and the banking structure for its implementation. The banking arrangements are often administered between a prime international bank (probably the principal banker to the transaction), in concert with the central bank in the LDC.

Settlement between importer and exporter within the LDC would be made in local currency via the central bank.

Counterpurchase goods are often overpriced or of an inferior quality by world market standards. In order to tempt a prospective buyer, an incentive must be given. The supplier of the principal products must subsidize the cost of the counterpurchase goods by paying a rebate or 'disagio' (see later explanation) to the buyer.

In Figure 17.2 we see an example of a counterpurchase transaction. An LDC wishes to purchase buses from West Germany. Coffee is made

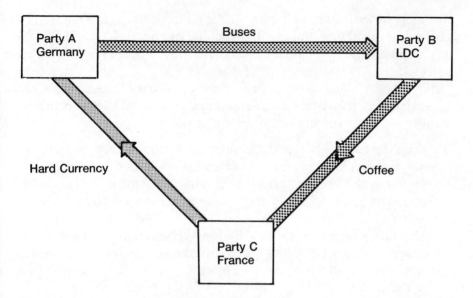

Figure 17.2   A classic counterpurchase structure

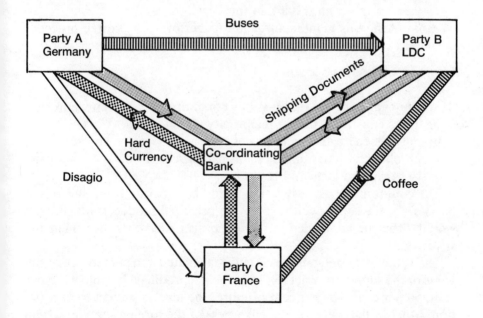

Figure 17.3   Classic counterpurchase structure showing the banking arrangements

available in settlement. A buyer for the coffee is found in France. The coffee is shipped first, thus neutralizing the risk on the LDC. The buses are shipped with settlement coming from the proceeds of the coffee sale.

Figure 17.3 relates to the same transaction with the banking structure superimposed. The overseas international bank would act as principal banker for the transaction. Let's look at the transaction again.

1 Once the coffee is shipped, the shipping documents are presented to the overseas bank under the coffee L/C. The documents are presented to the French coffee buyer against payment in convertible currency. Simultaneously, the bus manufacturer will pay the disagio to the coffee buyer.

2 The coffee proceeds are held by the overseas bank on an interest-bearing proceeds or 'escrow' account, until the buses are shipped in accordance with the terms of the bus L/C opened by the central bank in the LDC.

3 Upon presentation of (conforming) shipping documents for the buses, the German manufacturer is paid in convertible currency to the debit of the proceeds account. The shipping documents are passed to the central bank in the LDC.

4 Should the bus manufacturer fail to perform, the coffee proceeds would be held at the disposal of the LDC.

Counterpurchase obligations

'If we buy your goods you must buy some of ours' – counterpurchase obligations constitute simple reciprocity.

In order to secure an overseas sales contract, a foreign exporter enters into an obligation to make reciprocal purchases of the importing country's own products and resources.

The counterpurchase obligation would be separate from, but run in parallel to, the supply contract for the principal products, which itself would either be concluded on a cash basis or have its own financing structure.

The value of an obligation is usually calculated as a percentage of the value of the supply contract for the principal products. It could be 25 per cent, 50 per cent, 100 per cent or more: the level is subject to negotiation. Much will depend on the eagerness of the foreign supplier to win the contract, the level of competition and the priority given to the purchase of the principal products by the importing country. The lower the value of the counterpurchase obligation, the lower the potential cost to the foreign supplier.

Counterpurchase obligations are often evidenced by a memorandum of understanding (MOU) outlining the terms of the arrangement. Fulfilment of the obligation would be through the purchase of probably part traditional and part non-traditional products, which would be listed in the MOU.

Whilst the MOU would be signed by the foreign suppliers, provision is usually made for the counterpurchase obligation to be fulfilled by a third party trader on their behalf.

In its simplest and arguably cheapest form, an obligation might represent a simple statement of intent to purchase on a best endeavours basis. But it is more usual for a formal MOU to be involved which might call for a performance guarantee or at least a penalty clause to cover non-fulfilment. Non-fulfilment would probably harm the image of the foreign supplier at least in the eyes of the importing country.

Countries that have countertrade policies based on counterpurchase obligations (for example, East European countries, India, Indonesia and Malaysia) can often raise credit in international financial markets. Their countertrade policy is used to increase exports, to find new markets for their products and to help balance trade and therefore foreign exchange expenditures in an overall sense, rather than on a transaction by transaction basis (see also 'Offset', below).

Compensation or buy-back

Compensation, or buy-back, is an arrangement whereby the supplier of capital plant, manufacturing equipment or technology accepts payment, or part thereof, in goods subsequently manufactured by the equipment supplied.

This mechanism is often associated with large project-related and/or long-term contracts which can involve a lead-in time of several years before output commences. The sale of the relevant equipment would probably be the subject of a financing package in which case the proceeds of the plant output would be used in repayment.

The simple example in Figure 17.4 relates to the supply of a cement manufacturing plant by the USA to the USSR. The suppliers accept payment in the form of 30 per cent convertible currency and 70 per cent in cement produced by the plant they supplied. They may find markets for the cement themselves or engage a trader to do so.

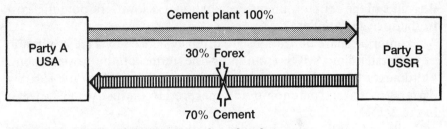

Figure 17.4   Compensation or buy-back

Through buy-back the purchasing nation can benefit from the development of its industrial base, technology transfer and assured export markets for the products subsequently manufactured.

Offset

Offset is a form of countertrade usually between industrialized nations and often associated with high-value contracts for the supply of civil or military aircraft, defence equipment and high-technology products. It is also becoming more popular with certain importing countries (Australia and New Zealand for example) seeking to accelerate their industrial development and increase export capacity.

The export contract, the subject of its own financing arrangements, is conditional upon the importing nation receiving a reciprocal benefit in return for making such a major purchase. The reciprocity could take the form of local investment, a transfer of technology or by orders being placed for the purchase of the importing nation's own products.

Direct offset

Direct (related) offset is where the principal products being supplied and the reciprocal arrangements are related:

(a) where materials, components or systems used by the exporting company, possibly but not necessarily in the manufacture of the products to be supplied, are procured from within the importing country; and/or

(b) the supply contract incorporates an element of technology transfer; and/or

(c) the products to be supplied, or at least major sub-assemblies, will be manufactured under licence within the importing country.

An example was a much publicized £850 million contract for the purchase by the UK of American Boeing AWACS aircraft, conditional upon companies in the AWACS consortium placing orders in the UK for materials and products for a total value equivalent to 130 per cent of the value of the aircraft purchased. The items procured in the UK did not have to be used in the manufacture of the aircraft, but had to be for use by AWACS consortium companies.

Indirect offset

Indirect (unrelated) offset is where the exporting company agrees to make purchases of unrelated products from the importing country.

For example, an exporter of high-technology communications equipment agrees to make purchases of unrelated industrial products which can either be sold on the home market or laid off elsewhere by a trader (similar to a counterpurchase obligation).

Some potential advantages of offset to an importing country are:

(a) reduction in imported content of a contract;
(b) elimination or at least reduction in the effect of a sizeable import on a country's balance of foreign trade and foreign currency reserves: a foreign exchange inflow could occur;
(c) transfer of technology and increased industrial development;
(d) increase in exports and/or export capability;
(e) creation of jobs.

Bilateral trade agreements

Although government-to-government trading mechanisms, bilaterals are still regarded as countertrade and a considerable volume of trade is conducted in this way. The countries involved typically have centrally planned or controlled economies and foreign exchange shortages. Bilaterals offer them assured markets for exports, regular sources of raw materials for import and balance of payments benefits.

An arrangement can vary from a statement to develop mutual trade on a best endeavours basis to a formal agreement, often with the following features.

1 An agreed volume of goods would flow in each direction during a specified period of time (say twelve months).
2 The goods to flow in each direction would probably be specified.

3 Monetary settlement between the countries should normally not be involved. Instead the each-way flow of goods is monitored by the central bank in each country through notional 'clearing accounts' maintained in an independent 'clearing currency' (usually a convertible currency such as US dollars).

4 Any imbalances which occur, whereby one country ships more goods than the other, would be cleared periodically or at the end of the term of the agreement by a balancing shipment of goods (or by a payment in convertible currency).

5 Settlement between importers and exporters within each country would be made in local currency through the central or foreign trade bank.

Bilateral trade agreements are an important feature of trade of East European countries between themselves and with LDCs and SICs. Notably, many East European countries have agreements with Brazil and India.

Figure 17.5 shows an example of a bilateral trade agreement between East Germany and Brazil involving the use of clearing accounts, maintained by the central bank in each country, to record the two-way flow of goods.

When Brazil ships goods to East Germany, instead of being paid in convertible currency it would be given a credit in the clearing account maintained by the East German central bank, equivalent to the value of the shipment. When Brazil receives goods from East Germany the clearing account would be debited. The central bank in Brazil would do the reverse and therefore the two clearing accounts should mirror each other.

Switch trading

Switch trading is a specialized form of countertrade which relates specifically to the imbalances in trade that often occur under bilateral trade agreements.

For example Brazil might have shipped substantially more goods to East Germany than it has received in return, creating a large credit balance on the clearing account maintained in East Germany (mirrored by a similar debit balance on the account maintained in Brazil).

East Germany is indebted to Brazil and should provide goods, or perhaps convertible currency, to settle the shortfall. In order to reduce

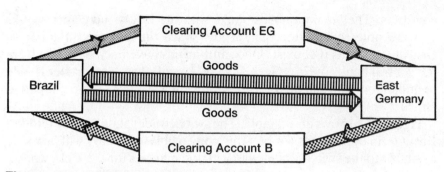

Figure 17.5 Bilateral clearing accounts

this and bring the clearing accounts more into balance, it is sometimes possible for goods sourced from a third country to be shipped to Brazil instead.

An exporting company in a third country, say the UK, interested in using bilateral clearing mechanisms to penetrate overseas markets, in this case Brazil which has stringent import regulations, would normally seek an introduction to a specialist 'switch trader'. These are banks and trading houses experienced in handling trade with East European

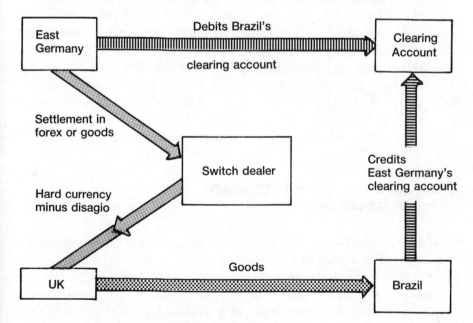

Figure 17.6 Switch trading

countries. They maintain close links with the FTOs and central banks and are able to monitor the surplus space on the large number of clearing accounts that exist. Once authorities have been obtained from the central banks in East Germany and Brazil, the switch trader is able to implement a switch operation to allow the UK goods to be shipped to Brazil.

Figure 17.6 shows an example. The switch trader stands in the middle. East German products (or possibly convertible currency) will be made available to the switch trader who will find markets for them elsewhere. The proceeds are paid, less a disagio (see later), to the UK exporter whose goods are shipped to Brazil. East Germany debits its clearing account with the appropriate value, Brazil passes a corresponding credit entry and the clearing accounts are brought more into balance. The whole operation is essentially a swap of East German goods for UK goods.

Some advantages of such switch trading are:

(a)   the East European country benefits because not only has its indebtedness to its foreign partner been reduced, but this has been achieved at an advantageous cost, since it probably provided goods to the switch trader for an equivalent value of less than 100 cents in the dollar;

(b)   whilst the third party exporters received less than 100 per cent of the quoted price for their goods (reflecting the disagio costs of the operation), they were able to make an export that otherwise would not have been possible;

(c)   the foreign partner, that is, Brazil, receives goods it has a preference for;

(d)   the clearing accounts are brought more into balance.

PARTICIPANTS IN COUNTERTRADE: THE 'COUNTERTRADERS'

The above review of the six basic countertrade mechanisms should only be regarded as a very loose guide.

In reality, countertrade is very much an *ad hoc* activity. Every transaction is different and it is difficult strictly to categorize them. There are neither ground rules nor standard procedures and the mechanisms vary according to the needs of the individual transaction. It is the countertrader's job to engineer, or tailor, a countertrade solution to a particular set of trade-related circumstances. In doing so, the countertrader will consider such things as local regulations (including countertrade policy if there is one), the type of goods being traded and the requirements of the parties involved. The result could be a structure very similar to one of the six mechanisms reviewed; it might be a hybrid incorporating elements drawn from two or three of them or, perhaps, an innovative solution which breaks new ground.

It is often costly and extraordinarily difficult to put a transaction together and bring it to fruition and a successful conclusion. It is fraught with a seemingly endless catalogue of pitfalls, problems and delays. It is a minefield for the amateur.

An involvement in countertrade requires special skills and knowledge which should be introduced at the earliest opportunity. If introduced too late, a lot of straightening out and undoing might be necessary to place the transaction on to an acceptable footing and it could also mean that costs are higher than might otherwise have been the case. The introduction of a specialist countertrader early on could mean the difference between success and failure. Experience counts.

There are a few exporting companies, usually the major multinationals, which use their trading experience and worldwide network of resources and contacts to maintain an in-house capability to handle countertrade. They are seeking to maintain and expand export markets and therefore use it not only in response to requests from buyers, but also offer it, as an extra incentive in order to win contracts. But, for the majority of those considering countertrade, it is usually essential to employ the services of a specialist. So who are the specialists, the 'countertraders'? Excluding the large corporates mentioned above, there are three principal types of player in the market place. These offer their expertise to exporters interested in countertrade:

- Large commodity traders
- Banks
- Independent consultants/agents.

Large commodity traders

Leading trading houses may specialize in trading a particular commodity or commodity group, be it metals, grains, fruit and vegetables, oil or whatever. Some have the capacity to handle a wide range of products and goods, including industrial products and consumer goods sourced from SICs.

Many such traders actively countertrade in the following ways:

1 They will use it selectively to maximize their trading returns.
2 Like other exporters they might be obliged to countertrade to penetrate a particular overseas market.
3 They use to advantage their worldwide trading ability to trade in those products offered under countertrade transactions. As buyers thereof they can reduce the costs and improve profit margins through the receipt of disagio payments.
4 They engineer countertrade transactions on their own behalf using their in-house expertise to trade out the offtake products and look for suppliers of suitable return products who are willing to absorb the required disagio, in order to make an export which might otherwise not be possible.

Those most actively involved in countertrade can therefore provide a wide range of useful services and opportunities for the exporter.

1 They will help structure, negotiate and document the countertrade transaction and, most importantly, act as principals in contracting to purchase the offtake products. They are nevertheless reliant on their bankers to provide the necessary services which constitute the banking structure for the transaction.
2 They can simply act as buyers of and thus take title to, the offtake products. In so doing they are prepared to be a signatory to counter-trade arrangements structured and administered by banks and large corporates.
3 For a market-related fee, they are willing to take over responsibility for the fulfilment of counterpurchase obligations.
4 The countertrade transactions engineered by the traders themselves can open up useful opportunities for exporters seeking to penetrate potential overseas markets which are short of foreign exchange and/or unable to raise credit and/or which have compulsory counter-trade requirements.

Banks

A common misconception is that banks are not countertraders at all, that their only use is as providers of traditional banking services and as administrators of proceeds accounts required under countertrade transactions arranged elsewhere. Let's look at the reality.

Banks have long-standing relationships with governments, central banks, companies and traders worldwide – in fact, all the parties likely to be involved in countertrade. However, although Viennese banks have been involved with East European countertrade for many years, it was only in the early 1980s, which saw a significant increase in the volume of countertrade, that some of the major international banks perceived the important role they could play in countertrade arrangements.

Today, some banks that have accumulated countertrade knowledge still take a relatively passive role. They will only go as far as assisting an exporter in an advisory capacity, preferring subsequently to make an introduction to a trading house which ultimately would be better placed to satisfy the exporter's requirements.

But there are a handful of very much more active banks that place themselves competitively in the forefront of the countertrade market. They have set up specialist units which can combine a comprehensive range of countertrade skills, traditional banking services and both conventional and non-conventional financing products to provide innovative solutions to trade-related problems.

Like everything else in countertrade, the role of such banks will vary from transaction to transaction, but the services they can provide include the following principal elements.

1 To review a company's export opportunities, identify potential for countertrade and implement a programme.
2 To introduce parties to a transaction, as appropriate, and bring them together in complete confidentiality.
3 To review the details of the underlying circumstances, propose how a countertrade solution should be pursued and suggest ways of overcoming operational difficulties and minimizing risks.
4 To structure the transaction and create the necessary countertrade documentation.
5 Those banks that have a trading capacity may act as principals in purchasing the offtake products.
6 To introduce, as appropriate, specialist suppliers and/or takers of specific products traded under countertrade transactions. (Through worldwide networks of clients and contacts, the banks

have special relationships with product suppliers and end-users as well as with the trading houses.)

7   To assist with the negotiation of the countertrade with the commercial parties involved and with the acquisition of the necessary government and central bank authorities and approvals that are usually necessary before a transaction can proceed.

8   To act as principal banker for the transaction, maintaining full control over its operation from start to finish and providing the required banking facilities to the parties concerned (subject to the bank's usual credit criteria). Such banking facilities could include the opening, advising and confirming of L/Cs, the operation of proceeds and/or evidence accounts and the issuing of bonds or guarantees, as appropriate.

9   The ability to introduce finance into a transaction (see 'Financing', below).

10 To work closely with the private insurance market. It is possible to cover a number of non-bankable performance/political risks through specialized markets in London and New York. Policies can be tailored to a given set of circumstances.

11 To act as countertrade advisers to governments, central banks, development banks, companies and individuals worldwide.

One of a bank's primary strengths in countertrade is its ability to act as an impartial intermediary to both sides of the transaction. Although the bank will primarily be representing its client, whichever party that is, it can be viewed by all the parties to the transaction, be they importers, exporters, government ministries or central banks, as a major financial institution that will wish to ensure that not only does the transaction proceed satisfactorily, but that its own name and reputation remain unblemished. For this reason, a bank's involvement can often enhance the chances of a transaction being brought to fruition and successfully concluded.

Some banks have built up enviable reputations based on successfully concluded transactions and will handle all types of countertrade, from barter to switch. Their approach is often both reactive and proactive, with clients bringing deals to them and the banks engineering transactions to take to their clients.

Independent consultants/agents

These are usually individuals or small companies. Some simply provide advice and assistance on countertrade matters, whilst others offer a more extensive range of services encompassing the structuring of transactions, the placing of countertrade products and the management of the arrangement. A few will consider taking title to countertraded products.

Most consultants may be dependent on the banks and trading houses to complement the services they can provide. At the same time they will also be competing with them for business.

For the exporter, the consultant can provide valuable assistance, particularly those that specialize in particular types of countertrade (for example, product related buy-back or offset) or specific markets (such as Eastern Europe, India, Indonesia or China).

THE COSTS (AND THE SAVINGS)

Each of the specialist countertraders will charge for their services. Their fees will vary according to the nature of the services provided and the size and complexity of the transaction, but they are competitively based and generally good value for the expertise and work involved. Out-of-pocket expenses, including any travel costs, may be extra. In addition, the exporter must also consider any banking cost of the operation which may fall outside the countertrader's fees. The latter might include L/C fees, including any confirmation charges (which could be significant) and funds transmission costs. But the countertrader's fees can often be relatively insignificant when compared with the costs of selling the counterpurchase or offtake products into the world market. This is the real cost of countertrade.

LDCs and SICs will often not allow their staple, cash-earning products to be used for countertrade unless surpluses exist and/or new, additional markets are being created. It is more usual for second-string, non-traditional products to be offered, but these may be of an inferior or substandard quality in world market terms. In order to protect the existing export markets for their goods and ensure additionality, stringent destination restrictions may be imposed which make the placing of the goods even more difficult. To compound all of this, the supplying country will have its own idea of pricing for the goods, which is often in excess of the world market value.

So why should potential buyers change their normal purchasing pattern and consider countertraded goods? They must be given an

307

incentive. In practice the supplier of the principal products back into the country concerned will be responsible for paying a 'disagio' (that is, a subsidy) to the buyer of the offtake goods to bring their cost down to an acceptable level.

In Figure 17.3 the French coffee buyer will have negotiated a price for the coffee with the supplier in the LDC. Based on this pricing, the French buyer must pay 100 per cent of the coffee proceeds into the proceeds account maintained by the co-ordinating bank (for the purpose of purchasing the buses). *Simultaneously* the West German bus manufacturer will pay a disagio to the French coffee buyer to subsidize the cost of the coffee and reduce it to an acceptable level.

The cost of the disagio must be built in to the costings of the suppliers of the principal products (the buses). They must consider how far they are prepared to reduce their profit margin to absorb the disagio cost and/or whether the price of the principal products to be supplied can be increased to compensate.

Unless an LDC can be persuaded to offer the counterpurchase goods at market pricing in the first place, it is generally unusual for the LDC to bear the cost of the disagio.

The size of the disagio would be negotiated between the buyer of the offtake goods and the supplier of the principal products. It will be calculated as a percentage of the LDC cost of the offtake goods and its size can vary considerably. The subsidy might be 3 per cent, 10 per cent, 30 per cent or even more. Much will depend on the original LDC cost of the goods, the quality and demand. It is when the disagio costs are realistically estimated and the full impact is known, that many potential countertrade transactions fall apart.

In theory, it follows that if good quality, traditional products are offered for countertrade at a competitive price and at a time of buoyant demand, the subsidy required by the prospective buyer should be a relatively small one. In practice it is rarely so simple.

Disagio costs might be reduced if the counterpurchase goods can be used in-house by the supplier of the principal products. Such opportunities are most likely to occur in relation to the offtake of goods under counterpurchase obligations or reciprocal orders for goods under offset requirements.

During the structuring and negotiation of a countertrade transaction a considerable amount of work is involved in identifying suitable counterpurchase products, finding a prospective buyer and estimating the likely level of disagio which must be absorbed. The definitive cost of the disagio will not be known until the final negotiations and contract signature, although a reasonable estimate can usually be made early on in negotiations. However, counterpurchase obligations are different. Because of the nature of these obligations, it is usual for them to be fulfilled by third party traders who, given certain basic information, are often willing to quote what is tantamount to a market price for the business. An exporter negotiating for the supply of products to, say, India or Indonesia can therefore obtain an accurate estimate of the cost of the countertrade early on in the negotiations.

As regards 'the savings', it follows that, depending on how attractive the disagio is, it is possible for a manufacturing company to reduce costs by sourcing its raw materials through countertrade. The savings that can be made by buying offtake products and therefore taking advantage of disagio payments represent one of the main reasons why trading houses have developed their expertise in trading the types of goods offered by LDCs and SICs for countertrade.

SOME RISKS

Delivery/performance risks

Countertrade is a trading medium whereby a country's goods, rather than its precious foreign currency reserves, are being used to generate either settlement for specific imports or at least some form of reciprocal benefit. The risks therefore generally relate to non-delivery or non-performance in respect of the offtake goods, rather than directly to non-payment.

In the majority of cases such risks can be reduced, if not eliminated, by ensuring that the *counterpurchase goods are shipped first* and that the proceeds are held safely on the proceeds account, with the co-ordinating bank, *outside* the country concerned, before the principal products are shipped. In the case of term transactions, involving a number of shipments of offtake goods, it would be a matter of ensuring that there are always sufficient funds on the proceeds account to cover work completed under the contract for the supply of the principal products. The co-ordinating bank might, however, be able to inject some flexibility into such a structure if it is prepared to add its confirmation to the LDC/SIC L/Cs for the import of the principal products, thus allowing the suppliers to ship when they like, regardless of whether there are sufficient funds in the proceeds account to cover.

More difficult risks to cover occur when it is agreed that the principal products should be shipped early on under a countertrade arrangement, with the counterpurchase goods, possibly perishable items, being supplied over a longer period of time, perhaps a number of years. It is possible to insure the associated delivery and political risks in the private insurance markets – such as Lloyd's of London and the American International Underwriters (AIU) – but the premium would be another significant cost which must usually be borne by the supplier of the principal products.

Contract risk

As a general rule it is not usually advisable for the supply of the principal products and the purchase of the offtake goods to be the subject of the same commercial contract. If, for example, a problem associated with the offtake goods occurred, then the whole contract could be endangered. Far better to have separate commercial contracts linked by the countertrade documentation. This way there would probably be a far better chance of solving the problem, perhaps finding a new buyer or substituting the offtake goods (which might even necessitate a completely new contract), without bringing down the whole structure.

The overzealous sales executive!

There are many jokes about overzealous sales executives who, in order to win supply contracts, readily sign on the dotted line to make reciprocal purchases of a country's own goods without in the slightest realizing the implications of what they are doing. It really does happen, even in the largest companies. Under normal circumstances, a contract for the offtake of goods should not be signed in isolation or without the countertrade being properly assessed and structured. The underlying commercial contracts and the countertrade documentation should preferably be signed simultaneously.

Disagio risks

There are two main areas of disagio risks.

1 Disagios are normally paid to the buyer of the offtake goods *simultaneously* with the remittance of the goods' proceeds to the co-ordinating bank for credit of the proceeds account.

As mentioned above, to cover the delivery risk on the LDC, it is advisable to arrange for the offtake products to be shipped first. This means that the suppliers of the principal products would make the (first) disagio payment before their products have been shipped and therefore prior to their receiving any payment from the funds on the proceeds account. The disagio therefore represents a real up-front risk.

In most cases the principal products would be shipped as soon as the funds are credited to the proceeds account, so that the disagio risk is short-lived. But this is not always the case. An advance payment under the supply contract, in convertible currency (possibly from the proceeds account), might be the best way of covering the disagio risk. An alternative could be penalty clausing in the supply contract providing for the payment of a penalty, equivalent to the disagio payment, from the funds on the proceeds account, in the event of default by the LDC.

2 Under countertrade transactions involving more than one shipment of offtake goods, it might not be in the buyer's interest to agree a fixed purchase price (and therefore disagio) at the outset of the contract covering all the shipments, which might be made over several months if not years. A buyer will only be prepared to bear the pricing risk for a limited period of time, for example one, three or six months, depending upon the nature of the offtake goods and the relative market for them.

This could mean periodic price negotiations and a fluctuating level of disagio, from shipment to shipment. It might also mean that shipment opportunities are missed because the disagio required is too great. The offtake of more goods must wait until the differential between the LDC pricing and the market value closes to an acceptable level. Hence the advisability of ensuring that there are always sufficient proceeds on the proceeds account to cover work completed under the contract for the supply of the principal products.

Currency risks

An exporter should consider the currency risks in the usual way, but for the purposes of the smooth operation of the countertrade transaction, it is best for the whole structure (including both commercial contracts) to be denominated in a single convertible currency, for example US dollars. If, for example, a supply contract is denominated in the LDC's local currency, with the proceeds of the offtake products paid in convertible currency, a conversion formula for reference purposes can be built in to the countertrade documentation, but it only leads to unnecessary complexities and potential problems. Far better to use a single convertible currency to avoid confusion.

FINANCING

Financing relates to the timing of payment, whereas countertrade involves the kind of payment.

A countertrade transaction often involves a country's products being used to generate payment in convertible currency, but finance can be introduced to add flexibility to the timing of the payment. Though financing is not strictly part of countertrade, the two can thus complement each other. Be it the simple provision of pre-shipment finance to an exporter, with repayment coming from the proceeds of the offtake products, or a large buy-back transaction involving an export credit, finance is an additional marketing tool which is playing an increasingly important role in countertrade transactions, particularly where banks are involved. However, the ability to introduce finance will depend very much on the bank's appetite for the credit and country risks involved.

Example of the role of financing

1　An LDC wishes to import chemicals, foodstuffs and spare parts (the principal products) for a total value of US$5 million, on 180-day credit terms.
2　The LDC offers settlement by way of shipments of sugar at the end of the 180-day period.
3　The exporter of the principal goods requires payment at sight, that is, upon presentation of the shipping documents.
4　A major international bank is introduced to structure a classic counterpurchase-type transaction.
5　The bank identifies a buyer for the sugar.
6　The bank agrees to advance funds to the supplier of the principal products, enabling him to extend 180 days credit, against the following security:
   (a)　an assignment of the sugar contract;
   (b)　an assignment of the proceeds of the letter of credit covering the sale of the sugar;

312

(c) the guarantee of the central bank of the LDC covering the delivery of the sugar or, failing that, payment of the equivalent value in convertible currency.

Repayment of the borrowing would come from the sugar proceeds.

7 The sugar buyer might arrange delivery risk insurance, in the private insurance market, covering non-delivery of the sugar. The bank would be named as the loss payee.

8 Recourse would be maintained to the supplier of the principal products for warranty and exclusions under the insurance policy.

A PRACTICAL EXAMPLE OF COUNTERTRADE

Although a relatively simple transaction, based on the classic counter-purchase structure, the following example emphasizes what can be achieved through the clever use of countertrade. Figure 17.7 relates to a countertrade transaction for the redemption of overdue debt.

An LDC owes money to a foreign supplier who is the holder of past due notes evidencing the debt. The foreign supplier has no idea when or if payment will be received.

An intermediary (probably a bank or trader) proposes a solution whereby:

1 The noteholder agrees to accept less than 100 cents in the dollar for cash now, or at least over an agreed period of time.
2 The LDC debtor makes available non-traditional goods (or a mix of traditional and non-traditional goods) to the trader for export, the proceeds of which are used to:
(a) pay off the notes;
(b) pay the intermediaries' fees.

Figure 17.7 outlines the operation of the transaction. The importance of the banking structure is emphasized. The bank's role would be to:

(a) monitor the levels of LDC goods being traded;
(b) handle the flow of shipping documents presented under the relative L/Cs;
(c) receive the convertible currency proceeds and hold them in a proceeds account;
(d) pay to the noteholder the agreed percentage of the notes (probably together with interest and overdue interest);
(e) cancel the overdue notes and pass them back to the central bank in the LDC.

313

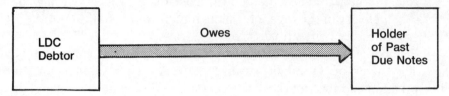

An exporter to an LDC has not been paid

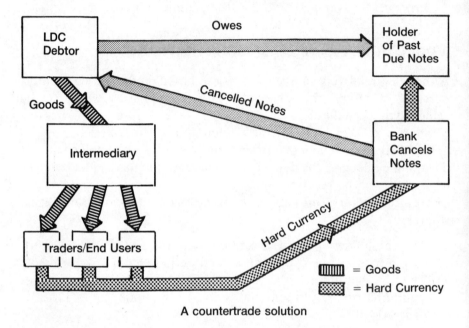

A countertrade solution

Figure 17.7   Countertrade to redeem overdue debt

The LDC benefits through a reduction in foreign debt, increased exports to new markets and the creation of new jobs.

ANATOMY OF COUNTERTRADE

How is a transaction constructed? What are the stages which a counter-trader must work through?

314

Conception of the proposal

An exporter might consider countertrade for any of the following reasons.

1 It might be required by the importing country which may have a well-established and controlled countertrade policy.
2 It might be the only way of selling to a nation short of foreign currency and unable to raise the necessary credit.
3 Reciprocity might be offered as an extreme incentive to win a contract.

Whatever the reason, a trading opportunity will present itself which is conditional upon settlement in goods, rather than money, and/or some other form of reciprocal benefit accruing to the country concerned.

Our example of classic counterpurchase (Figures 17.2 and 17.3) would probably fall under (2) above. The LDC has an urgent requirement for new buses, but does not have the necessary convertible currency available. Consideration is given to the provision of surplus staple products (coffee) in settlement.

Research and assessment

The following basic background information should be properly assessed in relation to the importing country.

- Economic and political backdrop
- Credit rating
- Trading reputation
- Performance record
- Level of public sector involvement in foreign trade
- Import and export regulations
- Exchange controls
- Export products, volumes, values and markets
- Countertrade policy
- Countertrade track record.

Through this exercise and previous knowledge and experience, the countertrader will be able to draw some initial conclusions as to whether a countertrade proposal is worth pursuing or not.

The countertrade products

In our counterpurchase example, the LDC has a priority import requirement for buses, but what goods can it offer in settlement? Consider the following points.

1 Obtain a list of goods *available for countertrade.*
2 Who is responsible for the marketing of the goods *and* the allocation to a specific countertrade transaction?
3 Are the goods traditional or non-traditional? Traditionals should be the objective.
4 Consider the quality and grade of the product(s) by national and international standards.
5 Obtain specifications and, if possible, samples.
6 Ascertain quantity and availability for shipment.
7 Pricing – how does it compare with the world market value? What sort of disagio will be required?
8 Marketability – are there any destination restrictions?
9 Examine the LDC's infrastructure and its ability to perform.
10 Who might be prepared to buy these goods?
11 Do the goods really exist? Have they been sold several times over in the market? – it does happen.

Identification of the players

In our counterpurchase example, we have a manufacturer (exporter) and a buyer (LDC importer) of buses. It has been agreed that coffee will be made available in settlement and a coffee supplier (LDC exporter) has been identified. In this example, the co-ordinating bank, which is providing its specialist countertrade services to the bus manufacturer, has identified a prospective buyer in France for the coffee.

It is often at this point, when the counterpurchase products have been identified and are being assessed, a buyer for them is being sought and an estimation of the disagio is known, that many potential transactions fall by the wayside.

The structure

Once the parties have been identified, the countertrader can get down to formulating an operating structure for the proposed transaction. It should be kept as simple as possible. The countertrader will consider the following:

(a) the terms of the underlying commercial contracts;
(b) the requirements of the parties to the countertrade;
(c) local regulations (including any countertrade policy);
(d) timing;
(e) how to minimize risks and overcome any operational difficulties;
(f) any financing requirements;
(g) how will the countertraders receive their fees?

The result will be a unique structure tailored to a unique set of circumstances.

The countertrade documentation

It has already been stated that there should be separate commercial contracts, one for the primary products (the buses), the other for the offtake goods (the coffee). The purpose of the countertrade documentation is to put a written legal framework around the countertrade structure. In so doing it will:

(a) link all the parties together;
(b) state the purpose of the countertrade;
(c) state the responsibilities of the parties;
(d) outline how the transaction will operate;
(e) seek to maximize the protections for the customer.

All countertraders will have their own method and style of documenting a transaction. The type and complexity of the transaction will dictate its format. There might be a single document or there could be several. Many countertraders have a preference for the existence of a separate document between the co-ordinating bank and the central bank of the LDC, outlining the *modus operandi* of the transaction (or what is often called 'the banking structure').

Some LDCs and SICs with an established countertrade policy provide their own countertrade documentation, which may or may not be negotiable.

Negotiation and the authority process

This is the most frustrating and troublesome stage, when another large proportion of proposed transactions fall apart. There are so many potential problems and pitfalls, that negotiations can take an inordinately long time and they can collapse at any moment. From inception of the proposal until signature and implementation of the transaction can take three months, six months, eighteen months or even longer. Much will depend on the willingness of the parties to co-operate and compromise and on their appetite for success.

There are seemingly endless negotiations not only between the contractual parties, but also with government ministries and the central bank in the country concerned. A competent, well-connected local agent is a valuable asset and could represent the difference between success and failure.

Because of the nature of countertrade, its potential effects on a country's economy and its sensitivities, it is a government-led trading medium and various approvals and authorities may be necessary from within the LDC before a transaction is allowed to proceed. Commonly found requirements are as follows:

1 Authorities from the ministry responsible for the import and the ministry responsible for the export.
2 Separate authorities may be required from the ministry of foreign trade and/or the ministry of finance.
3 Who should give the final overall approval for a transaction to proceed? This could be the prime minister or president himself.
4 Written evidence that the offtake products have been specifically allocated to this countertrade transaction.
5 Central bank approval for the non-repatriation of the foreign currency proceeds of the offtake goods where they are to be held on a proceeds account by a bank outside the country concerned.

Operation and 'the banking structure'

Once all the authorities are in place and the commercial contracts and countertrade documentation have been *simultaneously* signed, operation of the transaction can begin. How trouble-free the transaction proves to be will not just depend on the integrity of the preparations, negotiations and agreements that have gone before.

A countertrade transaction can collapse at any time before or during implementation. It is never a success until the last nut and bolt has been shipped. The banking structure of the transaction and how professionally it is implemented is all-important.

This is where the countertrade units of the banks come into their own. They provide not only the specialist expertise to set up a transaction, but also:

(a) as a first class financial institution they can stand in the middle as an independent intermediary giving integrity to the transaction and its operation;

(b) they can provide, in-house, the necessary traditional banking services on which the transaction depends;

(c) they may add flexibility to the transaction by the introduction of an element of finance;

(d) above all else they are able to maintain close control over the operation of the transaction including the flows of shipping documents and payments.

COUNTERTRADE CHECKLIST

Even if specialist expertise is employed to handle a countertrade, certain information will be required at the outset. Here is a list of points that the countertrader will need to know and which will help the exporters in their approach to a countertrade proposal.

1 Why countertrade and are there any alternatives?
2 What is the proposal and what are the benefits for the exporter?
3 Has the country any countertrade policy and/or a track record in countertrade?
4 What are the local import and export regulations?
5 What products are being offered for countertrade? In particular consider:
   (a) specifications and samples;
   (b) quality (in world market terms);
   (c) volumes and availability;
   (d) pricing (how does it compare with the world market value);
   (e) infrastructure and ability to perform;
   (f) marketability and destination restrictions;
   (g) whether the goods really exist.
6 Who would buy such goods? Make sure the prospective buyer is willing to take all the risks involved in the purchase of the goods.
7 Disagio.
8 Have the offtake goods been specifically allocated, in writing, to this countertrade transaction?

9 Have the necessary government and central bank authorities been given for this business to be transacted on a countertrade basis? If not, what authorities will be required? Who has the last say as to whether a transaction will proceed or not?

10 Has the exporter's local agent the tenacity, motivation and connections to play a significant role in negotiations and in obtaining the necessary authorities?

11 What are the risks and how might they be covered?

12 What happens if the offtake goods are not forthcoming? If a proceeds account is used, make sure that there are always sufficient funds available to cover work completed under the supply contract should it be necessary to stop work at any time.

13 Consider advance payments or penalty clausing to cover up front disagio costs.

14 Consider arbitration clausing in case things should go wrong.

CONCLUSION

So is countertrade just an unwelcome necessity when trade with certain developing countries is contemplated, or is it an innovative marketing tool?

Many companies shun countertrade, believing it to be more trouble than it is worth. They should not be deterred. In truth, it can be complex, expensive and fraught with setbacks and frustrations, but the rewards are there and, as more and more countries adopt it as a trading medium, a willingness and ability to countertrade can mean the difference between exporting, possibly even increasing market share, and not exporting at all. If a company cannot accept this point, it is likely that its competitors will.

But an increasing number of exporters acknowledge the rewards countertrade can bring and many are now adopting a proactive approach towards it. They know that the inclusion of an element of reciprocity in an offer can tip the balance. They realize that in order to penetrate some new markets (China for example) they must 'invest' in them rather than simply sell to them. They must give as well as take. This could mean two-way reciprocal trade, technology transfer or perhaps joint venture contracts with local entities, all of which are countertrade in their own way.

As a consequence of this positive approach to countertrade, its parameters are forever widening. The banks and traders respond to their customers' requirements with ever more innovative structures which combine reciprocity with both conventional and non-conventional financing techniques.

The tools are there. The choice is for the exporter to make. Reactive or proactive?

Recommended reading

Francis, Dick. (1987) *The Countertrade Handbook*. Cambridge: Woodhead-Faulkner. Gives an overview of countertrade and offset techniques in general.

Department of Trade and Industry. *Countertrade: Some Guidance for Exporters*. DTI London, Project and Export Policy Division.

PART VI
GETTING PAID

18

Collecting overdue debts

Brian Clarke

One of the foundations of good international credit management is the establishment of the most appropriate methods of payment for each and every transaction.

The more cautious will elect to use the most secure methods and turn away a good deal of business as a result. The more enlightened will appreciate how, taking calculated risks, much profitable business can be generated from marginal accounts. But the corollary to that kind of policy is the inevitability of some debts going overdue and some perhaps becoming irrecoverable. It is said that the really effective credit manager will at times have to write off a bad debt, but such a loss will be within the scope of the calculated risk policy and can normally be shown to have been unavoidable in spite of an efficient debt recovery policy and system.

It is also noteworthy to observe that in most companies the effects of delayed payment of overdues has a far more detrimental effect on profits than absolute write-offs.

So what constitutes an effective overdue debt collection policy and system? This chapter in general addresses that question in relation to overdues arising as a result of *customer* action (or non-action!) Debts blocked by foreign *governments* are discussed in Chapter 19.

DEBT PROGRESSION POLICY

All too many companies have no formal policy about progressing overdues and tend to regard the function as an extension of the ledger-keeper's job – a very shortsighted attitude, because the moment there is a conflict of priorities, the bookkeeping and cash allocation work has by its very nature to be done first. Indeed, how can you progress an overdue debt with any credibility until you are sure it has not been paid?

But far more companies simply fail to understand the importance to their survival of getting their money in on time.

Resources

Primarily the policy should be about resources – human and systems.

It is remarkable how many companies will readily employ highly paid staff to handle the task of obtaining export finance at the finest rates, whilst ignoring the fact that if they dedicated staff of equal calibre to chasing up payment of money rightfully due to the company, the need for external finance would diminish anyway.

The same may also be true of systems, with the correct emphasis being placed on hardware and software for, say, cash management but little upon the generation of such cash in the first place.

Like these other functions, debt recovery is a task which justifies adequate resources in terms of both quantity and quality. It is usually sensible to separate the task and the staff from other related functions such as maintaining the ledger. There will nevertheless be times when too much work is demanding the attention of a normally adequate staff and the policy must take account of this situation as well as the fact that there is always a short-term conflict about which debts to progress first.

Priorities

Incoming cash being the life-blood of any manufacturing or trading entity, the policy should inevitably be to 'go after the big ones first'.

The Pareto ratio, highlighted in Chapter 10, is equally relevant here. Most companies will be able to demonstrate by analysis of their sales ledgers that some 80 per cent of their overdue debts are due from some 20 per cent of their customers. So, rather than have the collection function work laboriously through the ledger from A to Z, cashflow requirements must demand that the largest overdues get chased first. Most international corporations are nowadays accustomed to maintaining their ledgers and credit control systems on computers and it should be straightforward to sort customer accounts according to overdue value.

All of this is not to say that smaller overdues can be left indefinitely, but they may have to be chased a day or two later. In circumstances of resource shortage, a regular sweep-up of the smaller overdues must be built in as a regular feature of the debt progression policy.

Targeting

In the light of current business conditions, corporate management should set realistic targets for credit and collection staff to aim to achieve, to demonstrate their collection performance. These targets are often expressed as days sales outstanding (DSO – see Chapter 8 for a discussion of this concept), but it is also useful to translate these into the cash values which it is hoped to achieve.

When to chase?

The obvious policy answer is when a debt goes overdue. By overdue, most credit managers will mean when the due date plus a reasonable time for the transmission of the cash has expired. When that condition is met, of course, it is reasonable to chase any other debts that are just on their due date.

But what about debts that are becoming near due? Some companies regard it as sensible gently to remind customers of any large debts as they approach due date. This needs to be handled carefully but there is surely nothing wrong in politely asking whether, for instance, a customer has all the necessary documents available to ensure that their payment, due next Monday, will not suffer any undue delay in the banking system! Alternatively, an exporter might genuinely have a forward currency contract dependent upon prompt delivery of the customer's funds. What harm can there be in pointing this out to the customer?

The sales manager may of course object to this line of action if he or she thinks the customer is going to be offended – which brings us to back to the policy and another policy matter.

Co-operation with sales department

In debt progression, as in many other areas, there is always scope for conflict between sales and credit.

Whilst a little tension between the two, reflecting their apparently differing aims of increasing sales and decreasing overdue debtors, may be healthy and avoid complacency in the corporation, it has to be recognized that both functions have the same corporate aim – to increase profits.

Debt progression is best served by a high level of co-operation between sales and credit, and particularly a high level of communication, keeping each other informed about customer situations, disputes, sensitivity and a whole host of other relevant matters.

The need for such co-operation should be set out in the corporate scheme of organization and given high-level support.

Multinationals

Companies which collectively comprise a multinational group have an added policy dimension, with options for centralized or decentralized control. These options and the additional collection opportunities available to multinationals are discussed in Chapter 4.

ROUTINE DEBT PROGRESSION METHODS

Within the policy framework laid down, those responsible for collection of overdues need an action plan, supporting systems and an arsenal of techniques to use in their quest for prompt payments.

Action plan

Each corporation or multinational group should establish its own action plan for progressing overdues, custom-built to meet its own particular pattern of trade, organization and policy. Fundamental to any plan, however, should be the following features:

1   When the debt-chasing process should begin.
2   How regularly follow-up should occur.
3   How soon severe remedies such as legal action should be embarked upon.
4   How performance should be measured and monitored against cash targets.
5   How senior management should be kept informed of performance, to facilitate overall control of the business and the working capital employed in it.

Supporting systems

The range of systems available to international credit managers is described in Chapter 25, and computer systems for the collection of overdues are covered in detail.

For debt progression, some cross-reference between various sales ledgers may be necessary for the following reasons.

1   Multinationals will need to co-ordinate their various national ledgers (export and domestic) to ensure that customers supplied from more than one of their source points can be pressed for payment of all debts overdue to the group as a whole (Chapter 4 discusses the options available to multinationals).
2   Corporations may be exporting via local merchanting houses, and recording such sales as domestic transactions, as well as exporting direct.

Where for any reason a customer has accounts in more than one group ledger, it makes sense for only one of the ledger holders to act as a focal point for progressing all the group's debts. Failing this, customers very quickly learn to play off one part of the organization against another, diligently paying one source point's bills whilst delaying another's and changing the pattern when the first one complains.

The only other matter to emphasize here is the need for such systems to be kept up to date at all times. Nobody can maintain credibility for long if they chase up debts for which payment was made weeks ago but is still waiting to be posted to the ledger, or which have been cancelled but the cancellation credit notes have not yet been recorded in the ledger.

Using the local agent

Exporters often sell direct to customers against direct indent orders processed under a local agency agreement. Normally, external agents are involved, but the agency may be held by an associated company or even a subsidiary (affiliate). The agent usually receives a commission for processing direct indent orders from customers and it is normal for these commissions to be withheld from payment until the underlying invoices have been settled. This acts as an incentive to the agents fully to earn their commission by seeing the transaction through to payment.

To facilitate this latter function, agents should be provided with regular analyses of unpaid customer debts relative to their agency, whether overdue or not. The better agents will marry this detail with copies of invoices, documentary remittance letters, and other documents already in their possession and, as an extension to their 'case of need' activities, will take the necessary action without prompting, when debts go overdue (or maybe a few days beforehand). The less reliable agents will need further prompting. Chapter 3 develops these themes in depth.

Who to chase?

When debts are flagged as overdue it may not mean that it is the customer who is delaying payment. It may be the bank, or even the exporter's own organization (or lack of it).

Debt progression systems need to identify the cause. If it is in-house, then speedy rectification of the problem – dispute, short-shipment, wrong goods, or whatever – is called for.

If a bank is found to be at fault and undue delay can be proven, then it is right and proper for some kind of redress to be sought, normally by way of interest.

On most occasions, however, it will be the customer.

If commission agents are involved, then as indicated above the first approach to the customer should be through them. If the chosen method of settlement was a documentary collection, then concurrent with any approach to an agent, the remitting bank should be reporting on the status of the debt.

If there is no third party involved and the customer has to be chased direct, it is a good tactic to address the approach to a specific individual, preferably the one who has the greatest vested interest in seeing the exporter's debts get paid on time.

Through which medium?

Obviously the fastest and most effective method of communication should be used. That will normally be by telex, telephone or facsimile (fax). For international debts, letters are too slow and the stereotype variety go straight into the waste paper basket.

Post

Letters can still be effective for multinationals' subsidiaries operating in a domestic market. They can be accompanied by copy invoices, thus providing the fullest of detail and avoiding time-wasting responses of the 'what was our order number?' variety.

It is said that first and subsequent dunning letters in different colours can be especially effective in expediting payment. One envisages the scene: a harassed accounts payable officer, waving an initial dunning letter on olive-green paper and screaming 'Quick, send them a cheque before the puce one arrives!' On the other hand, the accounts payable officer may be an avid collector and may decline to pay until he or she has the full multi-coloured set!

Progressing debts abroad, however, needs speed and electronic transmission.

Telephone

The telephone has become the popular medium for initial chasing in the USA and elsewhere, but such approaches need careful control. Preparation for a telephone call should be as thorough as when sending a written communication – probably more so because all possible responses need to be anticipated and catered for. A firm conclusion, hopefully a promise to pay immediately, should be reached – no woolly 'perhaps' or 'maybe' – and the conclusion should immediately be confirmed by telex along with any other important detail.

The timing of an international telephone call is also important, having regard to the various time zones around the world. Credit managers should keep abreast of the exact time difference in each case and pick the right moment to go into the level of detail often necessary to resolve a complicated account situation.

For those trading, say, with the Far East out of Europe, it pays to have an insomniac on the credit and collections staff who doesn't mind taking his or her work home and having the company subscribe to the domestic telephone bill.

Telex

Telex is undoubtedly the most effective and probably the cheapest medium for progressing overdues. For the older credit executive there may still be a subconscious reflex to keep telexes short and staccato, like the old telegram or cable language. This is not necessary however. The telex should be long enough to convey all necessary points clearly and unambiguously, with the recipient left in no doubt as to which debts are being chased. Some other basic rules are:

(a) keep explanations simple, especially if the telex is in a language foreign to the recipient (see also below);

(b) be polite, but firm;

(c) never make threats it isn't your company's intention to carry out.

Fax

Facsimile machines are still far from universally available, but if there is one at each end it is an extremely efficient way of progressing overdues and ensuring that all necessary details are conveyed.

Which language?

Chasing overdues, like many other aspects of international trade, invariably gets a better result if conducted in the 'other guy's' language. Few English-speaking exporters find it appropriate to recruit credit staff on the basis of language ability, but staff can be encouraged to acquire a language, especially if it is evident that it can be used directly in their job. Learning languages in these circumstances can greatly enhance job interest and help develop the function to the mutual benefit of employer and employee.

WHEN INITIAL APPROACHES GET NO RESULT

In domestic credit control, failure of initial approaches to elicit either payment or an explanation can quickly lead to threats of legal action. For exports, however, this is very much a last resort and, as we shall see, is rarely recommended. Obviously, lack of response demands a prompt follow-up via a swift transmission medium. The stage can be quickly reached where the customer must be approached in very strong language and made to understand that failure, at the very least to explain the reasons for non-payment, will result in serious action being taken.

More often than not, reasons will be given and these need to be tested to see if they are genuine. Thereafter the choice of action will depend upon the circumstances, and the various options are discussed below.

Local assistance

If there are no local agents, or their ability to assist has been exhausted, who else can one turn to locally? The local chamber of commerce may be able to help, to use a little of their influence to get things moving. The local embassy or consulate? – different credit executives will give you different reactions, ranging from pleasure at the help they once got, through to hysterical laughter. The simple fact is that embassies and the like have not been established to handle the nitty gritty of credit control. They have weightier things on their minds. But if the debt is big enough and there is the right connection, there may just be the chance that a word in the right ear from a senior official over a post-prandial brandy may unblock a payment log-jam.

Collection agencies

For most countries it is possible to find an agency – or sometimes perhaps a lawyer – whose business it is to collect difficult debts. This can often be on a 'no collection, no fee' basis. Successful collection, however, normally attracts a substantial fee.

Collection agencies are normally well advertised in the financial press.

Personal visits

Unlike their export sales colleagues, international credit managers often appear to have difficulty in justifying the cost of travelling to their markets, although almost invariably a journey to collect difficult debts can be easily cost-justified.

In practice, because of the distance and time involved, it normally makes sense to combine a debt recovery mission with other objectives – assessing the market and customers, learning more about local regulations and conditions, and above all getting to know the people who matter now and who are going to be important in future credit management and other activities.

Once credit managers have met the people who hitherto they had only corresponded with, or at best spoken to on the telephone, relationships are invariably improved. Now, when the credit manager telephones a customer, they can picture each other (they probably had a drink together) and suddenly there is a heightened degree of co-operation.

Because of their financial background, credit managers tend to look at a market from a different – and complementary – angle from that of the export salesman. Pre-planned visits to local banks can provide a great deal of useful information. Visits to other institutions, customers and competitors can complete the scene.

A word of warning though: there is absolutely no point in visiting a foreign country for the above purposes unless the credit manager goes thoroughly prepared. This means:

Establishing up-to-date analyses of customers' accounts

Really up to date! With all pipeline cash, returned goods and the like properly recorded. It is better not to sit in front of customers pressing for payment, than to run through a set of accounts with them only to find that they are out of date and unreliable. Credibility is immediately lost and it would have been better not to have broached the subject in the first place.

In such situations credit managers must have totally reliable accounts analyses at their disposal and it pays valuable dividends to bring them up to date by a quick telephone call back to base just before the appointment with the subject customer.

Researching all about the customers and their country

What do the sales people know? Can the banks offer advice? In the UK, the Department of Trade and Industry, through its Overseas Trade Department, has a wealth of information and there are similar sources in other countries (the Appendix at the end of the book describes a number of these sources).

What are the current import and exchange control regulations? The credit manager will need to be able to test the genuineness of the apparently official reasons (or excuses) given for non-payment. What are the normal exchange delays and delays within the banking system?

And how should one behave in the country? Almost every country has its own peculiar customs and attitudes; and even if English is spoken, certain expressions may not have the same meaning as in our home country. (Was it not indeed Sir Winston Churchill who commented that the UK and the USA were divided only by a common language?)

The golden rule for any travelling businessmen or businesswomen is to remember they are guests in the foreign land, to respect their hosts' manners and customs and not unduly outstay their welcome.

Going with a mandate to negotiate on behalf of the company up to well-defined limits

As will be seen below, the resolution of 'hard core' debts can involve renegotiation of terms and in certain cases some forgiveness of debt or other advantage. In such circumstances it does not help the credit manager's cause or image if, every time he or she is called upon to take a minor decision, it becomes necessary to refer back to base. It helps therefore if the extent of the credit manager's mandate is determined before the overseas visit and written into the remit described below.

Setting down a brief remit

Before leaving, the credit manager should set down a short list of the visit's aims and objectives; and upon return to base, a brief exercise should be undertaken to measure success against the remit. This need not be a long drawn out bureaucratic affair. But the formal discipline goes a long way towards reassuring all concerned that such a trip, far from being a 'Cook's tour' represents a serious, cost-justified and valuable part of the credit manager's job.

Face to face with the customer

The very fact that the credit manager may have travelled thousands of miles to keep an appointment with a delinquent customer ought to indicate to the latter that he or she is in deadly earnest to obtain payment. (Indeed, the very suggestion that a visit is to be made can set the money flowing – but there is a limit to the number of times one can 'threaten' a visit and not carry it out.)

The customer, however, just may not be able to pay immediately. In that event, the credit manager's earlier enquiries should already have prevented that fact from coming as a complete surprise and in such circumstances he or she can only resort to creativity and hope that the customer may be persuaded to give some measure of priority to his or her company, before considering the other alternatives outlined later in this chapter. What creative ideas might arise?

1   Does the customer have funds elsewhere which might be used to pay

     or part pay the debt, or be offered as a guarantee until formal payment can be made?

2   Can the customer offer guarantees of a personal or bank nature to support any debt-restructuring agreement (see later)?

Veiled threats

With recalcitrant customers a suggestion that, in view of their payment delinquency, their bankers are to be approached for a reference, will sometimes activate payment. The customers probably do not want their bankers to gain the impression that they are unable to pay their way as this might prompt the bankers to curtail their financing facilities. Similarly, if the supplier is a member of a credit control organization or common interest group, where past customer payment performance statistics are exchanged between members, why not make slow-paying customers aware of the fact? The customers surely do not want to get a bad name amongst all their suppliers. If all this sounds slightly unethical, is it any more unethical than the customer's refusal to pay on time?

Debt restructuring

When customers are patently unable to pay their debts, but alternatives to legal action are preferred, consideration might be given to restructuring the debt, agreeing to have it paid off by instalments whilst continuing to trade with the customers on a more secure basis.

    Much will depend upon the customer's current management quality, market opportunities and support from financial institutions. But if, after thorough investigation, it appears that the factors which caused the near collapse of the business have been overcome and, with support, future prospects are good, it may be worthwhile the supplier take a lead from any confidence expressed by the local bankers and entering into a restructuring agreement.

    This agreement would probably take the form of a repayment plan whereby the debt would be extinguished over a set period, perhaps with interest. The repayments might be evidenced by, say, a series of bills of exchange avalized or guaranteed by the customer's bankers. At the same time the customers would continue manufacturing/trading, taking supplies from their patient creditor and paying for them by some secure method. Such arrangements need a high level of confidence on the part of both creditors and bankers but, if the right kind of conditions exist, restructuring can prove to be a more profitable solution than legal action, with far more long-term benefits.

Doing a deal

Sometimes half a loaf is better than none and if, *in extremis*, it seems likely that any formal action against a delinquent one-off customer is going to be less than cost effective, it may be worthwhile negotiating a payment for less than the invoice value, in full and final settlement of the debt. This may sound defeatist, but it is often the (fortunately rare) price which a supplier must pay for otherwise successful trading with marginal accounts. In a deal like this, the customer being let off the hook should understand that the arrangement is to be kept confidential between himself, the supplier and, if one is involved, the agent. It is preferable that the word should not get around, lest other potential marginal customers decide to try the same game.

Legal action

For the multinational operating abroad, litigation might always be considered for the recovery of overdue debts within the 'home' market.

For export debts, however, any legal action can pose a variety of problems to the extent that all other alternatives to litigation should always be seriously considered.

If a supplier is contemplating legal action abroad, good sound advice should be sought as to the feasibility of obtaining a judgment and having it enforced stringently enough to recover the debt or such part of the debt as would justify the cost of the action.

In Western Europe, North America and other 'First World' countries, legal action can often be viable. Outside these areas, however, the likelihood of success must always be questionable.

Chapter 26 covers a variety of legal aspects including litigation, but when taking professional advice on the advisability of an action, exporters should bear in mind the following points.

1 Failure to take severe action can sometimes earn a supplier the reputation of being a 'soft touch', prepared to put up with long-delayed settlements of debts from any customer in the area.
2 Conversely, the public relations effect of a successful legal action putting a customer out of business and throwing his employees on to

an already swollen labour market might need to be considered. A judgment may not be much consolation for the 'wicked foreign corporation' in those circumstances!

3 Legal actions abroad can often be protracted affairs, lasting a year or more, and legal costs can be very high. Obviously lawyers acting for the plaintiff should always seek a judgment which includes costs.

4 At the commencement of a legal process (for example when a bill of exchange is protested) the value of the debt will be converted into the currency of the debtor's country and in that value it will remain until a judgment is given. If, therefore, the invoices covering the debt are not in the customer's currency, the supplier takes an exchange risk during the period of the action; and if the customer's currency is weak and non-convertible, it is likely to lose value against harder currencies during this period, so even if the action leads to a successful outcome, a substantial exchange loss may result upon realization.

Write-off of bad debts

In the final analysis, sometime, somewhere a bad debt will have to be written off. That is the price of taking risk management to the limit. When it happens, all steps must obviously be taken to mitigate the loss. Are any of the goods recoverable? What are the tax angles? What lessons can be learned for the future?

And then the credit manager must swallow hard and get back to the larger task of winning new, sound business without further detriment to the company's cashflow.

Recommended reading

Edwards, H. (Editor) (1985) *Credit Management Handbook*. 2nd edn. Aldershot: Gower. Comprehensive guide to granting and controlling credit in the UK with contributions by twenty-one experts.

Edwards, H. (1982) *Export Credit*. Aldershot: Gower. Strong on information sources and export credit management procedures.

19

Exchange controls

Hans Belcsak

INTRODUCTION

For most of us in the mainstream of international business today, barter – the exchange of goods against goods – is a thing of the distant past. Of late, to be sure, particularly since the eruption of the debt crisis in the developing world, which began to make headlines with the near-default by Mexico in 1982, there has been a modest revival of money-less transactions in the cross-border flows of goods and services. Even now, though, such deals, important as they are individually, constitute only a tiny fraction of world trade. And given the obstacles involved, which range from the difficulties of proper valuation to the problems of insurance, financing, quality control, after-sales service and finding markets for resale, one must seriously doubt that the proportion will grow very much in the years and decades to come.

World trade would be a pale shadow of its present volume without the use of currencies. Contrary to the border-crossing nature of international trade, however, currencies remain very much national creations with – for the most part – very limited supra-national qualities. This is true even for the world's major monetary units. An export company in Great Britain earning most of its income in US dollars would not dream of paying its employees at home in greenbacks. An Italian manufacturing firm selling the bulk of its output in Germany will need lire rather than marks to finance its inputs. A Dutch concern borrowing Euro-Swiss francs to generate low-cost operating capital will have to convert the proceeds to Dutch guilders to achieve the objective.

Foreign exchange thus has its roots, as a wise French economist once observed, in the co-existence between the internationalism of trade and the nationalism of currencies. In its narrowest sense, foreign exchange is the act of converting the currency of one nation into that of another. In a wider sense, in the manner in which it is mostly understood today, foreign exchange also defines assets, or more precisely all claims to another nation's currency that are payable abroad, whether they consist of funds held in foreign monetary units with banks abroad, or bills, cheques, or other financial instruments. And foreign exchange rates are the 'equalizing prices' that link different currencies.

From fixed to floating exchange rates

Ideally from the international credit executive's point of view, these prices, these foreign exchange rates, would be fixed, subject to only occasional alterations of their respective values, and all the currencies would be fully convertible. This was, indeed, one of the aspirations behind the world-wide monetary system that some of the most astute representatives of some of the most powerful nations set out to create when they met in a sleepy New Hampshire, USA, resort town by the name of Bretton Woods, right after World War II.

The Bretton Woods System, marrying the ideas of the British economist John Maynard Keynes and his American colleague Harry Dexter White, had the US dollar as its lynchpin and a newly created organization, the International Monetary Fund, as its supervisory agency. It provided for fixed par values between currencies, with fluctuation ranges of at most one per cent on either side of par, and for a direct link (through the dollar) to gold. It allowed for devaluations of individual monetary units, but these were rather infrequent. And although the mechanism was initially geared primarily to the world's foremost currencies, smaller nations had a variety of incentives to join and, over time, most of them did.

From then until the late 1960s, the reliability of exchange rates under the Bretton Woods System was a major contribution to the explosive growth of trade and cross-border investment that the world experienced. The key to the mechanism's smooth functioning was the fact that the USA entered the postwar period with the globe's strongest currency, and one that was scarce to boot. With 75 per cent of the tallied global gold reserves in its coffers, with its banking system in the most liquid condition since the founding of the Federal Reserve, and with a massive productive capacity waiting to be fully exploited for peaceful purposes, the USA, through its dollar, became the world's banker.

The dollar's position did not remain unchallenged for very long, however. In 1950 the US balance of payments shifted from surplus into deficit and, gradually at first, then with increasing velocity, the international dollar shortage turned to glut. In 1971 the US dollar's firm link with gold was cut. There was a brief attempt to preserve the currency stability of the Bretton Woods System with a somewhat more flexible arrangement minus gold, the so-called Smithsonian Agreement, which envisaged fluctuation ranges of 2.25 per cent on either side of each currency's central rate, but the new structure creaked from the very start and collapsed in February of 1973.

For the past fifteen years, therefore, international business has had to make do without the comfort and the assurances provided by stable exchange rates. One vestige of the fixed-rate era does survive to this day. The European Economic Community, in its attempts to make at least some modest progress toward the long-sought goal of monetary union, had decided in principle well over a decade ago to keep the fluctuations among member currencies within narrower bands that would have resulted from those permitted against the US dollar. Out of this special arrangement has developed today's European Monetary System (EMS). It links the German mark, the Belgian and Luxembourg francs, the Dutch guilder, the French franc, the Italian lira and the Irish pound to one another through a complex cross-rate grid of parities, ceilings and floors.

Within the EMS, fluctuation limits must be strictly observed and parity changes are permissible only with the consent of the other members. Otherwise, though, central banks today have a wide variety of options from which to choose in their selection of the most suitable method of exchange rate management, as may be seen from the chart in Figure 19.1. And for international credit executives as for all others involved in international business, the most notable consequence has been a surge in the risks related to foreign exchange.

Examples of the options shown in Figure 19.1 are:

- Independent float: Canadian dollar, British pound
- Group float: German mark, Belgian franc, Dutch guilder
- Crawling peg: Brazilian cruzado, Korean won, Uruguayan peso
- Peg to US dollar: Venezuelan bolivar, Hong Kong dollar
- Peg to other units: African CFA-franc to the French franc
- Peg to the SDR: Iranian rial, Kenyan shilling, Zambian kwacha
- Peg to other basket (often trade-weighted): Swedish crown, Finnish markka.

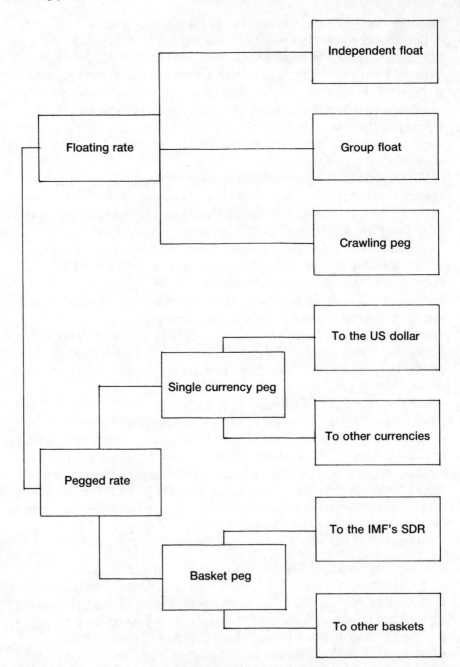

Figure 19.1 Options available to central banks for exchange rate determination

DEALING WITH THE RISK OF CONVERTIBLE CURRENCY VOLATILITY

There remain a number of currencies, mostly those of the top OECD nations, that continue to be fully convertible and that are traded in large, efficient global markets, with their values fluctuating strictly in line with supply and demand. Companies dealing in these currencies need not worry much about the foremost risk confronting them in other lands, the so-called transfer or convertibility risk. They must realize (and manage) the dangers or opportunities arising from often volatile exchange prices, but if they decide that exchange rate speculation does not fit into their corporate policy and that they prefer to eliminate the risk wherever possible, they find that they can do so at a usually quite acceptable cost.

The foreign exchange market, in which the world's leading currencies are traded, is not an organized trading place in the same sense as stock or commodity exchanges. There is no single, physical site where buy and sell orders are executed. Rather, the exchange market consists of an enormous, highly sophisticated and efficient global communications system in which most transactions are verbally arranged by the two parties and executed by telephone or telex. In this market, banks are the natural intermediaries between supply and demand. Their dealing activity tends to establish uniform price ranges for individual currencies throughout the financial centres of the world, since any deviation too far from the average in a given geographic location will quickly be eliminated by arbitrage.

The exchange market operates around the clock, twenty-four hours a day. It revolves around a number of major centres – London, Frankfurt and Zürich in Europe, New York, Chicago and Toronto in North America, Tokyo, Hong Kong and Singapore in the Far East – but modern communications have made it unnecessary for companies wishing to access the market to be physically close to any one of them.

Among the participants in this market, the banks, particularly the large commercial banks, are the dominant 'players'. They maintain dealing rooms both to trade for their own account and to service their corporate customers' needs. By contrast, corporations are real end-users of the market. They are the importers needing foreign currency to pay their suppliers, or the exporters seeking to sell their exchange receipts. They are companies investing abroad, borrowing in capital markets around the world, repatriating profits and dividends from overseas subsidiaries, or receiving royalties and licence fees. Still, their transactions constitute, in terms of volume, a mere fraction of the total inter-bank market.

Since in this market transactions directly related to actual international trade and investment constitute a very small proportion of overall deals, with the remainder generated by inter-bank activity and (more or less) speculative flows of funds, it stands to reason that exchange rates other than those that are semi-fixed by special arrangement (such as the EMS cross-rates) tend to be highly volatile.

This has sharply heightened the risks confronting international business, making it close to impossible to predict how currency values will move in the medium and long term, or even in the immediate future. In foreign trade, exporters can of course insist on invoicing shipments in their own currency, and importers on being billed in their domestic monetary unit. But a change in the billing currency does not really alter the risk. It merely shifts the responsibility for bearing it from one party to the other – in the case of the exporter to the foreign customer, in that of the importer to the supplier abroad.

On one or the other side of a cross-border transaction, the risk will have to be accepted, or protected against. Fortunately, the exchange market offers a number of ways in which this can be done, for the most part at an acceptable cost. To become familiar with these means for exchange risk management, one needs to take a closer look at the transactions that are possible in the market. The three basic ones are:

- Spot transactions
- Forward transactions
- Options.

All these methods of foreign currency exposure management are described in Chapter 22. In this chapter we look at the economic forces, controls and other circumstances that influence them.

Spot transactions

By definition, spot transactions are purchases or sales of foreign currency for 'immediate' delivery. In every exchange deal there are normally two key dates involved, the 'transaction date', on which the respective contract is concluded, and the 'value date', on which settlement, that is, the actual delivery of funds, must take place. Trading 'spot' implies a value date two good business days after the transaction date, with 'good' meaning that the banks are open in both centres involved.

For instance, a French franc/US dollar spot deal concluded on a Tuesday would call for delivery the following Thursday, assuming Wednesday (and, of course, Thursday) is not a holiday in either France or the USA. Likewise, a transaction on Thursday would be settled the following Monday, and one on Friday would have the next Tuesday as delivery date.

The objective of this arrangement is 'compensated value', meaning that both parties to the deal should receive, and make, delivery on the same business day, so that neither loses out on the use of funds. Given the time differential between, say, Europe and the USA, compensated value could not be achieved with same-day delivery, and often not even with next-day settlement. Thus, the two-day rule holds true for most currencies and markets, but not without exceptions.

There are some centres, especially in the Far East, which deal spot for delivery the following day, and some which trade for settlement on the same day. In New York currencies within the same time zones (the Canadian dollar and the Mexican peso) are normally traded for next-day delivery. Even in other currencies and markets, 'cash' or 'value' the same day or next day is usually feasible as a contract condition, but the party initiating the deal must make its preference clearly known in advance and will be charged one or two days' interest, which will be built into the quoted exchange rate.

Spot is the all-important exchange rate. It forms the basis for all other transactions, and quotations for delivery or settlement on any other than the spot date will be calculated from this rate. If customers contact a bank with the expressed wish to buy or sell currency without specifying the delivery date, it is automatically assumed that they want to deal spot.

Table 19.1 shows some typical examples of spot rates for major currencies against the US dollar. From these it will be seen that in most cases the 'direct' quotation is used, which indicates how many units of a given currency are equivalent to one US dollar. At one time exchange traders in the USA used the 'indirect' method of quoting, which expresses the US dollar equivalent of one unit of another currency. While US$1.00 = DM 1.6705 is the direct quotation, for instance, DM 1.00 = US$0.5986 would be the indirect one.

Today, US traders, too, quote direct. But there are exceptions to the rule. For example, when Great Britain did not have a decimal system, it

Table 19.1
Selected New York closing rates

Currencies	Bid	Offer
US$/DM	1.6720	1.6740
US$/SFr	1.3740	1.3770
US$/Hfl	1.8840	1.8855
US$/FFr	5.6748	5.6800
US$/Lit	1230.0	1240.0
US$/DKr	6.4200	6.4300
US$/SKr	6.0245	6.0345
US$/Y	135.00	135.20
UK£stg/US$	1.7800	1.7820

was traditionally easier to quote the value of the pound sterling in terms of the foreign currency (including the US dollar), and this practice has been retained although the UK does now employ the decimal system. Thus, Table 19.1 shows how many US dollars one pound will buy, not the other way around.

The same holds true for a small number of other currencies, such as the Australian dollar, or the Irish pound, or the New Zealand dollar. The South African rand until quite recently was also quoted (and traded) indirectly, but with effect from 1 March 1988 this practice was changed. Instead of, say, 0.4663 (US cents per Rand) the unit is now quoted 2.1445 (Rand per US dollar).

An exchange rate quotation normally has two sides, the 'bid' and the 'offer'. The 'bid' is the rate at which a bank buys foreign exchange if the quotation is direct, or buys its own currency if the quote is indirect. The 'offer' is the rate at which the bank sells foreign exchange if the quotation is direct, or sells its own currency if the quote is indirect. Since a bank will, of course, always buy at the low price and sell at the high price, this means that in the German mark example in Table 19.1 the bid side of DM 1.6720 shows the rate at which the dealer will buy dollars (and sell marks), while the offer side of DM 1.6740 gives the rate at which he or she will sell dollars (and buy Deutschmarks).

The important point to remember is that bid and offer mark the bank's position. Logically, therefore, assuming that a rate is being quoted directly (bid and offer are for foreign currency from the bank's point of view), an exporter selling foreign exchange will need the bank's bid rate for the transaction, while an importer buying foreign currency will need the bank's offered rate.

Forward transactions

As will be fully explained in Chapter 22, foreign exchange can be bought and sold not only on a spot or cash basis, but also for delivery on a stipulated future date (beyond two days), with both the settlement date and the price being agreed upon at the time the contract is made. Theoretically, the forward price for a currency can be identical with the spot price, and on very rare occasions this may indeed, be the case. Almost always, though, the forward rate is either higher (premium) or lower (discount). And these margins, contrary to a widely held notion, are not an indication as to where the exchange markets expect a particular currency to move over the indicated period, but are essentially a reflection of the differentials between interest rates prevailing in the two centres involved.

On occasions, however, there will be other forces at play. If there are strong devaluation rumours surrounding a currency, these may very well produce discounts substantially exceeding what the so-called 'interest-rate parity' calculation would indicate. Relationships can also be distorted by governmental exchange controls, taxation, reserve requirements and other factors impeding the free operation of market forces. And the forwards of minor currencies, for which large, sophisticated external deposit and lending markets do not exist, will as a rule not conform with interest-rate differentials. But the principle does, by and large, hold for the major monetary units.

Options

Should customers not know exactly when they will need the foreign currency they intend to buy, or will receive the exchange payment they expect from abroad, banks can accommodate them with a so-called option contract. Options in foreign exchange forward contracts have existed since the 1960s, but initially their unconventional nature drastically limited their use.

Such old-style options (which still exist) are not like put and call options in stocks or shares, which need not be taken up. Foreign exchange options of this kind must be executed, whether the underlying transaction materializes or not. What is optional in this case is merely – within a set frame – the delivery date.

Genuine currency put and call options, which were first tried out in Philadelphia, USA, are presently in the experimental stage in a few major centres. For the time being, both the types of currencies and the amounts and maturities for which such transactions are possible are quite limited. The depth (volume) of the market is relatively shallow, particularly when compared with that of the ordinary forward market in currencies. The banks operating the market find it rather difficult to hedge their own exposures arising from true options, and the cost to corporate customers is, accordingly, quite high.

International business in its various forms generates a real need for genuine options contracts, however, and it seems safe to assume that the market will grow rapidly in the years to come. Banks will become more confident as they gain more experience. The volume of supply will rise closer to the level of demand. Forward discounts and premiums are apt to shrink and, increasingly, even smaller players will find the market to be a useful vehicle for exchange risk management.

In sum, then, credit executives and others active in international business have several tools at their disposal for eliminating or at least drastically reducing the risks that arise from the fluctuations of the world's leading currencies.

But what about currencies which are not convertible?

DEALING WITH THE RISK OF INCONVERTIBILITY

If currencies were all traded like those of the leading OECD nations, the exchange risk in international trade would be fairly easily identified, measured and hedged. Protection has a cost, but if one disregards the potential loss of opportunity (that is, if one rejects speculation) this cost, too, can be identified and measured in advance.

Unfortunately, however, the number of monetary units that are traded on open markets relatively unfettered by government controls is quite limited. More or less stringent official restrictions prevent the free play of market forces for the great majority of the world's 150-odd currencies.

Where government fiat decrees an (often artificially overpriced) exchange value, the logical consequence is usually the emergence of a black (illegal) or grey (officially tolerated) 'parallel' market, quoting far weaker rates for the unit in question. Frequently, moreover, a government – finding its currency under irresistible pressure – will set up a two-tiered or multiple exchange rate mechanism with different prices applicable to different, specified transactions. In such instances there will usually be one rate that is permitted to float freely, and it then becomes a useful gauge of a currency's weakness.

Many currencies, moreover, are subject not only to restrictions on rate fluctuations in response to supply and demand forces, but also to limitations of their convertibility. These range from minor encumbrances, preventing conversion for certain purposes (for example, the remittance abroad of a dividend that lacks prior approval by the authorities) all the way to curbs reducing a unit to a non-convertible 'inland' currency (such as the monies of Eastern Europe). The following gives an overview, by no means exhaustive, of some of the exchange controls that currently impede cross-border movements of funds virtually throughout the Third World and even in some of the more developed industrial nations.

Summary of exchange controls

General

1 Limitations on moving funds into or out of a country, put into effect either as overall ceilings, or as maxima for specified purposes.
2 Bans on transactions with particular countries for national security reasons, for example between the USA and North Korea.
3 Prohibition of transactions involving countries subject to UN sanctions (for instance, the former Rhodesia).

Controls on banking activities

1 Reserve requirements on funds borrowed from foreign branches.
2 Foreign exchange position limits.
3 Lending is being restricted to certain classes of countries.
4 Ceilings are clamped on the granting of foreign credit.
5 There can be restrictions on the maturities of foreign credit granted.
6 The subsidiaries of foreign-owned companies may be denied access to local-currency credit.
7 Imposition of taxes on foreign deposits resulting in negative interest rates.

8 Imposition of taxes on local deposits resulting in negative interest rates (for example Switzerland at one time, Hong Kong now).
9 Direct limits on non-resident deposits.
10 Limitations on the use of local currency financing of all foreign trade.
11 Limitations on the use of local currency financing of trade between third countries.
12 Exemption from reserve requirements on non-resident local currency deposits.
13 Prohibition on transactions with non-residents that would lead to the forward sale of the local currency.
14 Required surrender of foreign exchange beyond established permissible spot positions.
15 Application of more or less favourable exchange rates to funds borrowed abroad under a multiple exchange rate system.
16 Requirement of non-interest-bearing prior deposits on foreign borrowings.
17 Ceilings on the volume of forward exchange sales to non-residents.

Controls on foreign borrowing and lending

1 Withholding taxes on interest and dividend payments to non-residents when those payments result from foreign borrowing by resident companies or their offshore financing subsidiaries.
2 The use of special exchange rates for capital flows under multiple exchange rate system (financial versus commercial exchange rate).
3 Ceilings on the granting or raising of foreign loans.
4 The requirement for overseas subsidiaries of multinational companies to retain funds raised locally in the host country.
5 A mandate that funds borrowed abroad in foreign currency must be surrendered for local currency.
6 Prohibitions on foreign borrowing in order to finance direct foreign investment.
7 Prescribed minimum or maximum maturities.
8 Prescription of currencies in which loans may be granted or received.
9 The restriction of foreign lending to foreign buyers of the home country's exports.

Controls on the payment of dividends, royalties and technical assistance fees

1 Limitations on such remittances to a specified percentage of the value (book value or otherwise) of the assets held (as in the case of Andean Pact regulations).
2 Ban on inter-company netting with offsetting payments.
3 Prescription of currency in which remittances may be made.
4 Complete prohibition on certain categories of remittances.
5 Restrictions on the 'leads' and 'lags', i.e., on delay or prepayment of scheduled remittances.

Controls on direct foreign investment flows

1 Ceilings on direct foreign investment (inbound or outbound).
2 Limits on the re-investment of earnings.
3 Limitation of investment outflows to certain specified geographical regions (for instance to less developed countries).
4 Application of an unfavourable exchange rate for investments under a multiple exchange rate system.
5 A requirement that a certain percentage of an investment must be financed by foreign interests.
6 A requirement that residents of the host country must own a certain percentage of the equity.
7 A requirement that foreign investors deliver proof their venture will generate positive balance of payments effects (which is to say it will generate net foreign exchange earnings) within a prescribed maximum time period.
8 A prescription of local-currency deposits in non-interest-bearing accounts equivalent to a specified percentage of the investment outflow.
9 Mandatory repatriation of the proceeds from any liquidation of foreign investments.
10 Investments may be undertaken only in prescribed currencies.

Controls on capital flows linked to portfolio investments

1 Interest equalization taxes equivalent to a given percentage of the value of foreign securities or equity held.
2 Restrictions clamped by the host country on portfolio investment in

351

specific industries (frequently those deemed to be of national security interest, such as defence or broadcasting, and services such as banking.)

3 Application of a special, unfavourable investment exchange rate under a multiple exchange rate system.
4 Prescription for residents and/or non-residents of the use of an 'investment currency pool' for which a free-market premium must be paid.
5 Requirement of non-interest-bearing local currency deposits equivalent to specified percentage of investment outflows.
6 Required repatriation of any proceeds from the liquidation of foreign portfolio investments.
7 Prescription of the currency in which foreign investment may be undertaken.
8 Prescribed minimum terms for foreign notes and bonds in which residents may invest.

Controls on export receipts

1 Mandated surrender of foreign exchange receipts to the local authorities within a certain period of time (to prevent hoarding of such receipts in foreign exchange).
2 Restrictions on the export credit terms that may be granted.
3 Restrictions on the acceptance of prepayment for exports.
4 Prohibition of inter-company netting of offsetting export and import payments.
5 Prescription of the currency or currencies in which exports may be invoiced and payments may be received.
6 Availability of forward exchange cover only at non-market rates.
7 Application of special exchange rates for trade transactions with certain countries under bilateral agreements.

Controls on import payments

1 Non-availability of foreign exchange for certain categories of imports (generally non-essentials).
2 Application of differing exchange rates for various classes of imports under multiple exchange rate systems.
3 Limitations on, or prohibition of, prepayment.

4 Prescription of maximum or minimum credit terms that may be accepted by the importer.

5 Prohibition of inter-company netting of offsetting export and import payments.

6 Prescription of a limited number of currencies in which payment may be made.

7 Prior deposit requirements, that is, mandated local-currency deposits in non-interest-bearing accounts equivalent to a certain percentage of the invoice value, for a specified period of time.

8 Application of penalty interest rates or taxes on trade credits of certain maturities.

9 Prepayment permitted only with foreign funds borrowed from local banks.

10 Availability of forward cover only at non-market rates.

11 Application of special exchange rates for trade under bilateral agreements with selected countries.

12 Limitation of forward hedging contracts to underlying merchandise trade transactions.

13 Restrictions on the maximum maturity of forward exchange hedging contracts.

14 A requirement that the maturity of forward exchange contracts taken out to hedge an import payment must coincide, or nearly coincide, with the commercial payment date.

15 Availability of forward exchange contracts for specific transactions at non-market rates.

16 Required deposit in local currency of a portion of all forward exchange purchases.

Even from this incomplete and merely indicative list it will be seen that governmental inventiveness knows no bounds when it comes to devising restrictions and controls that impede the free flow of goods, capital and foreign exchange. The main reason is that – while the world's economies are becoming ever more integrated into a truly global market for goods, services, and capital – economic policies fashioned by national governments are still very much designed with strictly national concerns in mind. To make this possible, governments need walls of control and restrictions lest their national designs be overwhelmed by the forces of international currents.

The global debt crisis that began in the late summer of 1982 – when Mexico came within a hair's breadth of insolvency and informed its creditors at a history-making meeting at the New York Federal Reserve Board that it would have to declare default unless it were granted a long-term rescheduling at favourable interest rates as well as massive new loans – has predictably led to a proliferation of exchange controls worldwide, as country after country has sought to limit imports and boost exports in a desparate (often IMF-prescribed) effort to earn enough foreign exchange to service what is owed abroad. The crisis has also put paid to the quaint notion that 'there is no such thing as sovereign risk', since 'countries never go bankrupt'.

Indeed they do not. But as every credit manager learns in the first few days on the job, the ability of a debtor to pay is only half of what needs to be assessed. The other half is the debtor's will to make timely, full interest remittances and to settle principal when it is due. Today, for many of the less developed countries, the ability to pay is in serious doubt. And for a growing number, the existence of the will must be questioned as well.

Back in the early 1970s the total foreign debt of the less developed countries (LDCs) amounted to roughly US$100 billion. The portion that needed to be rescheduled at the time was perhaps US$1 billion. But in 1983, one year after the eruption of the debt crisis, the aggregate LDC debt came to a staggering US$860 billion, plus US$80 billion or so in obligations by Communist Eastern Europe, for an overall total of US$940 billion.

More than half of this sum was owed to private banks. Reschedulings under way involved twenty-four countries, fifteen of them in Latin America, owing US$360 billion in all. Restructurings were needed and pending in the magnitude of at least US$40 billion in that year and in 1984. Just seven nations – Mexico, Brazil, Argentina, Venezuela, Chile, Yugoslavia and Poland – owed one-third of the total debt, and some 80 per cent of the obligations to be rescheduled.

Since then, we have seen much activity on the international financial scene. But behind the smokescreen of reschedulings, refinancings, stretch-outs and all kinds of other financial acrobatics, no real solutions have been found. In effect this means that international credit executives dealing with LDCs must be keenly concerned with not only exchange rate fluctuations, but also sovereign risk and transfer or convertibility risk.

Sovereign risk, by definition, refers to the inability or unwillingness of a government entity to raise sufficient amounts of foreign exchange to service its foreign currency debt obligations. Transfer or convertibility risk rests with the inability of companies in the private sector to raise enough foreign exchange to meet their overseas obligations, even though they are in good financial condition domestically.

Sovereign risk

The sovereign risk arises because in international trade a large volume of business is conducted on credit between private or public sector exporters and foreign governments through their various agencies, departments, ministries or state-owned productive enterprises. Many exporters tend to assume that, because they are dealing with a government, their risk is less than if they were doing business with a private company; others similarly tend to believe that a public sector customer is 'safer' than a private sector one.

In reality, neither generalization is accurate. As a rule, when a country runs into serious balance of payments and exchange availability problems, government entities confront many of the same difficulties that private companies are exposed to. Frequently, though, they are being given privileged access to the dwindling foreign currency reserves.

During the cited Mexican payment crisis in 1982, for instance, the state-owned oil concern Pemex (Petroleos Mexicanos) retained an excellent payments record, while private companies very quickly began to build up arrears. By contrast, exporters that had granted trade credits to government entities in Venezuela found payments blocked – and more recently have been forced into eight-year reschedulings – while most of their private sector customers tried hard, and often successfully, to keep payments reasonably up to date.

Transfer or convertibility risk

The concept of sovereign risk thus overlaps the broader one of transfer or convertibility risk, which in essence defines the danger that on due date an importer may not be able to obtain – at acceptable exchange rates – the foreign currency needed to pay the foreign supplier. The reason is usually a severe exchange shortage in the importer's country, which has prompted the government to impose more or less drastic controls.

Where these controls are already in place, the supplier can take them into consideration and structure an export deal accordingly. The real danger lies with situations where controls leading to total or partial inconvertibility of the importer's currency are clamped on after the export shipment has been made, but before payment has been effected. Unfortunately, since the eruption of the international debt crisis, the cases of countries plunging rather abruptly into exchange difficulties and responding with equally abrupt control efforts have multiplied, and a reversal of this trend is nowhere in sight.

Precautions

There are a number of precautions exporters can take to guard against this eventuality. Often in LDCs the availability of foreign exchange for overseas purchases is linked to an import licence; where such a document is required, it behoves the exporter to make sure – before shipment – that the customer does, in fact, have a licence. Where foreign exchange in the importing country is allocated in line with an officially stipulated priority schedule, the exporter must ascertain that the goods to be shipped are high enough on the priority list to be assured foreign exchange.

Certainly, when exchange controls prescribe how credit may be extended, under what terms (type and maturity) and for what purposes, the exporters must see to it that the envisaged arrangement meets regulations. If there is a multiple exchange rate system, the supplier should know precisely at what rate the customer will have to remit payment. If there is a 'waiting list' for import payments, the supplier should have a good idea about whether the goods shipped will wind up near the top or the bottom of the list. In LDCs existing country regulations usually determine the make-up of foreign trade transactions, including credit terms, the availability or non-availability of confirmation on letters of credit, and the required documentation. An exporter to such countries can greatly reduce the risk of not getting paid on time simply by making sure that all existing regulations are complied with.

Options when it is too late for precautions

There are no guarantees, though, that such regulations will not be changed overnight if exchange shortages become dramatic. While an exporter can and should use discretion in the provision of credit, to hedge against the danger of adverse regulatory changes 'in mid-transaction', so to speak, for instance by tightening terms from 180 days to sight draft, or from ninety-day date draft to cash in advance, the world is a competitive place that will time and again force sellers of goods and commodities to choose between sales on risky terms and no sales at all.

The consequence can be 'blocked funds', that is, payments that the importer either has made or could make in local currency, but which cannot be converted into foreign exchange for remittance abroad. Caught in this kind of situation, an exporter no longer has any 'good' choices. Still, there are ways of getting blocked funds out. These are as manifold as are the restrictions that have created them in the first place.

Sometimes, when foreign exchange has become unavailable through official channels, there are parallel markets that are tolerated or even encouraged by the authorities. In Venezuela importers who brought goods into the country prior to the devaluation of February 1984, and were subsequently confronted with the inability to make outbound payments at any one of the officially controlled 'preferential' exchange rates, were never denied the possibility to effect payment via the free market for bolivars, where dollars could be had all along, albeit only at a drastically downgraded rate.

A Brazilian importer of services facing obstacles in paying the foreign supplier service fees, royalties, technical assistance fees and the like, can use the parallel market for cruzados to satisfy such obligations abroad. Mexico has a very extensive free market for pesos, through which large amounts can be transacted (if usually at considerably more unfavourable exchange rates than offered by the controlled market).

At times an importer in an LDC has the possibility of effecting payment from accounts held abroad. Many Central and South American companies have accounts in the USA (frequently in Miami) in which they collect earnings from various overseas operations. Similarly, African companies may have accounts in Paris, and Middle Eastern companies in London. These accounts are generally maintained in violation of the parent country's exchange regulations, but this can be viewed as the importer's problem; for the exporter shipping against payment from such accounts, there is usually no onus attached.

Occasionally an investor can be found who is interested in acquiring foreign trade debts (at a discount) for which the supplier is paid in dollars or other convertible currencies, while the investor uses the local-currency funds paid by the importer to fund the investment. As the international debt crisis sharpened in recent years, many over-borrowed countries have, in fact, set up rules and systems to encourage debt-equity conversion. In response, debt capitalization techniques have become an important, unorthodox tool with which Third World countries can reduce their foreign obligations. Holders of such IOUs can whittle down their exposures, investors can garner cheap funds for capital projects and intermediaries can earn fat fees.

In its simplest form, a debt-equity swap involves (1) the purchase by a third party of a debtor country's foreign-currency denominated obligations at a discount; (2) their subsequent redemption at a smaller discount or even at face value in the obligor's local currency; and (3) the investment of the proceeds in equity in the debtor country. Ideally, the end-effect of the process is that the foreign holder of the LDC's paper has worked down the loan exposure, the country in question has trimmed its overall indebtedness abroad, and thus its interest bill, and the investor has obtained capital for much less than if the local-currency funds had been bought in the normal manner.

Countries with active debt–equity swap provisions on their books include Chile, Mexico, Brazil, Argentina and the Philippines. The concept is likely to spread, and while at present it is mostly bank debt that is converted in this manner, supplier credits will, most likely, play a growing role as well.

Trade debts secured by government bonds (for example, the stabilization bonds in Guatemala or Ecuador) can on occasion be sold (at discounts) to investors willing to hold them and to gamble that they will be paid at some future date. There are secondary markets for such bonds, and so long as there is some prospect of the paper being redeemed 'eventually', buyers will exist (with the discounts demanded by them depending on their perception of the debtor country's reliability).

Payment in kind (in merchandise) can sometimes replace cash when foreign exchange becomes unavailable. As stated at the outset, LDCs and their suppliers are seeing a revival (of sorts) of barter trade, despite the difficulty of constructing such transactions to the satisfaction of all the parties concerned. At times, moreover, exporters seeking to ship to a 'problem' country may be able to do a 'back-to-back' deal, in which the LDC customer effects payment in local currency to the local subsidiary of a third party, whose overseas parent then pays the exporter in foreign exchange.

All these options, however, involve a usually very substantial cost. The exporter will, as a rule, receive only a fraction of the original invoice value. It is, therefore, far better to put the greatest possible emphasis on researching the sovereign or transfer risk before an export contract is entered into, and structure the terms in keeping with this assessment. If the risk is deemed difficult to gauge, cash in advance or confirmed letter of credit should be chosen. If neither is available (as can easily happen in the case of some of the more over-borrowed among the LDCs), export credit insurance from government or private sources remains an option. If insurance is not available either, one should seriously consider not going through with the deal at all.

PART VII
FINANCE AND CASH/CURRENCY MANAGEMENT

20

European and US export finance

Brian Clarke

In many corporations, the raising of external funds to finance exports and the management of all funds, earned or borrowed, tends to be on the periphery of the credit management function, whilst in certain others it is deeply embedded within it. Whether the international credit manager is directly or only indirectly involved, however, he or she needs to have a sound appreciation of the ways in which funds can be raised and the techniques for managing them, be they in national or foreign currencies. Part Seven of the handbook is thus devoted to these matters.

The expression 'export finance', like so many others used in international credit, can mean all things to all men. In its most general sense it is often taken to comprehend many inter-linked export credit activities but in this and the following chapter it is used in its narrower and purer sense to denote the raising of monies specifically to help finance the manufacture and sale of exports.

The best and cheapest source of finance is of course the prompt collection of trading debts properly due to the corporation. Some degree of additional finance is, however, often necessary, particularly if the relatively long periods of credit associated with exporting are to be covered adequately.

The range of sources available will vary according to the country in which the requirement arises and the nature of the business – capital project items requiring long or medium term credit, or consumer goods on short term credit. Many of the sources depend upon separate guarantees being available from credit insurance agencies and the like, and in recent years these have not been so easy to come by, because of the number of countries left in financial difficulties by the world debt crisis.

EUROPEAN SOURCES OF FINANCE

The European money markets are still amongst the most highly developed in the world, and, because of their long established involvement in world trade, offer the most comprehensive range of export finance services.

London still leads the way in these specialized areas and a detailed description of the services available in the UK is given in Chapter 21.

Other financial centres in Europe such as Frankfurt and Zurich compete strongly with London and this competition is expected to become even fiercer as, on the one hand, the stagnating effect of the world debt crisis continues to be felt and, on the other, the 'single market' targeted for 1992 approaches.

In particular, all of this means that the commercial banks and their specialized subsidiaries are concentrating more and more on providing custom-built deals which offer the precise form of finance required by each exporter; and the credit agencies which support them with guarantees are also having to be more inventive to keep their business flowing with such devices as using the international securities market to refinance their export credits.

EC regional aid

In the European Communities, as part of the run up to the single market of 1992, the EC Commission plans to increase its EC regional aid grants to more than fourteen billion ECUs by the year 1993. These structural funds will be allocated primarily to the poorer nations of Europe for financing major public works and capital projects.

This in turn should create export opportunities not just for European corporations, but also, consequent upon the liberalization of public procurement, for corporations from other countries which are able to meet the competition.

USA SOURCES OF FINANCE

By comparison with Europe, the USA export finance market as a specialist area is relatively undeveloped. In the past the average US businessman was not so internationally minded as his European – or Japanese – counterpart and was not accustomed to offering longer terms of credit for exports and having to find ways of financing all or part of the extra waiting period. All that, however, has gradually been changing; in 1972 only four per cent of the US gross national product was derived from foreign trade. In 1988 the percentage was around fifteen making the USA, because of its sheer size, one of the world's largest exporters in trade value terms. However, the USA also imports rather a lot and if it is to overcome its severe balance of payments deficit, its exports must surely go on increasing and the specialist export finance market must some way expand.

At present the sources of finance in the USA are as follows.

Commercial banks

Whereas, say, in the UK there are a relatively small number of large, well organized banks, in the USA there are thousands of local and/or regional banks, many of which have never had to address themselves to international trade. Because of regulation, they were until recently unable to expand beyond state boundaries and there was thus a tendency for their banking services to be specific to the requirements of the local industry – perhaps, for instance, exclusively agricultural – with their fortunes rising or falling in line with that industry.

Deregulation is now taking place, with a beneficial trend towards interstate banking giving the larger groups more opportunity to develop their range of international services. Some of the really large groups, however, even more so than their European counterparts, are still saddled with massive, virtually uncollectable Third World debts and are reluctant to look far beyond their domestic market for any future expansion of lending.

In the meantime, some of the European banks are expanding across the Atlantic, largely by acquisition in the case of the British banks, at least one of which has declared its aim to provide large USA corporations with the same range of corporate finance services that it offers in London to their UK counterparts.

Eximbank

The Export–Import Bank of the United States is an independent federal banking corporation established in 1934 to promote US exports by way of loans, loan guarantees and export credit insurance.

Its export credit insurance policies are issued and serviced through

365

the Foreign Credit Insurance Association (FCIA), a group of US property, casualty and marine insurance companies with which Eximbank has an agency and re-insurance agreement.

Eximbank's programmes fall into two main categories – buyer credits and supplier credits.

Buyer credits involve the making of direct loans to foreign suppliers or guaranteeing loans made to them by commercial banks or other private sector lenders. The trade involved is normally of the large capital project variety requiring a long term credit period.

Supplier credits cover fixed rate bank funding or loan guarantees and generally relate to medium term exports requiring credit periods up to five years. One of the supplier credit programmes, however, the Working Capital Guarantee Program, can assist creditworthy small to medium sized companies in pre-export financing, by guaranteeing up to 90 per cent of working capital loans which private lending institutions would otherwise be unwilling to make.

Interest rates

Interest rates applicable to Eximbank's loans vary according to the length of the repayment period and the country to which the export is being made. Countries are categorized Rich, Intermediate or Poor, according to the classification adopted in the OECD Arrangement on Officially Supported Export Credits, known as the Consensus and described in Chapter 10.

Export credit insurance

Export credit insurance cover available through FCIA offers a wide range of options from one year blanket policies insuring short term credit sales through to medium term single buyer policies. The policy proceeds are usually assignable for financing purposes.

Current levels of activity

Like the commercial banks, Eximbank has seen its operations shrink of late because of low demand for project finance following the world debt crisis; and like other credit insurance agencies it has suffered large losses through payment of claims deriving from Third World debt.

Its ability to make direct loans is governed by the USA budget, currently severely restricted. Indeed out of its allocation for the whole of the 1988 fiscal year, nearly two-thirds had already been authorized by the end of the first quarter.

Recent changes in Eximbank's programmes allow higher fees to be charged for loans to some of the riskier countries, thereby enabling them to stay in those markets. Thus in early 1988 only fifteen of the world's most risky markets were out of bounds, in addition to twenty-seven politically unacceptable 'Marxist-Leninist' countries.

Another move towards increased liquidity for export finance is Eximbank's decision to make all its guarantees comprehensive and unconditional and fully transferable to a secondary market. Eximbank's ability to support a sustained increase in US exports, however, will rely upon a less frugal budget approach from the US government and, perhaps, some once-off recapitalization.

A detailed 'Map of Eximbank Programs' is available. This and other information can be obtained from their Marketing Department at 811, Vermont Avenue, NW, Washington, DC 20571, USA.

Other sources

Whether for export activity or any other requirements, US industrialists have traditionally been able to finance their businesses by borrowing in one way or another from:

1 Factors – who will buy accounts receivable and advance up to 90 per cent of invoice face value for a fee plus interest up to the date of the customer's payment. (The different aspects of factoring are described in Chapters 9 and 21).
2 Asset based lenders – who put primary emphasis upon the borrower's collateral, fully intending to liquidate it in the event of non-repayment of loans.
3 Venture capitalists – who normally take up an equity position in the borrowing company as consideration for the risks involved.

AID FUNDS

The stark economic imbalance between the developed nations of the world and the less developed countries (LDCs) has led to a variety of international aid schemes designed to make funds available to enable the LDCs to purchase the capital equipment and plant which they desperately need – and which the developed nations desperately wish to sell.

These schemes are put together by foreign governments and international agencies in one of the following ways and take the form of grants or loans.

1   Bilateral aid, where one donor country provides all the funding.
2   Multilateral aid, where the money is accumulated by an international agency from several different sources.

Exporters of capital project equipment, wishing to take advantage of such schemes in order to sell to the LDCs, are advised to keep abreast of the negotiations that take place from time to time between the Third World governments seeking aid and the richer governments and agencies who are likely to provide it. These donor conferences, as they are called, are, where appropriate, overseen by the World Bank (see below) and the International Monetary Fund to ensure compatibility with any national development plans and overall economic objectives. They normally result in the announcement of an aid programme, or line of credit available for suitable projects.

The main sources of aid finance for the LDCs are:

The World Bank

The World Bank, or to give it its proper title, The International Bank for Reconstruction and Development (IBRD), is based in Washington DC, USA, and offers low cost or 'soft' loans to the poorer countries through its International Development Association.

The World Bank obtains its funds by way of contributions from the richer countries of the world, the USA being its largest contributor. It enhances the availability of funds with a process of co-financing, finding partners in the private financial sector who are prepared to make similar loan funds available, on the basis that no Third World government is likely to default on repayments and risk the wrath of the World Bank.

For the credit manager concerned with large Third World contracts, the beauty of World Bank funding is that, for approved contracts, payment is made in full and on time.

Regional agencies

The better known regional agencies are the Inter-American Development Bank in Washington DC, USA, the African Development Bank and Fund in Abidjan Cote d'Ivoire and the Asian Development Bank in Manila, The Philippines.

Opportunities for funding capital projects are publicized through various embassies in Washington, Abidjan and Manila.

In the EEC, the European Development Fund invites bids for the community financing of African and other projects. Elsewhere there are a number of other overseas sources, notably in the Arab world.

Individual governments

The extent to which governments may subsidize interest rates and offer so called 'soft loans' to foreign countries according to how rich or poor they are is laid down by the OECD Consensus mentioned earlier. The funds are obviously provided only on the condition that they are used for the purchase of capital equipment from the donor country. Competitions between manufacturers of such capital goods is fierce in the pursuit of key overseas contracts and many accusations are made of governments getting around the consensus rules by incorporating straight aid funds into their commercial financing deals or making use of other 'softening' devices. Whether this is considered to be sharp practice or just being realistic in the face of competition, it makes sense for exporters of capital goods to be constantly on the alert for such opportunities.

In the UK, overseas development aid is channelled through the Aid and Trade Provision (ATP) from which grants of around 25 per cent of a project's value can sometimes be obtained to assist in the quest for hard won important overseas contracts.

Japan and France make similar provisions but the USA has abandoned the 'USA War Chest' which it originally set up to defend its international trade in the face of other countries' soft loan facilities.

Recommended reading

Ludlow, Nicholas. (1988) *A Practical Guide to the Development Bank Business*. Washington D.C. Development Bank Associates. A handbook for exporters of capital equipment interested in bidding for overseas development projects funded by the World Bank and the multilateral development banks.

21

UK export finance

Roger Pilcher

The purpose of this chapter is to define the needs for export finance, mainly of the short-term variety, and the ways in which an exporter can satisfy those needs both securely and profitably. Inevitably, there is a strong inter-relationship between this subject and many of those dealt with in other chapters; areas of overlap are kept to a minimum and readers should refer to the relevant chapters for in-depth information on other topics. However, one that cannot be divorced from finance is foreign exchange, as the exporter seeking to maximize sales by meeting currency preferences of foreign buyers may well tap the same sources for both money and foreign exchange protection; so greater reference will necessarily be made to this subject.

Before getting into detail on the question of export cashflow and sources of finance, it is perhaps worth dealing at this stage with one issue that frequently gives rise to misunderstandings whenever export finance is discussed: 'recourse'. One often sees reference, both in advertising and other forms of publicity to 'non-recourse finance'. Before pursuing any particular opportunity, exporters should be clear in their minds as to the meaning of this expression; experience demonstrates that there are those who believe that a without recourse facility provides them with a secure source of finance, completely protected against any misadventures, claims or disputes of whatever nature that may subsequently arise. Most banks or finance companies offering such facilities make it clear that they are subject to repayment should the exporting company not honour its contract of sale with the buyer or the terms of any supporting credit insurance policy. On the other hand, some facilities are completely without recourse so far as the lender is concerned but leave the exporter, in the final analysis, liable to arbitration and possible litigation at the instigation of an aggrieved buyer.

A perfectly fair arrangement, one might say, but beware falling into the trap of believing that financial institutions are prepared to take the direct risks of any unfulfilled contracts.

FEATURES OF EXPORT CASHFLOW

The aim of any well run company must be to keep borrowings at the lowest possible level, so the starting point has to be a clear evaluation of cashflow implications given the longer credit usually offered to overseas buyers and the related greater costs of financing sales.

Overseas buyers in many markets expect, or more often demand, sixty-day, ninety-day or even longer credit for transactions that in the home market would be on thirty-day terms. The short-term exporter, selling to a spread of overseas markets, may well be looking at a debt-turn more in the region of eighty to ninety days, rather than, say, forty-five to sixty days given good credit control procedures in domestic business. It is therefore essential to ensure that terms offered are no more generous than for comparable industries in each overseas market, that stringent collection procedures are applied based upon proper understanding of local trading practices and, dare it be said, that follow-up communications to slow payers should, whenever possible, be in their own languages. Effective use of credit insurance provides protection against bad debts; its misuse in the sense of delayed reporting of overdues and submission of claims results in unnecessarily prolonged waiting periods which seriously undermine cashflow. Compliance with the correct procedures at the outset ensures that collections are completed on time, whereas sloppy work in this area always leads to a slowing down in cashflow.

The various features referred to above are the concern of efficient export administration. In this context, it is surprising how many companies run a consolidated sales accounting system with foreign buyers intermingled with those in the home market. Apart from the dilution of effective control implied by this arrangement, the ability to communicate constructively with buyers so as to sell on the right terms in various markets, to ensure efficient collection procedures and, above all, to measure export cashflow and the cost of funding sales as separate entities from domestic business must be questioned. Ideally, customer accounting on a country by country basis allows the most efficient measurement both of the cost of sales and the extent and cost of finance specifically supporting the export side of the business.

Given professional planning and control, cashflow once brought to the point where further improvement is difficult to achieve will determine the lowest possible level at which funding has to be paid for. However, in this exercise equal care must also be taken to recognize the effect of seasonal peaks and troughs and, most important of all, to plan for adequate financial support for profitable expansion.

SOURCES OF FINANCE

Long/medium-term finance

Much long/medium-term finance is available through a variety of well-structured forfaiting schemes and lines of credit.

Forfaiting

Forfaiting of capital projects developed in trade with the East European countries and the main centres of financial activity were in Zürich and Vienna, close to the Comecon borders. London has now assumed a dominant role.

In a forfaiting operation involving long- or medium-term credit, a series of trade bills or promissory notes is usually avalized either by a state bank or some other major bank and the bills are readily discountable by a forfaiting bank without recourse.

The exporter thus achieves front end financing and is relieved of any future credit risk or exchange risk; and as the arrangement is off balance sheet and the risk has been shifted, the exporter's banking facilities are not eroded. (Chapter 9 considers the various ways of sharing the risk.)

Lines of credit

Lines of credit are arranged by banks to cover the export of particular types of capital goods to specific markets or groups of markets.

Each line will be for a specific total amount and will specify minimum contract values which the bank will consider for qualification and the range of credit periods acceptable.

The lines are well advertised but, remarkably, are not always fully utilized.

Overdraft

Traditionally, overdrafts are by far the largest source, with over 70 per cent of UK short-term export finance being provided by the clearing banks by this means. In the great majority of cases, the overdraft is not specific to a company's export business, but is a line of finance with a fixed but renegotiable ceiling, made available as a source of additional day-to-day working capital.

The size of facilities, their cost and the collateral required by a bank will depend upon the standing of the customer in terms of balance sheet strength, trading prospects, perceived quality of management and, where called for, the value of security available.

The overdraft is primarily intended to meet short-term needs and, whilst the majority of companies enjoy reasonable facilities on a continuing basis, it should always be remembered that advances on overdraft are repayable on demand, such demand being made either as a result of a bank's changed attitude to its customer's business or external restrictions which result in a general curtailment of lending. When an overdraft facility is arranged specifically in support of export sales, banks frequently seek collateral through the assignment of an export credit insurance policy and by a specific charge over export receivables.

The cost of overdraft borrowing, as already stated, varies considerably from company to company. In addition to interest, the exporter must expect to pay arrangement fees for setting up the facility and an annual renewal fee, quite apart from the normal charges related specifically to export business, for example, for the handling of documentary collections and foreign currency transactions.

With regard to foreign currency risks, these can be covered through the banks by taking out forward contracts under which the bank guarantees in advance the payment of a fixed amount of sterling against the invoiced foreign currency for a fixed term – usually thirty, sixty or ninety days (see Chapter 22 for details of this and other methods of foreign exchange management). Forward contracts do not, of course, constitute an additional financial facility; indeed, the exporter needs to be satisfied in advance that the reverse is not actually the case, that is, that the bank will not reduce its customer's financial facility as collateral against possible non-receipt of the foreign currency due under the forward contract.

Foreign currency overdrafts

Overdrafts can also be arranged in the principal trading currencies, with interest being charged as a margin over the banks' prevailing base rates for each individual currency. This facility provides exporters with the opportunity to borrow in the currencies in which they are selling, or in third currencies, so as to take advantage of the considerably lower interest rates available in some markets by comparison with those at home; exporters should, however, be aware that significant fluctuations can occur at short notice in many overseas interest rates. In the final analysis, whilst the proceeds of such borrowing may be converted immediately to the exporter's domestic currency, eventual repayment has to be in the currency borrowed and thus, if the exporter is using this technique to finance sales in a variety of currencies, it will inevitably result in somewhat complex administration. It also becomes more difficult to achieve an effective match between borrowing requirements and cashflow.

Short-term finance schemes

In 1960 a scheme was introduced in the UK by ECGD, which offered an exporting company, holding comprehensive short-term insurance cover, the ability to obtain an ECGD guarantee to its bank, known as the Comprehensive Bankers Guarantee (CBG), in return for which the bank would provide finance at 5/8 per cent over base rate plus the bank's normal handling and bill collection charges. The ceiling on each facility was set by ECGD, which charged an additional premium (over and above that charged for the credit insurance policy) of a minimum 25p, maximum 40p per £100 of the agreed limit. The arrangement was available in support of business transacted both by means of bills and notes and on open account. Many exporters made use of this scheme; but whilst the cost of borrowing appeared exceptionally low, in combination with the additional premium – charged whether or not the facility was fully drawn-down – it was less attractive to larger companies already able to command very fine interest rates. However, the arrangement was eventually withdrawn in 1987 following losses incurred by ECGD resulting from operational difficulties inherent in the scheme.

Bank schemes

To replace this facility, most of the banks announced formalized short-term schemes with similar characteristics to the Smaller Exporters schemes that several had introduced from 1979 onwards. At the time of writing, such schemes have now been introduced by all the UK clearing banks.

The purpose of all the schemes is to enable exporters to obtain advances of the credit insured value of their sales as soon as possible after shipment. As the format of the schemes varies in a number of ways from bank to bank, it is impossible here to do more than give a general description of the variations; details of each scheme are, of course, easily obtained from individual banks. Some schemes are totally undisclosed to overseas buyers whilst others require specific instructions to be given on invoices, to the effect that indebtedness has been assigned to the lending bank.

Without exception, the schemes were originally available against the background of credit insurance provided by ECGD; recently, some banks have agreed to accept policies from the private sector. The majority of facilities were set up based on the banks' own 'Managers' policies taken out with ECGD. Under this arrangement, the exporting company deals with the bank in obtaining credit sanctions, reporting overdues and making claims, as opposed to dealing direct with ECGD or via brokers. Following this route, the level of funding is controlled by the bank, which also has to ensure that the exporter complies fully with the terms of the ECGD policy, as it has no recourse to the insurer should problems arise due to maladministration or malpractice. In the event, the earlier schemes were modified and the later arrivals set up to incorporate the opportunity for exporters to obtain the facility, using their own policy direct with ECGD, without having to go through the bank as intermediary. However, whilst bank attitudes vary on this point, there remains a tendency to restrict the use of exporters' own policies to larger customers.

Whilst nearly all the schemes require reporting of each individual transaction, with full evidence of shipment and detailed accounting for collections, in some cases banks take no specific security (beyond any charges they may already hold over the exporting company), whilst others take a formal assignment of receivables and one, Barclays, offers an option under which it makes an outright purchase of the goods being

375

shipped, thus becoming title holder and undisclosed principal with the exporter acting as its agent for the sales and collection of proceeds. In virtually all cases the banks offer more than one scheme in recognition of the different characteristics in export businesses of varying sizes. For example, Lloyds Bank refers exporters with sales of less than £1 million per annum to its group factoring companies for facilities (see later).

Facilities involving the assignment of receivables or the sale of goods to the bank providing finance may generally be treated as 'off balance sheet', but the exporting company would be wise to take advice from its auditors on this point. To cover the direct funding cost of the facilities there is a commonly applied charge (albeit under a variety of labels!) at a mark-up over base rate, with the rate varying according to the characteristics of the customer's business. In addition, there is a variety of other charges for setting up and renewing facilities, charges for credit insurance when this is provided under the umbrella of the bank's own policy with ECGD, charges per transaction and currency charges when sales are invoiced in foreign currencies. Not all are applied under these headings by banks, so a careful analysis must be made by the exporter so as to interpret the true likely cost of funding business in this way.

Foreign exchange protection for sales invoiced in currencies is not an integral part of the schemes, but is available from all the banks through the use of forward contracts (discussed at greater length in Chapter 22). Again, as suggested in the section above on overdraft borrowing, the exporter should take care to ascertain whether the use of forward contracts will have any adverse effect on the size of financial facility available.

Similar schemes, though as yet promoted on a less formal basis, are offered by subsidiaries or branches of several foreign banks in London.

Exfinco

A specialist financial scheme, rather more comprehensive in its nature than the bank schemes as it embraces foreign exchange protection as an integral part, is that introduced in the UK by The Export Finance Company Limited (Exfinco) in 1985. Not a bank, but a finance company backed by major institutional shareholders, Exfinco was established as a result of a survey of financial export facilities carried out by the British Export-Finance Advisory Council, which identified a number of needs not otherwise covered at that time.

In practical terms, the company was set up as a corporate treasury, having the sole function of supporting the short-term finance and foreign exchange needs of British exporters. It is not involved in any other form of business and its services can be described more as being complementary to, rather than competitive with, those of the banks, as in the majority of cases they do not impinge on the mainstream banking relationship between the exporting company and its bankers.

The Exfinco scheme is similar to those of the banks, in that it provides payment of the credit insured value of sales following shipment. In two respects this payment differs: settlement of the credit-insured value is made immediately following receipt of simple evidence of shipment; and the uninsured balance (less any credits raised or adjustments made by the exporter) is automatically paid on the average date of payment of the exporter's overseas customers as a whole, as opposed to settlement as and when each individual buyer pays. Payment is made to exporters either in sterling or, if preferred, in convertible overseas currencies.

The main differences between this 'package' and that of the banks is the way in which foreign exchange cover is totally integrated (should it be required) with the financial facility. This relieves the exporter of the administration involved in handling forward contracts, other than having to inform Exfinco of cancellations of shipments and significant variations in terms that may arise between order and shipment.

Exfinco obtains security through the background of the exporter's credit insurance policy (that of ECGD or equivalent cover from the private sector) and by becoming undisclosed principal in each transaction. In essence it makes a standing offer to buy from the exporter goods ordered by overseas customers; and the exporter accepts this offer by evidencing shipment to Exfinco.

As purchaser for cash of the goods exported, Exfinco takes a cash discount, which is calculated at a margin over the average of clearing bank base rates. Discount on payments taken in foreign currencies is calculated by reference to the individual base rates for those currencies. The discount is charged for the average time that the individual buyers take to pay. The net result, therefore, is directly comparable with the rate over base rate charged on overdraft but there are no arrangement or renewal fees, transaction or foreign exchange charges. As an additional service, tender to contract options are available, as is also a documentary collection service.

The Exfinco arrangement can be treated by exporters as off balance sheet with the discount being netted against the value of the sales.

Overall the scheme can assist exporters to sell in currencies preferred by their buyers, without risk and with the advantage of fully predictable cashflow.

Discounting accepted drafts/bills of exchange

Documentary credits which provide support to a large proportion of short-term export transactions and, when used efficiently, provide both more controlled cashflow and more effective security than are available in open account trading, also serve as a useful basis for financing. The various forms of documentary credits are covered in some detail in Chapter 16, so it is appropriate here simply to comment that tenor drafts drawn against acceptance credits are, when accepted, usually specifically discountable by banks and some finance houses. Alternatively, they may form the basis for all or part of the financing arrangement through a specific export scheme, for example those of the clearing banks or Exfinco.

Similarly, bills of exchange attached to documentary collections (two topics dealt with in detail in Chapters 14 and 15 respectively) can usually be discounted, though rarely without recourse.

Export finance and confirming houses

Export finance and confirming houses have traditionally held an important place in supporting the sale of British goods abroad. The fundamental difference between the two is that the former normally purchase goods for their own account and then on-sell the goods as agent for the exporter or on their own account. In doing this they are generally involved in overseas marketing of the goods, carrying stocks necessary so as to provide a quick service to buyers, administering the sales and taking the risk (on their own shoulders or by taking out credit insurance) of non-payment by overseas customers. The latter, confirming houses, act on behalf of overseas buyers by confirming orders placed with UK manufacturers. In doing this they may grant the overseas buyers extended credit, without any responsibility on the part of the manufacturer.

In both cases the manufacturer is relieved both of export administration and the credit risk on overseas buyers and, whilst the sales can still be categorized as exports, they are in a practical sense being made to UK based companies. As a result, the question of export financing clearly does not arise, though the exporter may well require facilities to cover the time taken to pay by the export or confirming house, which is something that can usually be simply arranged through the banking system.

Most companies in this field are members of the British Export Houses Association (incorporated into the British Exporters Association) from whom details can be obtained. (See also Chapter 9.)

Short-term forfaiting

Forfaiting was originally designed to provide without recourse finance to manufacturers usually selling on medium- or long-term credit up to as long as eight years or so. It is provided at a margin over base rate plus a commission charge against receipt, by the exporter's bank, of promissory notes or bills of exchange avalized by an acceptable bank in the buyer's country.

Although there has been a growing market in London, forfaiting is still relatively little used in support of short-term business. Whilst interest rates charged are much in line with facilities available for similar terms of credit, commissions payable on single short-term transactions tend to render the cost disproportionately high by comparison with the various sources of short-term finance that have already been described.

Factoring and invoice discounting

Factoring

As a means of providing a combination of services and finance, the latter only available on the back of the former, factoring has been extensively used in the USA since early in the nineteenth century and has grown steadily in Europe since it was first introduced in the UK in the early 1960s. After a somewhat shaky start-up period, during which there was a tendency for companies to fear the attitude of both their suppliers and their bankers if they were known to be using factoring, the involvement of all the major clearing banks, either directly or through finance house subsidiaries, has amply demonstrated the credibility of the service and projected factoring to the stage where in 1987 the Association of British Factors reported a total volume of business of the order of £7 billion.

Over this period of years, factoring has come to have a number of meanings, but for our present purpose it is enough to define the basis of export factoring and that of invoice discounting, a service also provided by the majority of factoring houses.

Export factoring is usually offered on a non-recourse basis, with the factors providing maintenance of the export sales ledger, credit control of overseas buyers, 100 per cent protection on approved transactions and collection from customers. This service constitutes 'maturity' factoring. The factor is also usually willing to provide up to 80 per cent against the value of indebtedness for sales falling under the contract, thus converting maturity factoring to 'financed' factoring. This form of factoring is generally fully disclosed to buyers, notification being given by the supplier to customers that payment must be made to the factor. In order to provide security for the factors and to facilitate their collection activities on behalf of suppliers, the latter's indebtedness is assigned to the factor with the result that the arrangement is an outright sale of assets and can be treated as off balance sheet. Recourse export factoring, provided by some companies, offers no credit protection, this risk having to be borne by the exporter or laid off through credit insurance.

It is the factor's responsibility to maintain the supplier's sales ledger, regardless of currencies invoiced, in exactly the same way as in the home market. The factor makes an immediate conversion to sterling for the exporter's account of the total value of invoices submitted for factoring and is then responsible for collection from the customers overseas in their own currencies and on the terms most appropriate for their own industries and markets.

Credit cover is usually 100 per cent on approved customers and there is no necessity for the exporter to submit reports and claims in respect of slow and defaulting customers, as is the procedure under a credit insurance policy. Customer collections are handled in most of the principal export markets, either by the factors' own offices, staffed by locally employed specialists, or through correspondent factors – this means that customers are in most cases dealt with in their own languages with the effect that delayed payments and disputes are dealt with in the shortest possible time. Similarly, funds collected overseas find their way more quickly to their destination than is usually the case when exporters have to make their own individual collection arrangements in each market.

Factors make two charges. Firstly, a service charge in respect of credit risk, ledger administration, collection and other costs and, second, interest at a margin over base rate for the financial facility. The former will depend on the volume of risk and work involved and is expressed as a percentage of sales turnover, with exporters usually paying around 1 per cent and upwards. The margin over base rate tends to be similar to that charged on overdraft or slightly higher.

A variation on straightforward export factoring is the arrangement whereby an exporting company arranges for factoring services to be provided locally to its sales subsidiaries by the overseas offices or associates of its domestic factor. The implications of this, particularly in the European Common Market, are evident: by nature, an overseas sales operation is usually motivated and controlled by sales-orientated management and the administrative efficiency and credit and collection security afforded by the factor play an important part in achieving a balanced growth for the sales company.

The full range of services provided varies somewhat from one factoring company to another. In the UK there are at present four international factoring organizations with British members; three of these operate on a 'correspondent' basis between members with clear-cut disciplines with regard to credit procedures and accounting; and the fourth has its own network of regional offices, covering Europe and North America, tied to a central processing and clearing system in the UK.

Invoice discounting

Ironically, whilst the real development of invoice discounting in the home market has been in the hands of the factoring houses, some of the recently established short-term export finance schemes offered by the banks (some of them parents of the factoring companies) can, due to their being based on the assignment of receivables, also be described as invoice discounting.

However, the principal factoring houses offer discounting facilities to exporters and it is important that this service should be clearly understood by comparison with the full service arrangements of non-recourse factoring.

The purpose of invoice discounting is to enable a supplier to raise funds against the security of debtors, or more precisely against the indebtedness of selected well-rated customers buying on a regular basis. An invoice discounting arrangement does not provide any form of sales ledger or credit control and protection service; and interest rates can be above those normal in factoring. However, this service offers particular advantages to some companies, in that they are able to obtain short-term relief from liquidity problems by taking advances without having to commit themselves to full factoring services. In some cases, particularly where one or two well-rated customers make up the bulk of a supplier's business, this is a very practical way of releasing cash to take advantage of better terms for raw materials or whatever. As an 'off balance sheet' arrangement, invoice discounting is proving increasingly popular to large companies wishing to make better use of their debtor asset without disturbing their normal banking arrangements. Generally, the exporter is not required to hold a credit insurance policy specifically to support the invoice discounting arrangement, but a quid pro quo for this is that the percentage of receivables discounted is likely to fall well below the 80 per cent ceiling customary in full factoring. The discount charge related to clearing bank base rate, together in some cases with a commission, is charged based upon an evaluation of the likely type and level of business involved in each case and is likely to be somewhat in excess of the cost of a bank overdraft.

Invoice discounting may be either undisclosed or disclosed. It should be borne in mind that most forms of agreement between invoice discounters and their clients give the former the right to notify and collect direct from customers, should anything prevent a supplier from repaying the discounting facility.

WHICH WAY TO TURN?

With such a proliferation of short-term export finance facilities evolving in the market place over the past few years, it is inevitably difficult even for experienced exporters to assess the best possible source for their individual needs and it is certainly more baffling for those new to the export scene.

The only sensible course is to evaluate a sample of each type so as to ensure that the exporter's critical needs are satisfied. Any facility that itself helps to accelerate and regularize cashflow at a reasonable cost and without complex administration is obviously to be preferred to those involving a higher degree of 'bureaucratic' paperwork and complex communications. With export services it is of course helpful to get as close to real expertise as possible, so the question of point of contact and the ability to respond both quickly and effectively to the exporter's needs are significant requirements. If profitable advice is to be gained by pricing in buyers' currencies, this also has to be built in with the minimum of risk, administration and cost. All of the institutions that have been referred to will provide exporters with advice without charge and this is clearly the starting point in any comparative analysis.

Recommended reading

Brooke, Michael Z. (Editor). *International Financial Management Handbook*. Lancaster: Kluwer Publishing Ltd. Regularly updated loose-leaf handbook with over thirty financial experts contributing.

Gmur, Charles J. (Editor). (1986) *Trade Financing*, 2nd edn. Milton Keynes: Euromoney. A general overview of the many different techniques employed to finance international trade deals.

Guild, Ian and Harris, Rhodri. (1985) *Forfaiting*. Cambridge: Woodhead-Faulkner.

Pelkmans, J. and Winters, A. (1988) *Europe's Domestic Market*. London: Chatham House. A preview of the 1992 Single European Market in broad perspective.

22

Foreign exchange exposure management

Nick Douch

It is normally said that there are three main types of exposure: transaction exposure, translation exposure and economic exposure. This is not strictly correct as transaction exposure can be defined as merely a sub-set of economic exposure. However it is useful to make the distinctions between the three, as it is to order them from the easiest to the most difficult to perceive.

TYPES OF EXPOSURE

Transaction exposure

Most companies would recognize that they have a transaction exposure if they either import or export, or carry out international trade in any way. Very simply, if goods are bought or sold overseas and the transaction involves a foreign currency, then a transaction exposure exists. The actual payment does not have to be in a foreign currency – indeed by pricing in the company's base currency you do not eliminate the transaction exposure, although you may transfer it in the short term. However, if the transaction is part of a long-term trading relationship, then even the transfer of the problem is not true. For example, in the case of importing, although the company may pay for its goods in sterling, it is certain that in the medium term the base currency price will be linked to the overseas supplier's price in its domestic currency, and hence directly to the exchange rate.

Transaction exposures are usually relatively easy to identify; typically they will be derived from invoices or expected sales or purchases over a finite period. However, it is important to identify them as quickly and as accurately as possible. Just the same as anywhere else in an organization, inaccurate or incomplete information will lead to bad results, no matter how well the methods of handling the information are developed.

Transaction exposures will have a direct impact on profits and the profit and loss account. Companies tend, therefore, to be well aware of the problems of transaction exposure, although too often they confine their examination and worrying to the present or the next financial period, as if in some magical way the company will cease to exist or will be able to change direction at the end of this period.

Translation exposure

Whereas transaction exposure was related to the profit and loss account, translation exposure is related to the balance sheet. That is to say translation exposure is connected to asset and liability cover and is a stock concept, whilst transaction exposure is a flow concept.

Because translation exposure is balance sheet orientated, it is often thought to be too nebulous to hedge. Furthermore the cynical might say that it is ignored because it does not impinge on the day-to-day cashflow, and as balance sheets are only published twice a year or so, it can safely be left till then. This is of course rubbish, because although losses or gains on translation are taken below the line in reserves, a translation loss still dilutes the value of shareholders' funds and to that extent may well leave the company vulnerable to takeover, for example.

When deciding what to do about translation exposure, it is important to ask why the overseas assets (for example) have been acquired. If the decision was made to diversify the company away from its domestic economy, but not from its domestic currency, then the 'neutral' position on translation exposure would be for the assets/liabilities to be fully hedged. If on the other hand the decision was in any way taken to diversify away from the company's domestic currency, then clearly the 'neutral' position is for the company not to hedge its translation exposure.

Neither policy can be said to be right or wrong, and both are equally acceptable. However, it is important to state the rules by which you are playing explicitly to your shareholders before the event, and not implicitly after the event when you unexpectedly announce losses to your reserves. It is unsettling to discover how many companies attribute such losses to unexpected exchange rate movements, when in reality no exchange rate movement is unexpected, only unpredicted. There is more than just semantics in the distinction, because the former implies that there is no planning in the company, whilst the latter suggests there is planning, but the realities of the inadequacies of forecasting exchange rates are well recognized.

It is fair to say that translation exposure is difficult to grasp, but that is not a good excuse for ignoring the problem. Indeed it would be helpful if all companies took in translation repercussions before acquiring an overseas company rather than after, when it is often too late.

Economic exposure

Economic exposure really encompasses transaction exposure, but because companies tend to recognize transaction exposure, but fail to recognize, or ignore, economic exposure, they are usually treated separately. However, it should always be borne in mind that the distinction is artificial, and really the area to be looked at is the much wider economic exposure.

The normal definition of economic exposure is the effect on the company's future cashflows from future exchange rate movements. There is no time limit to the definition and hence, theoretically, economic exposure stretches to infinity. In reality, of course, the life of a company is something a good deal less than infinity. The use of economic exposure should be realistic, but at the same time it should not be confined to some artificial time period, say for example the length of the planning cycle.

The most important determinant of the length of time economic exposure exists is the time it would take the company to change direction. If, for example, the company was importing components from Japan, and it would take two years to switch suppliers, then the economic exposure to the yen is also two years. Similar considerations would apply to selling in an overseas market, but in some cases such markets are so crucial to the livelihood of the company that they can never be abandoned. In such circumstances the exposure to that market's currency is to all intents and purposes infinite, or until the eventual demise of the company.

One of the most difficult aspects of economic exposure is that it is extremely tricky to identify. Typically, companies can isolate transaction exposure by way of invoices or by forecasting expected sales. However, economic exposure goes beyond these, and there are rarely hard and fast facts to rely on. This makes it extremely difficult to collate any information and, some would argue, makes the whole exercise a waste of time. The main reason for the difficulty is that companies misunderstand the reason for looking at economic exposure. It is not just to decide what currencies should be hedged or left unhedged; more important, it is to discover how vulnerable the company is to changes in exchange rates. It is useful to think in terms of sensitivity analysis, and to establish pain thresholds – the levels at which an exchange rate movement would start doing real damage to the company.

It is not sufficient merely to examine the effects on the company of the forecast exchange rate. It is just as important to look at all possible outcomes and to decide which of these would be disastrous. No forecast should be thought of as perfect – at best it is the most likely outcome, but it is vital that the company goes through the exercise of looking at other possible outcomes, and decides which are good and bad for the company. It may even be useful to ascribe probabilities to these outcomes. Most companies will tell you that their exchange rate forecasts are not that accurate, yet far too often they then proceed as if the forecast were the only possible outcome.

Indirect exposure

It may seem that if a company always buys its goods in its domestic currency, and always sells its goods in its domestic currency, there is no currency exposure, especially if it confines both its buying and selling activities to its own domestic market. Unfortunately this is just not the case. As soon as one of the company's competitors decides to buy or sell into other markets, there is an implied exposure.

The obvious example is where a competitor chooses to buy components or finished goods from overseas. In these circumstances, if the competitor gains an advantage from favourable currency movements, then the domestically-orientated firm will be disadvantaged. Less obvious, but just as real, is a competitor firm which chooses to export, and which gains from a favourable currency movement. They may of course decide to take the extra profit and leave the remainder of their trading activities the same; alternatively, they may decide to use this good fortune to boost their presence in the domestic market by using the 'windfall' profits to subsidize their domestic position.

Other examples are somewhat obtuse. In most cases a company's competition does not come from solely domestic sources. It is apparent that, like it or not, the domestic company is at the mercy of its overseas competitor establishing a 'lucky' currency advantage.

This indirect exposure is important to recognize, as it can lead to some far from obvious conclusions. For example, if we take the example of a company exporting from the United States to Germany, then clearly if it chooses to sell in the domestic currency of Germany it will have a transaction exposure of Deutschemarks to US dollars. However, if the only competitor is Japanese, then the competitor will face exactly the same Deutschemark problems. The economic exposure (or indirect exposure) is actually between US dollars and Japanese yen.

Indirect exposure is really a form of economic exposure, but it is so important as to deserve special mention. It is all too easy to focus entirely on the currency problems caused by invoicing in a foreign currency, and to ignore the longer-term problems caused by competitors' currencies. There is no justification for such a policy, save that a company which focusses on the short term will never appreciate the problems involved – until it is too late.

TECHNIQUES FOR HANDLING CURRENCY EXPOSURES

The techniques that can be used to hedge exchange rate exposures can be broadly grouped into two areas, non-market and market methods. Many practitioners will jump straight to the latter, but in fact non-market techniques can often be a cheaper and more efficient way of dealing with the problem. It therefore seems logical to start here.

NON-MARKET OR INTERNAL METHODS

Before any corporation can even begin to think about using non-market hedging procedures, it is absolutely vital to ensure that the information available on currency exposures is accurate, or at the very least the best that is available. Too many decisions based on inaccurate or incomplete information are prevalent in corporate thinking. However, if the assumption that the information is good can be made, then, before doing anything else, the company should first look to matching exposures.

Matching currency exposures

One of the simplest methods of reducing currency exposure is to match flows in and out in the same currency. For example if a UK company sells to the USA in dollars, and buys components from the USA also in dollars, it makes sense to match these two flows. This may seem painfully self-evident, but many companies fail to take this simple action.

There are a number of reasons why this should happen. The first is that the treasurer of the company does not have full information in a timely fashion. Consequently the treasurer may only know about the inflow of dollars when it is too late – that is to say, when he or she has already hedged the outflow.

Secondly, there may be a mismatch between the timing of receipts and outgoings. If we assume that there are no exchange controls precluding the use of currency accounts, then the simplest method of removing the timing difference is either to deposit the foreign currency if it comes in first, or to borrow the foreign currency if the payments out are the first to materialize. In either case the exposure is no longer of a currency nature, but has been turned into an interest rate exposure.

Thirdly, matching is not undertaken because a company is obsessed with converting everything to its base currency. There is some logic in this, but what is illogical is to assume that such actions do much to reduce exposure. They can in fact do the exact opposite and increase exposures. Indeed, it could well be said that the greatest currency problem facing any company is its base currency. This may seem an absurd statement, but what is often overlooked is that an exchange rate is by definition something that involves two currencies. The only currency that is common to all a company's exchange rate decisions is the base currency, and it is in that sense that it provides the problems.

This obsession with the base currency can lead to matching opportunities being missed. Obvious examples are the premature conversions of receipts and payments so as to get both back to the base currency, but less obvious are flows in currencies that are closely related to one another.

Although it is true to say that the exchange rate system now in existence is of a floating nature, in fact very few major currencies actually float. (At the time of writing those that do are the US dollar, sterling, Swiss franc, Japanese yen, and Australian, Canadian and New Zealand dollars.) Many currencies move in line with another. Obvious examples are many countries in the Caribbean whose currencies are more or less irrevocably intertwined with the US dollar. Another excellent example is the European Monetary System (EMS) whose currencies are kept in narrow bands. Many other currencies (for example the Scandinavian currencies) are linked to a basket of other currencies. The important point is that these near-relationships enable further matching to be achieved.

For example, a company has receipts in Deutschemarks and payments in French francs. Because they are both linked within the EMS, it makes little sense to convert both back to the base currency – say sterling – as both transactions would create exposures that otherwise would not have existed. It is vitally important that cashflows are analysed not just in individual currencies but also by groupings that tend to move together. A company must guard against artificially converting everything to a base just to make bookkeeping easier. There is nothing against such a practice if it is restricted to a notional basis, but it should stop short of actual deals.

Forced matching

Forced matching may be too strong a word; and maybe planned matching might be more appropriate. Whatever term is used, though, the essence of the idea is that companies should not match those currency exposures that just arise in the normal course of business, but should actively plan to take exposures that would either exactly match or go some way to matching existing exposures.

An obvious example is seeking overseas suppliers in a country where the company already makes sales, but the idea could obviously work the other way round, where companies seek buyers in countries where they are forced to buy components.

Tendering for foreign contracts is another case. Very often the company tendering will be at a great advantage if it tenders in the domestic currency of the buyer (indeed it may be precluded from doing anything else). In such circumstances one way of reducing the exposure is to look for suppliers in the same currency. These suppliers will of course still face the contingent cashflow problem, but it will at least be in their own currency. If this is done it is obvious that the main contractor must purchase the components in the tendering currency and not in its domestic currency.

MARKET METHODS

Spot exchange rates

Spot exchange rates do not really provide a method of hedging exchange rate exposure – more of a non-method. One option always available to a company is to do absolutely nothing until the foreign exchange cashflow materializes. In such circumstances the exchange transaction will be carried out at the spot rate (which is most people's idea of what an exchange rate is). That is to say, the exchange will take place two working days from the point at which the deal is struck.

Although using spot exchange rates is not really a hedging method, it is of course a perfectly acceptable way of managing an exposure, so long as the company takes a positive decision to wait until dealing at the spot rate, rather than the non-decision of just waiting.

Forward exchange rates

A forward exchange rate is a means by which you can fix an exchange rate now for a given time in the future. It is made up of two parts – the spot rate and a forward margin. The forward margin is actually equivalent to the interest rate differentials between the two currencies involved, and is not necessarily the market's expectation of the future. A simple example will explain why this must be so.

If the interest rate on US dollars for twelve months is 8 per cent, and the interest rate on 12 months' Deutschemarks is 4 per cent, then if a company holds Deutschemarks it can increase its yield on these funds by 4 per cent if it converts the Deutschemarks to US dollars and deposits the dollars for a year.

Clearly there is a risk that the exchange rate for the dollar against the Deutschemark will weaken by more than 4 per cent, so that at the end of the period the company will be worse off for making the exchange.

However, instead of just converting the Deutschemarks to dollars at spot, the company could also (at the same time) have undertaken a forward exchange contract to sell the dollars for Deutschemarks in twelve months' time. The spot rate on both contracts would be the same (so long as the deals were struck simultaneously), the only difference between the rates being the forward margin.

If that is not exactly equal to the 4 per cent difference in interest rates, an arbitrage opportunity will exist, and market operators will soon transact deals that will ensure them a guaranteed profit, but which will very soon work the arbitrage opportunity out of the market.

If the forward rate is not the market's expectation of the future, then in no sense can it be said to be a target to be beaten. It is, however, the one certainty, in that you can guarantee your base currency proceeds. Therefore, to decide not to cover forward certain exposures implies that the company is confident that it will see better exchange rates in the future. The last is rather a hard statement, but it is true to say that, elsewhere in a business, there is a premium on certainty, and there seems no reason why it should not also apply to foreign exchange exposures.

Premiums and discounts

Forward margins are expressed either as a premium or as a discount. A low interest rate currency will be at a premium to a high interest rate currency, whilst a high interest rate currency will be at a discount to a low interest rate currency.

If you are buying a currency which is at a premium on a forward basis, the exchange rate will be 'worse' than the spot rate; whilst if you are buying a currency which is at a discount, then you will receive a 'better' rate than the spot rate.

Fixed forward contracts and option forward contracts

A fixed forward contract establishes the rate at which the exchange transaction will be carried out on a fixed date in the future, whilst an option forward contract will fix the rate at which the exchange transaction will be enacted between two dates in the future, say between one month and three months.

In general terms it is always better to deal in fixed forward contracts, because option forward contracts will always be charged at the worst rate applying to the period. Therefore the company will only break even if the currency is actually delivered on the date on which the worst rate applies.

If the company is not certain on which date the funds will materialize, then it should make use of currency accounts or extend the contract if the monies arrive late, or take the contract up early if they arrive ahead of schedule.

Extension and early take-ups of forward contracts

A fixed forward exchange contract is far more flexible than the name suggests. In the real world it is impossible to predict accurately the exact date of paying away funds, let alone the date of receipt of incoming funds. It is this uncertainty which is often used as an excuse either for using option forward contracts or, worse still, for not covering forward at all. In fact it is easy to adjust the maturity date to allow for this.

The example that follows illustrates the extension of a forward contract, but the arithmetic is the same for an early take-up of a forward contract – only reversed

Example

A company in West Germany expects to receive US dollars in six months' time, and wishes to hedge the proceeds into Deutschemarks. The spot rate for selling dollars into Deutschemarks is DM 1.70, and the dollar is at a discount of 4.5 Pfennigs to the Deutschemark (the Deutschemark is of course at a premium of 4.5 Pfennigs for the six-month period). Therefore the company will receive a rate of 1.70 − 0.045 = 1.655.

If the dollar receipts amount to $1 million, then the company will receive DM 1 655 000 in six months' time, when it exchanges the dollars.

There is a delay in the shipment of the goods and the receipt of the dollars will be delayed one month. Therefore at the end of the six-month period, the company will not have the dollars to satisfy the commitment of the forward contract. It has to extend the contract.

This is done by entering into a pair of contracts. A spot contract to buy dollars and sell Deutschemarks (this will settle the outstanding forward contract), and a forward contract to sell dollars and buy Deutschemarks one month forward. Provided the deals are simultaneous, the spot rate will be the same for both contracts – though not necessarily the same as that on the existing forward contract (in fact this is very unlikely).

The spot rate for selling dollars against Deutschemarks is now DM 1.50, and the dollar is at a discount of 0.5 Pfennigs for one month. The forward rate will be DM 1.50 − 0.005 = 1.4950.

At spot the company will have to buy one million dollars, which will cost it DM 1 500 000, and will receive DM 1 495 000 when it eventually delivers the million dollars in one month's time. At spot value, the company will receive DM 1 655 000 and will pay away DM 1 500 000 – an apparent profit of DM 155,000.

However, in one month's time it will now receive only DM 1 495 000. Thus in total it will receive DM 1 495 000 + 155 000 = 1 650 000.

This is exactly the same as the original expected receipts, adjusted for the fact that there was an extra month's premium because of the delay in the receipt of funds. There was no extra profit (nor would there have been a loss if the exchange rate had moved in the other direction). The exchange rate differences are a cashflow problem, not an exchange rate problem.

The real risk in early or delayed payments when a fixed exchange rate contract is in place is an interest rate one. This is not surprising given that forward margins are based on interest rate differentials. Fixed exchange rate contracts are a flexible tool, not an inflexible strait-jacket.

Currency accounts

An alternative to extending or bringing back fixed forward contracts is the use of currency accounts. If money comes in early, it can be placed on (interest-bearing) deposit until such time as the fixed forward contract matures.

On the other hand, if money comes in late, then the proceeds to satisfy the forward contract can be taken by way of loan on a currency account (see also 'Foreign currency overdraft' in Chapter 21 for further comments).

In either case, the result will be analogous to the effect of altering the maturity date of a forward contract, because, once again, with forward margins based on interest-rate differentials the earning or paying of interest on currency accounts instead of the earning or paying of interest on the base currency account will be more or less the same.

Currency accounts are most useful where the payment size is small, and a large number of regular payments are received. They cut down on administrative effort and are therefore cheap to operate. However, they are not as efficient (in an economic sense) as fixed forward contracts, and should be avoided where large individual payments or receipts are the order of the day. In such circumstances the extending of fixed forward contracts is a more efficient method.

394

Currency futures

Currency futures are a hedging tool mostly used in the USA where the forward exchange market has not been as developed as in Europe. The product grew out of necessity, but nevertheless makes a useful contribution to the techniques available. However, its use in Europe is far more restricted because of the greater flexibility provided by the forward exchange market.

The currency future enables a company to hedge expected cashflows and so remove the risk of unexpected exchange rate movements. Just like a forward exchange contract, the price is fixed for a fixed date in the future for a given exchange rate contract.

The main differences between the two techniques emanate from the fact that the future is a tradeable instrument, whereas the forward exchange contract is an agreement between two parties, neither of which has the explicit right to pass on its liability to third party without the express agreement of the other party to the original agreement. This ability to buy or sell a future makes the technique particularly attractive to a speculator. However, there is little difference between selling onwards a future and liquidating or closing out a forward contract. In the latter case if you no longer have the expected cashflow, or if you decide to cash in the profit or loss on the contract, the company merely needs to undertake the equal but opposite foreign exchange contract, the cash difference becoming payable at the maturity of the two contracts. Because of the great interchangeability between the two concepts, their pricing must be the same or very similar, otherwise it would be possible to arbitrage between them. Therefore there will rarely be significant price advantages in trading regularly in one market or the other – particularly for pure hedging transactions.

Where forward contracts score is in their greater flexibility of use, as the comparisons below show.

1 Forward exchange contracts can be for any amount, whereas currency futures are sold in set contract sizes – normally US$25 000 on most exchanges.
2 Forward exchange contracts can mature on any working day in the future, unlike futures contracts which only mature on four days a year.
3 Forward exchange contracts are fixed at the exchange rate ruling at the time, but futures contracts are priced at set intervals – in the case of US dollar/sterling at five-cent intervals. There is an advantage in

futures in the sense that you can choose more than one price when you fix the deal, although each will of course be worth more or less the same, after allowing for the cost of each future.

4 Having taken out a forward exchange contract, there is nothing to pay until the maturity of the contract, whereas with futures contracts increased margins may become payable if the futures contract becomes worth less – that is, the currency moves adversely. Companies can find this topping up of margin administratively cumbersome.

On the whole, forward contracts tend to be the more useful for hedging, except in two areas: first, where the liquidity of the forward market is not as good as the futures market – the Chicago Mercantile Exchange is certainly more liquid in its time zone than the equivalent forward market. Second, because a forward contract is between two parties only, each takes a credit view of the other. If the company does not have a strong balance sheet, then counter-parties may be unwilling to extend forward exchange facilities. However, as long as the company can meet margin calls, there is no such restriction of access to the futures market, and all underlying risks are underwritten by the exchange involved.

Currency options

The advent of currency options in the last few years has meant a significant advance in the techniques available to companies for hedging exchange rate exposure. It has enabled company treasurers to handle a much wider range of uncertainties than was previously possible.

Essentially, a currency option is a contract whereby the buyer of the option has the right, but not the obligation, to undertake a given exchange rate contract at a given rate during a fixed period of time.

The buyer therefore has all the rights and none of the obligations. Conversely, the seller of the option has all the obligations but none of the rights. Not surprisingly, the sellers of the option will exact a price for giving up all of their rights, and this will be the premium payed by the buyer.

The world of currency options is full of jargon, most of which can happily be ignored. There are some terms that do need defining though.

American and European options

An American option is an option which can be exercised at any time during the term of the option, whereas European options can only be exercised at the maturity date of the option. Most currency options sold are of the American type.

Strike price

The strike price of an option is the exchange rate at which it can be exercised.

'In the money', 'out the money' and 'at the money'

These terms all relate to the position of the option's strike price versus the prevailing exchange rate at that moment. Thus 'in the money' options are those where the strike price is at an advantageous rate to the option holder compared with the market price; 'out the money' options are at a disadvantageous rate, and 'at the money' options are at the same rate.

Traded options and 'over the counter' options

Traded options are those bought and sold on an options exchange, for example Chicago or LIFFE in London. They are freely negotiable and can therefore be bought or sold at any time from or to any third party. 'Over the counter' options are not negotiable, the contract being restricted to the buyer and seller. It is possible to sell the option (if it is American) back to the original seller at any time, but the title cannot be passed to any third party.

However, although 'over the counter' options are not traded, they are flexible in other senses. Traded options have only four maturity dates a year; the strike prices are at regular intervals, but you can only deal in between by buying a combination of options; amounts are fixed (usually US$25 000) and it is not possible to get a fixed price in advance for a very large deal. In all these respects the 'over the counter' option has the advantage, with maturity dates, strike prices and amounts all being chosen by the option buyer.

It is impossible to say whether one type or another is better, but traded options are obviously more flexible if in fact the company does intend to trade options, whereas 'over the counter' options tend to have greater flexibility when it comes to hedging underlying exposures.

Uses of options

Options are invaluable when a company is facing uncertainty in its hedging decisions. It could well be argued that there is always uncertainty in such circumstances, and indeed options are always suitable as a hedging tool. However, the big snag is the premium. Option premiums are high because they reflect the high risks the seller of the option is accepting. Very simply, option premiums are based on:

(a)   amount of option;
(b)   length of option;
(c)   strike price of the option;
(d)   volatility of the two currencies involved;
(e)   interest rate differentials between the two currencies involved;
(f)   American or European option.

Not surprisingly, the longer the option the larger the amount and the better the strike price; and the more volatile the currencies, the greater the premium that must be paid.

Whilst it is not necessary for an option buyer to understand the full mathematics of option pricing, it is important to calculate the premium that the company reckons to be appropriate for the uncertainties and risks being removed. If the option premium is equal to or less than the figure calculated, then in no way can the option be described as expensive.

Therefore it is important to understand the uncertainties that an option can be used to hedge.

Uncertainty of cashflow

This is without doubt the most classic use of options. Until they came along, a company was unable effectively to hedge contingent cashflows. This is no longer true. An option can be bought to cover the contingent exposure. If it materializes, then the company can either exercise its option or it can deal in the market if the rate is more favourable. (In other words the option was 'out the money'.) If the contingent exposure never becomes a reality, then the company need do nothing. It can throw away its option – its loss being restricted to the option premium – or if the option is 'in the money', it can exercise the option, recover its premium possibly, or on occasion actually realize a profit.

Such contingent cashflows occur when a company is tendering for a contract in a foreign currency or when a company hedges its expected sales or purchases. In the former case, the exposure only becomes real if the company wins the tender. In the latter case, expected flows are unlikely to be the real flows; there will always be a margin of error either side of the expectation. If reality errs on the low side, the company will find itself over-hedged, with the converse true if the expectation is on the high side.

Options can be used to remove this problem, the company retaining the ultimate flexibility as to whether and when it should deal.

Uncertainty as to competitors' actions

One of the greatest problems facing a company when looking at hedging their exposure is what their competitors are doing. However well you hedge your exposure, your competitors may still be better off than you if they do nothing, and yet the exchange rate moves quite fortuitously in their favour.

An example may help to explain this. A company is importing goods from Japan to France, and has to pay for the goods in yen. Being prudent, the company always hedges the payments for the imports forward, so that it knows what it will have to sell the goods for in French francs. However, a competitor does nothing. The yen subsequently weakens against the French franc, and our company is left either facing a price disadvantage versus the competitor or significantly reduced profits, or both.

If, however, the company had hedged its import exposure using options, it could have torn up the option and covered in the market in the same way as the competitor. It would now only be worse off to the extent of the option premium.

Uncertainty as to exchange rate movements

Facing every company is the continual problem of what exchange rates are going to do in the future. All too often the response is: 'We do not know, so we will do nothing.' Doing nothing really means that the company has a very strong view that it will see more advantageous rates in the future. In fact the true 'don't know' position is to be 50 per cent hedged.

An alternative is to use options. If the rate in the market is better, the company deals there, if not it will utilize the option. With the benefit of hindsight, the option will never have been the right thing to have done, there will always have been a better course. However, the option will never have been the worst course either, and it is this that makes it an attractive tool for the company that is really concerned about reducing risk.

Derivatives of options

The world is now full of option acronyms, all of which are derived from the original option contract. Almost without exception, the purpose of these derivatives is to reduce the up front premium. It is not within the scope of this chapter to cover this area in great detail, and in any case new products appear to be arriving almost daily. One observation is worth making though if the premium is reduced, then it is certain that the benefits of this type of option will be less than those of a full currency option. It is imperative that a company discovers what it is giving up when it buys a derivative product, and to decide whether it can live without the lost benefits.

Currency swaps

A currency swap is exactly what it sounds – the swapping of one currency into another for a given period of time (normally a number of years) with the reverse swap taking place at the end of the given period. This facility has always been available in the forward market, but was restricted to shorter periods depending on the liquidity of the forward market.

Currency swaps take advantage of the fact that there may be counter-parties who have the opposite interest to other companies, and who would be willing to swap these interests at a mutually agreeable price. To enable the parties to find each other, banks or other financial institutions act as middle-men, so that the risk of doing the deal is with the bank, not with the counter-party, who may not even be known to the original company.

There is another main difference between this type of currency swap

400

and those available in the forward exchange market. In the latter, the price at which the currencies are originally swapped will be the rate ruling for the date of the swap – usually spot, and no further adjustment will take place till the maturity of the swap. The difference that will then be paid will represent the interest differential that ruled for the period of the swap.

In currency swaps, however, the rates at which the swaps are made are the same at the beginning as at the end. The adjustment is made by way of annual payments, with, in general terms, the holder of the high interest rate currency making a payment roughly equivalent to the interest differential to the holder of the low interest rate currency. All these adjustments are known and fixed at the time of the original swap, and therefore the currency swap can be an ideal hedging instrument for long-term exposures.

The market is now well developed in the major currencies, where there are many reciprocal interests, but, as could be expected, is very thin or non-existent in currencies where little or no forward trading exists. Nevertheless, currency swaps are now a widely used tool, and should be considered whenever the cost of hedging an exposure needs to be amortized over the length of the hedge, rather than taken in one hit on final maturity.

USING THE TECHNIQUES TO HEDGE DIFFERENT TYPES OF EXPOSURE

Having regard to the diverse composition and policies of corporations, it would be impossible to give more than a cursory summary of how to use these techniques, but some simple guidelines can be set out, and one or two practical hints conveyed.

Transaction exposure

Transaction exposure is the most easily understood of all exposures, and the use of the various techniques is also the best understood. Forward contracts are an obvious tool, as are spot contracts. Currency accounts should also be used to counteract unexpected differences in the movement of funds in either direction. Currency options can also form an integral part of transaction exposure, especially if the flows or competitors' actions are uncertain.

Translation exposures

Translation exposures are more difficult to hedge, partly because there is no underlying cashflow, and partly because they are only really measured when balance sheets are prepared.

The simplest way of handling a translation exposure is to set up a matching asset or liability in the same currency, so that when the underlying asset or liability is valued back into the base currency, any resulting movement across the reserves will be exactly matched by an opposite movement in the revaluation of the matching hedge. There are a number of ways of achieving this, but unfortunately all have disadvantages. There is no right or wrong way overall to handle the problem. Each company must choose the most appropriate method for its own purposes.

Matching currency loans (or deposits)

As most translation exposures arise because of overseas investments, all the examples used will be from this point of view. However, in all cases, if a company chose to borrow overseas the hedging procedure would be the exact opposite.

If a company decides to purchase a company overseas, a simple way of eliminating translation exposure is to borrow the money for the purchase in the same currency as the asset. At the time of making up the balance sheet, there will be matching assets and liabilities in the same currency.

The first problem is the differences between the purchase price of the company and its real worth. Most purchases will include an element of goodwill, which presumably the purchasing company will want to write off as soon as possible. It would therefore be inappropriate to borrow foreign currency for the whole purchase price, only for the 'real' value of the business.

The second problem is much more intractable. It is a reasonable assumption that the new investment will release a stream of earnings over time. If these earnings are retained in the overseas company, then the underlying value of the overseas asset will be increasing in local currency terms. To ensure that the translation hedge remains complete, the company will need to increase its currency borrowings. This means it cannot use the overseas earnings to reduce its borrowing, and could –

theoretically at least – end up borrowing its own money at a margin – a not very satisfactory state of affairs.

The limitation then of matching borrowings is its inflexibility if the overseas earnings are intended to be retained there.

Forward exchange contracts

If a company has an overseas asset, then another way of hedging the translation exposure is to undertake a forward exchange contract to sell the same amount of currency forward. On balance sheet date this forward contract will be valued at the same exchange rate as the asset, and the change in value of the forward contract will compensate for the underlying change in the value of the asset.

The forward contract overcomes the problem of increasing the value of the asset by retained earnings. It is after all simplicity itself to increase the value of the forward contract to allow for the increase in the value of the asset. The forward margin on the contract will very nearly equal the difference in interest rates between the two currencies, and will not therefore act as a drain on earnings any more than a borrowing in the base currency would have done.

The problem in forward contracts arises because, when they are rolled over or extended, the rates are based on the then ruling market rates, and not on the rate of the original contract. Although this has no effect on the value of the hedge (see the section on extending forward contracts), it can give rise to cashflows which at their worst could be harmful to the liquidity of the company, and at their best can give rise to accountancy treatment problems.

Currency swaps

Currency swaps overcome the problem of forward exchange contracts because they are taken out for a number of years, and because the exchange rates at the beginning and end are the same. There is no problem with annual roll-overs, and the payment or receipt each year is exactly equivalent to the interest differentials. In the case of currency swaps, there is the added advantage of knowing the fixed amount of this difference at the beginning of the contract for the duration of the contract.

The difficulty that currency swaps pose is that, because the swap is for a fixed length of time, there is an implied assumption that the asset will last for the same length of time. Thus, if the asset is sold before the swap has matured, there is the problem of unwinding the swap (with possible losses involved) or of leaving the swap in place, and having an unhedged translation exposure, but now by way of a liability rather than an asset.

Either way, the risk of loss may deter the company from undertaking what would otherwise be a sensible long-term disinvestment decision.

Currency options

In many ways the currency option is the perfect translation hedge. It guarantees the worst case for translation, yet there is the chance of making a fortuitous gain.

Translation hedging by using options involves the company in buying an option to sell the currency in which it has an asset, or to buy the currency in which it has a liability. In the case of the translation of an asset, if the value of the asset has fallen because of adverse currency movements, then the value of the option to an equal and opposite amount.

The problem of options once again revolves around the premium. In every case there will be a premium to pay, and many companies find it difficult to justify for something as intangible as a translation exposure. That is not a good reason, but a better one is the fact that option premiums may well not be allowable for tax relief when used as a translation hedge, yet any gains from the value of the option may be treated as current income rather than as a capital gain. This unequal fiscal treatment of currency options under some tax regimes does make their use more expensive than appears justified.

Conclusion

There is no perfect hedge for translation exposure – all of the methods have their pluses and minuses. However, the fact that no one method stands head and shoulders above the rest is not a reason for doing nothing. The only real reason for ignoring translation exposure is if the company has clearly stated – in advance – that doing nothing is the declared policy.

Retained profits in a foreign currency

One of the most thorny problems is how to treat retained profits overseas. From a translation point of view, it may well be company policy not to hedge the exposure, but deliberately to diversify the balance sheet away from the base currency. Unfortunately, retained profits have a once-and-for-all effect on the profit and loss account, and hence on transaction exposure. Thus in year one retained profits will have to appear on the profit and loss account, but thereafter will be confined as a reserve item on the balance sheet. Most companies will hedge their transaction exposure in terms of dividends, and ideally would like to hedge the exposure for retained profits as well, but somehow have to unwind the hedge (at no cost) to return the retained profits to the overseas currency.

The only method of doing this is by way of currency options, whereby any shortfall in the value of the overseas profits can be made up by the increased value of the option. If the value of the retained profits has risen in base currency terms, the option will merely be thrown away.

The difficulty is once again the premium, which many companies will find expensive. It is worth repeating that there is no other way to protect this type of exposure.

Economic exposure

At the beginning of this chapter it was said that transaction exposure was part of economic exposure. It should come as no surprise, therefore, that the methods of hedging economic exposure are the same as those for transaction exposure. However, the uncertainties that both increased time and competitors' actions bring mean that there must be greater difficulties in deciding what to do.

In general terms, currency options become more attractive because they enable the company to change direction easily if it has made the wrong hedging decision. However, once again the cost of the premiums mitigates the attractiveness of currency options as an instrument. Instead, many companies seek to hedge only part of their exposure – say one half – so that, whatever happens, they are not totally exposed to an unfavourable currency movement. The antithesis of this is that the company cannot fully benefit from any favourable exchange rate movement, but most see that as a small price to pay for avoiding the worst.

Nevertheless, it is important to realize that hedging economic exposure is very far from easy, and it may well be that the company benefits more from establishing exactly what risks it faces from possible exchange rate movements, than it does from hedging these long-term problems. At least if it knows where the risks are it can make adjustments to its actions if the unfavourable movements become more of a probability than a possibility.

SUMMARY

This has been a long chapter. Rightly so because the problems that floating and hence volatile exchange rates pose for companies are some of the worst to be faced. The chances of this volatility receding seem as far away as ever. Almost the only safe forecast on exchange rates is that they will be more volatile in the next year than in the last.

The difficulties of identifying exposures and the even greater difficulties involved in trying to get rid of these exposures unfortunately encourage some to think that the whole exercise is fruitless. This total reliance on fate seems inappropriate for any business let alone major multinationals. Perhaps the movement of exchange rates should be thought of in the same way as sailors view the sea: not something to be totally scared of, but certainly something to respect; and like sailors the company should ensure that it does all that is possible to protect itself against the risks.

23

Treasury/cash management

Peter Cecil

The successful management of cash makes a considerable contribution to the reduction of a corporation's costs and preserves the most liquid of its assets. The management of many of the risks involved requires a forecasting system that is also an essential support to the management of foreign exchange risk.

Detailed planning of cash pays off. Balances that do not earn interest are of no more value to a company than if they were in a customer's bank account. Borrowing resources are usually finite and will be more effectively used if their size can be targeted. Perhaps most important of all, the process of forecasting and monitoring results concentrates the mind and identifies bottlenecks in cashflow and makes it possible to measure improvement or deterioration from an initial standard.

CASH FORECASTING

It is surprising how many, even large, companies regard cashflow forecasting as a waste of time. They look at their balance sheet, recognize its strength, that borrowing facilities are far above that which is required to fund the day-to-day business and then decide that money spent on cash forecasting would be wasted. It always comes as a shock to these companies when they finally accept the need, usually because of a sudden crisis, to find that the benefits far outweigh the costs.

Most areas of financial management interlink and a primary use for cashflow forecasts would be to assist in the control of foreign currency exposure, especially if economic risks are to be managed. Thus, all but the smallest companies should aim to produce multi-currency cash forecasts with the conversion from foreign currency to domestic feeding through into the domestic cash forecast. Inputs into a cash forecast will

407

come from many areas of a company. Sales income, both export and domestic, and charges will have the main impact but account should be taken of all income, including royalties and any other miscellaneous items and all cash expenditure. Non-cash expense such as depreciation and provisions should be excluded.

The forecast should be repeatedly fine tuned by reference to a separate cash report. Most benefit will be gained from this in the early period as previously unidentified cashflows are picked up and forecasting becomes improved as a result of the feedback provided. The total duration of a cashflow forecast and associated reporting will vary from industry to industry as will the time units into which the forecast is divided. It will usually be an additional benefit if the immediate future is divided into as short a time unit as possible, that is, daily, to obtain fine tuning of the cash position.

LIQUIDITY MANAGEMENT

Short-term borrowing

Overdrafts

Most companies should use the opportunity, if it is available, to borrow using an overdraft facility. Such facilities have the advantage of supplying immediate needs and of giving immediate value to receipts, because their credit to the account reduces borrowings. Thus, in almost any liquidity management situation, an overdraft-type account, if available, is of great value. A company that runs a net surplus position will still find it pays to have a small overdraft, provided the overdraft is targeted at a size that will absorb unexpected payments and that the gap between borrowing and depositing interest rates is not too large. If, for example, a company's daily receipts from customers are between $250 000 and $500 000, a $500 000 targeted overdraft position every night will mean a maximum borrowing level of $250 000 and a minimum of nil, without ever suffering a non-interest-earning deposit. If the cost of borrowing is 10 per cent and an overnight deposit earns 8 per cent, it will always pay to run the overdraft position if the instance of high receipts is greater than two (interest gap) in eight (deposit rate). If high receipts are less frequent, a point will be found at which guaranteed interest pays for limited borrowings.

Overnight funds

Overdraft borrowings alone will not usually be sufficient to finance a company's short-term needs and if those needs are substantial, there may be cost-effective alternatives. The major money market centres of London, New York, Frankfurt and elsewhere make available overnight funds. The price of these varies with short-term supply and demand but they are often a cost-effective substitute for the majority of short-term overdraft requirements.

Unlike overdrafts, overnight borrowing does require daily fixing and can be subject to considerable variation in price. Thus, it would not be prudent to borrow overnight more than could be repaid from an overdraft borrowing if rates in the overnight market should move significantly above overdraft rate. Even more important, in certain market conditions overnight money might not be available and it would then be essential to have an alternative available. When making a decision to move to overnight funding, it is useful to set target rates that will recognize the cost of transferring funds and the cost of paying interest daily instead of at the overdraft interest frequency.

Longer-term inter-bank funds or acceptance credits

These may be available depending on market conditions and the borrowing status of the trading company. Loan facilities organized to raise these funds are normally secured or subject to financial co-venants but can be used to support any working capital need within a company. Borrowings can be taken normally for fixed periods of one, two, three, six or twelve months and thus periods can be selected that will support a company's view on interest rates, the life of the assets to be financed or the period of finance requirement. If any flexibility is required, because borrowing requirements fluctuate, it is important to negotiate a revolving facility that enables drawings under the facility to be subdivided and repaid on individual maturities, without cancelling part of the facility or incurring penalties. It is normal, especially in markets where the total availability of facilities is restricted, to pay a commitment fee of perhaps 30 per cent of the facility margin on the portion of the facility that is unused at any time. There may also be arrangement fees, and if the facility is large, syndication fees.

Specific short-term funding schemes

Specific short-term schemes are available in certain markets and provide lenders with security and convert receivable assets to cash for the trading company. These may take the form of factoring arrangements, receivables financing, various bank schemes and, in the UK, an undisclosed export finance scheme operated by Exfinco. A useful benefit of specific funding is that the duration and size of borrowings are matched effortlessly to the underlying asset. This is a very competitive area of lending, especially in the UK, and the institutions try hard to gain a marketing advantage. It is not normal to pay commitment or arrangement fees and extra services can be combined with finance to control associated risks.

A company should always aim to ensure that it has sufficient committed facilities available to finance the maximum requirement identified by its cashflow forecast after adding an appropriate safety margin. Thus, one of the roles of the cash forecast is to identify possible restrictions of funding capacity that would prevent operational plans being achieved. Forewarned, a company is able to negotiate such needs at an early stage. This can be very important as banks respond much more favourably to planned facility increases than to sudden panics.

The larger and stronger companies may well be able to negotiate facilities which do not incorporate security requirements or even strong financial covenants. This puts those companies in a position to negotiate with a wide range of suppliers and, without involving the banks as intermediaries, to use the alternative of commercial paper which, backed by standby facilities, may well provide the best low-cost funding alternative. Other companies will be subject to financial security and strong financial covenants that will make the achievement of alternative sources of funds much more difficult as lenders will not want to put themselves in a secondary security position without taking a substantial risk premium in the rate charged. The alternative for these companies, if they wish to achieve flexibility, is to seek out those areas of their business which can be financed by alternative means and use those to supplement their lead bankers who enjoy the majority of security.

One of the great advantages gained by companies who fight for an alternative source of finance is that it sharpens the previous monopoly supplier's need to be competitive. Most companies would not consider it prudent to have a monopoly supplier of the basic materials used in production of their goods and yet many companies have a monopoly supplier of finance. Those who change usually find that the alternative achieves cost savings for them, both from the beginning and later when their original banker seeks both to gain back lost business and to become more competitive on remaining business, to ensure that it is retained.

Cash surpluses

The first aim of a cash surplus management policy must be safety. It is essential to be 100 per cent confident that funds deposited will be returned. There is no point in going for a 1 per cent better return on a deposit with a high-risk taker as the average corporation is not in a position to assess the risk represented by financial institutions. It follows therefore that a prudent management will set up an authorization system that will approve certain names of deposit takers and the limits of deposits that can be placed with them. This will have the effect of both ensuring that deposits are only placed with risk-free institutions and that in large companies there is not an undue concentration with, perhaps, organizations which entertain the treasurer particularly lavishly. This may seem fanciful but it has been known for those hungry for deposits to go overboard on entertainment and then not pay a fully commercial price for the funds placed with them. Proper internal controls can prevent all this.

It is important to ensure that interest-free balances do not occur, even with the safest of institutions; money not earning interest is wasted. It was explained earlier in this chapter that overdrafts have a role to play in surplus cash management and they should be taken advantage of when available. If this is not practical or possible, the first line of defence is an interest-earning current account. These are available in almost all markets, though the interest rate offered may not be very attractive. An offset of non-interest-earning balances against bank charges is frequently offered. While preferable to nothing, this tends to draw attention away from the size of bank charges, which in normal circumstances should be the subject of efforts to control and reduce. 'Free' bank accounts do not exist. It is almost always better to manage both interest received and bank charges paid, separately.

Unnecessarily large numbers of bank accounts being held are often a reason for certain accounts being overlooked and balances left idle. In some markets, facilities are available to group all balances, positive and negative held with the same bank, to achieve a net balance at a central control account. This facilitates efficient management of large numbers of bank accounts, provided they are all in the same currency. Unnecessary accounts should be identified and closed.

The period of deposits is the next area to consider. There is usually an overnight market but it is unlikely to maximize the return on cash deposits and if funds can be placed for longer periods, extra benefit will be earned. Thus, if it is known that funds will not be needed for a period of ninety days they can either be placed on a fixed term deposit for ninety days or a ninety-day certificate of deposit can be purchased. The advantage of the latter is that it can be resold on the secondary market should a new demand for funds be identified but, being more liquid than a fixed deposit, it will have the disadvantage of earning slightly less interest.

It is important not to bring new risks into the management of surplus cash resources. Therefore, putting funds on a long-term deposit, without the certainty that those funds will not be required, may not be advisable. The temptation may exist, if a view is taken that interest rates will fall in the future, to place funds on deposit for, say, six months, because it is assumed that interest rates will be lower when those funds are required and will therefore earn more money on deposit now than they would cost to borrow in the future. While sounding attractive, the very real risk exists that the forecast will be inaccurate and that future funds may be more and not less expensive. An alternative to placing funds on deposit would be to take advantage of suppliers' discounts that may be offered for early payment. If none is at first obvious, it could be that certain suppliers would be willing to offer quite generous discounts if paid early. These are often, though not always, those who chase with the most vigour for payment. It is a simple matter to calculate whether the discount offered would be greater than the amount which could be earned on a bank deposit, though the paying of suppliers early can better be compared to a long-term investment and is therefore really most suited to companies with a continuing surplus cash position.

International float management

One of the principal winners in international trade is always the bank involved in the transaction flow. The greatest cost associated with international payments is not the declared cost of bank charges but the hidden cost of banking float – money being transmitted through the international banking system. Everyone is used to calling or telexing customers and demanding to know where their payments are, only to be told they paid yesterday, last week or last month – in Italy perhaps even two months ago. It is sometimes felt by credit managers that the customer is being less than honest, but very often what has happened is that the customer has parted with the money but the exporter has not got it; the people who have it are the international banks. The cause of the problem may be exchange control regulations in the customer's country but more often it is an imperfect payment instrument or unplanned payment routes. A little knowledge about how international transfers work is therefore very handy if one is to reduce the float involved and thus save a great deal of lost interest.

Export customers will quite naturally, if given an open choice, choose the slowest way of making a payment or perhaps adopt a procedure commonly used in the domestic market but which will be totally unsuited to international payments. For example, cheques are very inefficient international payment instruments from the exporter's point of view though, in most countries, fine from the importer's viewpoint because their account will not be debited until their bank finally clears the cheque. Even international payments made by telegraphic transfer or wire can take a great deal of time if some thought has not been given to the account to which funds should be paid.

The cheque payment cycle for a shipment from say Atlanta, USA to Manchester, England is a good illustration of an apparently simple international payment that takes a long time to clear. Let's say the importers draw a cheque for $100 000 on their bank, the First National Bank of Atlanta for payment to the Manchester-based UK exporter. This is mailed by air but, given the inefficiencies of the international mail service, takes five days to get from Atlanta to Manchester. The exporter then goes along to his bank with the cheque and presents it across the counter and that night the Manchester branch sends the cheque to its nearest international branch, where it will be batched up with other international cheques received and sent to the UK bank's London international headquarters. From there, now a further two days later, the cheque is passed to either the UK branch of the foreign bank on which the cheque is drawn, if there is one, or sent to the UK bank's New York office. These transfers will be sent by courier and will therefore take only one more day; but, having arrived in New York, the cheque will probably be mailed to First National Bank of Atlanta, taking another, say, four days to reach its destination. Upon receipt, the

First National Bank of Atlanta will, assuming funds are available on the account, honour the cheque and transfer the funds to its correspondent account in the UK, which may well not be the exporter's bank. This takes a further two days. The correspondent, having received the credit, will then transfer the funds to the account of the exporter's bank in London, which through its international branch network will advise the exporter. If the exporters have daily statements, they should have funds on their account and an advice of the funds received two days from receipt by the international bank.

Thus, a cheque for $100 000 has taken a total of sixteen days to be cleared and credited to the exporter's account. Bank charges on the transfer might have been $25 but the hidden lost interest cost is, assuming an 11 per cent cost of funds, $488. This assumes the exporters choose to have the cheque collected; they could have chosen to negotiate the cheque which has the advantage of providing instant cash but will incur a charge for the equivalent to the bank's lost interest for the period it would take to clear the cheque. The other disadvantage of negotiated cheques is that, should the cheque not be honoured on final presentation, the exporter's account will be debited with the original value of the cheque and this could be as long as six or even twelve months after negotiation. This clearly presents a credit manager with a significant problem when trying to decide how much is outstanding from customers.

Telegraphic or wired transfers overcome the cheque float problem and normally provide a much more efficient payment method. To gain full advantage of international funds transfer it is essential to provide very clear instructions, preferably in their own language, to customers and banks and if possible to specify a payment route and value date. If this is not done problems can occur, especially in Third World markets, though for large fund flows the problem can be eased by opening accounts with banks which are correspondents of either the exporter's bank or, if that is not possible, at least the major bank in the importing country. Communications are bad in Third World countries and banks tend to be small and staffed by a limited number of skilled personnel. Figure 23.1 illustrates both an original transfer chain for a sale from the UK to Niger and a revised chain which significantly improved transfer times. In this particular illustration, a French bank has been chosen because Niger is part of French-speaking Africa and thus there is a good chance of finding someone who can telex out to chase payment in the appropriate language. In addition, the local currency, Central African

Original payment route	Revised payment route
Importers give instructions for Central African franc payment at Banque Centrale des Etats de l'Afrique de l'Ouest, Zinder for credit to Midland Bank, London French Franc Account.	Importers give their bank, BCEAO, Zinder instructions to pay via BIAO Niamey, Central African francs for credit to Banque Nationale de Paris, Paris.
↓	↓
BCEAO sends banker's draft to head office in Niamey.	BIAO, Niamey telegraphs BNP, Paris.
↓	↓
BCEAO head office sends draft to Banque Internationale pour l'Afrique Occidentale.	BNP, Paris credits customer account and advises BNP, London.
↓	↓
BIAO, Niamey telegraphs to BIAO, Paris.	BNP, London advises customer.
↓	
BIAO, Paris sends draft to Banque Paribus for credit to Midland Bank account and advise.	
↓	
Midland advises customer funds received.	

Figure 23.1   Improving transfer time

francs, is directly convertible into French francs.

One of the largest challenges in the developed world is the Italian market. Italy has a strong well-developed manufacturing base but an incredibly archaic banking system. It is almost essential, if one wishes to achieve efficient payment, to trade with Italy on a form of documentary collection. Open account trading courts disaster, as the Italian importers may transfer funds with the genuine intention of moving them swiftly to the exporter's account, and their account may well be debited; but it can still take anything up to six weeks for the money to emerge from the Italian banking system.

Domestic float management

Domestic cashflow management is usually much less complex than international. Nevertheless, attention to a few key points will help to ensure that funds are credited promptly to bank accounts and leave them at the last reasonable date.

It is obviously a sensible discipline to ensure that funds are banked daily and, if appropriate, remotely rather than to have cheques collected by a sales team or branches and sent by post to a central point for banking. If the facility is available, the use of standing orders or direct debits will add a degree of certainty to cashflow and ensure that payments are made on time by customers. Retail stores and other large cash recipients may find that post offices or other institutions will accept cash on non-banking days and thus improve both security and the interest-earning ability of funds collected.

It is not intended to devote any time here to the description of controls for payments to be made to suppliers, but it is worthwhile to ensure that high-value payments are targeted for specific value dates. The uncertainty of when a cheque may arrive through the post can be removed by paying suppliers by value dated credit transfer, which ensures that the paying company receives value for its funds until the last possible date, while the recipient company is paid at an acceptable time.

The main exception to standard rules is the USA, where the current concept of one-state banking slows down the likely clearing cycle for cheques. Most major US banks have lock-box services which will speed the clearing of out of state cheques and can therefore greatly assist in speeding cashflow.

MULTINATIONALS' FUND MANAGEMENT

Fund management in multinationals normally has to be based on central guidelines, but operational management will probably be more efficient if delegated to well-trained personnel in each country of operation. There are at first sight possibilities for improving efficiency by pooling cash, but these are often made impossible, or at the very least not advisable, by foreign exchange risk or regulations, tax complications or the overall policy and style of management of the group of companies.

Policy is a good point to start from. It is very difficult to try to impose on a company a cash policy that differs radically from its overall management policy. If a group is decentralized in terms of production and profit accountability, it is unlikely to make sense to try to remove funds from one company within the group in order to avoid borrowing in another. To do so would produce a culture clash, as the management of the company authorized to place a deposit with another in the group fights to retain the autonomy which they see being removed from them. If, however, a group has integrated production facilities and foreign exchange management it may be possible to achieve the integration of funds as well, so that surpluses available in one part of the group can be used to avoid the need for borrowings in another. The foreign exchange management element is obviously very important, as to move funds between countries usually means to acquire foreign exchange risks that far outweigh the potential savings that may occur if more use can be made of surplus funds.

Assuming the policy problems have been overcome, probably the next main hurdle would be foreign exchange regulations making it impossible for companies in certain countries to transfer funds to others, even within the same group, domiciled in other countries. There is also the risk that funds lent on could not be returned because of the imposition of foreign exchange regulations after a deposit had been made. The risk of foreign exchange rate changes can be overcome by the centre taking responsibility for the risk which it can lay off on the foreign exchange markets on behalf of both the deposit placer and taker. This does, though, obviously rule out the involvement of subsidiaries that may well have a pressing need for funds in countries where there is no effective foreign exchange market. The cover of foreign exchange risk is essential but does not remove the major element of potential savings. Say a group wishes to use funds earning 2 per cent in

Switzerland to fund the operations of a UK subsidiary, paying base rate of 10 per cent plus a 1 per cent margin for its money. At first sight the saving is $11 - 2 = 9$ per cent. But the true saving may only be 1.5 per cent, the discount payable on the foreign exchange deal, necessary to hedge the value of sterling when the loan is repaid, absorbing the rest. The reasons for the existence of the discount are explained in Chapter 22.

For the really large multinationals, opportunities can arise for the cash management activities of subsidiaries in West European and North American countries to operate a centralized cash management activity, utilizing processes of reinvoicing and netting. This is described in Chapter 4.

Inter-group transfers

International transfers and the problems that can befall exporting companies were considered earlier. The same sort of problems can befall the subsidiaries of multinationals trading with each other. In this case there is a clear need for the benefit of the group as a whole to be considered, as the only beneficiary of sloppy systems would be the international banking sector. The key is to use value dating for all significant payments, so that payments made have included in the instruction a specific date on which value should be given on the recipient's bank account. This should be the same as the day on which the transferee's bank account is debited, thus ensuring that no value is given away to the banks. It is often a good routine to have a common settlement date each week, or even each month, within a group so that all involved know when intercompany accounts are to be cleared and the value dating routine becomes firmly established.

Recommended reading

Brooke, Michael Z. (Editor). *International Financial Management Handbook*. Lancaster: Kluwer Publishing Ltd. Regularly updated loose-leaf handbook with over thirty financial experts contributing.

PART VIII
ORGANIZATION AND SYSTEMS

24

Organization and policy

Tom Auchterlonie

Credit is a separate discipline within finance, in support of selling and for management of the investment in accounts receivable.

Granting credit is an investment process because it commits capital of the business to outsiders for varying periods with the risk of it being lost.

Ideally there should be a Vice President-Credit. This allows the perspective of investing short term in the customers of the company to be liberated from Sales and Comptrollership bias. Credit is the customer-orientated element of the financing of the company and thus is naturally aligned with the marketing sales function. Credit is a key element in bad debt loss and thus is also aligned with control in regard to costs and protection of assets.

Credit is in fact a hybrid, not traditionally viewed as separate as are accounting and selling. Consequently, over time it has been assigned variously to sales, control, treasury or law according to the nature of its recognition by management. The author recognizes credit to be a customer-orientated investing function of finance in direct support of selling, charged with management of risk to control credit loss within parameter(s) designated by the business plan.

Credit should report to the management level responsible for the results of the company. The common locations for the credit function have been in finance or in sales. The specific location of credit – to whom it reports – often determines its characteristics. Table 24.1 lists characteristics of the environments spawned by the finance and sales functions.

The hospital environment for credit, in the author's opinion, is one largely:

- Custodial
- Judgemental

421

Table 24.1
Characteristics of environments

Finance		Sales
Treasury	*Control*	
Custodial	Conforming	Outgoing
Planning	Record keeping	Planning
Appraising	Statistical	Permissive
Future-orientated	Historical	Contemporary

- Risk-taking
- Future-orientated

or close to the author's assessment of the treasury environment.

FUNCTIONS

Wherever located in the company, credit has functions to perform. They are often the following:

(a) approval, extension, and termination of credit to customers;
(b) review, correction and approval of letters of credit on behalf of the company in combination with other functions impacted by letter of credit requirements;
(c) timely collections with sales assistance;
(d) control of bad debt losses;
(e) control of cost of credit management;
(f) maintenance of any associated record keeping assigned to credit (accounts receivable, and so on).

Credit policy

Guidance is necessary. Acceptance and implementation of the international credit function in the company requires a policy. Too often the policy is not articulated or, at best, a policy is assumed or develops through precedent.

In support of selling and for management of the investment in accounts receivable, a policy modelled after the following is appropriate.

1 Establish credit lines for all customers and do so on the basis of risk, profitability and ability to pay. Once the limit is established, credit will monitor the account balance and paying habits of each customer

to protect the firm's investment.
2 Maintain direct relations with customers.
3 Perform periodic reviews of the appropriateness of assigned credit.
4 Shipments cannot be released without prior credit approval. The customer's class of risk, historic and present payment performance and credit line are major factors in determining the type and degree of approval arrangements necessary.
5 In regard to letters of credit:
   (a) shipments are not to be made until the supporting letter of credit is in-house and approved, including amendments;
   (b) security interest in the goods sold is to be retained until payment is received or unconditional commitment to pay is obtained from the controlling bank as designated in the letter of credit. Measures to protect the security interest in the goods could be as follows.
   ● Consignment to order of shipper is preferred.
   ● Faulty documents are not to be sent on approval nor is the bank to pay under reserve. Faulty and late documents are to be held at the bank to which presentation has been made until advice of their acceptance or authorization to pay is confirmed.
6 Sales representatives have an accountability to help collect in accordance with terms. Bank collections and other items (invoices) which are not paid when they are due are a responsibility of credit with the assistance of the sales representative.

ORGANIZATION

There are various organization options available to accomplish credit functions. How the company chooses to organize the credit function is critical only to that company. One commonly expects credit to be carried out by a person or a department. It can be done part time or accomplished by a department which performs a variety of (other) functions. The author believes the best results flow from an organization matrix which fosters objectivity and allows the concept of accountability – what one is answerable for – to have full play in what has to be accomplished. Whether a department or individual or a function such as sales, finance or law is answerable, accountabilities should define what is to be accomplished and ideally associate measures and goals to evaluate results.

Accountabilities

Some examples of accountabilities are:

- Establish and maintain financially responsible credit lines for assigned customers
- Administer and maintain collections
- Direct and effectively use related services
- Accomplish personal development through reading, professional societies and formal instruction.

Measures

Measures are yardsticks for the determination of achievement. Examples of measures associated with accountabilities are:

- Bad debts
- Financial ratios
- Business plan parameters
- Percent receivables current
- Balances late more than sixty days
- Academic or professional curricula
- Activity in organizations.

Goals

Examples of goals associated with accountabilities and measures are:

- Benchmark loss rate
- Ratio criteria
- Expected, approved loss rate
- Timeliness of remittances from customers
- Action accomplished on late balances
- Accomplishment and/or level of study
- Participation (nature and accomplishment).

Organization revisited

Accountabilities, measures and goals evaluate and direct accomplishment. They are applicable to the performance of credit by persons, units or (other) functions such as finance, sales or law; they work together as criteria. Table 24.2 shows the integration of four accountabilities, goals

Table 24.2
Performance

Accountability	Goal	Measure
Establish and maintain financially responsible credit lines.	Bad debt losses less than a specified year or chosen period.	$x per $100 of sales or a stated specific total amount.
	Approved bad debt loss rate budgeted to meet incremental sales and profit goals.	Losses compared to business plan parameters.
	Specify the financial ratios and variance indicative of financial strength and performance management wishes to see in the customer base per business segment	Actual ranges of the selected ratios derived as averages of the ratios calculated from the financial statements of all the customers approved for credits during specific periods, by business segment. Approved exceptions to goal standards.
Administer and maintain collections.	Percentage of receivables current judged to be appropriate to the business segment(s).	Percentage of receivables current derived from periodic A/R aged trial balances.
	Percentage of receivables current deemed controllable by credit function.	Percentage of receivables current derived from period A/R aged trial balances *adjusted* by factor to account for portion of the percentage not controllable by credit function.
	Maximum number of items for which reason(s) for non-payment is unknown. Non-risk 3 Semi-risk 5 Risk 1	46 to 90 days overdue.
Direct and effectively use related services.	Consolidate number of collection agencies to improve control and reduce cost.	No more than three active agencies; cost of services of each not to exceed 7 per cent of assigned collections.

425

Table 24.2 (concluded)

Accountability	Goal	Measure
Accomplish personal development through reading, professional societies and formal instruction.	Participation in International Credit Club.	Timely and appropriate sharing of experience, conduct one credit seminar during (this) year.

and measures to illustrate evaluation and direction of accomplishment. The selection is in no way meant as 'the only' or 'most important' or 'as is to be worded.' The selection instead is drawn to show how criteria are formed by the integration of accountabilities, measures and goals, and how such criteria apply to direction and evaluation of performance.

The standard for accomplishment by the credit function should be established by the management level responsible for the results of the company. The standard for accomplishment – tempered as it may be by cost – induces the extent and kind of organization to carry out the credit function. Credit policy provides guidance. How the company actually chooses to organize the credit function is critical only to that company.

Necessity for balance

The best results flow from an organization matrix which fosters objectivity. Checks and balances evolve from implementing the credit policy. Accountabilities, measures and goals focus accomplishment on what the company wishes to achieve (the business plan). A function of credit is approval, extension, and termination of credit to customers. The related accountability is 'Establish and maintain financially responsible credit lines for assigned customers.' Integration of this accountability with goal and measure creates criteria for accomplishment of control of bad debt loss. The role of credit in the company evolves from the constellation of function, policy, accountabilities, goals and measures. Tone is set by the characteristics described earlier in this chapter.

Participative role of credit

Customer-orientated credit operations support selling without sacrifice of control.

The credit role in sales can be shown as follows:

1 Credit services:
   ● Credit lines
   ● Bank collections
   ● Review of letters of credit
   ● Information
2 Exposure control:
   ● Co-ordination with sales
   ● Pre-shipment release
   ● Collections
3 Other:
   ● Field work with customers, sales and overseas representatives
   ● Consultation
   ● Review

The above is consistent with the functions, policy and accountabilities demonstrated earlier.

Harmony with control

Control exercises protective oversight of the assets of the company. Controller concern for the safety of the company's investment in accounts receivable is pervasive. Potential bad debts and disputes subtract from the realizable value of accounts receivable.

Bad debts are investment losses. Many are preventable. Preventable bad debts can be identified in the early stages by various means. One means is the ageing of accounts receivable from reference points such as the date invoices were to have been paid by customers. The interval between the date an invoice was to have been paid and the date reckoning is done can indicate late payment which should be investigated for why it is late. A pattern of lateness can emerge which identifies potential bad debt loss preventable by appropriate immediate action. Watchfulness and timely corrective action satisfies controller concern for safety of investment in accounts receivable.

Reserves for bad debts, or similar reserves maintained in jurisdictions where law prohibits writing off a debt due from a party not yet 'officially' bankrupt, are also a concern of control *when* their adequacy should conform to accounting standards, company policy or lawful regulation.

The bookkeeping role requires control to maintain records for accounts receivable, or assure adequate records are maintained. The credit function and the control function both benefit from well-kept accounts receivable.

Credit lines are a control device. The effectiveness of credit lines in the control of exposure (investment in customers) is improved through the use of information generated by accounts receivable. Credit and control thus have direct interest in and dependence on accurate accounts receivable. The scheme of business requires co-operation between functions to control loss in pursuit of profit. Necessity binds.

Loss control

Loss control is critical because it impacts pride in performance, the effectiveness of capital and cost.

The participative role of credit requires risk taking. Profits are usually not gained without risk. The author defines credit as an investment process because it commits capital of the company to outsiders for varying periods with the risk of losing it. Credit's role is to support selling by finding successful arrangements to invest short term in customers.

Just as sales should be profitable, so should credit's commitment of capital be effective. Obviously results will be mixed as there are unprofitable sales and (for credit) bad debt losses.

Preoccupation with loss can be as detrimental as fixation on volume. Both encourage loss because profitable opportunities are passed which, in fact, could be managed, or risk is undertaken without regard for informed counsel. Loss control is shared and should be continuous to be effective.

In the main, credit and sales work to produce effective results. Credit's concern with risk of loss is to be regarded as positively as sales' concern for profitable margins.

Balance between sales and credit

There is considerable lore on the adversarial nature of the relationship of sales and credit due to the goals of their respective functions. Their relative responsibilities are in fact not adversarial when credit is understood to be an investment process. Credit is the customer-orientated element of the financing of the company and thus is naturally aligned with sales. Table 24.3 presents the relative responsibilities of sales and credit, and shows them to be synergistic. It points to the added value of the role of credit in accomplishment of sales plans.

Table 24.3
Relative responsibilities of sales and credit

Credit (investment)	Commercial (sales)
Decides whether to make an investment in the customer.	Decides who to sell to.
Decides how much investment to make (credit line).	Decides on a sales plan: product, price, characteristics and quantity to sell.
Assesses customer's ability to pay.	Assesses customers' needs (sales plan).
Monitors cashflow within agreed terms.	Sets terms of payment and creates an accurate, legal invoice.
Advises the commercial department of customers who do not honour commitments to pay within agreed upon terms.	Informs customers when payment is not made within agreed upon terms.
Informs commercial department of disputes.	Resolves disputes.
Manages loss control.	Informs credit when customer will have difficulty paying.

Reconciliation

When a sales plan requires investment (in accounts receivable) exceeding the amount which credit is willing to make in a customer, based on the customer's ability to pay, the *gap* between ability to pay and the sales plan *can be*:

(a) eliminated by reducing sales or shortening payment terms;
(b) supported with collateral, liens, guarantees, or a transfer of risk (insurance or discount without recourse);
(c) charged to the income statement of the product or business as a reserve against future losses.

In the event of disagreement between sales and credit as to the treatment to be afforded a customer, the management level responsible for the results of the firm decides the case. The author recommends that in no event should decisions on cases be within the power of a management level equal or less than the highest level to which sales and credit report. This principle encourages amicable resolution of difference. It preserves balance and fosters objectivity.

Table 24.4
Risk classification

Classification	Characteristics
A Best	Excellent financial strength with good payment performance.
B Good	Strong financial strength with reasonably good payment performance.
C Semi-risk	Financial strength ranging from adequate to strong. Compared to higher rated risk, semi-risk is more susceptible to adverse economic conditions or changing circumstances which weaken ability to pay.
D Risk	Limited financial strength. Risk is considerable with respect to conformance with terms. Customers in this category are highly susceptible to adversity.
Cash basis	High-risk accounts which do not rate a line of credit because of likelihood of loss.

Marginal risk/incremental sales

A marginal risk and an attractive incremental sale will often coincide. This can lead to the use of reconciliation as described above. Many such sales, however, are made without reconciliation, using instead tight co-operation between sales and credit. Tight co-operation is usual in category D in Table 24.4. However, various degrees of reconciliation should be unfailingly employed when investing in the lower range of D.

Overall, a rating system should be applied to all investment candidates.

Collection

Value not punctually remitted by customers is subject to collection. The interests of control, credit and sales rapidly converge when money due is not punctually remitted (see Table 24.5).

Collection is an accountability of the company. How collection is managed, maintained and accomplished should be determined by the management level responsible for the results of the business. Tact, firmness and sensitivity are important. Perseverance is essential. How the company chooses to accomplish collection is critical only to that company.

In the author's opinion sales should collect money not remitted in accordance with terms (customer relations, good standing). Credit should assist, but perform a secondary role until it is evident there has

Table 24.5
Overdue debts: convergance of interests

Control	Credit	Sales
Safety of investment ● Stewardship	Investment turnover ● Reopen credit ● Justify exposure	Customer relations ● Maintain good standing ● Maintain respect
Redemption of value ● Loss control ● Bad debts	Loss control ● Maintain respect ● Minimize loss	Loss control ● Protect margin ● Minimize loss

been no timely remittance. Sales and credit should thereafter agree on their roles in the performance of the collection (loss control, customer relations). Should a potential bad debt ensue, recovery can be pursued by credit or control, with cognizance of sales (minimize cost, minimize loss).

Visitation

There is no substitute for field experience at home or abroad. Feel cannot be developed without contact. Visitation is primary to reciprocal relations – with customers, and with the elements of the firm. A credit function which does not interact with customers – personally – will not mature, nor will it be effective.

Personnel selection

Because credit is the customer-orientated element of the financing of the company, this complexity requires versatile personnel. Job value and company-specific requirements also influence selection.

Effective credit personnel exhibit:

● a taste for adventure
● the need to interact with people
● good knowledge of the business
● an excellent sense of finance
● a practical understanding of selling, distribution and law
● orientation toward profit
● no fear of risk

Organization and systems

Credit is not the preserve of accountants. Effective credit personnel are drawn from all disciplines. While manufacturing and law are not obviously thought of as sources, sales, public relations and business development are apparent sources, as is accounting. No one background is best. How the company has chosen to accomplish credit and the nature of its recognition by management, in the end, determines selection.

Training and the credit manual

Most credit training presently is accomplished on the job. A body of knowledge has been documented, and is taught, by the National Association of Credit Management in the US and by the credit institutes around the world (see the Appendix for a discussion of this and other sources). Extensive literature is available, more is being written.

A form of credit literature is the credit manual, usually written in-house and specialized to the company. A credit manual is a useful resource for training (and for audit) if written sensitively to meet the needs of sales, credit and control. The credit manual can encompass:

1 Policy:
   - Guidance
   - Accountabilities
   - Role
2 Standards:
   - Measures
   - Ratios
   - Risk classification
   - Letters of credit
3 Procedure:
   - Credit approval
   - Reconciliation
   - Loss control
   - Collection
4 Relations:
   - Balance between sales and credit
   - Harmony with control
   - Organization

In the training and development of the credit function within the firm, an alert management will recognize the importance and vitality of (credit) training to the business plan as essential, and progressive.

Definition revisited

Credit is a separated discipline within finance in support of selling and for management of the investment in accounts receivable.

Granting credit is an investment process because it commits capital of the business to outsiders for varying periods with the risk of it being lost.

COMMENT

This chapter has addressed various issues derived from the author's concept of credit, and its station in the hierarchy of the company. Caution has been exercised to avoid company-specific presentation of the material. For this reason, the temptation to show a department organization chart has been resisted.

25

Supporting systems

Robert T Lambert

The international credit executive, like his or her domestic counterpart, needs current information on the status and trend of customer accounts properly to manage the investment in accounts receivable. For today's credit professional, this is best provided by an automated system which among other things identifies the exception accounts requiring attention while by-passing those accounts which do not require any action.

Everything begins with the sales order. From the order entry system, it proceeds through the invoicing or billing system and into the accounts receivable system. Along the way, inventory records and sales history are updated.

Later the customer's payment is received, matched to invoices in the customer's account receivable and the paid items are removed to a paid item history file. The customer's record is then updated with payment trend, high credit and other accumulated statistical data.

SCOPE OF CREDIT SYSTEMS

While the above description represents a skeleton outline of a total system, the purpose of this handbook is to provide practical guidance to international credit executives. This objective requires an examination of the various elements of the credit and collection systems; and the assumption is made that today's international credit executive will be utilizing some level of computer automation.

Export sales ledger

The export sales ledger may also be called the export accounts receivable ledger. An international accounts receivable system has many similarities with a domestic one, but it also has some noticeable differences. It can therefore be a very bad mistake for a company new to exporting to try to use a domestic system to handle its export receivables.

The first section of information in the export sales ledger is the customer information master file. If an on-line system is in use, this would be accessed through the customer information screen. The customer master will include all the basic, and mainly reasonably permanent, information: correct name and trade style, complete billing and shipping addresses, credit limit and, possibly, high credit or highest exposure recorded.

The recommended customer master or customer information screen would contain additional information to facilitate the credit manager's handling of the account. Modern systems can display customer information data on-line to the credit manager, which was previously available only in the credit file. Included in this additional information ought to be the following.

- Name and address of customer's bank
- Salesman and sales manager codes
- Customer risk classification
- Last payment date and amount
- High credit date and amount
- Customer's quoted terms
- Customer contact's name
- Telephone, telex and facsimile numbers
- Account status with past due ageing
- Pending orders and values

The customer's export ledger is updated as new billings are reflected in the system, and the data will include transaction number, shipment date, currency, invoiced amount, terms and due date.

The accounts receivable system should in particular be able to handle multiple currencies as well as bills of exchange (drafts). Exporters often prefer to price shipments in their domestic currency and thus avoid any currency devaluation risk. In today's markets, however, competition may make it necessary to price in a currency other than the exporter's currency. This may then require billing in the customer's currency or even in a third country's currency. The accounts receivable system should be able to handle different currencies down to individual transaction level and to report in both the billed currency and the exporter's currency. The system should accumulate receivables by currency and by country and produce routine reports for the purpose of currency revaluation and country risk exposures.

A significant number of exports are sold on draft/bill of exchange terms. The accounts receivable system should if required allow application of accepted time or sight drafts by offsetting the invoices and setting up a new receivable, created by the draft, with the due date. The transfer of funds in payment of the draft will then simply offset the open draft receivable. Because foreign drafts do not have the same degree of security as domestic drafts, some exporters prefer not to run an export bills receivable book. In such cases, unpaid invoices will remain in the original customer accounts. If however they are 'tagged' as covered by drafts, a suitable system can still extract those items and create a notional bills receivable book.

Modern systems accept data transfer of remittance information and automatic updating of the accounts receivable detail at the customer and invoice or draft level. Data arrives from the bank in the evening of the day the funds are received at the bank. The bank prepares a data tape which is transmitted to the exporter's data centre each evening. If there are multiple banks in the collection system, a consolidator may receive each bank's data and consolidate it into one data tape for transmission to the data centre. Update of the customer's account then occurs overnight during the system's nightly processing cycle.

At a minimum, the export accounts receivable system should provide weekly or semi-monthly detailed aged trial balances with the status of the export accounts receivables. Some form of delinquency notice should be produced of past due items as they become past due.

The export accounts receivable system may also provide for automatic dunning of overdues by preparing and transmitting telex or facsimile communications to the customer with copies to the appropriate salesman. This automatic routine follow up of overdues allows the export credit manager to concentrate on the exceptions with the routine follow up handled by automation. It is advisable, however, for a 'manual intercept' feature to be available to prevent sensitive debts, subject to mitigating circumstances, from being chased.

Intercompany accounting

Companies forming part of a multinational group can use their computerized intercompany accounting procedures to enhance their credit and cash management functions. This involves harnessing available computer technologies to process and network their data for the following purposes.

Re-invoicing sales to customers

No matter from which parts of the multinational group the goods are sourced, they will always be invoiced by the local company in their own country. This technique, using local printing facilities, enables the customer to treat with one local company in a familiar language and environment. It also permits the local company to control credit on behalf of all supplying members of the group.

Re-invoicing through a specific centre

This technique is described in more detail in Chapter 4; it enhances the currency management of a multinational group. It can be followed by the local re-invoicing process described above.

Blending debtors and order/invoicing data

This displays to all parts of the group the overall receivables/payables position of each customer/supplier. This facilitates negotiation of terms, 'stop shipment' routines, netting procedures and 'debit control' as well as credit control ('debit control' in this sense meaning not paying promptly a supplier who in the guise of customer is delinquent on payment of debts due to another part of the group).

Netting off intercompany cashflows between different parts of the group

Where companies within the same group are both buying from and selling to each other, bank charges and especially float time can be greatly reduced by a process of netting, provided it is not prohibited by local exchange controls. Appropriate systems can examine data relating to proposed cashflows, convert currencies according to set rules to one common currency, and determine the minimum amounts of money that need actually flow after netting. Accounting entries give effect to the sums that would have flowed had netting not taken place.

Risk assessment

The business periodicals carry almost daily articles concerning the present economic, political and social instability of many countries of the world. Exporters can no longer assume that all foreign countries have either the ability or the willingness to meet their financial obligations. Therefore, the present conditions dictate that exporters must develop formal approaches to evaluating and dealing with the risk in their export credit administration.

World-wide economic conditions and continuously changing political conditions require that exporters have a systematic process for evaluating the country risk and a clear-cut corporate policy for the guidance of the credit administrators.

Reviewing articles and discussions with others dealing with export credit all too often suggests that many companies have no systematic process for evaluating the country or sovereign risk in export credit sales. This may be due to the many differences in multinational companies' organizations, management philosophy, strategic plans or their profitability.

The techniques of risk assessment are covered in Part II of this handbook. From a systems viewpoint the following is recommended as just one solution for providing consistency in the management of export credit risk in receivables.

A suggested country risk evaluation system

The system should provide specific standard terms of sale for each country, variable perhaps by product group, with background information on the restrictive ones. The final decision to restrict sales to a country, either through terms or termination due to the political risk, is usually the prerogative of the manager or director who has profit responsibility. However, the international credit manager should now have the ability to provide a more accurate risk assessment to aid in the decision-making process.

The credit manager should systematically review information on country credit and financial conditions from financial newspapers and periodicals, major banks and at least one country risk-rating service. The information gathered should be analysed and standard terms established for each country. Using the same information, a country risk classification might be established on a scale of one to five, with one the lowest risk and five the highest risk. Risk ratings are, at best, a subjective judgement. However, one set of guidelines for a risk rating system is defined as follows.

1 No foreign exchange problems or slowness reported.
2 Minor foreign exchange problems or slowness of thirty to sixty days reported.
3 Serious foreign exchange shortage or slowness of ninety days or more reported.
4 Very limited foreign exchange or slowness of 180 days or more reported.
5 Unstable politically or funds blocked for the foreseeable future.

Using the convenience of a microcomputer, a database should be established of the countries with which the corporation is trading or considering trading. Each country file on the database should at the very least contain:

(a) units or locations selling into the country;
(b) assigned risk classification;
(c) currency exposure of each unit;
(d) payment survey results;
(e) exchange delays;
(f) rating service rating; and
(g) miscellaneous comments.

The currency exposure by country is updated at least monthly. A monthly country risk exposure report is prepared and distributed to management (see Figure 25.1).

A country recommended terms report is printed out monthly and distributed to exporting units' sales personnel for use in quoting terms to customers (see Figure 25.2). Upon request, a print-out of the file of a specific country is obtained and distributed (see Figure 25.3).

The country risk database and reporting facility can be implemented on either a mainframe, MIS-supported system or a microcomputer with 'off the shelf' database software. The microcomputer system can normally be implemented and easily changed or improved by credit personnel, without the assistance of any professional systems personnel.

Any company exporting in today's international financial climate must have a system of protection against the country risk exposure. This system must be either one of systematic evaluation of the country risk or transferring the risk to a third party through such means as insurance or

Country Risk Report

Group	Country	Terms	Risk Rating	Exchange	Unit 1	Unit 2	Unit 3	Unit 4	Unit 5	Country T1
Europe	France	Sight Draft/Open Account	2	91.7	30	325,000.00	92,000.00	53,000.00	87,000.00	11,000.00	568,000.00
Europe	Italy	Letter of Credit	4	74.3	45	45,000.00	312,000.00	98,745.00	34,056.00	12,345.00	502,146.00
Europe	U.K.	Open Account	1	94.3	15	245,888.00	36,542.00	981,324.00	15,000.00	64,567.00	1,343,321.00

SUMMARY

Tuesday March 29, 1988

Sum for Risk Class : 7
Sum for Rating   : 260.3
Sum for Exchange : 90
Sum for Unit 1   : 615,888.00
Sum for Unit 2   : 440,542.00
Sum for Unit 3   : 1,133,069.00
Sum for Unit 4   : 136,056.00
Sum for Unit 5   : 87,912.00
Sum for Country T1 : 2,413,467.00

Printed 3 of the 3 records.

Figure 25.1 Monthly country risk exposure report

Recommended Terms Report

Group	Country	Terms	Risk	Rating	Pay Good	Pay Fair	Pay Poor	Exchange	Comments
Europe	France	Sight draft/Open Account	2	91.7	30.0	50.0	20.0	30	Anticipate Devaluation
Europe	Italy	Letter of Credit	4	74.3	10.5	60.2	29.3	45	Expect Devaluation
Europe	U.K.	Open Account	1	94.3	50.1	40.9	10.0	15	Economy Improving

SUMMARY

Tuesday March 29, 1988

```
Sum for Risk Class :   7
Sum for Rating     : 260.3
Sum for Pay Good % :  90.6
Sum for Pay Fair % : 151.1
Sum for Pay Poor % :  59.3
Sum for Exchange   :  90
```

Printed 3 of the 3 records.

Figure 25.2 Country recommended terms report

Database Name: COMPUTE   Description: recommended terms

Group   [Europe   ]
Country   [France   ]
Terms   [Sight Draft/Open Account]
Risk Class   [2]
Rating   [91.7]
Pay Good %   [30.0]
Pay Fair %   [50.0]
Pay Poor %   [20.0]
Exchange   [30]
Comments   [Anticipate Devaluation   ]
Unit 1   [325,000.00]
Unit 2   [92,000.00]
Unit 3   [53,000.00]
Unit 4   [87,000.00]
Unit 5   [11,000.00]
Country T1 $ [568,000.00]

┌──┐
│ MODIFY   │
│   Action: ┌─Modify PgUp─Previous PgDn─Next ESC─Exit │
│ Insert Mode   (Alphanumeric field)   │
└──┘

Figure 25.3 Print-out of a country file

factoring. Without one or the other, rapidly changing international conditions may jeopardize the timely collection of the company's export receivables.

Computer systems can also help with customer risk assessment, particularly in the area of evaluating customers' financial statements and establishing credit limits. These areas and that of customer categorization are dealt with in Chapters 7 and 8.

Collection

The collection system is usually incorporated into, or is a by-product of, the accounts receivable system. A state of the art system identifies the exceptions, overdues in range or amounts, without the credit personnel having to leaf through computer print-outs or ledgers, visually to identify overdue items for collection activity. In addition, routine collection follow-up activity can be automatic with either telex or facsimile output. Finally, the collection system should allow easy access for report writing for both regular and special reporting.

Where bills of exchange are used to collect overseas debts, the first step in preparing for collection activity may be to update the accounts receivable system by offsetting individual invoices with time or sight drafts (see earlier remarks under 'Export sales ledger'). In such cases the draft then becomes the receivable. The system should allow offsetting of invoices included in the draft, journal entries for miscellaneous charges and establishment of the draft with its individual due date as the new receivable. The application of the draft should be recorded in the paid history file for later investigation, if necessary.

Initial dunning of overdues should be automatic but with a manual override. There is no substitute in collections for a prompt and persistent request for payment. For routine collections, the first – and perhaps the second (follow-up) – chasers can be sent to the customer or agent by automatically generated telexes or facsimiles. The system should also contain a provision for designating specific customers or disputed items as exempt from the dunning cycle, to enable them to be handled on an individual basis.

Modern systems have an electronic notepad and the ability to establish an automatic reminder of the next follow-up. Notes on previous collection activity can be recorded and remain with the account as activity continues.

A modern on-line credit management and accounts receivable system should have an exception model for automatic searching of the accounts for items which meet particular criteria. The credit manager may set up a model with any or all of the following variables:

(a) country;
(b) salesman or agent;
(c) credit analyst or manager;
(d) currency;
(e) multiple branches of a common account;
(f) overdue category;
(g) minimum and maximum monetary amounts;
(h) exceeding credit limit; and
(i) due for follow-up.

The model is usually established as the credit manager sets the criteria for his or her review.

The credit manager may, for example, decide to review accounts which meet the criteria of customers who:

(a) are located in France;
(b) are sixty days or more overdue;
(c) have overdues exceeding 1000 monetary units; and
(d) have exceeded their credit limit.

The system will search the file and display the names and amounts owing of customers meeting the model criteria. Individual accounts may now be called up and reviewed along with payment history and any previously entered collection notes.

Alternatively, the credit manager may decide to review the electronic notes which are designated for current follow-up. In this case the system will prompt for accounts with a designated follow-up date. This routine is simply an automated version of the old systems of assigning a bring-up date and placing a piece of paper in a tickler file. Indeed, all of the automated functions described in the state of the art system are simply electronic replacements of time-honoured manual or paper systems available to the credit professional in years gone by. But they are infinitely faster and more accurate.

Bad and doubtful debts provision

Each country has its own rules and conditions for the actual timing as to when a write-off of a bad debt may be taken for tax purposes. However, many companies establish a reserve position for the write-off of bad or doubtful accounts as a hedge for the current year's operating plan. A reserve of this nature simply protects the company from having to establish an unplanned reserve mid-way into a year because of the sudden bankruptcy of a customer or a blockage of funds from a country with a sudden deterioration in its economy.

Many methods of establishing a reserve are utilized. Some of the more common are:

(a)   a percentage of sales;
(b)   a percentage of the accounts receivable balance; and
(c)   historical rate of write-offs.

None of these more common methods really reflects the actual degree of exposure in the receivables portfolio on a periodic basis. One disciplined method is described below which requires assessments and updates on a monthly, quarterly, semi-annual or annual basis.

Many credit organizations utilize risk classification codes to designate the amount of perceived risk of the customer base. One system, for example, utilizes the following four classification codes, with One the least and Four the greatest risk.

- One: Prime, least risk, no bad debts
- Two: Good, some risk, few if any bad debts
- Three: Limited, more risk, some bad debts
- Four: Marginal, high risk, highest bad debts

This system is an easy microcomputer application and can be further automated by down-loading data from a mainframe system. If the customer master file contains a risk classification code, these codes can be utilized in the reserve evaluation. Using one of the commercially available programs, a spread-sheet can be established with columns for the following information:

(a)   customer name and location;
(b)   amount owed;
(c)   percentage risk assessment;
(d)   multiply amount (b) by (c) and total the answers.

The credit manager can then apply his or her own percentage assessment to the amount totalled in (d) above. An example of this spread-sheet is illustrated in Table 25.1.

This method of evaluating the adequacy of the reserve for doubtful

Table 25.1
Worksheet for doubtful accounts reserve

Reserve for doubtful accounts worksheet (US$)			
Name and location	Total A/R	Probability factor (%)	Adjusted amount
French customer Paris, France	45 617	25	11 404
Mexican customer Mexico City, DF	24 091	80	19 273
Brazilian customer Sao Paolo, Brazil	71 398	65	46 409
Total	141 106		77 086
Credit manager's probability factor and recommended reserve amount		35	26 980

accounts, if used consistently over time, will force the credit manager into a discipline of looking at the marginal accounts on a consistent basis. Some accountants may not endorse this method, however, preferring a fully statistical approach to a subjective judgement.

Integration with other systems

Depending upon the business activities and size of a corporation, its credit management systems might be integrated with a variety of other systems, particularly the order invoicing system and those which help manage cash and currencies.

Cash and currency management

Cash and currency management is concerned with the forecasting of incoming and outgoing funds and the disposition and raising of such funds (Chapter 23 covers this topic). Good credit management ensures that borrowings are kept to a minimum (or deposits and investments to a maximum), whilst credit management supporting systems can be a contributory source of much of the data required for forecasting and monitoring the forecasts.

The accounts receivable can very easily be analysed by currency and due date, and the resulting data married with other receivables and similar data from accounts payable, to produce the initial building blocks in a forecasting/monitoring system. Data can also be copied over from the order/invoicing system to pick up values and due dates for orders in the pipeline; and estimates then have to be made as regards any future orders and shipments which should figure in the forecasts. The accuracy of these estimates and therefore of the forecasts can be progressively refined in the light of experience and the actual cashflows measured in accounts receivable, accounts payable and elsewhere.

The order/invoicing (billing) system

As a matter of priority, the order/invoicing system should be integrated with credit management.

When the salesman or agent writes an order or, as we see today, enters the order into a portable computer, there is a definite cycle from the order entry to the general ledger.

Many sales people now carry portable computers which provide a database of information about their customers. In addition, the portable computers are used to write customer orders for later transmission into the mainframe computer. The portable computers keep the sales person up to date on prices and promotions plus the status of orders and shipments for their customers.

The order input to the main computer, whether by transmission from the sales person's portable computer or encoding orders from other sources, will enter an order processing routine. In this routine the customer order is lined up with current exposures and pending orders and is cleared against the customer credit limit. Either automatic or manual credit approval is then obtained.

Product availability is checked by reference to the inventory records and pending, unshipped orders. The order processing system prepares warehouse pick, or plant production documents and shipping documents, using information from the customer's master file record.

Invoices and other documents are then produced in an invoicing system and other sub-systems. The accounts receivable files are updated along with sales history information files.

When the corresponding funds are received from the customer, the

447

accounts receivable are updated with them. Payment adjustments such as discounts, freight charges, bank charges, and any other charges accepted by the exporter are fed to the general ledger from the accounts receivable system. Payment history and other statistical data update the customer master file. The cycle is complete and repeats itself when the next sale is made.

COMPUTER VERSUS MANUAL SYSTEMS

Is there really any contest today between manual and computer systems for accounts receivable and credit management?

Very few credit operations today function in a manual environment. Even a small credit operation can utilize a microcomputer for maintaining accounts receivable and producing the usual credit output. In addition, the microcomputer can provide a simulated on-line account status environment.

One small word of warning though. We should not be so bedazzled by computers that we try to apply every exceptional activity to them. International credit control is full of small exceptions which are best handled manually.

Nevertheless, the managers of today must become computer literate if they are to be the managers of tomorrow. Everyone is aware of the recent computer upsurge. Computers which once required large, special temperature-controlled rooms with false floors for their large cables can now be compressed into a small lap-top computer running on batteries and weighing ten to thirteen pounds.

The rapid advances in computers and computing power, coupled with those in communications, will continue for the foreseeable future. So, credit manager, educate yourself or be left behind!

STAGES OF COMPUTER SYSTEMS DESIGN

There are several fairly distinct stages in the design of a new or improved credit management system.

The problem study

The need for a new system only becomes apparent if there are significant problems in the operation of the old system, be it manual or computer.

448

Is there really a problem? And does it need an automated solution; or would a manual solution suffice? So the scope of the problem needs to be ascertained and all concerned convinced that it really does need to be tackled.

If there is to be a new or improved system, someone must have a vision of the future. Without that vision, people rarely make a conscious effort to see what might be in the future and can easily content themselves with saying the present system cannot be improved. But when the vision for that new on-line real-time system is caught, it's still a long way from implementation!

Feasibility study

Next, the expenditure in time and money to develop and implement a new system, whether purchased package or developed in-house, must be justified to management. Several approaches may be used:

(a) need to automate and update the function;
(b) provide timely and accurate information for cash forecasting and planning;
(c) reduce cost of clerical work through automation;
(d) improve the turnover of receivables; and
(e) reduce bad debts.

All of this needs to be expressed in terms of estimated cost-effectiveness. At the feasibility stage, a full system evaluation obviously cannot be undertaken but the proposed concept must be studied sufficiently to provide adequate indications of the following.

1 The benefits and savings expected to accrue from the new system.
2 The anticipated time scale to implementation.
3 The capital cost of systems purchase/design, programming, testing, staff training and implementation.
4 The running costs of the new system, compared with those of the old.

A completely open mind should be maintained by those making the study; and it should not be automatically assumed that it will result in a 'Yes' answer, with a recommendation to go ahead with the proposed project. Many feasibility studies rightly come back with a 'No' recommendation pointing those who commissioned the study towards a cheaper more effective alternative solution.

The remit

Given, however, that a feasibility study recommends a computerized solution acceptable to management, the latter must next set down a remit for the project, indicating the objectives, agreed timetable, resources to be made available, project organization and costs. It also makes sense for someone in authority to be given the task of 'auditing' the project against this remit throughout the whole of its development.

Initial design

The resource allocation in the remit should allow for user representatives to work alongside the MIS group systems analysts. Indeed the first step in designing (or evaluating the purchase of) a new computer system is to determine the users' needs. A serious mistake is often made when the MIS group unilaterally decides on a package or system design without extensive input from the users. Although there is the risk of a committee-designed system (and it is well known that the camel is a horse designed by a committee) the users will have pride of ownership if they have meaningful input into the many decisions that will need to be taken.

Early on in the design stage, all the users should be gathered together to go through the proposed system. The group will challenge, argue, find alternatives and make trade-offs, but the end result will be a design in which all the users will have ownership.

Thereafter, representatives of the users should come together regularly as a group to monitor progress, solve problems and eventually help test the system thoroughly. During this and subsequent stages, management must be aware that considerable additional work will fall upon the staff and should take all possible steps to alleviate the inevitable pressures.

A few pitfalls to be avoided

Systems people cannot be expected to know the peculiar requirements of all the professions they work for and it is unlikely that they will appreciate the importance to international credit people of matters such as the following.

1   Credit control is an ongoing exercise and does not treat the month-end as sacrosanct in the way that accountants have to. It makes sense

therefore for the system to allow month 2 postings of sales and cash and up-to-date reporting, irrespective of whether or not month 1 has been closed off.

2   International competition and foreign exchange considerations demand flexibility. So if a user requests a multi-currency facility, it doesn't just mean a given currency for a specific country or a given currency for a specific customer. It means that the user is likely to trade in *any* currency with *any* customer. So the facility is required at invoice/transaction level.

3   As with currencies, terms of payment for international trade can be many and varied. They are best coded in two parts – the method of payment and the effective number of days having regard to any qualifying clauses (for example, sixty days after delivery). The important points are that they should apply down to the level of invoice/transaction and that the system should therefore be capable of calculating meaningful due dates for payment.

4   The system should try to cater for all the changes that could arise during its estimated life span: How large might the volumes grow? Are there possibilities of acquisitions? How would new laws at home and abroad be likely to affect credit matters depending on the system? In Europe specifically how might reporting and collections be affected by the emergence of the single market expected in 1992? Is the devaluation of any given currency, or a large expansion of trade in that currency, likely to cause accumulators to overflow in the proposed system? It is always wise to allow generously for large expansions in values, numbers of transactions and the like.

Functional specifications

Whilst the systems people are writing or adapting the systems specifications, the users should be producing their own written functional specifications. These will form the basis for a User Manual but meanwhile can be used as a discussion and information document amongst all users and, as firmed up, can be checked against the systems specifications.

Systems specifications

The systems specifications are written by the MIS group analysts to be used ultimately by the programmers. They also serve as permanent documentation to be kept up to date with any subsequent changes to the system.

The degree of custom written documentation will obviously depend on whether the system is being written entirely in-house or purchased from outside with some adaptation.

Coding and testing

The next step is for the MIS programmers to do the hard coding of the system (or adapt and test the purchased package). In addition, new interfaces from the billing system and output interfaces to the general ledger will have to be designed and hard coded.

Complete testing of the new system is absolutely necessary and cannot be over-emphasized. During the testing period, samples of real data should be used and the aim should be to duplicate the real environment as much as possible.

Acceptance

By now, enough is known and documented about the new system to enable management to say whether they accept it against the concepts expressed in the original remit. If so, the timetable needs to be firmed up, as several target dates during the ensuing very busy period will prove to be critical.

User Manual

With comprehensive computer systems, a User Manual can prove invaluable for training, ongoing reference – and keeping the auditors happy! It should be based on the functional specifications mentioned above and should extend to all associated clerical functions.

Many cynics will say it cannot be kept up to date and will quickly fall out of use. Except for initial training, it does not need to be constantly in use, but give it an index and it will be found to be a useful work of reference, encouraging management and users to refine it and keep it up to date.

Training

Train, train, train all the staff affected by the new system prior to going live with it. Human nature dictates fear of the unknown and implementing a new system only confirms this statement. Much of the fear can be dispelled by adequate training prior to going live. If possible, use the test data to give credit personnel hands-on training. Ask each credit person to spend, say, thirty minutes per day, for two weeks prior to going live, in training. Do not exclude supervisors and managers, as clerical personnel will take their lead from the management. And make full use of the User Manual.

When going live, have trainers available to assist the personnel. Regardless of the training time, the crew will suffer from opening day jitters. Mistakes will be made. More training will be needed, so be patient. The start-up day and the way it is managed can be crucial for the future full utilization of the system.

Plan for additional training fifteen to thirty days after installation. The follow-up training sessions should concentrate on answering any difficulties encountered in operation and for full utilization of the 'bells and whistles' of the system.

Parallel operation

It is most unwise to implement a new system without running parallel with the old system for a period of time. There are several reasons for this.

1 If the new system 'blows up', the old one is still intact.
2 It will really test the new system.
3 It makes sure all parts of the new system are working.
4 It makes sure the new system yields exactly the same results as the old one.

For most corporations, it is normally sufficient to take a representative segment of the ledger, debtors system, and so on to run in parallel (so long as the systems people replicate the data a sufficient number of times to reproduce the normal overall volumes).

The results of the parallel runs should be thoroughly checked, new system with old, to ensure that in the new system no data is being gained or lost and that all audit requirements are being met.

Implementation and afterwards

Comes the big day. Both management and staff, though probably weary from the additional work caused by the system development, should nevertheless be feeling considerable enthusiasm if the project has been handled carefully.

However, this is no time to relax. During the run-up period certain credit activities may have been neglected through development pressures and these will now require urgent attention.

The MIS analysts will usually remain with the project until the first month-end and then hand over to systems support.

Following initial installation, however, opportunities for fine tuning and improving the system will present themselves. Management and systems analysts should listen to the users. They will work with the system on a day-by-day basis and their input can be valuable.

At three-, six- and twelve-month intervals, the users should sit down with the systems analysts and review progress since the installation. Any problems or potential problems can be identified and resolved. The credit executive cannot afford to let the MIS personnel walk away from the project, regarding it as completed.

Conclusion

You, the credit executive, must catch the vision of where you want to be five years from now and begin planning how to get there. With a modern credit management and accounts receivable system, it can take two or three years from vision to reality.

Recommended reading

Rowe, Michael. (1987) *Electronic Trade Payments*. Byfleet: IBC Financial Technology Publishing. Describes how computerized techniques are beginning to link export/import documentation and related payment procedures, and analyses the issues involved.

PART IX
INTERNATIONAL LAW

26

Legal and regulatory issues

Michael Rowe

For people engaged in international business, the law is what happens when deals go wrong. Yet attention paid to drafting and regulatory requirements at the outset can repay itself many times over as a project progresses.

What law should apply to the contract? Shall we include an arbitration clause? Do I have any comeback if the bank refuses my documents, and what security do negotiable instruments give me? Are licences required to export materials and machinery, and who suffers the consequences if these are denied? Do those three stubborn negotiators on the other side of the table really have the authority to sign?

Legal issues affecting international credit management can be divided very broadly into two main camps. *Private* law deals with relationships between the parties to individual agreements; *public* law covers government regulations and official requirements laid down in the general interest.

Rules of the first type define the nature and consequences of business undertakings and fill in the gaps in agreements. The law of contract provides one general example. Provisions of the second sort direct and limit what the parties can do and the way they can do it. Examples are exchange control regulations, anti-trust rules, financial reporting requirements and – perhaps worst of all – taxation law.

In general, laws and regulations help define rights, duties and responsibilities, and prescribe sanctions, compensation and penalties. They provide security and define areas of risk. Accordingly the credit manager needs to take them into account when judging the form, viability and attractiveness of his or her transactions.

PRIVATE LAW RULES

General structure

The legal basis of international and other business deals is the twin concept that parties are free to agree the content of their deals, and that they are then obliged to perform what they have agreed. All systems accept these underlying principles, and all qualify and restrict them in different ways.

For instance, a party may be relieved from the obligation to perform, by an act of '*force majeure*' rendering performance impossible. Or, as another example, communist countries regard central planning as a vital aspect of their economic development, and submit contracts concluded by state agencies to detailed authorization procedures.

International business and finance have developed many uniform instruments and practices of global reach. Letters of credit, first demand guarantees, syndicated loans, forfaiting operations and countertrade arrangements provide characteristic examples. Typically, such arrangements evolved from business and banking practice and do not fit precisely into pre-established legal pigeon-holes. Their legal acceptance and effects rely heavily on general principles of the law of contracts and obligations.

Often the normal operation of such deals is covered by widely accepted standard ground rules. For instance, many large-scale construction projects are subjected to general conditions drawn up by FIDIC, the International Federation of Consulting Engineers, in Lausanne, Switzerland. Export contracts frequently incorporate INCOTERMS, the standard delivery conditions drafted by the Paris-based International Chamber of Commerce (ICC).

But there is still no comprehensive transnational business law, accepted on a uniform basis throughout the world. And there are no international business courts to hear disputes between battling business people. Contracts involving more than one country are still generally subject to national ('municipal') laws. Disputes are heard by national or local judges, unless the parties agree to a private arbitration procedure.

Harmonizing the laws

International commercial law-making has perforce followed a piecemeal pattern. Countries tend to agree to harmonize their rules when there is an immediate need in a particular sector, and are less interested in general principles.

Nowadays the United Nations (UN) provides the normal forum for agreeing laws ('conventions') between states. UNCITRAL, the UN Commission on International Trade Law, tries to co-ordinate activities in the business law field and also drafts conventions itself.

Such measures are discussed in specialist groups and may be the subject of vigorous horse-trading between representatives of countries with different ideas on laws and economics. The final product is formally adopted by a diplomatic conference. It then enters into effect when enough individual countries decide to ratify the measure and make it part of their own legal systems.

The number of acceptances required for entry into force will be set out in the convention. The measure will apply only in states that have ratified. Such countries agree to apply the new rules to international deals, but maintain their own domestic provisions for local transactions.

Trade laws

Most progress has been made in the area of international trade and goods transport. The majority of seafaring nations have ratified two uniform laws on maritime carriage of goods, the Hague Rules of 1924 and an amendment of 1968 known as the Hague–Visby Rules.

A similar convention, known as the Warsaw Rules, exists for air transport, though the measure of harmonization achieved is less than complete. Some countries have adopted the original version of 1929, whilst others have ratified a 1955 amendment called the Hague Protocol. Further revisions which not everyone has adopted were agreed at Guadalajara in 1959 and Montreal in 1975. Some states introduced variations to the basic texts when incorporating them in their national legislation. As a result, over forty different versions apply in different countries.

In 1978 the UN completed a new international convention for sea carriage, known as the Hamburg Rules. It has yet to collect enough ratifications to come into force. A 1980 UN convention on multimodal transport got enmeshed in political bickering between North and South, and looks unlikely to enter into effect.

Another measure finalized at the UN in 1980 is enjoying greater success. A convention on contracts for the international sale of goods entered into force in ratifying states on 1 January 1988. Countries that have accepted the new rules include the USA, China, France, Italy, Egypt and Argentina.

The convention lays down a uniform legal system for export/import deals. It covers formation of contract, delivery, obligations of buyer and seller, breach of contract and remedies. It applies only to physical goods; contracts for services are excluded.

UNCITRAL has also drafted conventions for cheques, bills of exchange and promissory notes employed in international operations. These have not yet come into force. (Chapter 14 discusses the draft conventions, and specimens of a proposed bill of exchange and promissory note are given.)

Trade practices

Legislation is not the only means by which uniform provisions are incorporated into contracts.

Merchants buying and selling goods gradually evolved standard trading terms for their dealings with one another. It became the understood practice that by using shorthand expressions such as FOB and CIF, the parties adopted specific delivery conditions by reference. In course of time, courts in different countries gave legal recognition to these standard delivery conditions. Often judges would hear expert testimony from the most experienced traders to establish the normally accepted content and meaning of these terms within the trade (see also 'INCOTERMS' below).

Uniform rules

Associations representing business interests frequently draft rules and contract forms for their members' and others' transactions. Some of these gain industry-wide acceptance internationally. Since they are drawn up by private bodies without legislative power, such provisions bind the parties to individual deals only if they agree to apply them – usually by express reference in the contract.

Examples include the International Chamber of Commerce's (ICC) Uniform Customs and Practice for Documentary Credits, and the same organization's INCOTERMS. The former are applied virtually universally to letter of credit operations throughout the world. In principle, the basis of application is contractual agreement; each credit issued refers specifically to the rules. In practice the rules are accepted as the common code of conduct by banks, and imposed on the other parties automatically. Lawyers refer to this type of arrangement as a contract of adhesion; 'take it or leave it' is the general idea.

INCOTERMS

The INCOTERMS are a codification of some of the most commonly adopted trade terms (delivery conditions). In part they set out in written form traditionally applied terms such as FOB and CIF. Courts in some countries, France and West Germany for instance, refer to these traditional INCOTERMS definitions as best evidence of the common trade practice even in cases where the contract does not state that the INCOTERMS apply.

More recently adopted INCOTERMS go beyond a simple codification of the accepted practice, and provide new conditions adapted to evolving transport techniques. For example, 'free carrier' (FRC) and 'freight carriage and insurance paid' (CIP) are especially appropriate in the case of multimodal transport. In these cases, it is essential that the contract should refer both to the particular term and to the IN-COTERMS specifically. The ICC recommends that this practice be followed in all cases.

The ICC has recently started work on revising the INCOTERMS once more, to bring them up to date with current trading practices and legal requirements. It is not yet certain what will be changed. One of the main reasons for revision, however, is the desire to adapt the conditions to increasing commercial use of electronic data interchange (EDI) techniques.

Essentially, INCOTERMS divide the risks and costs of transport between buyer and seller under the *sales* contract. They do not apply to the contract of carriage, nor do they deal directly with transfer of ownership (title) in the goods. In practice, title usually passes on shipment or delivery.

Reservation of title

If a seller manages to remain owner of the goods until payment is made, he or she can recover them in case of default. Otherwise the seller's only remedy is an action for payment against the buyer.

There is no general legal rule to prevent ownership from passing before payment has been made. The seller has to provide for this specifically by including a reservation of title (property) clause in the contract. Such a clause may also give the seller priority rights over the goods or the proceeds of any resale if the buyer becomes insolvent. The rules vary widely from one country to another.

Belgian law prevents a seller from using the clause against the buyer's creditors. German judges favour the reservation system and allow the clause to operate even when the goods have become mixed up with other materials. In France a law of 1980 gives the exporter or other seller some protection in case of bankruptcy of the buyer.

English court decisions wander back and forth unhappily. In several instances English courts have upheld a seller's right to preserve a priority claim to the proceeds in case of resale. In some jurisdictions, including the USA, contract clauses that reserve security interests are binding against third parties only if they are noted in a public register.

Force majeure and frustration

Wars, revolutions, natural disasters and economic upheavals may stop an international business deal in mid-course. The legal consequences resulting from such events are risk factors that the prudent credit manager must bear in mind.

Large-scale contracts usually contain detailed clauses to cope with such happenings. National laws also cover the subject.

If performance becomes impossible, or in some cases unrealistic, the law will take action to suspend or terminate the contract and sort out the mess. In England and other common law countries this is referred to as frustration of contract. Countries deriving their systems from European civil law traditions usually apply the principle of *force majeure*. (International contracts under both systems often include specific *force majeure* clauses. The scope of such provisions and their relationship with the applicable law are not always clearly defined.)

In some countries, West Germany and Egypt for instance, the judge can modify the terms of a contract that has run into difficulties and produce a revised deal that is fair to all parties. Relatively few courts enjoy this power, though some long-term contracts contain hardship clauses that provide for renegotiation of the contract terms if the economic foundations of the deal are swept away. The ICC offers model contract clauses on both *force majeure* and hardship.

All legal systems agree on one point: only in exceptional circumstances will parties be relieved of their obligations. After the Suez crisis of 1956, the House of Lords, the highest British appeal court, held that closure of the Suez Canal did not cancel sales contracts merely because the goods would have to be shipped around the Cape of Good Hope instead of going through the canal.

Normally the events relied on must be external to the party concerned, and of such a nature that the parties could not have foreseen them in the ordinary course of things.

Even with a carefully drafted clause in the contract, parties may be in for a few shocks when things go wrong. In one case an Asian company selling steel thought it no longer had to deliver when a government circular forbade exports of that product. The contract contained an arbitration clause. The arbitrator found that the circular was not legally binding and that accordingly the exporter was not relieved from the duty to deliver. He awarded damages of £1 million to the European buyer.

Often, failure to obtain an import or export licence is not accepted as a reason to break a contract, particularly if the contract does not mention licences at all. The assumption may then be that each party has impliedly accepted responsibility for obtaining the permissions it needs.

Companies doing business with state trading organizations need to remember that, legally, the organization is a separate entity from the government and that action by the latter will not usually be imputed to the trading agency. In 1974 the Polish government banned the export of sugar because of a crop failure. A Polish state trading agency had concluded a contract to sell sugar to an English buyer. The contract included a *force majeure* clause. The Polish organization successfully used this clause as a defence when the buyer took proceedings for non-delivery in the English courts.

Applicable law

An international contract may be governed by one of several different laws, for example the law of the country in which one of the parties is established, a legal system designated in the agreement, an intergovernmental convention, or a mixture of all of these.

Choice of law may have significant results on the rights of the parties and distribution of responsibilities. For instance, the right to bring an action for breach of contract is cancelled if not exercised within a specified time limit. This principle is known as prescription or limitation of actions, and the time limit differs from one country to another; thus the right to bring the case may be lost if one law is applicable but still subsist under another. Interest payable on damages is limited to a fixed 'legal rate' under some laws, whereas in other cases a higher prevailing market rate may be claimed.

Each country has developed its own rules to determine whose law applies to an international contract if a dispute arises and the contract is silent on the point. These are called conflict of law rules or private international law. The latter expression is particularly confusing, since the legal rules applied to select the law and the law chosen are generally both national laws. Only the dispute is international.

Factors that may be taken into account include the place where the contract was concluded and the residence of the parties. The modern tendency is to apply the law with which the agreement is most closely connected – sometimes referred to as the proper law of the contract. Often this is held to be the place where the contract has to be carried out.

In one ancient but still valid instance, a bill of exchange was drawn in England and payable in Spain. It was dishonoured by non-acceptance in the latter. No notice of dishonour was given. Such notice was required by English rules but not by Spanish law. The English Court of Appeal held that Spanish law applied to questions concerning acceptance and related formalities. It accordingly decided that the endorser of the bill in England was liable on it (*Horn* v *Rouquette* (1878) 3 QBD 514).

A handful of countries have agreed to apply standard rules to determine the national law applicable in the case of international sales contracts. The provisions are contained in a 1955 convention drawn up by an organization known as the Hague Conference for Private International Law, and amended in 1985. This is a separate measure from the 1980 UN sales convention which replaced national laws with uniform rules dealing with the substance of export/import deals.

Even when the substance of a contract is governed by a uniform international convention it may still be necessary to refer to national laws. For example, the UN sales convention normally applies only when both parties are resident in states that have ratified the measure, but even when this is not the case it may sometimes apply if the contract is subject to the law of a ratifying country.

Moreover, international conventions usually leave some of the trickier questions to be resolved by national laws. For instance, the conventions on sea transport deal with the responsibilities of carriers. The most important document issued by the carrier is the bill of lading.

This sets out the terms of the contract of carriage, provides evidence that the goods have been shipped in good condition, and may also act as a negotiable document of title. Buyers can endorse it to transfer ownership in the goods whilst they are afloat, or to pledge them by way of security to a financing bank. The rules on negotiability are left to each individual legal system.

Dispute settlement

The parties start squabbling and cannot settle their differences. They are established in at least two different countries; who will hear the case?

This is a different issue from that of deciding whose law is applicable. A court that decides it has jurisdiction to hear an international case may apply a foreign law; and the country whose law is applicable may not be the appropriate one in which to judge the dispute.

The approach differs from one country to another. Broadly speaking a court will agree to hear a dispute involving parties in different countries if it decides it has jurisdiction over the parties or the subject matter. Factors taken into account include the location of the parties and where the contract was to be carried out. The parties may be able to avoid the problem by agreeing in their contract whose courts are to hear the case.

Arbitration

If the parties wish to avoid going to national courts they can agree to submit any dispute to arbitration instead. The normal way of doing this is to include a general arbitration clause in the original contract. Alternatively the parties may agree to submit a particular dispute to arbitration at the time the problem arises, though typically by then they are unlikely to agree even on the time of day!

The arbitrator can be appointed by the parties directly, and they can decide on the procedural rules and administrative procedures that are to apply to the case. They will also negotiate the fees to be paid to the arbitrator or panel of arbitrators (arbitral tribunal). This is known as *ad hoc* arbitration.

Alternatively, the procedure may be administered by a specialized institution that offers formal administrative rules and handles financial aspects of the procedure. Examples are the International Chamber of

465

Commerce Court of Arbitration, the London Court of International Arbitration, the American Arbitration Association (AAA) and the International Centre for the Settlement of Investment Disputes (ICSID) attached to the World Bank.

Such bodies do not hear the cases themselves, even if the word 'court' is included in their title. They may appoint the arbitrators however. UNCITRAL also offers arbitration rules, but does not itself administer cases under the rules. Other institutions may do so.

The parties' agreement gives the arbitrator similar powers to those of a judge, though they are subject to more restrictions. His or her award can be enforced by national authorities like a court judgment. Some seventy countries have ratified a convention drawn up in 1958 (the New York Convention), by which they undertake to recognize and enforce valid arbitration awards rendered in other states without rehearing the case.

Arbitration proceedings are held in private. Like judges, arbitrators apply legal principles in arriving at their decisions. In some cases they may be less obliged to stick rigidly to the confines of a particular national system, and may show a greater readiness to give effect to accepted international business practice. They tend to place great emphasis on the obligation to respect contractual undertakings strictly.

Generally, there is no appeals system against arbitral awards. National courts may set awards aside or refuse to enforce them if they fail to meet specified standards of fairness or procedural requirements. Arbitral institutions claim that most awards are respected voluntarily. In other cases the award can be enforced through the national judicial machinery.

Litigation – debt recovery

Litigation proceedings may be brought for the recovery of a simple money debt, where there is no dispute as to liability or the amount owing. For instance, a buyer may have dishonoured his or her promissory note on maturity, and has not claimed any irregularities.

Many courts offer accelerated procedures for proving such claims and obtaining an order for recovery. Default proceedings under English law provide one example.

In these cases, court proceedings are likely to be more expeditious and less costly than arbitration. Arbitrators will normally have to insist on hearing the case in full, even if the defendant is not present and does not raise any defence or counterclaim. This is done in order to avoid problems with national procedural requirements if the award has to be enforced through the courts.

Parties normally decide to include an arbitration provision when the contract is drawn up. The clause then applies to any proceedings that may arise later. It is impossible to know when a contract is signed whether any such proceedings will be simple money claims or hotly disputed questions of fact and law.

PUBLIC LAW ISSUES

General remarks

Governments, like policemen, are often around when least wanted. Buyer and seller are eager to clinch their deal. The law gives them freedom to agree on the terms, but this freedom is limited by the state's views on the public interest.

Imports and exports may be regulated to protect the national economy, security, health or cultural heritage. Customs duties and other taxes are imposed on goods entering the country. In many areas exchange control rules still limit the flow of available funds. Transborder flows of data through electronic networks may be restricted by laws aimed at privacy protection or economic objectives.

A number of international agreements attempt to make life easier for the business executive carrying out deals across frontiers. Countries emerging from the destruction of the Second World War agreed to adopt the basic principle of free trade among nations as a means to help achieve prosperity and preserve peace. The International Monetary Fund (IMF), the General Agreement on Tariffs and Trade (GATT) and the World Bank were set up to pursue these objectives. Not all countries are members, and the economic crises beginning in the 1970s wrought havoc with the effective application of many of the original ideas.

Free trade

The GATT – which is the name given both to the agreement itself and to the Geneva-based secretariat that polices it – came into force on 1 January 1948. The agreement was supposed to be the first step towards the establishment of an international trading organization, but this grandiose vision was never realized.

The GATT's aim is to discourage protectionism in international trade. Member countries, the contracting parties, now number over a hundred. They subscribe in word, if not always in deed, to basic principles of fair play as well as to many detailed tariff schedules, agreements, protocols, *procès-verbaux* and codes running into several bulky volumes.

The cornerstone of the whole edifice is the concept of 'most favoured nation' treatment. Each member is supposed to treat every other member as favourably as it treats the nation which receives its most favourable treatment on imports and exports. Each contracting party negotiates maximum tariffs which it undertakes not to exceed towards other members.

Customs duties and import taxes are the most obvious barriers to free flow of goods, but by no means the only ones. Dumping and use of various subsidies constitute the most frequent abuse of GATT rules. Member states are entitled to impose countervailing duties on the goods concerned up to the amount of the subsidies. US legislation allows individual companies to petition the government to show that grounds for such action exist.

GATT rules cover trade in goods only. The USA and other industrialized countries are pressing for services to be added. Many developing countries resist this.

Exchange control

Exchange control regulations limit the amounts of currency that can be transferred into or out of a country, and circumscribe the purposes for which transfers can be made. They may be deployed in an emergency situation to block the flight of capital, or on a permanent basis as part of national economic policy.

Communist states adopt planned foreign exchange policies as part of their central economic strategies. Western countries have been dismantling their controls in recent years. Remaining barriers inside the European Community (EC) are supposed to be dismantled by 1992.

Member states of the IMF undertake to reduce exchange control restrictions and to facilitate current operations between countries. One of the IMF's original aims – that of promoting stability of exchange rates – was abandoned when floating rates were adopted in the 1970s.

Insolvency

When the party against whom a claim is made becomes insolvent, and winding-up proceedings are commenced by the creditors or by the insolvent company, the relevant procedures can vary widely from one country to another.

In any event, the claimants will have to give proof of what they are owed in the proceedings along with other creditors. The available assets are divided up amongst parties that have proved their claims, and each of them may finally receive a derisory percentage of the total due.

Security devices such as mortgages and other charges over assets may enable a claimant to assert priority claims over the assets concerned (see also 'Reservation of title', above). Great care is needed to minimize the risks of such devices being disallowed as fraudulent preferences. Bank guarantees, standby letters of credit and guarantees of a subsidiary by its parent company can also help in appropriate cases.

Some legal systems allow companies in trouble to apply to the courts for restructuring and postponement of creditors' claims. Proceedings under Chapter 11 of the US bankruptcy statutes provide one prominent example. A creditor's attitude to such goings on may be ambivalent. He or she is being deprived of a slice of bread today, but might postponement bring the addition of jam tomorrow?

Sovereign immunity

The doctrine of sovereign immunity prevents private parties from suing a foreign state without its consent, and stops them from seizing its property in satisfaction of an award. The basis of the doctrine is the idea that there is an overriding public interest in safeguarding the dignity of the state.

But what happens when the king steps down from his throne and sets up a market stall? Is he still entitled to protection if his fish are not fresh or he fails to pay suppliers? An unqualified application of the doctrine today would seriously prejudice business operations, in which states or state agencies are frequently involved.

Courts and arbitrators increasingly rule that sovereign immunity cannot be pleaded by a state party engaged in commercial activities. Several countries have enacted legislation on the subject in recent years, limiting the availability of such immunity. Examples are the US Foreign Sovereign Immunity Act of 1978, and the British State

Immunity Act of 1976. The latter gives effect in the UK to the European Convention on State Immunity of 16 May 1972, drawn up by the Council of Europe.

States may waive their immunity. Agreement in a contract to submit disputes to a particular court or arbitration system will normally be taken to constitute such waiver. (It may be easier to persuade a state to accept the decision of a neutral arbitrator rendered in private, rather than to submit to the jurisdiction of another country's public courts.)

Even if a state or government agency is not granted immunity from being sued, it may still be able to plead that certain of its assets cannot be seized to satisfy a judgment against it. The US Sovereign Immunities Act provides that assets can be seized only if they were used for commercial purposes and one of a number of alternative conditions is met – for example that the assets were implicated in the dispute or expropriated in specified circumstances.

French courts distinguish between sums held in France for traditional government activities which cannot be seized, and those held for commercial purposes, which can. English courts follow a similar line.

CONCLUSION

The international credit manager needs to establish a coherent global policy for the company's credit operations worldwide. This is necessary for proper management and optimum evaluation of performance.

Legal and regulatory issues must form part of this policy. Within the overall framework, a flexible approach is required, since specific rules differ from one place to another. For instance, general contract conditions and loan formalities will have to take account of any special requirements of local law; clauses giving the seller extra rights may have to be individually signed, for example.

A harmonized general approach is still possible, even if detailed application must vary according to geography and politics. Maximum use can be made of internationally recognized rules and conditions. Inter-governmental conventions help in some areas. A properly drafted arbitration clause may reduce some of the difficulties in a conflict situation.

The types of legal issues that need attention are broadly similar everywhere, though solutions may differ. This chapter has outlined some of the important questions. The credit manager can categorize the issues, and apply a consistent policy of covering them at the outset to minimize problems later.

Recommended reading

Ezer, Shaul. (Looseleaf update) *International Exporting Agreements*. Albany, NY: Matthew Bender. Provides precedents and information on US practice.

Hedley, William. (1986) *Bills of Exchange and Bankers' Documentary Credits*. London: Lloyd's of London Press.

International Chamber of Commerce (1988) *Rules for the ICC Court of Arbitration*, ICC Publication No. 291. Paris: ICC.

Reitman, Jeffrey B., and Weisblatt, Harold. (Looseleaf update, 1987.) *Checks Drafts and Notes*. Albany, NY: Matthew Bender.

Rendell, Robert S. (Editor) (1983) *International Financial Law* (two volumes). Milton Keynes: Euromoney.

Rowe, Michael. (1987) *Guarantees*. Milton Keynes: Euromoney. Looks at all the uses of bank guarantees and other security devices in international business. Includes chapters on practical procedures and key country studies.

Schmitthoff, Clive M. (1986) *Schmitthoff's Export Trade*. 8th edn. London: Stevens & Sons, 1986. The standard English work on this subject.

27

Maritime fraud

Ian R Hyslop

In late 1979 the *Salem* set sail from Kuwait with a cargo of crude oil worth $56 million, intended for Italy. However, the oil never reached Italy; instead the vessel diverted to South Africa and secretly discharged her cargo in defiance of existing sanctions. She continued up the coast of Africa until she was scuttled by her crew off Senegal.

At this point meticulous planning and execution began to degenerate into farce. The *Salem* sank in view of another vessel and left no significant oil slick. Her crew, rescued from lifeboats, claimed they had spent hours fighting an engine room fire, but were clean and neatly dressed. They were all carrying passports and suitcases, but not the ship's log.

Nine separate investigations of the *Salem* case around the world led to criminal convictions in Britain, the USA, Greece and the Netherlands. The legal consequences of the affair were probably played out only in 1987, when charges against a Dutch businessman, alleged to have been one of the ringleaders, were dropped by a Dutch court. The lack of evidence in this case resulted, at least partly, from the, unsurprising, reluctance of the South African authorities to co-operate.

THE INCIDENCE OF FRAUD

The *Salem* is probably the most celebrated and extravagant example to date of a maritime fraud. But it is symptomatic of a problem to which the transportation industry is particularly vulnerable. International trade brings together people of different traditions, laws and institutions. Relationships are based on trust. In the event of this trust being misplaced, or of something else going wrong, cultural difficulties between trading partners will be compounded by jurisdictional problems and by the fact that, once a ship has left port, it is not easy to know what she is doing.

Maritime fraud peaked around the time of the *Salem*. Much of it was the result of the sudden increase in wealth in the Middle East countries and, above all, in Nigeria. Nigeria's sudden surge in demand for imports was far from matched by improvements in the infrastructure for handling them. The resultant congestion meant that vessels sometimes had to wait months for a berth. The commercial consequences of this congestion were very harmful to shipowners, and many were tempted to dispose of their cargoes fraudulently, rather than wait and see their costs build up. And there were other negative results – piracy of ships waiting at anchorage became a growth industry in West Africa.

The amount of maritime fraud has reduced since the early 1980s, but it still tends to reflect opportunities offered by the prevailing economic and political situation. For example, at the time of writing advantage is being taken of the confusion caused by the Gulf War and the practical inaccessibility of various parts of the Lebanon.

Some 80 per cent of maritime fraud concerns the defrauding of the buyer rather than the seller. Nevertheless, international credit managers should be aware of the threats to both parties. Indeed, most corporations have to buy as well as sell and, if credit managers are truly the guardians of their corporations' cashflow, they should be as concerned about paying money for non-delivered or worthless goods as they are with parting up with goods without receiving money.

Although the range of maritime fraud is startlingly wide and, as in other types of crime, is constantly being expanded in line with the ingenuity and imagination of the people who practise it, it can still quite satisfactorily, and usefully, be analysed into classifications.

Deviation

The *Salem* was a case of deviation – that is, the unauthorized carriage of a cargo to a wrong port and its discharge there. When shipowners decide to deviate their vessels, or charterers decide to deviate vessels chartered to them, they sometimes protect themselves from the consequences of their theft and fraud, and from redress on behalf of the cargo interests, by liquidating their companies and disappearing, or by taking their vessels with their stolen cargoes to inaccessible parts of the world.

In contemporary terms this latter course usually means the Lebanon.

Deviations into Lebanon approached epidemic proportions in 1987. One example involved a cargo of cocoa from West Africa to Europe. The early stages of this voyage were confused by a number of 'red herrings' introduced by the shipowners. Firstly, the vessel was supposed to have called at a port *en route* to load an additional deck cargo of wood, which in truth never existed. Secondly, the vessel was supposed to have broken down off Italy. The shipowner sought to give such credibility to this fiction that he travelled to Italy, obtained a 'quote' from the Albanians for towing his disabled vessel into Albania, and purported to go to Albania himself. Albania is of course probably the only country in the world less penetrable than the Lebanon. In reality, the vessel was nowhere near Albania – she was in North Lebanon, out of reach, and had thus frustrated even the limited opportunities for negotiation which might have existed had her cargo fallen into the hands of Christian forces in Beirut.

Hull fraud

An alternative to disappearing in this way is to sink (or 'scuttle') the vessel, and pretend that the cargo was on her before she sank. This of course was attempted in the *Salem*. There is also scuttling 'for its own sake' – whether to make a false insurance claim or to get rid of a useless vessel, this is known as hull fraud. This is more common, as one would expect, in a depressed market.

Overlapping categories of fraud

A more recent case of deviation occurred in 1985. The account which follows is accurate, but place names have been altered, mainly out of concern for the personal safety of one of the members of the crew.

A vessel loaded a cargo of steel in Italy, worth $300 000, for the UK. Ten days later the vessel was reported sunk north of Morocco. The crew were picked up from lifeboats by a Spanish ferry, saying that a leak had developed in the engine room.

It did not take a great deal of imagination to deduce that there was something suspicious about this event. The vessel sank in calm seas. She sank in the early hours of the morning, when there was no other ship in sight, but among busy shipping lanes where 'survivors' were certain to be picked up. Further, Moroccan industrialists had made several approaches to the Italians to obtain the type of steel which the vessel was carrying. Finally, it appeared that the master was one of the owners of the vessel.

The crew was landed by the ferry in Bilbao and dispersed. However, a group of them was later traced to a French prison where they were accommodated having been convicted of smuggling drugs in a different vessel. The captain insisted that the first vessel had sunk accidentally. However, one of the other crew members admitted that she had been scuttled, and that the cargo had earlier been discharged in Morocco. The vessel had also been used regularly for drug smuggling, but it was getting old and had outlived its usefulness.

There was therefore an element of hull fraud in this deception. This indicates that analytical categories of fraud, although they are useful, often overlap.

Documentary frauds

Many maritime frauds are really documentary frauds, which of course involve the use of false or forged documents calculated to deceive. In the maritime context, these documents are usually bills of lading and commercial invoices – or sometimes nothing more elaborate than a telex message.

As stated above, buyers and sellers are often separated by political, legal and geographical barriers. Sellers have a natural reluctance to part with goods until the purchase price is paid. Conversely, buyers prefer to pay on delivery of goods. The gap between payment and delivery of goods is often bridged by the documentary credit system (see Chapter 16 for a full description). The mechanism of this system is well known. The buyers instruct their bank (the issuing bank) to open a letter of credit in favour of the seller. The issuing bank instructs the paying bank in the seller's country to hand over the purchase price when the seller tenders documents confirming shipment of the goods.

Alternatively, in a documentary collection arrangement (described in Chapter 15), for example a payment against documents (D/P) transaction, the payment takes place in the buyer's country. The seller instructs a bank in the buyer's country to hand over the documents of title to the goods to the buyer upon receipt of payment. Both the documentary credit and the collection arrangements rely on the honesty of the trading partners and are easily abused. A fraudulent seller can cash the letter of credit by presenting bogus documents for a non-existent cargo. Alternatively, the cargo can be of lesser quality or quantity. Sometimes the same cargo is sold to two or more buyers, and the purchase price collected from each. This was attempted several times in 1987 with Nigerian oil. Finally, a fraudulent buyer can present forged bills of lading in a D/P transaction and collect the cargo without paying for it.

The *Helga Weir* case

A classic documentary fraud concerned the vessel *Helga Weir*. In autumn 1981 an Egyptian buyer agreed to purchase a number of second-hand vehicles from a Belgian exporter, whom he had known for some time. In October 1981 the Belgian travelled to the Cairo offices of the buyer with a German associate. He explained that he was unable to provide the second-hand vehicles, but that his colleague from Germany could. A pro forma invoice was produced and indicated that the potential supplier company was registered in Liechtenstein. The buyer thought that he was getting an extremely good bargain and agreed to proceed.

The following day the Egyptian buyer went to his bank and arranged for a letter of credit for Deutschemarks 350 000 to be opened in favour of the Liechtenstein company, which had an account at a Swiss bank. Only two documents were called for under the letter of credit – a clean bill of lading and the beneficiary's invoice.

The German exporter, on receipt of notice that a letter of credit had been opened in favour of the Liechtenstein company, obtained a bill of lading on which a company called Red Med Lines appeared as the carrier. This company had in fact gone into liquidation some nine months previously. The German exporter, who had no intention of making any shipment, completed the bill of lading to show that five Mercedes Tipper Trucks had been shipped on the *Helga Weir* on 4 December 1981 at Hamburg. In reality, the *Helga Weir* was in fact discharging cargo at Lisbon on 4 December. The bill of lading together with an invoice which showed the seller as Vias Establishment of Vaduz were duly presented to the Swiss bank in Zürich, where payment was made to the beneficiary.

The Egyptian did not become suspicious until about mid-January when his vehicles had still failed to arrive. At first he made attempts to contact the German exporter but, when he proved untraceable, he turned to the Belgian exporter for assistance. The Belgian, however, claimed that he had only acted as an introducer of the business and was reluctant to become involved in any attempts to resolve the matter.

Although a criminal offence took place in Zürich, as a result of the uttering of a forged bill of lading to obtain the money, the Swiss bank refused to become involved in any criminal complaint as they had suffered no loss, having been reimbursed from Cairo.

The Liechtenstein company was controlled, as many companies are in that country, by a lawyer who was prevented by law from disclosing its true owner.

One thing which emerges from this case is that one can be deceived even when dealing with known and trusted people – the Egyptian importer thought he could rely on the Belgian exporter.

The *Pluvius* case

It is worth in this context considering a further case from the early 1980s. The year 1982 was a time of great political uncertainty in Hong Kong – when the future was unknown. In that year an English company wished to buy 300 tons of antimony, a special mineral ore, imported from the People's Republic of China. A Hong Kong company, Wang Shun, offered to provide this antimony, but proposed that it should be conveyed by a feeder vessel to Taiwan and from there on the *Pluvius* to Rotterdam. The reason given for this was that if the government of the People's Republic thought the product was going to Taiwan, they would treat the matter as a domestic sale and demand a lower price.

This was a lie, and in retrospect it seems hardly convincing. The People's Republic would have been more likely to impose an embargo on Taiwan than to offer them a discount. Also, it was a peculiar route – it would be more logical to sail from Taiwan to Hong Kong and on to Europe than the other way round.

In any case, the English company accepted these terms. But Wang Shun shipped nine containers of scrap – not antimony – on the feeder vessel. The master issued nine bills of lading for scrap, which was what he had loaded. Wang Shun substituted for these bills false documents procured from a shipping company, Cosmopolitan Lines. Like Red Med Lines in the *Helga Weir* case, Cosmopolitan Lines were in liquidation. These false bills were presented, together with a certificate of origin which Wang Shun had no difficulty in forging, to the negotiating bank, which made payment for the antimony.

Wang Shun simply went into liquidation before the fraud was discovered and the offenders have never been traced.

Another letter of credit fraud

The facts of the following, almost subtle, documentary fraud, which occurred in 1987, are correct as stated. However, this time for legal reasons, place names have again had to be altered. Terms were agreed between a fish exporter in Sri Lanka and a buyer in Manila. As a result, a letter of credit was opened stipulating, first, that the cargo should be inspected by a nominated representative of the buyer and, second, that it should be shipped to Manila. A Sri Lankan bank negotiated the letter of credit in due course but failed to notice either that the nominated representative had not inspected the cargo, or that it had been shipped to Davao, not Manila. The cargo lay at Davao until it disappeared, presumed stolen. The consignees were able to take action against the bank for not complying with the terms. However, it was strongly suspected that there was collusion between the exporter and the bank to disguise the fact that the goods were not in the correct condition when shipped.

When the letter of credit itself is fraudulent

In June 1987 a major international bank was approached by telex by a man identifying himself as the managing director of a London business services company. He requested financing facilities for several million dollars and claimed that his company was the beneficiary of standby letters of credit issued by a bank in Costa Mesa, California, to the value of US$5 million.

The bank became suspicious when they were unable to trace the bank in Costa Mesa, and therefore did not respond to this initial approach. However, after receiving several more telexes they did reply, declining interest. But the applicant remained undeterred and finally arranged a meeting at the bank, supporting his case with documents.

The first document described a major agricultural project in West Africa for which the London company was to supply agricultural and transport equipment, and for which the letters of credit had allegedly been opened.

The applicant also produced one of the letters of credit. It was by no means a convincing document, even to a non-specialist. A further problem with it was that the telephone number of the bank quoted on it was found to be out of service.

Thirdly, the applicant provided a financial statement relating to his

Costa Mesa bank prepared by accountants in Los Angeles. This was accompanied by other miscellaneous documents purporting to establish the credibility of the bank.

Fourthly, he produced a profile of his company. The profile stated that the company had fifty years' experience in marketing and exporting, and that it operated in conjunction with a company specializing in industrial catering.

At the meeting the applicant explained, with some evasiveness, the fact that his bank could not be traced by referring to a recent change of name, and by its constitution as an investment bank rather than a commercial bank. When it was suggested that it was surprising that a small bank in a residential west coast community should be selected for such a major international transaction, he replied that one of the instigators of the project had contacts with the bank through real estate interests in Texas. He was less forthcoming on the question of how he came to be the beneficiary of letters of credit issued by a bank about which he knew so little.

Not surprisingly, the bank did not, as a result of this meeting, reverse its decision declining interest.

Investigations revealed that the address given by the Costa Mesa bank was in fact a room in a high-rise block occupied only by a female employee for a few hours each morning. The address given by the accountants, although they were registered as tenants of it, appeared in reality to be wholly occupied by another company, to which their relationship was, at most, tenuous.

This matter is still being investigated by law enforcement agencies in the USA and the UK. However, on the face of it, it seems a classic, if slightly crude, attempt to negotiate fraudulent letters of credit.

Charter party fraud

Clearly, very many sea voyages are made under the terms of a charter party. The success of this type of voyage depends on each party – the shipowner, the charterer and the cargo owner – fulfilling their obligations. When one or more of the parties fail to do so, the resulting contractual mess usually requires a great deal of investigation and negotiation if anything is to be salvaged. Failures occur for two reasons, which often become blurred in practice – fraud and business failure.

A typical fraud will concern a time charter party, under which a vessel is hired on a *per diem* basis and hire is usually paid in fortnightly instalments in advance. The first hire is paid by the time charterer and the vessel proceeds to the loading port where the cargoes are loaded. The shipowner authorizes the release of freight prepaid bills of lading to the charterers, who pass them on to the cargo owner in exchange for freight (that is to say, the shipowner's transportation charges). In other words, the shipowners are releasing a document acknowledging the charterers' title to the goods on board their ship, and this document can be negotiated as representing these goods. They do this in recognition of the fact that their freight has been paid, although in fact all that has been paid is the first two week instalment. The charterer then passes the bills of lading, and thus evidence of title to the goods and of the fact that the freight has been paid, to the cargo owner, in exchange for the *entire* freight for the voyage.

What happens next is that the ship sails from the loading port to her destination and the charterers abscond with the entire freight which they have collected from the cargo owners. The shipowners are contractually bound to deliver the cargo under the bills of lading, which they have issued. But since they are no longer receiving their freight they may not have the financial resources to do so.

The cargo owners almost always lose when a charter party fails. They usually pay for the goods soon after the issue of a bill of lading and are faced, at best, with a long wait, possibly aggravated by penalties for late delivery, before they get paid. As soon as something appears to go wrong, the buyer may try to stop payment, for example if under a letter of credit, by finding technical deficiencies in the documents. The cargo owners may sometimes also find themselves helpless against a shipowner who, in a variation of charter party fraud, claims an exorbitant amount to repair 'engine damage' after a voyage has started. Further, the crew of a stranded ship may be tempted to start selling the cargo, sometimes with the consent of the shipowner, and sometimes 'legally' with the help of unscrupulous local lawyers who are prepared to take advantage of the fact that the genuine cargo owner is far away, in another jurisdiction.

On a scale of vulnerability, the shipowners are in an intermediate position. When a default occurs, they can take the time to examine their options, knowing that their vessel is safe from arrest by the cargo owner on grounds of delay – as long as they act reasonably.

The charterers, especially when their company is registered in a country of convenience, and the beneficial ownership is difficult to trace, have least to lose. If there are any problems they can often just walk away and disappear.

The frequency of chartering failures, and the absence of real sanctions, create a climate favourable to the fraudster. As in many other types of fraud, charter party fraudsters can protect themselves by saying that they failed through a series of bad business decisions rather than criminal intent.

There was a classic charter party default in 1987. A vessel was chartered by a Lebanese company for a voyage from Spain and the UK to the Middle East. Part of the proposed cargo was loaded in Spain, and the vessel then sailed to England to load the rest. After ten days the remaining cargo failed to appear, and the charterers defaulted, declining to pay the shipowners any freight.

The perils of over-invoicing

The following over-invoicing fraud can, in a sense, be viewed as a moral tale. It took place in the late 1970s, at a time of severe foreign exchange and import controls in Nigeria.

A Nigerian importer contracted with a Danish exporter for the supply of rice and salt, which was actually worth $25 000. The importer and exporter agreed that the goods would be invoiced for $250 000. The intention was that the Nigerian would pay $250 000 for the goods – ten times what they were worth. This money would go to the Dane, who would keep $25 000, as payment for the goods he had supplied, and probably another $25 000 for his trouble. The remaining $200 000 he would remit to a secret offshore account (in the Caymans or somewhere) belonging to the Nigerian.

The Nigerian's intention was to get money out of the country. There have been examples of this type of fraud where the importers have arranged for the goods to be 'stolen' on arrival, and then claimed for the inflated value on their insurance – thereby defrauding their insurance company. But this was not the case here, the intention was only to evade exchange control regulations.

The mundane commodities – rice and salt – were chosen because they would not attract attention and would not require an import permit. Goods such as rosary beads were notoriously used for this purpose in Nigeria at the time – and Nigeria appears to have imported sufficient baby carriages to service the whole of Africa. The Nigerian authorities have tightened controls to prevent this type of abuse – but it is still a risk.

The ship arrived in Nigeria. The arrangements were *payment against documents*, that is to say, the buyer himself was to see the documents before paying. The importer went to his bank, paid his $250 000 and got the documents. He then took these documents, including of course the bill of lading stating that he was entitled to the cargo, to the shipping agent, but discovered that his rice and salt were not manifested. The agent made enquiries and discovered that they had never been loaded and that the bill of lading was false. This was therefore a straightforward documentary fraud of the type discussed above.

The Dane had committed this fraud in the belief that the Nigerian could not complain about it because of the exchange control irregularity.

However, the $250 000 which the Nigerian had paid into his bank never reached the Dane – it disappeared somewhere. Almost certainly it was taken by an astute bank clerk who realized what was going on, and forged the Dane's signature of receipt. He did this in the confidence that the Dane could not complain because of his documentary fraud.

The matter only came to light because the shipowner was worried that his vessel would be arrested by the Nigerians for non-delivery of cargo – this can be done quite easily by a Nigerian national in Nigeria. He therefore caused investigations to be made by his insurers, his 'P & I (Protection and Indemnity) Club'.

Insurance frauds

Finally, as would be expected, many frauds turn on insurance. The intrusion of insurance into maritime fraud is very diverse. Two examples of such intrusions follow.

Firstly, in 1986 a Nepalese 'entrepreneur' accepted instructions from several local firms to go to Hong Kong to purchase electronic and other goods. He was entrusted with the money to purchase and insure the goods. He obtained blank insurance forms issued by a reputable Far East insurance company, altered them to indicate a different company at the same address, inserted details of the goods he had agreed to insure and kept the money advanced to him for this purpose. When the goods were pilfered on the way through India, the consignees claimed on the insurance and found that the 'insurance company' did not exist.

Secondly, also in 1986, a Chicago insurer received a substantial claim for the total loss of perishable goods. The insurer was suspicious because the casualty had been reported three days after the placement of cover. An examination of telex traffic proved that the assured had indeed known of the casualty when he placed his cover, and the underwriters were therefore able to repudiate the claim.

THE AVOIDANCE OF FRAUD

International trading will always involve some risk, for the reasons elaborated above. However, this risk can be minimized by taking certain preventive measures.

Know your trading partners

Most important, since everything depends on trust, traders should as far as possible restrict their dealings to established companies which they know something about – even if, as seen from the case of the *Helga Weir*, this is not foolproof. This ideal may further be rendered problematical by the absence of well-known carriers on certain routes, and the effective anonymity of some charterers and owners. Nevertheless, there are several organizations, including the UK International Maritime Bureau, in a position to provide topical information on potential trading partners, if requested. A requirement to seek and assess this type of information is indeed formalized in the Institute Cargo Clauses.

Use payment methods properly

Secondly, traders should consider how the documentary credit and documentary collection systems can best be used to their advantage. Payment against documents, as defined above, is certainly safer for the buyer – but it is not so satisfactory for the seller, since the buyer can default. Sellers should especially give careful consideration to the documents they require for presenting against letters of credit, and the need for *prompt* presentation.

Cargo owners

Cargo owners can insist on a pre-loading inspection of the goods or the vessel – although this of course adds to costs. Further, insurers can insert classification clauses, insisting that vessels used meet certain standards, or, as is rarely done in practice, they can require that the names of proposed vessels be notified to them. On a more basic level, it is easy, and elementary, to check that a proposed vessel does in fact exist, does have the necessary capacity to carry the cargo, and was where she was supposed to have been when the bills of lading were issued.

Cargo owners should also be aware of clauses in bills of lading which give them greater (or less) protection. For example, freight collect terms, under which the freight is payable only when the cargo is discharged, are clearly more favourable to cargo owners than freight prepaid terms. In general, cargo owners should be cautious of bills of lading which are subject to charter parties. The effect will be that they are being bound by a contract to which they were not a party (only the shipowner and the charterer are parties to a charter party), and which they have probably never seen.

Masters should ensure that cargo signed for on bills of lading is actually on board, and where practicable should themselves sign the bill of lading. Cargoes should only be released against a duly endorsed bill of lading.

At least in the case of valuable cargoes, masters should be instructed to radio their position at certain times during the voyage. There is also the possibility of appointing a 'supercargo' to travel on the ship to ensure the security of the cargo, although this can clearly be expensive.

Six warning signs

Finally, there are six clear warning signs which should put traders on their guard.

1 The goods may be in strong demand or not readily available.
2 Low prices may be quoted or the source of supply may be unusual.
3 The method of payment may be unusual, or it may be required to be made to a third party, or to an intermediary.
4 The names used by companies involved may resemble those of well-known business houses.
5 There may be pressure for fast acceptance, or fast issuance of documentary credits.
6 It may be proposed that a bill of lading be accepted even though the goods are inconsistent with it – this is in fact granting indemnity for an incorrect document, and is illegal in many jurisdictions.

Appendix: Sources of advice and assistance

Brian Clarke

There is a wealth of information and practical help available to international credit managers, if only they know where to find it.

In addition to the invaluable help obtainable from the banking industry, associations, risk assessment agencies and other sources mentioned elsewhere in this handbook, a great deal is provided by official bodies, both government and private, sometimes free, sometimes for a membership or service fee.

This appendix details the better known organizations which provide such advice and assistance. It is by no means exhaustive either as regards country or type of service.

THE INTERNATIONAL CHAMBER OF COMMERCE (ICC)

In its many types of activities during nearly seventy years, the very simple objective of the ICC has always been, and continues to be, making it easier to do business across frontiers.

In so doing, it has become the world's largest business organization with members in some 110 countries, more than half of which function with National Committees. Members in the remaining countries belong, in most cases, to the central Chamber of Commerce or other principal business organization of the country concerned, but there are some direct individual memberships.

Members are drawn from virtually every sector and aspect of international trade, both directly and indirectly – manufacturing, oil interests, mining, services and various professions. Employer organizations and those representing specific sectors of industry are also included and, while the ICC itself is not an overriding chamber of commerce as such, membership includes many local chambers of commerce in a number of countries.

The ICC is thus unique, both in the geographical spread of the membership in countries in every stage of development, and in the business sectors it represents.

Committed to open and fair trade, to encouragement of investment across frontiers and to maximum freedom of movement of information, the ICC stands for free enterprise and self-regulation, where practicable, by responsible business.

By influencing governments and inter-governmental organizations, the ICC seeks at all times to create the right climate in which all business, large or small, can flourish. But within that concern towards influencing the development of long-term policies relating to trade and investment, it is not just a lobbyist – it also facilitates trade by establishing and promoting international rules which, if followed, can save traders many millions of pounds each year in overheads.

Of particular relevance to international credit managers are the ICC Uniform Customs and Practice for Documentary Credits – UCP (see Chapter 16), the Uniform Rules for Collections (see Chapter 15) and INCOTERMS, the standard delivery terms, well known to professional traders (see Chapter 11).

The latest development in this series are the ICC rules governing electronically transmitted data (UNCID), which fill the gap where the technology and the services using it are way ahead of any adaptation of the present legal framework. In addition, the ICC has drafted an international convention to be applied to the activities of pre-shipment inspection agencies, aimed at minimizing misunderstandings between the parties concerned.

The ICC Court of Arbitration, founded in 1923, is the oldest-established body of its kind for the resolution of international disputes.

Languages can be barriers in international trade, for which the ICC provides assistance with its five language glossary of over 1500 words and expressions used in trade, called *Key Words*. There is also an ICC booklet to give those concerned with protection against exchange rate risks basic information on the methods available and the special phraseology involved. While English is the basic language of ICC publications, official translations are available of several of the most widely used publications, and National Committees have undertaken local translations in a number of other cases.

The ICC *Business Guide to the New GATT Round*, in simple language and containing a useful glossary, explains the key issues in the current round of trade and services negotiations launched in Uruguay in September 1986.

ICC International Headquarters in Paris are led by the Secretary General, assisted by a permanent Secretariat, and the driving force of the ICC activities lies in the work of its central working bodies, the majority in the form of permanent Commissions. Some thirty in number, supported as necessary by committees and permanent or *ad hoc* working parties, all comprise practising business people and specialists from all sectors of economic life. They are responsible for drafting the specific codes and guidelines exemplified above, as well as the initiatives for presentation to governments and international organizations.

The Congress is the supreme assembly of the ICC. It meets every three years and all member companies and organizations are invited to send senior representatives. The venue is changed each time at the invitation of a National Committee. There is an annual conference in years when there is no Congress, similarly held at different venues and closely centred around a particular theme.

There are a number of specialized Divisions, amongst them the ICC International Maritime Bureau and the ICC Counterfeiting Intelligence Bureau based in the UK, whose activities include credit card and similar fraud prevention.

ICC International Headquarters are at:

38 Cours Albert 1er
75008 Paris
France
Telephone: (1) 42–25–86–63

In the UK and North America, information can be obtained from the national organizations at:

ICC United Kingdom
Centre Point
103 New Oxford Street
London WC1A 1QB
Telephone: 01–240 5558

The United States Council of the ICC
1212 Avenue of the Americas
New York
NY 10036
Telephone: 212–354–4480

The International Business Council
1080 Beaver Hall Hill (Suite 1630)
Montreal
Quebec H2Z 1T2
Telephone: 514–866–4334

CHAMBERS OF COMMERCE

Local independent chambers of commerce exist around the world to facilitate both domestic and international trade. Their strength is directly proportionate to the numbers and quality of their membership and their normal objectives are to provide the services, contacts and representations which enable business to prosper.

Properly organized, the larger chambers can offer help with export information, research, documentation, training and business travel.

International credit managers, whose local chamber is both substantial and strong on international matters, should seriously consider becoming members.

The US Chamber of Commerce is particularly active in encouraging more competitiveness in international trade by US companies and lobbying government to facilitate such trade with appropriate programmes. The latter would be mainly aimed at bringing down trade barriers, countering violation of international trading agreements and making the same flexible medium term export finance facilities available to US businessmen as their counterparts enjoy in some other countries.

Additional chambers of commerce exist to foster trade between two specific countries. Good examples are the American Chamber of Commerce (UK) and its counterpart 'across the pond' and the Anglo-Dutch Chamber of Commerce.

For the credit manager, such chambers are mainly sources of information on import/export regulations, tax laws and the like. Some offer credit reports on companies and occasionally a debt collection service. Credit managers whose corporations tend to concentrate their exporting effort on just one or two particular countries may find membership of an appropriate inter-country chamber to be of considerable assistance.

DTI EXPORT SERVICES (UK)

Working through the British Overseas Trade Board (BOTB), the Department of Trade and Industry (DTI) is an official UK government organization providing a range of export services. Its principal aim is to help British companies, large and small, new or well established, to achieve profitable business in overseas markets.

Its President is a government minister, the Secretary of State for Trade and Industry, and the Chairman and members of the Board are leading businessmen.

Most of the advice the DTI offers is free and ranges from tariffs and regulations to local marketing methods and current economic circumstances in specific countries.

The DTI can trace its origins back, through the old Board of Trade, to the 'Councell of Trade' instituted in 1660 by King Charles II. Its instructions to members included the ageless advice:

> You are to consider of the severall Manufactures of these our Kingdomes . . . and how they may be farther improved . . . so that the private profitt of the Tradesmen or Merchants may not destroy ye Creditt of the Commodity and thereby render it neglected and unvended abroad to ye great loss and scandall of these our Kingdomes.

These days 'creditt' has implications, not simply in terms of the credibility of goods sold abroad, but as regards the likelihood of payment coming back in return – and the DTI can advise on both aspects.

The DTI's ancient origins have ensured close ties with the British Foreign Office and its overseas embassies and consulates from which much of their information and advice derives. These ancient origins have not, however, prevented them from moving into the electronic era. Consequently, a whole library and database of statistics and market intelligence information is available to personal or telephone callers.

Although much of the service is geared towards helping exporters establish themselves in the right market, find appropriate agents/

representatives and keep abreast of importing conditions abroad, there is also a great deal of information for the credit manager by way of exchange control and documentation requirement advice, hints for travellers, and the general Export Intelligence Service.

Information publications include *Hints to Exporters, Export Handbook, Countertrade* and a variety of regular country profiles.

Full details of all services can be obtained from:

Department of Trade and Industry
1–19 Victoria Street
London SW1H 0ET
England
Telephone: 01–215 4853

THE SIMPLER TRADE PROCEDURES BOARD (SITPRO) (UK)

SITPRO is an independent executive body set up in 1970 by the British government and sponsored by the DTI.

Its terms of reference are:

to guide, stimulate and assist the rationalization of international trade procedures and the documentation and information flows associated with them and, where appropriate and in consultation with the DTI, to undertake consultancy work in the trade facilitation field in the UK and overseas.

SITPRO is run by a board comprised of eminent business executives, supported by a full time executive management group and working groups of experts drawn from British trade and industry. All of these people carry out sterling work in what must often seem to be a hopeless task of standardizing and simplifying international procedures. They have achieved great breakthroughs, particularly in Europe, but anyone familiar with, for instance, the import and exchange control regulations of third world countries, will appreciate the immensity of their task.

Much of SITPRO's thrust at present runs hand in hand with the drive towards paperless trade. Its other objectives include improving documentation, simplifying official controls, increasing international co-operation, freeing payment bottlenecks and advising international businesses.

SITPRO seeks to fulfil these objectives by arranging for its working groups and staff to take part in a wide variety of initiatives such as the introduction of the Single Administrative Document, which at the beginning of 1988 replaced customs forms throughout the European Community as part of a drive towards harmonization of customs procedures. It also works closely with the ICC when the latter's uniform publications are being reviewed; and it has a powerful involvement in the UN inspired Joint Electronic Data Interchange study as well as in what has become a national 'campaign' to improve the payment performance of letter of credit transactions.

Aiding and abetting these initiatives are a range of SITPRO products and services. Those which should be of direct or indirect interest to the international credit manager are:

1   The export documentation starter kit which explains the practical business of delivery and payment procedures.
2   Copier systems which enable sets of export documents to be produced through a copier with a once-typed or computer printed master document.
3   Spex 3 microcomputer software for exporters and Interbridge 4 software providing computer to computer links.
4   Management and Staff Briefing Guides and checklists for export related matters. SITPRO's export checklists represent valuable tools for optimizing the use of letters of credit and avoiding payment delays through poor documentation. *Cash by Express* shows how to speed export payments through the international banking system. *Instant Export Payments* is a review of the new bank and finance house schemes.
5   'Customs Now' training materials have been designed to give some knowledge on how to meet customs requirements, minimize operating costs and raise efficiency.

A free newsletter is also available and is supplemented by an information desk to answer telephone enquiries.

Information on SITPRO products and services is available from:

Customer Services
SITPRO
Almack House
26 King Street
London SW1Y 6QW
England
Telephone: 01–930 0532

US GOVERNMENT PUBLICATIONS

Through the Superintendent of Documents, the US Department of Commerce makes a variety of books and pamphlets available to existing and potential exporters.

For those intending to set up an export trading company (ETC), *The Export Trading Company Guidebook, 1987* is particularly relevant. Small businesses can benefit from the *Exporters Guide to Federal Resources for Small Business*.

The *Monthly Catalog of US Government Publications* details all government publications by author, title and subject.

INTERNATIONAL AGENCIES

For the credit executive seeking country and statistical information there are a wide variety of publications to choose from, made available by international agencies such as those listed below.

Many of the economic reviews, digests and surveys are of an annual or infrequent nature but they can often be updated by reference to a monthly supplement.

The United Nations, New York.
The Organisation for Economic Co-operation and Development (OECD), Paris.
The World Bank (the International Bank for Reconstruction and Development), Washington D.C.
The International Monetary Fund, Washington D.C.
The European Communities, Brussels and Luxembourg.
The General Agreement on Tariffs and Trade (GATT), Geneva.

TRADE ASSOCIATIONS AND GROUPS

A variety of bodies fall under this heading but the one thing they have in common is their sheer dependence for their existence upon their membership. Belonging to a credit group for a particular industry can often provide a valuable interchange of information and experience.

FCIB–NACM Corporation

Of all the relevant membership organizations, FCIB–NACM is probably the one most appropriate to the international credit manager. FCIB is an association of executives in Finance, Credit and International Business. It was founded in 1919 and was incorporated in 1972 as the FCIB–NACM Corporation, under the laws of the state of New York, as the international affiliate of the US National Association of Credit Management. The latter is a membership association, owned and governed by its US members, and dates back to 1896.

FCIB's objective is to provide information and assistance to enable members to export with confidence and thus facilitate the free flow of goods and services from one country to another.

Although originating in the USA, FCIB has established a significant chapter in Europe. There are also members in Australia, Canada and Mexico, and the first Asian members were recently welcomed.

FCIB complies strictly with the anti-trust and restraint of trade laws prevailing in the USA and EEC in offering the following services.

Round table conferences and seminars

Conferences are held every month in the USA. In Europe there are three international conferences per annum. The Pacific Rim now also has its own international conference once a year.

The conferences bring together credit and financial executives from many industries and countries to discuss general credit management techniques and specific country problems.

Allied to the conferences are other meetings of common interest industry groups where past experiences of both countries and mutual customers may be discussed. Occasional workshops are also held on broad credit issues and separate group meetings are held for those international credit executives who have responsibility for the collection functions of their overseas subsidiaries.

Publications

FCIB produces for its members a regular newsletter, country reports and international bulletins on conditions in world markets and a semi-annual survey of commercial and credit conditions, setting out trade terms and experience across some 115 countries. The survey is based on members' responses to a regular questionnaire, and has received recognition from major international financial institutions such as the IMF.

A monthly magazine called *Business Credit* is also produced by FCIB's parent, NACM.

Worldwide collection services

FCIB operates a collection service on behalf of members at competitive rates. This service is enhanced by FCIB's membership of the LIC (League of International Creditors) worldwide network.

Contacts

Probably the greatest benefit to be derived from membership of such an organization is the wide range of contacts that can be made as a result of active participation. FCIB publishes a membership roster which has become a sort of 'Who's Who' in the international credit sphere. Potential members perusing the roster may well ask themselves, can I afford *not* to be a member?

Further information on FCIB is available from its World Headquarters at:

520 Eighth Avenue
New York
NY 10018-6571
USA
Telephone: 212–947–5070

National institutes of credit management

Most of the developed countries have a national institute or association of credit managers similar to NACM in the USA mentioned in the previous section.

In the UK the Institute of Credit Management is a prime example, offering its members a focal point for all credit matters. It sets high professional standards and limits membership to those who can demonstrate the required levels of professional competence.

The UK Institute organizes extensive training for both students and qualified members and gives valuable advice to government, national bodies and other professions on appropriate topics. Its other services or activities include:

- a technical advice service
- a staff recruitment service
- production of a monthly journal, entitled *Credit Management*

494

- professional 'briefs' on topics of special interest or concern
- a directory of members

Further information can be obtained from:

Institute of Credit Management
Easton House
Easton on the Hill
Stamford
Lincolnshire PE9 3NH
England
Telephone: 0780 56777
Telex 32251

Here again, one of the reasons for the credit professional to be a member of such an institute is the personal contacts it provides and the strength of its collective membership in the pursuit of common aims; and for the multinational, membership cannot but assist its 'domestic' subsidiary operations.

Although predominantly home trade orientated, national institutes do not neglect exporting. Indeed, to take the UK Institute as an example again, it is currently playing a leading part in establishing the Federation of European Credit Management Associations (FECMA). This is an indication of its increasing influence outside the UK and its determination to encourage the adoption of its high professional standards abroad.

FECMA provides a forum for the exchange of views and practical trade and professional matters and encourages personal contacts between members of the different European credit management associations.

The Institute of Export (UK)

The Institute of Export is a professional association and registered educational charity, whose aims are to set and raise the standards of export practice and management through training, formal and informal education and the exchange of ideas and information between exporters.

Members are elected after successful examination or relevant experience.

The Institute publishes a well-regarded journal and acts as a focal point representing members' professional views to government. It runs an advisory service and a staff bureau and employment register.

Further information is obtainable from:

The Institute of Export
Export House
64 Clifton Street
London EC2A 4HB
Telephone: 01–247 9812

Index